The Russian Revolution

Blackwell Essential Readings in History

This series comprises concise collections of key articles on important historical topics. Designed as a complement to standard survey histories, the volumes are intended to help introduce students to the range of scholarly debate in a subject area. Each collection includes a general introduction and brief contextual headnotes to each article, offering a coherent, critical framework for study.

Published

The German Reformation: The Essential Readings
C. Scott Dixon

The Counter-Reformation: The Essential Readings
David M. Luebke

The French Revolution: The Essential Readings
Ronald Schechter

The Russian Revolution: The Essential Readings
Martin A. Miller

The Third Reich: The Essential Readings
Christian Leitz

In Preparation

The Italian Renaissance: The Essential Readings
Paula Findlen

The Enlightenment: The Essential Readings
Martin Fitzpatrick

The English Civil War: The Essential Readings
Peter Gaunt

The Cold War: The Essential Readings
Klaus Larres and Ann Lane

The Russian Revolution

The Essential Readings

Edited by Martin A. Miller

BLACKWELL
Publishers

Copyright © Blackwell Publishers Ltd 2001. Editorial arrangement and introductions copyright © Martin A. Miller 2001.

First published 2001

2 4 6 8 10 9 7 5 3 1

Blackwell Publishers Inc.
350 Main Street
Malden, Massachusetts 02148
USA

Blackwell Publishers Ltd
108 Cowley Road
Oxford OX4 1JF
UK

Library of Congress Cataloging-in-Publication Data

Miller, Martin A.(Martin Alan), 1938–
      The Russian revolution: the essential readings / edited by Martin Miller.
          p.   cm. – (Blackwell essential readings in history)
      Includes bibliographical references and index.
      ISBN 0-631-21638-3 (alk. paper) – ISBN 0-631-21639-1 (pb: alk. paper)
      1. Soviet Union–History–Revolution, 1917–1921. I. Title. II. Series.

    DK265 .M532 2001
    947.084'1 – dc21

                                                                    00-034319

British Library Cataloguing in Publication Data

A CIP catalogue record for this book is available from the British Library.

Typeset in 10½ on 12 pt Photina
by Best-set Typesetter Ltd., Hong Kong
Printed and bound in Great Britain by TJ International , Padstow, Cornwall

This book is printed on acid-free paper

To my students – past, present, and future

Contents

Acknowledgments

The editor wishes to express gratitude to the anonymous readers for the press who provided very constructive suggestions, and to the following colleagues whose assistance made it possible to stay within the demands set by the publication schedule: Barbara Clements, Warren Lerner, Alexander Rabinowitch, and Donald Raleigh. Thanks are also due to Tessa Harvey, Louise Spencely, and Helen Rappaport at Blackwell Publishers for their encouragement and help. The editor alone, however, was responsible for the selection of the articles that make up this volume. Finally, Venice International University provided a splendid environment for the completion of this project.

Martin A. Miller
Venice, April 2000

Blackwell Publishers, USA. Reprinted by permission of Blackwell Publishers.

Extract from Alexander Rabinowitch, *The Bolsheviks Come to Power*. Reprinted by permission of the author.

Extract from William G. Rosenburg, "Russian Labor and Bolshevik power: social dimensions of protest in Petrograd after October," *Slavic Review* 44 (1985). Reprinted by permission of American Association of the Advancement of Slavic Studies (AAASS).

Extract from Sheila Fitzpatrick, "Ascribing Class: The Construction of Social Identity in Soviet Russia," *Journal of Modern History* 65 (1993). (c) 1993 by the University of Chicago, 0022-2801/93/6504-0003501 00. All rights reserved. Reprinted by permission of University of Chicago Press.

Extract from Barbara Evans Clements, "The Revolution" from *Bolshevik Women*, Cambridge University Press, 1997. Reprinted by permission of Cambridge University Press and the author.

Extract from Ronald Grigor Suny, *The Revenge of the Past: Nationalism, Revolution, and the Collapse of the Soviet Union*. With the permission of the publishers, Stanford University Press (c) 1993 by the Board of Trustees of the Leland Stanford Junior University.

Extract from Steve Smith, "Writing the History of the Russian Revolution after the Fall of Communism," *Europe Asia Studies*, 46, 4 (1994) pp 563–78. Reprinted by permission of Taylor & Francis Limited.

Editor's Introduction

The Russian Revolution at the Millennium

Martin A. Miller

The events in Russia which took place in 1917 and which have come down to us as the "Russian Revolution" may have been somewhat misnamed. First of all, there were at least two moments during that tumultuous year that have traditionally been labeled as revolutions, one in February and the other in October. Second, it is far from clear that it was a specifically Russian affair since, depending upon our conceptual framework, we could be speaking of the participation of other nationalities in the upheavals. Third, and perhaps most important, many students of 1917 have grave doubts as to whether what took place was a revolution at all. The October insurrection which brought Lenin and the Bolsheviks to power has been frequently called a coup or a seizure of power; and when the term revolution has been used, the spectrum of adjectives used to define it have ranged from the derisive "unfinished" to the elegiac "great proletarian socialist." This in turn reminds us that so much of our knowledge of 1917 and its aftermath has been influenced by the often partisan and contrasting perspectives of the culture of the Cold War. For many writers on the subject, deciding whether 1917 was a revolution as authentic as that which France experienced in 1789 had much to do with the position one took in the consuming rivalry between the U.S. and the U.S.S.R.

To make matters even more confusing, we still have no agreed-upon chronology for the beginning and end of the revolutionary process. Should we start with the famine of 1891, as Orlando Figes does in his comprehensive account, *A People's Tragedy*? Are we speaking of the year 1917 from February to October, in which case the revolution was over the morning that the Bolsheviks took power from the previous regime, the Provisional Government? Or must we expand our lens to include the years of the Civil War up to Lenin's death in 1924? Or further to the First Five-Year Plan of centralized industrialization and the terrorism of the Great Purges of 1937–8 when Stalin's power was consolidated and victorious against all opposition, as Sheila Fitzpatrick has shown in her book, *The Russian Revolution*? And what criteria do we use to make our assessment?

These questions are as crucial as those which probe the deeper consequences of the revolution beyond the borders of the Soviet Union. Some historians, for example, have argued that the menace of Bolshevism after 1917 was so threatening that it contributed in a major way to the ability of the Nazi Party to gain adherents by fostering an image of itself as the supreme anticommunist force in Weimar Germany. Others have emphasized how in America and Britain during the Depression of the 1930s, Soviet propaganda was able to attract large numbers of writers and intellectuals. This is not to mention the debate as to whether the enormous number of lives lost during the intimidating years of Stalin's purges, forbidding labor camps and executions were perhaps even a logical and an inevitable consequence of the Russian Revolution.

It would be utopian to expect to answer all of these questions at this point, though the material in the essays that follow provides a great deal of information and analysis to help get closer to that goal. It should also be pointed out that no single volume can possibly attend to all of the layers of the Russian Revolution – from personalities to institutions to ideologies – in any comprehensive way. Nevertheless, now that we are over eight decades away from the revolutionary year itself and a decade away from the collapse of the Soviet Union, it is time to take a fresh look at the meaning of 1917 for Russia and the world, free of the biases of the Cold War. The demise of the U.S.S.R. has resulted in an archival gold mine for historians, which makes the study of not only the revolution but also the larger context of Soviet history possible in ways that were unimaginable in the past. Indeed, some of the chapters below include research that is based on those previously inaccessible sources.

There are further issues to consider before plunging into these essays, which will take the reader into the heart of the revolution. The material in this book has been written *post facto* by historians, who base their findings on the crucial foundation of contemporary evidence generally referred to as sources. However, as all historians know, sources can be deceiving as well as conflicting, and require careful corroboration with other evidence. Let us explore one example. In February, 1914, Peter Durnovo, a former cabinet official in the tsarist government and a man immensely loyal to the regime, sent Nicholas II a memorandum in which he argued in the strongest of terms that a war with Germany must be avoided because of the social unrest it would provoke at home. In the event of a defeat in such a war, Durnovo predicted that "social revolution in its most extreme form is inevitable."

Several months later, in the summer of 1914, the *National Geographic* editors and photographers toured Russia from the capital to the Caucasus. The title of the report they published, which filled the entire November 1914 issue was "Young Russia: The Land of Unlimited Possibilities." The Great War, the consequences of which Durnovo feared so greatly, had already begun when the article appeared, but there is only one photograph dealing with it. The tone of the article is close to inspirational, predicting that Russia is about to come alive with "unlimited possibilities" in all areas of development under the tsars, whether political, religious, economic, or social and cultural. Durnovo's memorandum, which foresaw a revolutionary upheaval, languished in one of tsar's drawers, probably unread and certainly without known influence; the *National Geographic*, which had a huge readership and undoubtedly was a factor in constructing the West's image of Russia at the time, could not even imagine a revolution in Russia. Both are crucial in our understanding of the revolution, not when seen as isolated pieces of differing evidence, but only when placed into a proper context. Examples of how this is done should be evident from the careful analyses conducted in the essays below.

Modern revolutions (the term comes originally from Copernicus' book on astronomy), born in late eighteenth-century America and France and extended in Russia in 1917, are fought over many things, not least of which includes the popular demand for a legitimate polity that would recognize the rights, property, and dignity of all citizens. Unlike the earlier revolutions, however, Russia experienced three forms of legitimacies in that single, fateful year of 1917. Until the February uprising, the country was an autocratic empire justified on the antiquated principles of divine right. All of Nicholas II's documents include references to God's help, will and vengeful might. From February to October, the country was transformed into a republic based on the principles of popular sovereignty. The Provisional Government ruled awkwardly as a government without a parliament, promised after elections, alongside a network of workers' and peasants' soviets with its center in the capital, which operated as an elected parliament without a government. Finally, after the Bolshevik insurrection in October, Russia shifted into an unprecedented third form of political legitimacy – government by ideology, in which the revered texts of Marxism, as interpreted by the newly empowered Leninists, were to chart the country's destiny. The desire for a resolution to this crisis of political instability and multiple legitimacies spread to all levels of society.

In Russia, the revolutionary events of 1917 and their aftermath were shaped by a long history of tension between the forces of authoritarianism in politics and forms of opposition and resistance from both above and below. In the eighteenth century, regime changes were often determined by "palace coups" organized by coalitions of the elite sectors of the court; military leaders were frequently mobilized to support a successor. Even the celebrated Decembrist rebellion of 1825 was largely confined to the same elites, except that this time the confrontation was organized by secret societies and was resolved with bloodshed not in the palace but on the public square outside. The gathering storm of revolutionary activity, driven by resentment of the symbols and the realities of tsarist power, began in earnest during the 1860s, when it become clear that the reforms of Alexander II were too limited for the establishment of a polity acceptable to the new self-appointed spokespersons of the Russian masses. For the next decades, this movement of protest achieved the status of a permanent force in Russian society, composed as it was of a variety of ideologies and tactics, including the creation of the Western world's first terrorist organization in 1879, the People's Will.

Missing from the oscillating intensity of this drama of the regime and its police against a militant revolutionary underground was the emergence of a democratic alternative. We should, of course, recall that there were no democracies anywhere outside of the U.S. until the French Revolution, and once that was extinguished, no country in Europe with the important exceptions of France and Britain had a democratic government before the First World War. Russia, it would appear, was no different. In fact, however, there were some distinctively Russian traits at work. The long heritage of reliance on serfdom as an economic system and as a cultural way of life cost the country dearly. Among other penalties, it solidified a rigid class division in which ruling elites appeared to determine the choices for the vast, impoverished and largely illiterate peasantry whose condition they saw little need to alter so long as obedience was maintained. These distinctions were far greater than anything that existed in the West. In Russia, capitalism itself was inhibited, as was the possibility of a shared civic order of different economic strata, nationalities and religions. In addition, Russia moved into the twentieth century without the parliamentary institutions of citizenship that even the monarchies of Western Europe possessed. Political parties and labor unions, which elsewhere fostered this new civic identity and provided access to the realization of expanded rights within the framework of the modern nation-state, were absent in Russia until the 1905 revolution. Even then the concessions wrought from the regime after an extended year of revolutionary upheaval were severely constrained.

Russian history as a field of study only emerged in a systematic way after the Second World War. Until that time, there were very few specialists in Western countries who taught and wrote about Russia in a scholarly manner. Beginning in the 1960s, exchange programs between the former Soviet Union and Western countries permitted noncommunist scholars to enter Soviet archives for the first time on a regular basis. Materials were limited for some time to prerevolutionary documents, but even this led to a professionally sophisticated historiography of the entire history of Russia and of the revolution in particular. Over the course of time, orientations have reigned, melted and been replaced by others. At the start of the twenty-first century, we now have a solid body of work on the revolution from a variety of perspectives, including intellectual and cultural history, political and diplomatic history, and social and economic history. Much of this rich literature is represented in the selections below. Perhaps most significant in this regard is the recent collaboration between Russian and Western historians, which had been virtually impossible in the public arena before the collapse of the Soviet Union. It may seem archaic to contemporary students, but for decades Soviet historians, either by compulsion or desire, regularly vilified their colleagues in the West, who of course responded in kind, albeit in more polite terminology in most cases.

We can now proceed to the essays that make up this volume. To help students navigate the often challenging waters to come, the editor has provided a brief introduction to each essay. At the end of the essay a glossary identifying major names, political parties, and Russian terms is appended, followed by a list of suggested English-language further reading that is meant to be selective rather than comprehensive in any way. There is a vast literature on the origins, dynamics, and consequences of the Revolution in Russia, composed of both documents and authorities, and due to space limitations, many outstanding books could not be included. In most cases, books discussed in the introductions to the essays will not be repeated in the further reading sections that follow. Anyone wishing to do further research can make use of the excellent bibliographies that appear in the books that are listed, all of which cite books and articles in English and Russian as well as other languages.

When reading the essays, the reader should bear in mind that Russia maintained the Julian calendar until the Bolsheviks, who rejected most bourgeois customs, (hence, commissars instead of ministers or secretaries in the government center), ironically accepted the Gregorian calendar which had been used in the West for centuries. Thus, in the twentieth century, 13 days separated the two calendars, with the confusing result that the overthrow of the Romanov dynasty in February 1917 (old Julian style) actually took place in March (new Gregorian style), and October occurred in November. Spellings, a notoriously contentious subject among linguists, have here been standardized with general consistency along the lines of the Library of Congress system except where readers have prior familiarity (e.g., Trotsky instead of Trotskii, as it should be transliterated).

Part I
On the Eve:
Toward Revolution

1

The Battleground

Edward Acton

Originally appeared as "The Battleground," in *Rethinking the Russian Revolution* by Edward Acton (London: Edward Arnold, 1990): 5–27.

Editor's Introduction

Edward Acton has written extensively on Russian history, including a biography of the pioneering nineteenth-century radical thinker Alexander Herzen, and a widely used textbook. The essay which follows is the introductory chapter to a book in which Acton reassesses the Revolution in Russia. Readers will find a useful analysis of the background to the revolutionary events of 1917 and beyond. He begins with the landmark legislation issued by Emperor Alexander II in the early 1860s concerning the abolition of serfdom, the reform of the military and the establishment of a modern judiciary system. For students unfamiliar with the events of the decades prior to the collapse of Romanov power in 1917, Acton discusses the 1905 Revolution, the national Duma set up in its aftermath, the strike movement of the new proletariat, the role of the Russian intelligentsia in the years leading up to the First World War, the impact of the war, and the revolutions of 1917 culminating in the Bolshevik seizure of power in October.

Though not mentioned by Acton, it should be pointed out that an unresolved debate remains in the literature about the relationship between the war and the revolution. Put simply, one school of thought (and it is the majority opinion) argues that the war was a critical factor in making the revolution possible. The assumption made is that the war destabilized the country politically, divided and demoralized educated society, and ruined the economy which actually had been showing signs of improvement in many areas. The conclusion drawn is that without the war, in all likelihood there would not have been a revolution in Russia, and further, a moderate constitutional monarchy would have evolved instead of a communist regime with all its attendant (most assumed to be negative) consequences.

On the other side, a number of historians are persuaded that the war's effect was the opposite. Just prior to the outbreak of the Great War as it was to be called, strikes in various parts of the country were intensifying to such an extent that it appeared the regime was literally losing control over the militant sections of the labor movement. The key example was the Lena goldfields disaster in 1912 when the army was called in to quell a disturbance and ended up firing on the unarmed mineworkers. Once the war began in August 1914, the labor movement shut down. The decision for most workers was obvious when faced with the choice between striking for better working conditions or fighting to defend the fatherland against the Germans.

Regardless of how one interprets the evidence in this matter, many other forces were in progress at the historical moment when the Russian government announced its participation in the outbreak of international hostilities, and Russian society found itself suddenly drawn into the war which it was quite unprepared to wage successfully. The "battleground," as Acton makes clear in his analysis of the events, shifted from civil society before the war to the front once the war started. The consequences were to be immense.

The Battleground

Edward Acton

Introduction

The middle decades of the nineteenth century marked a watershed in Russia's modern history. The international pre-eminence the country had enjoyed since defeating Napoleon in 1812 was brought to an abrupt end by the Crimean War (1853–56). She was soundly defeated in her war against Turkey when Britain and France intervened for fear that Russia would establish her sway over Constantinople. The Tsar's forces were humiliated by land and sea and under the terms of the Treaty of Paris Russia was disarmed on the Black Sea. The defeat brought home in the most devastating fashion just how far the Empire's development had fallen behind that of her Great Power rivals in the West. It fully exposed her backwardness – military, economic, social, administrative. It served as a catalyst which greatly accelerated the pace of change within the Empire.

In the aftermath of the war the government of Alexander II (1855–1881) undertook a series of major reforms. The Tsar's authority remained unlimited but almost every area of public life was affected, and in preparing the reforms the government slackened censorship and gave unprecedented opportunity for different sections of society to air their grievances. The most far-reaching reform was the abolition in 1861 of serfdom, the supreme symbol of Russia's backwardness. The 22.8 million serfs privately owned by members of the nobility were emancipated. The principle of the statute was that the newly-freed serfs should retain their household plots and an allotment of land, but that they should pay for this land. The amount of land made available to them was, on average, less than that which they had tilled for their own subsistence under serfdom. The government provided compensation for the nobility, while the peasantry were to repay the government in annual redemption dues spread over a period of 49 years. Statutes of 1863 and 1866 enabled peasants on crown lands and state peasants to redeem their land on somewhat more favourable but broadly similar terms.

A series of other 'great reforms' recast much of the country's traditional institutional structure. Administratively, the most innovative measures were the local government statutes of 1864 and 1870 which established a network of elected provincial and district *zemstvos* and city *dumas* outside the regular bureaucracy. They were empowered to improve a range of local facilities from transport, credit, and insurance to health and education. Their autonomy, it is true, was carefully circumscribed. The chairmen of zemstvo assemblies were state appointees. The zemstvo franchise, while providing minority representation for urban and peasant proprietors, ensured the domination of wealthier members of the nobility, and the duma franchise was equally restricted. But the zemstvos in particular rapidly expanded their activities during the ensuing decades. They employed a growing number of teachers, medical workers, veterinary surgeons and other specialists, thereby introducing the so-called 'third element', often a radical one, into rural life.

The reform of the legal system (1864) was explicitly modelled on advanced western practice, and laid down that the law was to be overseen by an independent judiciary. Juries were to deal with serious criminal cases, elected justices of the peace were to hear minor criminal and civil cases, and trials were henceforth to be held in public. The appeals procedure was streamlined, court practice was refined, and the crudest forms of punishment were abolished. The reform of censorship (1865) was based on the principle that it was for the courts to decide when the press had broken the law, and pre-publication censorship was significantly reduced. Measures affecting higher education saw the universities granted greater autonomy in running their own affairs. In the 1870s, a series of military reforms gave new impetus to the professionalization of the officer corps, and sought to emulate the Prussian example by introducing universal conscription, building a reserve of trained men, and reducing the size of the massive standing army.

In each case, the reforms were hedged in with clauses designed to preserve leeway for the authorities. During the late 1860s and 70s, administrative powers were frequently used to override the principles of the reforms as the government took alarm at the critical attitude of a more assertive 'public opinion', at recurrent outbreaks of student protest, and at the emergence of a small but dynamic underground revolutionary movement. In 1878 diplomatic humiliation at the Congress of Berlin threw the government onto the political defensive at home, and during his last years Alexander II was subject to renewed pressure for further change. His own ministers even proposed the creation of machinery for a measure of consultation on national issues with representatives of 'society' drawn from the zemstvos and municipal dumas. In 1881, however, on the very day he had decided to accept some of these proposals, the Tsar was assassinated and his son, Alexander III (1881–1894), firmly reasserted the principle of autocracy.

From the 1880s the regime made plain its determination not only to halt any further movement in the direction of public participation but in some respects to reverse the reforms of the 1860s. There was a purge of ministers sympathetic to reform and office was entrusted to staunch conservatives. Emergency regulations empowered the government to declare virtual martial law at will. Steps were taken to restrict the autonomy of the zemstvos, to discipline the universities, to intensify censorship. In 1889 a new tier of provincial officials, the 'land captains', was created with both administrative and judicial powers to tighten the State's direct supervision of the peasantry. Police sections specializing in the prevention and exposure of underground political activity (the Okhrana) were developed. The regime attempted to impose narrow restrictions on the ability of the different classes and groups within society to organize and articulate their aspirations. This was the inheritance which Nicholas II (1894–1917) pledged to uphold when he ascended the throne. Yet while the last tsars sought to preserve the traditional order Russia was undergoing a process of profound economic and social change. Within a decade of his accession, Nicholas was to be confronted by a wave of social and political protest which shook tsarism to its foundations.

The Emancipation of the serfs made possible a gradual but sustained acceleration in the rate of economic growth, the development of the internal market, the division of labour, the accumulation of capital, technological innovation and urbanization. From the 1880s the State itself sponsored an upsurge in heavy industry. The focal point of the policy, most closely identified with the name of S. Iu. Witte, Minister of Finance from 1892 to 1903, was a massive programme of railway construction financed by foreign capital. A major stimulus in the industrialization of most countries, railways made a particularly powerful impact upon an economy uniquely handicapped by vast distances and poor communications. They linked the Empire's far-flung mineral resources with each other and with the centres of population; they enormously increased the volume of both domestic and foreign trade; and their construction generated a massive new demand for coal, steel, iron and manufactures. The social repercussions of Emancipation and accelerated economic development gave rise to a range of diverse pressures upon the regime.

For the landed nobility, the impact of Emancipation was deeply disturbing. The compensation granted them was not sufficient to prevent a steady decline in noble landownership during the decades that followed 1861. A growing proportion of the nobility lost their ties with the land altogether. This was reflected in a loosening of what had traditionally been a strong correlation between landownership and civil and military office, especially at the highest level. The privileged position of the nobility seemed threatened, too, by the growing professionalization of the bureaucracy and the army. Among those who remained attached to the land, the result was a new wariness in their attitude towards the government. Their resentment focused on the way industry seemed to be benefiting at their expense and they blamed the Finance Ministry's favouritism towards industry for the plight – and the restiveness – of the peasantry. Towards the end of the century their anger began to take political form. A politically active minority of provincial landowners voiced criticism of the arbitrary nature of the bureaucracy and the autocracy. They made maximum use of the forum provided by the zemstvos and drew them towards an alliance with the liberal and constitutional movement emerging in the cities.

Along with the development of the urban economy, the education system and public services, the decades after the great reforms saw a rapid broadening in the ranks of educated, urban-orientated society outside officialdom. The quickening pace of trade and industry provided new opportunities for industrialists and entrepreneurs, and generated a need for managers, engineers and clerks of every description. The development of the legal system, the press, education and public services saw sustained growth in the numbers of lawyers, doctors, teachers, journalists, writers, students, and specialists of various kinds. As different strata of the educated public became conscious of belonging to a substantial and articulate body of opinion, 'society's' self-confidence grew. And as the aspirations of the various professions, of students, of the 'third element' rose, so did their exasperation at continuing official inefficiency, corruption and oppression. Leading industrialists and businessmen, many of whom were involved in foreign-owned enterprises, generally remained as politically quiescent as the traditional merchant community. But the economically less powerful sections of the middle class became increasingly outspoken, exploiting to the full the limited opportunities for organization and public debate opened out by the great reforms. During the 1890s the demand for guaranteed civil liberties and public participation in state decision-making gathered momentum. The foundation in 1902 of the émigré journal *Osvobozhdenie*, edited by Peter Struve, was an important milestone in the emergence of a liberal movement. In 1903 a loosely structured organization, the Union of Liberation, was formed to unite all sections of opposition and to press for constitutional democracy based on universal, equal, secret and direct franchise. More radical sections of the educated élite looked beyond liberal and constitutional reform to socialist revolution. From the 1860s they created a succession of underground organizations culminating in the foundation, in 1898 and 1901 respectively, of the Marxist-inspired Russian Social Democratic Workers Party (RSDWP) and the rival, peasant-orientated Socialist Revolutionary Party (SR).

Discontent lower down the social scale was no less intense. For the peasantry, the terms of Emancipation, under which they were compelled to pay for the land, were a bitter disappointment. Moreover, in the following decades pressure on the land was constantly increased by explosive population growth. During the second half of the century the Empire's population rose on average 1.5 per cent a year, the total soaring from 74 million at Emancipation in 1861 to 126 million in 1897. The result was to force up the price both of renting and of buying land. The overall trend in peasant living standards during the period is hotly disputed. But recurrent harvest failures, the most notorious of which led to devastating famine in 1891, imposed severe hardship on many. Equally clear is the peasantry's sense of injustice over the Emancipation settlement, their resentment against the landowning nobility, and their yearning to see all noble land made over to them.

Village life and the peasant outlook were conditioned by the administrative arrangements adopted at Emancipation. Except in the most westerly provinces, the land was redeemed not by individual peasants but by the village commune. It was the commune that was to own the land and to be responsible for all peasant obligations, including the payment of redemption dues. In part to ensure that all households could meet their obligations, the traditional practice whereby the commune periodically redistributed the land between households according to the size of families was extended. These arrangements entrenched a distinctive land-owning pattern among the peasantry and perpetuated the peasantry's distance from other social estates. Despite increasing integration into the market, therefore, the village remained in large measure set apart from the world outside, regulating its own affairs through customary law under the tutelage of the police. Deprived of any effective legal mechanism through which to express their discontent, the peasants expressed it instead through rural disturbances. The incidence of rent and labour strikes and land seizures from private landowners rose during the 1890s. Serious crop failure in 1901 was followed by major peasant uprisings during 1902 in the Ukraine, the Volga area, and Georgia. Peasant protest, both in the countryside and among the rank and file in the army, played a major part in the revolution of 1905.

Although the peasantry continued to account for over 80 per cent of the population, discontent among the urban poor and especially the industrial working class was of scarcely less significance than the unrest in the countryside. By the turn of the century, some two million men and women, rather less than 5 per cent of the working population, were employed in mines and factories. As in the West, the early stages of industrialization were accompanied by harsh working and living conditions. Moreover, large-scale manufacture tended to be concentrated in a few industrial areas, of which St Petersburg, Moscow, and the major cities of Poland, the Ukraine and the South were the most significant, and the plants themselves tended to be markedly larger than in the West. The concentration of labour both facilitated organization among workers and heightened the political significance of labour protest. The government tended to intervene swiftly with police and troops when major plants or the railway system were disrupted. Although labour organizations were illegal, protest from the working class grew ominously from the mid 1880s. In 1896 and again in 1897 almost the entire textile industry of St Petersburg was briefly paralysed. From 1899 Russia was hit by a severe depression which temporarily weakened the strike movement but aggravated unemployment and urban discontent. Towards the end of 1902 and during 1903 there was a series of mass strikes in several important cities in the South, including Rostov-on-Don, Baku and Odessa. The Ministry of the Interior, anxious about the security implications of labour unrest, experimented from 1901–3 with police-run labour organizations through which it hoped to direct working-class energy from political towards purely economic and cultural aims. These 'Zubatov unions', so-called in honour of the police chief who sponsored them, tended to escape the control of their sponsors and contributed to the explosion of protest which shook the regime during 1905.

Mounting social tension was accompanied by the swift development of national consciousness among the Empire's ethnic minorities. At the turn of the century only 43 per cent of the population were Great Russians, and the tsarist government's overt identification with them and with the Orthodox Church alienated minority nationalities. A heavy-handed policy of Russification tended to push even relatively mild cultural movements, such as that in the Ukraine, in the direction of political protest. In areas such as the Baltic provinces and the semi-autonomous Duchy of Finland, the government's attempts to tighten its control and impose administrative and cultural uniformity created nationalist opposition where little had existed. Where there was a long history of nationalist resistance, notably in Poland, Russification provoked bitter resentment. Particularly harsh was the discrimination imposed against the Empire's 5.5 million Jewish minority. Nationalist unrest among the minorities in general, and the Poles in particular, constituted an important ingredient in the upheaval of 1905.

The Revolution of 1905

This complex pattern of social and political agitation was brought to a head by the outbreak of war between Russia and Japan (January 1904–August 1905). The war, which arose over the two countries' rival ambitions in Manchuria and Korea, was widely regarded in Russia as the product of intrigue at court and among a handful of entrepreneurs, and aroused little patriotic enthusiasm. A series of military and naval defeats, culminating in the loss of the war, generated fierce criticism of government incompetence, ministerial confidence was visibly shaken, and smouldering discontent burst into flames. During 1904, with the government on the political defensive, there was an upsurge of liberal and revolutionary propaganda. A campaign of banquets and public meetings was mounted to demand reform, a zemstvo congress drew up specific proposals for constitutional change, and a series of politically-orientated professional unions was formed.

At the same time, working-class protest and strikes intensified and on 9 January 1905 a massive demonstration gathered to present a petition for reform to the Winter Palace. Troops opened fire on the unarmed, hymn-singing men and women. The events of 'Bloody Sunday' had a profound effect on the political consciousness of all classes. In the following months, government efforts to open a dialogue with workers failed as their representatives pressed for changes too radical for the government to consider. Attempts to extract expressions of loyalty from the peasantry also backfired. An All-Russian Peasants' Union was formed and at its first congress, which met in secret in July, it demanded the abolition of private property in land and the convening of a constituent assembly. By August the government was trying to pacify protest by undertaking to summon an elected consultative assembly. But the following month saw a renewed wave of strikes paralyse St Petersburg, Moscow and many provincial cities. The new Union of Railwaymen brought the railways to a halt, a liberal Union of Unions and leading liberal figures proclaimed full support for the strikes, and many employers showed sympathy by lenient treatment of striking workers. The disparate movements of protest were for a moment united in massive resistance. The government looked so vulnerable that even irreproachable traditionalists among the landowning nobility concluded that political reform was inescapable. In desperation the Tsar appointed Witte to handle the crisis, committed himself to creating a unified cabinet under Witte's premiership, and on 17 October issued an historic Manifesto. The autocracy undertook to guarantee full civil liberty, to give major legislative powers to the promised assembly (the State Duma), and to base it upon a broad franchise.

The Manifesto marked a major turning-point in the revolution. It divided the forces arrayed against the Tsar. Once it had been issued, moderate unions, including the Union of Railwaymen, called for a return to work. Employers brought maximum pressure to bear on workers in order to restore order: recalcitrant strikers faced lock-outs. Liberals generally considered the Manifesto less than satisfactory but sufficient grounds for a return to normality. They formed the Constitutional Democratic (Kadet) party, dedicated to using the concessions of 17 October as a stepping-stone towards full parliamentary democracy. More enthusiastic was the Union of 17 October (Octobrists), a loose political alliance led by landed nobility and a few prominent industrialists, which was formed to work with the Tsar on the basis of the Manifesto. On the extreme Right, disparate reactionary groups formed the violently loyalist, nationalist and anti-Semitic Union of the Russian People to rally support for the Tsar.

On the other hand, much of the opposition to the regime remained unpacified by the Manifesto. Unrest continued among the most militant national minorities, notably in the Baltic and in Poland. The period from October to December saw a rash of mutinies among soldiers and sailors. From the naval base of Kronstadt near St Petersburg to the Far Eastern Army came reports of large-scale insubordination. Peasant protest – labour and rent strikes, land seizures, and direct assaults on noble manors – peaked in the same period. A second congress of the All-Russian Peasants' Union in November was satisfied neither by the Manifesto nor by the announcement that redemption dues were to be phased out altogether, and peasant disturbances continued through 1906 and into 1907. The working class was hardly more impressed by the Manifesto and in the weeks that followed it the government faced an unprecedented challenge to its authority, centred on St Petersburg and Moscow. On the very day of the Manifesto a central strike committee in the capital proclaimed itself the St Petersburg Soviet (Council) of Workers' Deputies. Its deputies were elected directly at factory level and subject to immediate recall, while on its Executive Committee members of the socialist parties played prominent roles. This novel organization rapidly gained the confidence of the capital's work-force, and helped to inspire the creation of soviets elsewhere in the country – among peasants and soldiers as well as workers. The Petersburg Soviet took on quasi-governmental functions, including the setting up of an armed militia. Early in November it called a second general strike. This time, however, employers' resistance was rigid and the strike soon lost momentum. When on 3 December the government arrested the Executive Committee and suppressed the Petersburg Soviet, the immediate sequel was an armed uprising in several cities, headed by Moscow.

Yet the government survived. It retained the loyalty of a sufficient proportion of the army to stamp out the mutinies, impose martial law in Poland, deploy troops on a wide scale in the countryside, and crush both the soviets and the week-long guerrilla-style urban uprisings of December. Moreover, the threat of social upheaval increased the anxiety of the government's more moderate critics to see the restoration of order. In the months that followed October the government gradually regained the initiative.

Pre-war Russia

Although the period following 1905 saw an extension in the freedom of the press and of assembly, the civil liberties granted fell short of the promises made in the October Manifesto. Equally, although the popularly elected State Duma promised by Nicholas was duly established, the franchise discriminated heavily against peasants and workers, elections were to be indirect, and votes were to be cast and counted by class and property groups (*curias*). Moreover, the powers entrusted to the legislature under the Duma Statute and Fundamental Laws issued in 1906 were severely limited. Ministers were not responsible to it and continued to be appointed and dismissed by the Tsar. The traditional supreme body within the bureaucracy, the State Council, was expanded to form an upper chamber half of whose members were appointed by the Tsar and half elected from such relatively privileged institutions as the Holy Synod, provincial assemblies of the nobility, and zemstvos. The Tsar retained the power to veto all legislation and should an emergency arise while the Duma was not in session, Article 87 of the Fundamental Laws enabled him to legislate by decree.

When the First Duma met in April 1906 it was dominated by Kadets, led by P. N. Miliukov, and peasant deputies loosely bound together in the Trudovik (Labour) Group. Efforts by the Tsar's ministers to persuade Miliukov and other prominent Kadets and Octobrists to join the cabinet were unsuccessful. Instead the Kadets took the lead in issuing a series of demands for far-reaching reforms, including the appointment of a government responsible to the Duma and the redistribution of private land. The government rejected these proposals out of hand and after two months dissolved the assembly. The Kadets led other radical deputies across the border to Vyborg in Finland where they issued a manifesto calling for protest in the form of passive resistance. The 'Vyborg Manifesto' elicited little response and those who took part were debarred from election to the next Duma.

The dissolution of the Duma coincided with the appointment of a new Prime Minister, Peter Stolypin. During his five years in office he combined vigorous measures to suppress continuing disorder with efforts to promote a programme of reforms which he hoped would prevent a recurrence of the upheaval of 1905. The centrepiece of these reforms was addressed to the issue of peasant landownership. He rejected the idea of compulsorily alienating noble land, but tried to alleviate peasant land hunger by providing additional credit for peasants to buy land and by facilitating resettlement on vacant land in Siberia. Above all he sought to dismantle the traditional peasant commune. Peasants were encouraged to register their communal holdings as private property and to consolidate their scattered strips into coherent farms. Stolypin described the measures as a 'wager on the strong', hoping to see the emergence of a class of efficient yeomen farmers with a firm stake in the status quo.

Stolypin's reforms found little sympathy in the Second Duma, which met in February 1907. Although the Second Duma saw a small increase in the number of right-wing deputies, more striking was the decline in the number of Kadet deputies and the advance of the extreme Left, including Social Democrats and SRs who had decided to abandon the electoral boycott they had staged during the elections to the First Duma. The government was bitterly denounced for the emergency measures it was taking to enforce order. Unable to establish any common ground between his proposals and the radical demands of the Left, Stolypin dissolved the Second Duma on 3 June 1907 and drastically altered the franchise on which subsequent Dumas were to be elected. The representation of the urban population (especially the working class), the peasantry and the national minorities was cut to a fraction.

The make-up of the Third Duma (1907–12) was markedly more conservative than the first two Dumas. The Left was reduced to a small minority and the tone of Kadet opposition became more cautious. A majority of the deputies were landed noblemen and the Octobrists, led by A. I. Guchkov, now formed the largest parliamentary group. The Octobrist leadership were broadly sympathetic to Stolypin's proposals for legal and administrative changes, and shared his hope that cooperation between Duma and government would strengthen the State's authority, check the pretensions of minority nationalities and reduce social tension. Yet Stolypin proved unable to enact more than a fraction of the measures he proposed. Not only were many of his proposals radically altered by the Duma, but he encountered stiff opposition from the State Council and the Tsar himself gave him no more than lukewarm support. Stolypin's problems were epitomized by the constitutional crisis that arose in 1911 over a bill to establish zemstvos in the western provinces. To ensure that the zemstvos would be controlled by Russian rather than Polish landowners in the region, the bill envisaged a cautious lowering of the property qualifications and the creation of electoral curias based on nationality. The majority in the State Council feared that these proposals would set a damaging precedent and, with the consent of the Tsar, rejected the bill. Stolypin's frustration was intense. He consented to continue in office only on condition the Tsar suspended both chambers, disciplined his leading opponents in the State Council, and promulgated the bill under Article 87. The Tsar felt humiliated, the majority in the State Council were furious, and the Octobrists joined in bitter denunciation of Stolypin's high-handed use of Article 87. The premier's downfall was widely predicted before he was assassinated, by an anarchist but with possible police complicity, in September 1911.

After Stolypin's assassination relations between ministers and the Duma deteriorated further. The parties at the centre of the political spectrum became more outspoken in their criticisms of the government. The core of the Octobrist party, which had suffered major defections to the Right, and a new Progressive party, led by a group of Moscow industrialists, moved close to the Kadets, who in turn intensified their opposition to the government. In the Fourth Duma (1912–17) the government showed little concern to defuse opposition or to exploit the deep divisions between its more moderate critics and the small minority of radical Left deputies. The Tsar proved wary of replacing Stolypin with a leader committed to any firm legislative programme. By 1914, when he appointed the aged I. L. Goremykin, the premier had become a mere figurehead in charge of no major department, and individual ministers reverted to reporting independently and in haphazard fashion to the Tsar.

The lack of clear leadership was underlined by the increasing isolation of Nicholas himself. The anxiety of the Tsar and Tsarina to shield their haemophiliac son led them to withdraw into a narrow family circle, incurring the displeasure of members of high society. The royal couple's prestige was further damaged by their devotion to the 'holy man' Rasputin. To the Tsar, and especially to the Tsarina, he seemed a gift from heaven endowed with miraculous power to stem the Tsarevich's bleeding attacks. On the other hand, in the eyes of even the most loyal ministers and the foremost grand dukes and prelates, he was no holy man but a charlatan whose doctrine of 'redemption by sin' was but a thin veil for crude depravity. No amount of censorship could quell public curiosity and disapproval.

Following the revolution of 1905 Russia experienced a further period of rapid economic and social change. A recession brought on by the disruption of war and revolution lasted into 1908 but thereafter swift industrial growth coincided with a series of generally good harvests. The pace of urbanization accelerated as did the development of civil society visible before 1905. The education system expanded at all levels. There was a rapid increase in the output of journals and books and in the range of and demand for newspapers. The number and size of business, professional and other independent organizations rose swiftly. The legal limitations on organizations representing labour remained more severe. Legislation passed in 1912 to establish funds for accident and illness insurance for workers created councils to which workers elected representatives. Trade unions, on the other hand, after enjoying a brief period of vigorous growth in the immediate aftermath of their legalization in 1906, were subjected to a variety of restrictions and reduced to a skeletal and precarious existence. Until 1910 organized labour protest was subdued but as the industrial boom gathered pace, bringing the number of workers in mining and large-sale industry to over three million by 1914, the relative industrial calm was broken. In 1912 over half a million workers across the Empire went on strike to protest when government troops opened fire upon a large crowd of striking miners in the Lena goldfields in eastern Siberia, killing some 270. No city proved more strike-prone than the capital where there was a general strike in the summer of 1914.

The strike coincided with international crisis. As the Ottoman Empire in Europe disintegrated in the late nineteenth century, leaving a number of small successor states, hostility mounted between Russia and Austria-Hungary over their rival claims to influence in the Balkans. Between 1908 and 1913, while Austria-Hungary sought to check the growth of Serbia, the most ambitious and assertive of the successor states, Russia lent her fellow Slaves diplomatic support. The conflict played a key role in exacerbating tension between the Dual Alliance of Austria and Germany, on the one side, and Russia and France on the other. In July 1914, after Serbian nationalists had assassinated the Habsburg heir apparent, the Austrian government resolved to crush the Serbian menace once and for all. Fully confident of German support, Vienna issued Serbia an ultimatum which she could not fulfil, and declared war. Russia mobilized her army, Germany immediately followed suit, and the First World War ensued.

The Revolutionary Intelligentsia

A significant role in the disorder that plagued the last decades of the Russian Empire was played by the so-called 'revolutionary intelligentsia'. A watertight definition of the elusive social category 'intelligentsia' is difficult to frame. The term is generally taken to denote that section of the educated élite – an élite deliberately nurtured by the tsarist regime to man the civil and military establishment – which became critical of the existing order. A radical minority of the intelligentsia took their criticism beyond intellectual dissent, broke their ties with conventional society and made a conscious commitment to the revolutionary overthrow of the tsarist order. Emerging in significant numbers in the 1860s, this revolutionary intelligentsia established a tradition of revolutionary thought, organization, propaganda and agitation. Until the last years of the nineteenth century it was they who posed the most visible challenge to the status quo. It was they who introduced and developed the political vocabulary in terms of which protagonists of the Left interpreted the revolutionary drama. It was they who, at the turn of the century, founded the socialist parties which came to dominate the political scene in 1917. And it was from their number that the most prominent socialist leaders of 1917 were drawn.

In the decades before Emancipation only a few isolated individuals had carried dissent to the point of revolutionary commitment. The most prominent of these was Alexander Herzen who emigrated in 1847 and in 1853 founded a Free Russian Press in London which launched a tradition of radical émigré journals smuggled into the Empire. From the late 1850s, as censorship was slackened and expectations of imminent and major reform rose, a small but steady stream of intelligentsia, largely drawn from students in higher education, became involved in radical dissent. At first much of their energy was absorbed in rebellion against the values and conventions, the patriarchy and religion, of the educated world from which they sprang. During the 1860s, however, cultural revolt became overlaid by concern for broader social problems. They drew upon the émigré press and upon a steady flow of western social, political, economic and scientific works. They drew, too, upon illegal literature put out by clandestine presses within Russia, and upon the legally published works of social critics who skilfully circumvented the censor, the most influential being the journalist N. G. Chernyshevsky.

The dominant theme of this literature was concern for the well-being of the peasantry. Castigating the terms of Emancipation as unjust and rejecting the prospect of Russia following the western path of capitalist development, they developed the 'populist' ideology adumbrated by Herzen and Chernyshevsky. At the centre of their vision of Russia's revolutionary transformation stood the peasant commune which, they argued, had preserved the peasantry from the corruption of private property. With its egalitarian tradition of periodic redistribution of the land it seemed to them to provide a basis on which Russia could bypass capitalism and make a direct transition to socialism. During the late 1860s and 70s a series of revolutionary underground organizations was formed. They attempted to propagate socialist ideas among the peasantry, and in 1874 two to three thousand young radicals 'went to the people' in the countryside. They made little impact and at the end of the decade some of them resorted to terrorist attacks on senior officials in an effort to destabilize the government. The most highly-centralized and coherent terrorist organization they created was the 'People's Will' formed in 1879. Despite the government's efforts, the People's Will succeeded in 1881 in assassinating the Tsar himself. The upshot, however, was not revolution but the destruction of the organization.

During the 1880s Marxism began to gain currency among the revolutionary intelligentsia. Its most influential spokesman was G. V. Plekhanov, who along with four other former populists founded the émigré 'Emancipation of Labour' group dedicated to spreading Marxist ideas in Russia. Plekhanov argued that Russia was bound to undergo capitalism and that the populist notion of direct transition from semi-feudalism to socialism was an utopian illusion. The commune was doomed by the spread of market relations and the peasantry were becoming divided between capitalists and propertyless rural labourers. Moreover, capitalism alone could generate the industrial base necessary for socialism and the class destined to overthrow the bourgeoisie and carry through socialist revolution, the industrial working class. The revolutionary intelligentsia, Plekhanov urged, must abandon its romantic and terrorist traditions, adopt the scientific perspective of Marxism, and devote itself to assisting in the development of a powerful revolutionary organization of the proletariat.

By the early nineties a significant proportion of young radicals had adopted Marxist ideas. At first they devoted themselves to self-education, fierce polemics against the populists, and propaganda among circles of selected workers. During the mid nineties, however, they began to turn to mass agitation at factory level. In 1895 the 'Union of Struggle for the Emancipation of the Working Class', among whose leaders were V. I. Lenin and Iu. O. Martov, was set up in St Petersburg and its members were active in the major strikes of 1896 and 1897. 1898 saw the foundation of the RSDWP. It was promptly shattered by police arrests, and following the economic downturn of 1899 there was a brief fall-off in strike action and contact between *intelligenty* and workers declined. But in 1900 Plekhanov's group, augmented by Lenin and Martov, set up *Iskra*, an émigré journal designed as a rallying point for like-minded Social Democrats. In 1903 a second founding congress, held in Brussels and London and dominated by delegates loyal to *Iskra*, re-established the party.

At this congress the delegates split into two factions. The initial bone of contention was the question of the terms on which sympathizers should be admitted to the party. One faction (the Bolsheviks – 'partisans of the majority') favoured a narrow definition which would admit only dedicated and disciplined activists, while another (the Mensheviks – 'partisans of the minority') envisaged a much broader party embracing wide sections of the proletariat. Lenin, who had spelled out his ideas on the need for a tightly-knit, centralized party of 'professional revolutionaries' in his major tract on party structure, *What Is To Be Done?* (1902), emerged as the leader of the Bolsheviks. The Mensheviks, among whom Martov played a leading role, rejected Lenin's vision of the party on the grounds that it would institutionalize the gap between intelligentsia and workers, between party and class.

The following years saw repeated attempts at reconciliation between the two factions, and local activists showed markedly less interest in ideological divisions than did leaders abroad. During the revolution of 1905, when many of the émigré leaders briefly returned to Russia, there was considerable co-operation between them. Yet after 1905 the rift widened. Mensheviks in general adhered more strictly to the traditional Marxist assumption that in so backward a country as Russia the impending revolution would bring the bourgeoisie to power. They were willing to envisage greater co-operation with liberal representatives of the bourgeoisie and tended to place more emphasis on taking advantage of the new opportunities of the Duma era for the development of a legal workers' movement. Bolsheviks, on the other hand, were more dismissive of the revolutionary potential of the Russian bourgeoisie, saw the peasantry as more likely allies of the proletariat, and regarded legal activity as no substitute for underground preparation for revolution. During the Stolypin years, when the SDs were hard hit by repression and membership fell precipitately, factional strife amongst émigré SDs was fierce. Lenin clashed with the most intransigent Bolsheviks, led by the philosopher A. A. Bogdanov, who were hostile to even minimal use of such legal outlets as Duma representation and favoured concentration upon preparation for a new armed uprising. In 1909 Lenin succeeded in having Bogdanov expelled from the Bolshevik faction. In January 1912 he organized a conference of like-minded Social Democrats in Prague. A new Central Committee was elected and the Bolshevik faction became a fully-fledged independent party. A rival meeting in Vienna the same year, at which the radical Menshevik L. D. Trotsky took a leading role, failed to forge unity among the non-Bolshevik Social Democrats. Trotsky subsequently became identified with the 'Interdistrict' Committee which was formed in St Petersburg the following year in an attempt to create a bridge between rival party groups.

In the immediate pre-war years, as working-class protest resumed, the parties created by the revolutionary intelligentsia enjoyed something of a revival. Bolshevik publications, demanding an eight-hour day, a democratic republic, and confiscation of all noble land, achieved wider circulation than those of the Mensheviks. In the Duma elections of 1912 the Bolsheviks won six of the nine curias reserved for workers and by 1914 the Mensheviks had lost control of the trade unions and social insurance councils in the Moscow and St Petersburg regions to their more radical rivals.

By no means all revolutionaries were converted to social democracy. Many refused to accept the notion that the peasantry must pass through the mill of capitalism and be divided between rural capitalists and rural proletarians. From the 1890s 'neo-populists', whose chief theorist was V. M. Chernov, placed less emphasis on the peculiar virtues of the peasant commune than had earlier populists, but argued that since the vast majority of peasants rejected private landownership and depended upon the labour of their own hands, they were already semi-socialist in outlook. While accepting that in the cities events would unfold much as Marx had envisaged, with a phase of bourgeois rule culminating in proletarian revolution, they insisted that in the countryside peasant revolution could achieve the immediate 'socialization' of the land and abolition of private ownership in preparation for the ultimate transition to socialist production. Several local groups came together in 1901 to form the SR party, and were joined the following year by the émigré Agrarian Socialist League.

The party addressed much of its effort to workers and it enrolled few peasant members, yet the peasant question was central to its programme and during the revolution of 1905 it exerted considerable influence in the All-Russian Peasants' Union. The SRs suffered divisions over tactics – the older generation tended to disapprove of the wave of terrorist attacks mounted by younger members between 1901 and 1907. The repression of the Stolypin years took as heavy a toll on the SRs as the SDs and the party suffered a major blow to both its morale and organization in 1908 when E. F. Azef, the leader of its 'fighting organization', was exposed as a double agent working for the Okhrana. The level of SR activity declined sharply and in the pre-war period they took less advantage than did the SDs of the opportunities for legal activity. When the franchise reform of 1907 virtually ruled out the possibility of exploiting Duma elections for propaganda purposes among the peasantry, the party boycotted both the Third and Fourth Dumas.

The War and the February Revolution

The initial public response to the outbreak of war was an upsurge of patriotic fervour, at any rate among the middle and upper classes: the Kadet leadership in the Duma called for a political truce and national unity against the common enemy. Yet the war proved far longer and more destructive than had been generally expected. The news from the front was grim. Although Russia scored major victories against Austria-Hungary in 1914 and again in 1916, she could not hold her own against Germany. An initial invasion of East Prussia relieved German pressure on the French but led to disastrous Russian defeats at Tannenberg and the Masurian Lakes. During 1915 the Russians were forced to evacuate a vast stretch of territory reaching beyond Poland into the western provinces and 1916 saw further defeats. The number of deaths, casualties and prisoners taken spiralled remorselessly upwards. In both the navy and the army, which enrolled a total of 15 million predominantly peasant men, morale deteriorated. By the winter of 1916–17 the High Command had become seriously worried by rank-and-file disaffection.

The war effort imposed heavy burdens on the civilian population. As production for the front was stepped up, the output of civilian manufactures fell, prices soared, and peasants found less and less incentive to sell their produce. The market mechanism linking city and countryside began to break down, and was further disrupted by the inability of the railway system to cope with the exceptional wartime demands made upon it. The flow of grain to the cities – and to the army – dwindled. Real wages for workers declined steadily and in the winter of 1916–17 even those of skilled metal workers in the capital (renamed Petrograd in line with patriotic sentiment) plummeted. The length of the working day was extended and the incidence of accidents in mines and factories rose. At the same time, the hectic expansion of war industries swelled the industrial proletariat by no less than a third, there was a massive influx of refugees from front-line areas, and the cities became increasingly overcrowded, insanitary and disease-ridden.

The regime was held responsible. The High Command, and the Tsar himself, especially after he took personal command in the summer of 1915, were blamed for military incompetence. The War Ministry was blamed for the desperate shortage of arms and ammunition during the first two years of the war, and for the tardiness with which domestic industry was harnessed to war production. Civilian ministries were blamed for failing to ensure adequate supplies of food, for chronic shortages of every kind, for the endless queues. National minorities were given particular cause for grievance by the High Command's disregard for their sensibilities, epitomized by the wholesale deportation of Jews from the Polish provinces. Rumours of treason, corruption and massive war-profiteering gathered pace, fed by the Germanic origins of the Tsarina, the notoriety of Rasputin, the frantic jostling for office among government ministers, and the relative comfort enjoyed by high society.

Initially, mobilization had served to increase government control of public affairs. Civil liberties were further curtailed, disruptive workers were drafted into the army, censorship was tightened, legal socialist publications suppressed, and the Bolshevik members of the Duma arrested. Underground socialist organizations were hard hit by arrests. Émigré socialist leaders had greater difficulty communicating with Russia. Moreover, the war intensified factional disputes as socialists divided between 'defencists' who were prepared to support the war effort and 'internationalists', among whom Lenin was most uncompromising, who condemned it. Yet the authorities were unable to silence the expression of political opposition. Within the Duma the small contingent of Menshevik and Trudovik Deputies, led by N. S. Chkeidze and A. F. Kerensky respectively, became increasingly strident in their attacks upon the regime. In August 1915 a broad spectrum of liberal and conservative Duma deputies formed a 'Progressive Bloc' under Miliukov's leadership and called upon Nicholas to appoint a government enjoying public confidence. In November 1916 a speech by Miliukov created a sensation when he punctuated a list of the government's shortcomings with the rhetorical question: 'Is this stupidity or treason?' The Tsar rejected the Duma's demands and permitted it only the briefest of sessions. Yet as the war dragged on it served not only to increase the regime's unpopularity but also to give new leverage to the forces of opposition.

The professional and business classes, anxious to support the army with auxiliary services and medical care for the wounded, and to increase military production, organized their efforts through public organizations – the Union of Zemstvos, the Union of Towns and a network of War Industry Committees (WICs). These provided a forum and focus for public criticism of officialdom. The holding of elections for worker representatives to the WICs from 1915 created new outlets for agitation and organization among the proletariat. While Bolsheviks and radical socialists urged a boycott of the WICs, the predominantly Menshevik Labour groups that were established secured a new platform. Moreover, the direct dependence of the war effort upon industrial output rendered workers' resort to the strike weapon even more devastating than in peacetime, and from the summer of 1915 there was a resurgence of industrial stoppages. Equally, mobilization drew millions of peasants into closer contact with national affairs and, especially in the urban garrisons behind the lines, created a concentrated pool of peasant discontent far more threatening than that of scattered villagers.

In early 1917 the number of strikes in the capital rose and there was a series of demonstrations, notably on 9 January, the anniversary of Bloody Sunday, and 14 February, the day the Duma reconvened. News of impending bread rationing created panic buying and on Thursday 23 February, International Women's Day, female textile workers went on strike and demonstrated, closely followed by metal workers concentrated in the most militant and solidly proletarian quarter of Petrograd, the Vyborg district. In the following days the strike rapidly spread across the city and workers were joined by white-collar employees, teachers and students in mass demonstrations which converged on the city centre. Calls for the creation of a workers' soviet, including a summons by the Bolshevik Vyborg District Committee to form it at the Finland Station in the Vyborg district, became widespread. On Monday 27th many insurgents converged on the Tauride Palace, seat of the Duma, and that evening a group of predominantly Menshevik intelligentsia established a Provisional Executive Committee (EC) of the soviet in the palace and summoned factories and barracks to elect deputies to it.

The authorities failed to regain control of the situation. On Sunday 26th on instructions from the Tsar, troops opened fire on demonstrators and the Duma was prorogued. The following day General Ivanov was instructed to assemble loyal forces near the capital to restore order. On Monday and Tuesday, however, the government's forces in the capital disintegrated as soldiers in the garrison ignored orders and streamed from the barracks to fraternize with civilian demonstrators. By the Wednesday the revolution had spread to Moscow, Kronstadt and the Baltic Fleet and the High Command ordered a halt to Ivanov's expedition. On Thursday 2 March the military leaders recommended to Nicholas that he abdicate. He did so not only for himself but also for his son, in favour of his brother Mikhail, and when Mikhail declined the throne the monarchy disappeared.

On the same day that the Petrograd Soviet was set up, the Duma leaders, while accepting the prorogation ordered by the Tsar, held a private meeting and created a Provisional Committee. The Committee decided to form a government and by Wednesday 1 March Miliukov, who had emerged as the dominant figure, was drawing up a list of potential cabinet ministers. Radical socialists urged that the Soviet was in a position to establish a revolutionary government in defiance of the Duma Committee. Workers had rallied enthusiastically to the Soviet, and soldiers in the capital also seemed to have more faith in it than in the Duma leaders. This was borne out on the Wednesday when insurgent soldiers pressed the Soviet to issue an order – Order No. 1 – which severely circumscribed the authority of officers both by sanctioning the election of soldiers' committees with control over weapons and by laying down that officers' orders were to be subject to the Soviet's approval. Yet the majority of the Soviet EC favoured a government drawn from the Duma. On Thursday 2 March they reached agreement with the Duma leaders and the Soviet plenum voted overwhelmingly to offer conditional support to Miliukov and his colleagues. The following day the formation of a Provisional Government was proclaimed, headed by Prince G. E. Lvov, chairman of the Union of Zemstvos, with Miliukov as Foreign Minister, Guchkov as War Minister and Kerensky, the only socialist member, Minister of Justice.

February to October

The Provisional Government committed itself to a wide range of reforms. All the classical liberal demands were rapidly satisfied by decree: a political amnesty and full freedom of the press, speech, association and religion; an end to all discrimination based on class, nationality or religion; the abolition of the death penalty and the creation of a fully independent judiciary. Church and State were to be separated, local government democratized, and a Constituent Assembly elected by universal, direct, equal and secret franchise was to be summoned to settle the future form of the country's constitution and to resolve major social problems such as that of the land.

The early weeks of the new era saw far-reaching institutional change throughout the country. The tsarist police force disintegrated and was replaced by local militias. New commissars replaced the provincial governors. Zemstvos and city dumas co-opted new members in preparation for democratic elections and meanwhile had to contend with 'Committees of Public Organizations' which sprang up in most localities. Within the army, a hierarchy of committees was elected to represent the soldiers. Peasant representatives were incorporated into committees established to organize food supplies and make preparations for land reform. New bodies emerged to represent and press the claims of the more assertive national minorities. Workers established their own militia, factory committees and trade unions, and a complex network of regional, city and suburban soviets was elected to represent workers and in some areas soldiers and peasants. In March an All-Russian Conference of Soviets met in Petrograd and created a Soviet Central Executive Committee.

At the centre the authority of the new government was limited by the rival authority of the Petrograd Soviet, a situation dubbed 'dual power'. The issue which initially caused greatest friction between the two was that of the war. On 14 March the Soviet issued an appeal to the world for a democratic peace based on renunciation by all sides of annexations and indemnities. The Foreign Minister Miliukov, however, was determined to pursue war to victory. Demonstrations against his policy, which took place from 18–21 April, precipitated a cabinet crisis. Miliukov and the War Minister, Guchkov, resigned and the whole cabinet threatened to follow suit unless the socialist leaders of the Soviet agreed to form a coalition. A majority of the EC, in which the Georgian Menshevik I. G. Tsereteli had emerged as a leading figure, had by this time adopted 'revolutionary defencism', accepting that until peace had been secured they must uphold the front. Reluctantly, and after much soul-searching, they decided to respond to Lvov's invitation. On 5 May six socialists led by Tsereteli formed a coalition with Lvov and his liberal colleagues. The SR leader Chernov became Minister of Agriculture and the Menshevik M. I. Skobelev became Minister of Labour.

The First Coalition pursued two lines in the search for peace. Working through the Soviet, the Mensheviks and SRs tried to organize an international socialist conference in Stockholm, designed to rally anti-war feeling in all countries. M. A. Tereshchenko, the non-party liberal who succeeded Miliukov as Foreign Minister, proposed to the Allies that they revise their war aims to bring them closer to the peace proposals enunciated by the Soviet. While both approaches were being pursued with little success, the government made preparations for a new offensive against Germany and Austria-Hungary. The new War Minister, Kerensky, made a series of highly-publicized tours of the front to raise the men's fighting spirit. The offensive was launched on 18 June but was deeply unpopular with much of the rank and file and collapsed in the first week of July.

Meanwhile, the government was confronted by an array of problems. The incipient trade breakdown which had helped to spark the Petrograd insurrection accelerated after February. This exacerbated the growing shortage of food, fuel and raw materials. Industrial output was cut, prices soared, and urban conditions deteriorated. Conflict between employers and workers intensified, and the number of strikes rose. In addition, peasant unrest in areas where there was significant private landholding had reached serious proportions by May. Moreover, there was an upsurge in nationalist agitation: demands for varying degrees of autonomy were made by minorities from the Baltic to the Caucasus.

To make matters worse, the government was faced by increasingly strident opposition from the Bolsheviks. On 3 April Lenin returned from exile, travelling from Switzerland on a sealed train provided by the German Foreign Ministry, and denounced 'revolutionary defencism' as tantamount to supporting a 'predatory imperialist war'. In his 'April Theses' he called for a revolutionary government based on the Soviets and empowered to control the banks, production and distribution. He demanded the confiscation of all private estates, the nationalization of the land, and its management by local peasant soviets. At the Party Conference held at the end of April the Bolsheviks officially repudiated even the most heavily qualified support for the Provisional Government and adopted Lenin's programme which was disseminated in crisp, clear, and hard-hitting language. Until the late summer the Bolsheviks were outnumbered by moderate socialists in most popular forums. Menshevik and SR sympathizers dominated the soldiers' committees; among the peasantry the SRs enjoyed far more support than any other party; the Mensheviks were most prominent in the trade unions; together the two parties won large majorities in municipal duma elections which began in May; and in June they dominated the First All-Russian Congress of Soviets and consolidated control of its Central Executive Committee (CEC). Yet the size of the Bolshevik party increased, it gained widespread support in the factory committees, and developed a network of military organizations in the army and navy. On 18 June the CEC was taken aback when a demonstration in the capital which it had itself summoned featured Bolshevik anti-government slogans.

At the beginning of July, this array of social and political problems induced a renewed cabinet crisis. The Kadet ministers considered their socialist colleagues were pre-empting the decisions of the Constituent Assembly by making partial concessions to Ukrainian demands for autonomy and to peasant demands for the redistribution of private land. On 2 July the Kadets resigned. On 3 and 4 July mass demonstrations in which workers, garrison soldiers, and sailors from the Kronstadt naval base were prominent, converged on the Tauride Palace. Demonstrators urged the socialist leaders of the EC to break with their liberal allies and form a purely socialist, Soviet-based government. The EC refused and with the help of loyal troops restored order. The Bolsheviks were blamed for the 'July uprising', and Lenin was publicly denounced as a German agent. Leading Bolsheviks, including Trotsky who now joined the party, were arrested, their press was attacked, and Lenin was driven into hiding in Finland.

After prolonged negotiations, a Second Coalition government headed by Kerensky was formed on 25 July. Kerensky sought to consolidate the position of the government by holding a State Conference in Moscow (12–15 August). The Conference was met by a protest strike in Moscow and the Bolsheviks boycotted the proceedings. The middle-class organizations and parties who dominated the Conference gave a rousing reception to General Kornilov, the new Supreme Commander. Kornilov urged the government to take decisive measures to restore discipline in the army and quell disorder at home. The upshot was the 'Kornilov affair'. At the the end of August Kerensky abruptly denounced Kornilov for plotting to overthrow the government. He gained a free hand from his ministerial colleagues to reconstruct the cabinet and called upon the Soviet to help defend the capital against 'counter-revolution'. Bolsheviks and moderate socialists alike joined garrison troops, sailors from Kronstadt and workers' militia ('Red Guard') detachments in heading off the force despatched by Kornilov. Railway workers halted the troop trains, rank-and-file soldiers abandoned the expedition and Kornilov was arrested.

Kerensky's prestige was badly tarnished, the government was left in disarray, and the call for 'All Power to the Soviets' became more popular. The moderate socialists remained opposed to the formation of a Soviet-based government, but rejected co-operation with the Kadets whom they considered implicated in the Kornilov affair. After a Democratic Conference summoned to resolve the membership of the new government had failed, Kerensky was allowed to form a Third Coalition which took office on 27 September. The Kadets were again included. The moderate socialists who took office alongside them were lesser-known figures and included neither Tsereteli nor Chernov. The new government was to be responsible to a Provisional Council of the Russian Republic, or 'Pre-Parliament', drawn from democratic elements which convened on 7 October and was still in session when the Provisional Government was overthrown.

The Kornilov affair boosted the fortunes of the Bolsheviks. Trotsky and other party members arrested after the July Days were released. The Petrograd Soviet endorsed the call by their spokesman, L. B. Kamenev, for an exclusively socialist government. By the end of September the Bolsheviks had gained majority support in both the Moscow and Petrograd soviets, where Trotsky had become chairman. The moderate socialists still controlled the CEC elected by the first All-Russian Congress of Soviets in June, but acceded to demands that they summon a Second Congress which, following a series of regional soviet congresses, eventually met on 25 October.

On 14 September Lenin, still in hiding, began to urge his colleagues on the Bolshevik Central Committee to organize an immediate seizure of power. The Central Committee was at first unsympathetic but on 10 October, at a meeting which Lenin attended, it was resolved to make armed insurrection the order of the day. The decision was confirmed on 16 October at an expanded meeting which included representatives from the Petrograd city committee and other regional bodies. The decision was vigorously opposed by some sections of the party, including two of Lenin's leading lieutenants, Kamenev and G. E. Zinoviev. Meanwhile the Petrograd Soviet had voted to establish a Military Revolutionary Committee (MRC) to co-ordinate measures both against any German assault on the capital and against any attack on the Left by the Provisional Government. The MRC contained radical SR members but was dominated by Bolsheviks and it was through it that the October uprising was planned. On 21–22 October the MRC asserted its own control over the garrison. On 24 October its forces rebuffed efforts by the government to close Bolshevik newspapers and seal bridges linking working-class districts to the city centre. That night Lenin travelled incognito to Soviet and party headquarters and in the early hours of 25 October strategic points in the city were seized. Kerensky left the capital and tried with little success to raise loyal troops. At 10 a.m. Lenin drafted a proclamation announcing the fall of the Provisional Government, and that evening, shortly after the Second All-Russian Congress of Soviets had assembled, the Winter Palace was taken and the cabinet arrested.

The minority of moderate socialists at the Congress denounced the seizure of power and walked out. The majority, made up predominantly of Bolsheviks with a substantial bloc of radical SRs, approved the formation of a Bolshevik government, the Council of People's Commissars. Cadets from military schools and a force of 1000 cossacks from outside the capital tried without success to overthrow the new government. Moderate leaders of the railway and postal workers attempted to force the formation of an all-socialist coalition, a 'homogeneous socialist government'. Several Bolshevik commissars favoured such a compromise, but Lenin and Trotsky were adamantly opposed and negotiations broke down. In November the Left SRs, now formally established as a separate party, entered negotiations for the formation of what proved a short-lived coalition with the Bolsheviks.

The first steps of the new government included decrees on land, peace, the rights of national minorities and workers' control in industry. The peasants were authorized to parcel out the private estates while legal ownership of all land was vested in the State; factory committees were given broad powers to vet the actions of management; the minorities were granted the right of self-determination; each regiment was authorized to negotiate armistice terms. A general armistice was signed on 4 December and by the treaty of Brest-Litovsk the war was brought to an end. Urban soviets in many parts of Russia quickly declared their allegiance to the new government. Opponents were harrassed, an All-Russian Extraordinary Commission for Combating Counter-Revolution and Sabotage (Cheka) was created, and Kadet and non-socialist newspapers banned. Elections to the Constituent Assembly, which the Provisional Government had eventually scheduled for November, went ahead. But when the Assembly met for its first session on 5 January 1918 it immediately became clear that a majority of the deputies were hostile to the government and the Assembly was forcibly disbanded. The economic situation worsened dramatically in the months that followed October as soldiers flocked home and military orders to industry abruptly halted. Industry was nationalized and steps were taken to tighten discipline in the factories and extract food from the countryside. During 1918 the Right, the Mensheviks, the SRs, various minority national groups, and foreign powers sought to reverse different aspects of the revolution and in June 1918 large-scale civil war broke out.

Glossary

Ivanov, General N. I.   Chief of Petrograd Military District in January 1917.

Osvobozhdenie   Russian liberal newspaper *"Liberation."*

Struve, Peter   Intellectual who shifted from Marxist, to liberal, to anticommunist, 1890s–1920s.

Further Reading: General Background on Russia and the Period Leading up to the 1917 Revolution

General histories

E. Acton, Russia: *The Tsarist and Soviet Legacy* (Longman, 1995).

A. Brown, M. Kaser and G. S. Smith (eds.), *The Cambridge Encyclopedia of Russia and the Former Soviet Union* (Cambridge University Press, 1994).

L. Kochen and J. Keep, *The Making of Modern Russia* (Penguin, rev. ed., 1997).

H. Rogger, *Russia in the Age of Modernization and Revolution, 1881–1917* (Longman, 1983).

D. Saunders, *Russia in the Era of Reaction and Reform, 1801–1881* (Longman, 1991).

Specialized studies

A. Ascher, *The Revolution of 1905*, 2 vols. (Stanford University Press, 1988, 1992).

M. Ferro, *Nicholas II: The Last of the Tsars* (Viking, 1991).

A. Wildman, *The End of the Russian Imperial Army*. 2 vols. (Princeton University Press, 1980–7).

Anthologies of articles

E. Clowes, Samuel Kassow and James L. West (eds.), *Between Tsar and People: Educated Society and the Quest for Public Identity in Late Imperial Russia* (Princeton University Press, 1991).

Olga Crisp and Linda Edmondson (eds.), *Civil Rights in Imperial Russia* (Oxford/Clarendon Press, 1989).

Stephen P. Frank and Mark D. Steinberg (eds.), *Cultures in Flux: Lower Class Values, Practices and Resistance in Late Imperial Russia* (Princeton University Press, 1994).

Part II
Parties, Movements and Personalities in the Revolutions of 1917

2

Russia's Second Revolution: The February 1917 Uprising in Petrograd

E. N. Burdzhalov

Originally appeared as E. N. Burdzhalov, *Russia's Second Revolution: The February 1917 Uprising in Petrograd*, translated and edited by Donald J. Raleigh (Bloomington, Indiana: Indiana University Press, 1987): 296–319.

Editor's Introduction

E. N. Burdzhalov was one of the boldest of Soviet historians during a period when scholars in the USSR were being carefully scrutinized for their points of view. Historians in the Soviet Union, even in the less severe years after Stalin's death, were continually called upon to produce books and articles that maintained a sense of consistency with the ruling Communist Party's current ideological position on historical events. Biographies, for example, were virtually nonexistent (with the exception of the permitted repetition of Lenin's heroic achievements); certain subjects, such as the role of the Church and of the Russian middle class, were not really studied in any professional sense but were treated *en passant* with derision, dismissal or in negative terms as forms of opposition that communism successfully combatted.

When it came to dealing with the revolution itself, the ante was raised to the highest levels. There were a plethora of "official histories," such as I. I. Mints's voluminous history of the Russian Revolution. Though he and other historians commissioned by the party because of their ideological loyalty and their professional expertise certainly made use of relevant archival and published sources, their interpretations fell into specific categories. Basically, their perspectives in terms of asking questions and seeking out evidence for their findings were rooted in a predetermined framework of analysis and outcome. To be sure, there were quiet forms of dissension. Some historians followed the path of P. A. Zaionchkovskii, who was mentor not only to many Soviet students but also to a large number of American historians who formed the first generation of Western graduate students doing dissertation research in the Soviet Union. Zaionchkovskii, a specialist on the period from the 1860s to the 1880s, managed to pay obeisance to Lenin's alleged authority on all matters of history in the introductions and conclusions of his books, but, as he instructed his students, the actual work of history only appeared in his chapters of content. Indeed, he would often tell his charges that they should not waste time even reading the first and last chapters of Soviet historical works.

Burdzhalov's career, which is effectively described in the introduction to his book from which this excerpt is taken by Donald Raleigh, a noted American historian of the Soviet provinces during the period of the revolution, evolved from acceptance to criticism of the party's commanding interpretations of 1917. Indeed, he was the subject of a large and public denunciation which was fought out in the pages of *Voprosy Istorii*, the leading Soviet historical journal.

Readers have an excellent example from the extract below of Burdzhalov's vivid presentation of the complex events of the February uprising which brought an end to the monarchy; (full citations for the footnotes can be found at the end of the essay). He begins his narrative at the beginning of March 1917 when it had become clear to the Russian General Staff that the abdication of Nicholas II was a necessity if there were to be any hope of a successful completion of the ruinous world war. The court scandals over the inappropriate power obtained by the illiterate priest Grigory Rasputin had led to his assassination a few months before; food riots in the capital had merged with a number of street demonstrations led by a variety of militant revolutionary parties; and the tsar had lost all remaining credibility by going to the front to command his army, an act which coincided with further military disasters for Russia. For these and other reasons (see the previous article by Edward Acton in this volume), negotiations were opened between members of the Duma and the military to establish a democratic "Provisional Government" which would make a renewed commitment to support the war effort. At the same time, radical and working-class sectors of St. Petersburg worked to reestablish the "Soviet," or council, which had first been created during the first revolution in 1905. The tension between the two bodies began from day one. This is an example of Soviet historiography at its best.

Russia's Second Revolution: The February 1917 Uprising in Petrograd

E. N. Burdzhalov

At 10:00 P.M. on March 2 the discussion on the imperial train began. Guchkov spoke first. Quite upset, he avoided making eye contact with the tsar and detailed unpersuasively what had occurred in Petrograd. Judging by the protocols kept by the head of the field office, K. A. Naryshkin, Guchkov said that he had arrived with Shul'gin to apprise the emperor of the real conditions in Petrograd and to seek advice on measures that could save the situation. Guchkov reported the state of affairs in Petrograd was extremely threatening, the disorders had spread to the outlying regions, there was not a single reliable unit, troops arriving from the fronts promptly sided with the insurgents, and although a Provisional Duma Committee had been formed, it lacked power. Moreover, extremist elements considered the moderate Duma members traitors and were fighting to eliminate the monarchy and establish a socialist republic. "Besides us, a committee of the workers' party is meeting and we are under its influence and censorship. . . . The leftist elements are already beginning to sweep us away. Their slogan is: proclaim a socialist republic. The movement has infected the lower classes and even the soldiers, who are promised land." Guchkov pointed out that the contagion might spread to the front, that in view of the army's present mood it was impossible to preserve the throne for Nicholas. The only way out is to transfer power to others – the abdication of Nicholas II in favor of his son under a regency of Mikhail and the formation of a new government was the only way "to save the monarchical order to save the dynasty."[1]

Guchkov subsequently recalled that Ruzskii supported him, confirming that "there is not a single unit reliable enough to be sent to suppress the revolution. The tsar looked completely unshaken. The only thing that could be read on his face was that this long speech was unnecessary." And, in fact, the question of abdication had been resolved before the arrival of the Duma Committee's representatives. The protocols of the abdication compiled by Naryshkin state that Nicholas, having heard Guchkov out, commented: "I thought about this during the morning

---

1 "Protokol otrecheniia Nikolaia II (Po zapisi generala K. A. Naryshkina)," in *Otrechenie Nikolaia II*, ed. P. E. Shchegolev, pp. 185–86, Leningrad, 1927.

and in the name of general well-being, peace, and Russia's salvation, I was ready to abdicate in favor of my son, but now, reconsidering the situation, I have come to the conclusion that because of his illness I must abdicate at the same time both for my son and for myself, since I cannot part with him."[2]

Nicholas abdicated in favor of his brother Mikhail. The Duma representatives, arriving with a proposal to make Mikhail regent, not tsar, had not anticipated such a decision. They asked that they be given the opportunity to reflect on the "new terms" of the abdication. Then Guchkov announced they did not oppose the tsar's recommendation. Their confederates in the Duma subsequently criticized Guchkov's and Shul'gin's acceptance of Mikhail's candidacy. Attempting to justify his behavior, Shul'gin observed: "How could we have disagreed? . . . We had arrived to tell the tsar the Duma Committee's opinion . . . which coincided with the tsar's. . . . And if it hadn't, what could we have done? . . . We could have returned [to Petrograd] if they let us . . . for we, after all, had not resorted to 'clandestine violence' as was done in the eighteenth and the beginning of the nineteenth centuries. . . ." Shul'gin wrote that whether Aleksei or Mikhail would be tsar was, in the final analysis, a mere detail and that Mikhail's candidacy actually had some advantages. Mikhail could swear allegiance to a constitution to pacify the people, and if need be, he could renounce the throne like his brother, something a minor such as Aleksei could not do. The main thing was that time would be won.[3]

Guchkov gave the tsar the draft abdication manifesto. Nicholas left, returned shortly, and handed a paper to Guchkov. It was the document previously formulated at headquarters, and not the one presented by the Duma delegates. They had wanted Nicholas's successor to grant a constitution. They had argued that the greatest danger came from the leftist elements who were striving to declare a republic, and that if the new tsar were bound by a constitution this would weaken the position of those advocating a republic. As Shul'gin said: "We are preserving the country's symbol. . . . It's hell in the Duma, a real madhouse. We'll have to get embroiled in a decisive fight with the leftist elements and some sort of basis is necessary for this. . . . Should your brother Mikhail Aleksandrovich as the legitimate monarch swear to uphold a new constitution upon his ascension to the throne, this would contribute to a general pacification.[4] In accordance with this request, a phrase was added to the abdication manifesto that the new emperor must

2   Ibid., p. 186.
3   V. V. Shul'gin, *Dni*, Belgrade, 1925, pp. 270–71.
4   "Protokol otrecheniia Nikolaia II," p. 186.

take an inviolable oath to govern in concert with the people's representatives.

The tsar's manifesto said that "it has pleased God to lay on Russia a new and painful trial," that the newly arisen popular domestic disturbances imperil the successful prosecution of the war, which must be carried out to a victorious end no matter what happens. The document read: "In agreement with the State Duma, we think it best to abdicate the throne of the Russian State and lay down the supreme power. Not wishing to be separated from our beloved son, we hand down our inheritance to our brother, Grand Prince Mikhail Aleksandrovich, and give him our blessing on ascending the throne of the Russian State. We enjoin our brother to govern in concert and harmony with the people's representatives in legislative institutions on such principles as they shall deem fit to establish, and to bind himself by oath in the name of our beloved country."[5]

The Duma delegates did not wish to create the impression they had extorted the manifesto from the tsar. Although it was approaching midnight, the tsar, at the deputies' request, dated the manifesto 3:00 P.M. The document was typed in two copies, signed by Nicholas II in pencil, and countersigned by the court minister. N. Vishniakov, a bourgeois activist and Moscow City Duma deputy, gave an interesting interpretation of this curious detail. "The pitiful excuse for a tsar could not even see fit to sign his abdication in ink like a real man, but did so in pencil. It was as if he were so indifferent to it all, as others are when they scribble notes in pencil to a friend or make a list of dirty laundry. What despicable people! And it was precisely they who had controlled the fate of a great empire for centuries."[6]

The Duma delegates recommended Nicholas sign one more document. Guchkov said: "Workers and soldiers who took part in the disorders are convinced a return to the old system would result in reprisals against them and therefore a complete change is necessary. The popular imagination needs a crack of the whip that would change everything. I hold that the decision you have reached must be accompanied by the appointment of Prince L'vov as chairman of the Council of Ministers."[7] Nicholas signed the ukase to the State Senate in regard to Prince L'vov's appointment as chairman of the Council of Ministers and the Grand Prince Nikolai Nikolaevich as commander in chief. Insofar as Nicholas had already abdicated, his orders lacked authority. To impart "legality"

5   "Manifest otrecheniia Nikolaia II," in Otrechenie Nikolaia II, ed. P. E. Shchegolev, p. 189.
6   TsGAOR SSSR, f. 875, op. 1, d. 20, l. 272.
7   "Protokol otrecheniia Nikolaia II," pp. 186–87.

to them, they were dated 1:00 P.M., March 2, that is, much earlier than they were actually signed.

At the end of their conversation, Guchkov and Shul'gin asked the tsar about his personal plans following his abdication. He answered that he intended to spend several days at Supreme Headquarters, then visit his mother, and return to Tsarskoe Selo. The deputies assured him they would do everything in their power to facilitate his plans.

On the evening of March 2–3, the imperial train pulled out of Pskov Station for Mogilev. It was the train of the last representative of the Romanov monarchy. Nicholas II, branded by universal contempt and hatred, was even abandoned by the most loyal members of his retinue. Concerning the reaction of those closest to the tsar to the abdication, Guchkov wrote: "Literally no one tried to block us, literally no one supported the tsar. . . . Total emptiness surrounded the throne."[8]

The next day, March 3, the former tsar cabled Mikhail Aleksandrovich: "Events of the past days have forced me to decide unconditionally on such an extreme step. Forgive me, if we distressed you and failed to warn you. I remain eternally loyal to my brother. I am returning to headquarters, from where I hope to travel to Tsarskoe Selo in a few days."[9]

The tsar's abdication was not unexpected, but stemmed logically from all of the events that had preceded it. Dem'ian Bednyi wrote in *Izvestiia* on the occasion (March 4, 1917):

> Even without a manifesto we knew
> Tsar Nicholas had been deprived of his just due.
> Still, we must address the people and let them know
> So as to avoid confusion others might sow.
> "Candidates" one and all surely will moan
> When they learn there no longer is any "throne."

Had the victorious revolution resulted in the tsar's abdication or deposition? The latter, of course. The revolution had overthrown Nicholas II, and only afterward was this presented as a voluntary resignation. Nicholas II had not stepped down in the first days of the revolution when he still intended to drown the unarmed people in blood with the help of troops from the front. The tsar abdicated when the unreliability of these units became manifest, when the revolution had spread to Moscow and other cities, when the tsar's cause had failed and all options had closed. The insurgent people had dethroned Nicholas them-

8 TsGAOR SSSR, f. 5856, op. 1, d. 600, l. 9.
9 B. V. Nikitin, *Rokovye gody*, Paris, 1937, p. 202.

selves, and the "voluntary abdication" merely legalized this act by ante-dating it. Former subjects of the Russian tsar said he had abdicated himself long ago from the people.

Not for nothing did the bourgeoisie give the tsar's dethronement the form of a voluntary act. As Guchkov put it, "I was afraid that in the event he had refused to renounce the throne, the Soviet of Workers' and Soldiers' Deputies would depose Nicholas II."[10]

The tsar's so-called voluntary abdication freed the army from its oath and made it easier for it to join the revolution. It paralyzed the reactionary officers corps's opposition as well as that of other supporters of the old regime. Monarchists would not be able to defend the throne if it were vacant, if no one agreed to wear the crown knocked from Nicholas II's head. They had to accept the fall of the monarchy, at least temporarily.

The form in which the autocrat's abdication was presented, however, kept the path open for the monarchy's restoration. Calling for the abolition of the monarchy and establishment of a democratic republic, *Izvestiia* rightly noted that the dethronement was shrouded in such a manner that the possibility existed it would be overruled, that the path to restoring the monarchy was not closed. Nicholas's resignation on behalf of his brother and the latter's on behalf of the Provisional Government (see below) preserved the continuity of power and created more favorable conditions for the restoration of the monarchy than the direct deposition of the tsar and proclamation of a republican order.

Supporters of the autocracy depicted the tsar's abdication as a noble gesture, as a sacrifice he made for the well-being of the fatherland. They subsequently maintained that this measure, forced upon them, was illegal, that Nicholas II was not empowered to act for his son and that therefore the Romanov dynasty had not lost its rights to the Russian throne. Aleksandra Fedorovna held that things would return to normal. Believing that all it would take was granting a responsible ministry and constitution, she wrote her husband: "If you are forced to make concessions, you are not obliged to carry them out, since they were wrung from you. . . . It's absolutely criminal that you were compelled to do this simply because you lacked an army. Such a promise will no longer be valid when power is in your hands again. . . . God will save you and restore all of your rights to you."[11] Aleksandra Fedorovna continued to believe this even after Nicholas II had abdicated. On March 3 she wrote

10   *Poslednie novosti*, September 13, 1926.
11   *Perepiska Nikolaia i Aleksandry Romanovykh*, Moscow and Petrograd, 1923–1927, vol. 5, pp. 226, 229.

the former tsar: "I swear we shall see you once again on your throne which you will ascend with your people and troops for the glory of your reign."[12]

General V. I. Gurko, commander of the Special Army, who not long before the revolution had served as acting chief of staff, wrote the former tsar on March 4 that he hoped the country would return to its "legal sovereign" and that the present heir would be called upon to accept the throne.[13]

The tsar's voluntary abdication in favor of Mikhail did not end further efforts to abolish the monarchy. Workers and soldiers had to take new decisive steps to render Nicholas II and other members of the over-thrown dynasty harmless and to prevent a possible restoration of the monarchy.

The deposed tsar had appointed the head of the new Russian government. At 2:17 A.M., March 3, Guchkov and Shul'gin telegraphed Petrograd that the sovereign had agreed to step down on behalf of the Grand Prince Mikhail Aleksandrovich, under the condition that he be bound to uphold a constitution, and that he had entrusted Prince G. E. L'vov to form a new government. L'vov's appointment had clearly come too late. Guchkov and Shul'gin thought that the Provisional Duma Committee would hold off declaring the formation of a new government until their return, but upon their arrival in Petrograd they saw posters on the streets announcing the formation of a Provisional Government headed by that very L'vov, and set up not with the tsar's "blessing," but with that of the Soviet of Workers' and Soldiers' Deputies.

The proclamation of Mikhail Romanov as emperor of Russia did not correspond to the situation that had arisen in the capital or the rest of the country. The broad masses of the people opposed the monarchy in any form. Mikhail's accession to the throne under these conditions could set off a powerful revolutionary explosion that would destroy not only the new tsar but the Duma Committee as well as the Provisional Government, and could pave the way for genuine popular rule. In view of this the overwhelming majority of Duma members realized that if they did not submit today they could lose everything tomorrow. They yielded to the necessity of sacrificing Mikhail and agreeing to the con-vocation of a constituent assembly, thereby averting a new revolution-ary onslaught. In any case, the question of Mikhail's accession was subject to discussion. The manifesto recording Nicholas II's abdication on behalf of his brother had already been transmitted to the fronts and

---

12   Ibid., p. 232.
13   *Izvestiia tsentral'nogo ispolnitel'nogo komiteta i Petrogradskogo Soveta rabochikh i soldatskikh deputatov*, September 21, 1917.

military districts when the Duma Committee released a new command to delay its publication.

At 6:00 A.M. on March 3 Rodzianko informed Alekseev: "Events here have far from abated, the situation has become more threatening and unclear, and I urge you not to release any manifesto until you hear from me how we might put an end to the revolution." Rodzianko told Alekseev that Mikhail's accession to the throne could unleash civil war because his candidacy was unacceptable to everyone.[14] He added that he had failed to reach any agreement on this basis and that a truce was concluded by consenting to convoke a constituent assembly.

Within two hours Rodzianko told Ruzskii approximately the same. "The point is," he said over the Hughes apparatus, "that only with great difficulty have we held the revolutionary movement within more or less acceptable limits, the situation has not normalized, and civil war remains a distinct possibility. People would probably accept the accession of the tsarevich under a regency of the grand prince, but the latter's accession as emperor is totally unacceptable." Rodzianko emphasized that after the agreement with the Soviet to convoke a constituent assembly was reached "the troops slowly but surely returned to order during the night. The proclamation of Mikhail Aleksandrovich as emperor, however, would fuel the fire once again and the merciless destruction would begin of everything capable of being destroyed. We are losing and yielding all of our authority and nothing will be able to pacify the people, not even the return of the monarchy in the proposed form."[15]

It follows from Rodzianko's reports that the Duma leaders intended to restore the dynasty through the constituent assembly and that until its convocation, they hoped to preserve the Provisional Committee, the State Duma, State Senate, and the ministry responsible to them as organs of power. This decision did not please the high command. Promising Rodzianko he would hold back publication of the tsar's manifesto, Alekseev said: "That which you have informed me is far from pleasant. An uncertain situation and a constituent assembly – both are dangerous when applied to the army in the field."[16] Ruzskii regretted that the Duma Committee deputies who had gone to Pskov to negotiate with the tsar had failed to illuminate sufficiently the state of affairs that had arisen in Petrograd. Rodzianko responded it was impossible to blame the deputies. "A totally unexpected soldiers' mutiny had flared up, the likes of which I had never seen before." In fact the situation in Petrograd had become further strained on March 2 and the Provisional Duma

---

14   "Fevral'skaia revoliutsiia 1917 goda: Dokumenty Stavki," *Krasnyi arkhiv*, no. 3 (22), pp. 25–26.
15   Ibid., pp. 27–28.
16   Ibid., p. 27.

Committee had to retreat even further. Guchkov and Shul'gin had left for Pskov to save the monarchy by replacing the tsar, and now members of the Duma Committee were proposing to hold back proclamation of the new emperor.

Upon his return to Petrograd, Shul'gin addressed the soldiers that had gathered at the station, calling upon them to rally around the new tsar, Mikhail, and to obey him. "He shall lead us! Hurrah for the sovereign, Emperor Mikhail II!" It seemed to Shul'gin that the new tsar firmly occupied the Russian throne, that he had traveled to Nicholas II for the sake of the monarchy, and that the monarchy had been saved. Shul'gin was mistaken. Immediately after his speech, he received instructions over the telephone from Miliukov: "Don't release the manifesto. . . . Major changes have taken place." Shul'gin replied that he had already mentioned the new emperor Mikhail to the crowd of soldiers. "You shouldn't have done that," said Miliukov. "The state of affairs has sharply deteriorated since you left Petrograd. . . . They transmitted the text to us. . . . It is altogether unsatisfactory . . . for it is absolutely essential to mention the Constituent Assembly. . . . Don't take any further measures . . . grave misfortunes could follow."[17] Shul'gin promptly went in search of Guchkov to tell him what Miliukov had said.

Guchkov, meanwhile, was addressing a rally of railroad shop workers. Shul'gin recalled that when he entered the large shop where the workers had gathered, the chairman of the meeting was speaking.

> "Take for example the formation of the new government. . . . Who is in it? Do you think, comrades, that representatives of the people have been included? Of the very people who won freedom for themselves? If only that were the case! Here, read this . . . Prince L'vov . . . prince" (the crowd began to grumble). The chairman continued: "Why, then, did we make a revolution! . . . We've all suffered at the hands of these very same princes and counts. . . . We freed ourselves – and for you! Prince L'vov!" (the crowd began to seethe). He continued. "For example, who, comrades, is our new minister of finance? Who would you say? Maybe someone who has personally experienced how the poor live? No, our new finance minister is Mr. Tereshchenko who owns ten sugar plants, and a hundred thousand desiatinas of land. He's worth thirty million!"[18]

Another worker spoke out in the same vein.

> "They've arrived. And look what they've brought with them! Who knows them? Who knows what they've brought back with them? Maybe they've

17   Shul'gin, *Dni*, pp. 286–87.
18   Ibid., p. 289.

brought what the revolutionary democracy doesn't need. Who asked them anyway? . . . On whose behalf did they go? The people's? The Soviet of Soldiers' and Workers Deputies'? No! The State Duma's! And who belongs to the Duma? Rich landowners. I would advise you comrades not to let Aleksandr Ivanovich leave here."

The crowd responded to the speaker and shut the shop doors. "It was becoming most unpleasant," Shul'gin observed.

At that point an engineer spoke against taking Guchkov into custody. "We ourselves invited them," he said, "they trusted us and came here. . . . You want to lock the doors? Threaten them?" Cries rang out: "Open the doors!" The doors were opened. Guchkov began to speak. Then Shul'gin. In view of the mood at the rally they wisely did not attempt to support Mikhail's candidacy for the Russian throne. "At this very moment an important meeting is taking place in the State Duma between the Provisional Duma Committee and the Soviet of Workers' Deputies. Everything will be decided at it. Maybe the decisions taken will please everyone. . . . In any event, Aleksandr Ivanovich and I must leave at once." "Well, go then, who's stopping you?" they cried out in reply. "The crowd began to part and we began to make our way to the exit."[19] Thus ended Guchkov's and Shul'gin's attempt to proclaim Mikhail the new emperor.

How did Mikhail feel? After arriving from Gatchina he wandered about Petrograd for a long time, not risking an appearance at the Mariinskii or Winter palaces. He settled down in the private apartment of Princess Putiatina on Millionnaia Street, not far from the Winter Palace. It was there that he found out about Nicholas II's manifesto. News of the tsar's abdication in his favor purportedly dismayed the grand prince greatly. The crown of the Russian empire was bestowed upon Mikhail, and he not only lacked real force at his disposal, but he could not even find refuge for himself from revolution in the capital of his empire. He did not know what to do. He said that he had never wanted the throne anyway, and had not prepared himself for it, that the Provisional Government would function better without him. "How do you like L'vov," Mikhail asked N. Ivanov. "He's a smart one, isn't he? And Kerensky has character. Perhaps he'll gain control over the masses."[20]

On the morning of March 3 members of the Duma Committee and the Provisional Government assembled in Princess Putiatina's apartment to discuss whether Mikhail Aleksandrovich should ascend the

19   Ibid., pp. 291–92. Sources usually claim that railroad workers arrested Guchkov because he proclaimed Mikhail emperor. Judging by Shul'gin's account, however, the matter never came to an actual arrest.
20   TsGAOR SSSR, f. 6439, d. 3, l. 5.

throne. Only Miliukov among those assembled supported Mikhail's candidacy. Miliukov spoke at great length, detailing the situation in the country, arguing that it was necessary for Mikhail to accept the throne. Addressing Mikhail Aleksandrovich, Miliukov said: "If you refuse . . . Your Excellency, everything will be ruined! . . . Russia will lose the symbol that holds it together. . . . If you refuse, anarchy will set in . . . chaos, bloody confusion. . . . If you refuse, things will take a terrible turn . . . toward complete uncertainty." Shul'gin observed that "advice to accept the throne now means to head a loyal regiment and pit yourself against the socialists and cut them down with machine guns."[21]

What was Miliukov counting on by taking such a dangerous position? He later said he favored taking a risk, counting on the help of the Moscow garrison. Miliukov proposed going to Moscow to organize forces to support Mikhail Aleksandrovich. Like Miliukov, Guchkov felt Mikhail should accept the throne. However, taking present conditions into account, he made a conciliatory proposal and advised Mikhail to assume the throne not as tsar but as regent, and in this capacity lead the country until the constituent assembly decided who would rule Russia. What disturbed him most was the possibility that Mikhail's refusal to become tsar would break the continuity of authority and form a serious break between the old and new governments. Others protested Guchkov's suggestion, citing the law codes. There could not be a regent without a tsar. The overwhelming majority present concluded that there was no other alternative than to reject the throne and regency temporarily. Kerensky spoke up in favor of refusing the throne. He said to Mikhail Aleksandrovich: "I am a republican by conviction and am against the monarchy. . . . By assuming the throne you will not save Russia. . . . Russia needs complete unity to face the foreign threat. I implore you in the name of Russia to make this sacrifice. . . . I cannot vouch for your safety, Your Excellency." After consulting privately with Rodzianko and L'vov, Mikhail decided not to accept the throne.

The Duma Committee and the Provisional Government summoned the jurist Baron B. E. Nol'de to Princess Putiatina's, and he, together with Nabokov and Shul'gin, drafted a proclamation. They wrote it in Putiatina's daughter's study, sitting at a school desk, writing in a school notebook. It was established that Mikhail Aleksandrovich refused to accept the throne, and instead deferred the question to the constituent assembly. But who would hold power until it was convened? They decided to proclaim all power belonged to the Provisional Government. The draft document resembled the manifesto and began: "We by the

21   Shul'gin, *Dni*, p. 299.

grace of God, Mikhail, emperor and autocrat of all the Russias, etc." Mikhail was not tsar, however, and asked that these words be struck out. He also recommended including in the proclamation a call to pray for God's blessing and a request to all citizens of the empire to recognize the Provisional Government's authority.

An agreement between the Soviet and the Provisional Duma Committee had given rise to the Provisional Government. Now the last Russian emperor Mikhail gave his blessing. The Romanov dynasty had begun with a Mikhail and now ended with one. Mikhail signed the document, embraced L'vov, and wished him well. Turning to Mikhail, Kerensky said: "Believe me, Your Excellency, we will preserve your precious authority until the Constituent Assembly meets, not losing a single bit of it."[22] Nicholas II was dissatisfied with such a turn of events. He wrote in his diary that "it so happens that Misha has abdicated. His Manifesto ends with the call for elections to a constituent assembly through four-tailed suffrage within six months. God only knows who advised him to sign such nonsense."[23]

Subsequently explaining why the Duma monarchists opposed Mikhail Aleksandrovich's accession to the throne, Rodzianko wrote that the workers and the entire revolutionary democracy of Petrograd would not have allowed it.

> It was absolutely clear to us that the grand prince would reign for only a few hours before enormous bloodshed would occur in the capital, launching civil war. It was clear to us that the grand prince would be murdered immediately and all of his supporters with him. He did not have any loyal troops at his disposal and therefore could not rely on any armed force. Mikhail Aleksandrovich asked me point-blank whether I could guarantee his life if he accepted the throne and I was compelled to tell him no. . . . Nor was it possible to slip him out of Petrograd secretly, for not a single automobile or tram would be allowed out of the city.[24]

That very day, March 3, an extra supplement to the fourth issue of *Izvestiia* carried the headline: "Abdication from the throne. Deputy Karaulov appeared at the Duma and announced that the sovereign, Nicholas II, has abdicated in favor of Mikhail Aleksandrovich who in turn has abdicated to the people. Grandiose rallies and ovations are taking place in the Duma. The rapture defies description."

22   B. E. Nol'de, *Dalekoe i blizkoe: Istoricheskie ocherki* (Paris, 1930), p. 145.
23   A. A. Sergeev, "Dnevnik Nikolaia Romanova," *Krasnyi Arkhiv* no. 20 (1) (1927), p. 137.
24   M. V. Rodzianko, *Gosudarstvennaia duma i Fevral'skaia 1917 g. revoliutsiia*, Rostov-on-the-Don, 1919, p. 45.

In preparing the abdication documents for publication, arguments arose over what to call them. Were they the manifestos of two emperors? Could Mikhail Aleksandrovich be considered emperor and autocrat of all the Russias? Some argued that he did not have any power and therefore did not reign. Others disagreed, maintaining that he had been emperor from the moment Nicholas II abdicated, that is, almost for a full day, that young and feeble-minded monarchs also had lacked authority, but they had reigned, and that Mikhail's abdication made juridical sense only if it was agreed that he had been emperor. "The disagreement got bogged down in state law," said Bublikov. "Finally, about two o'clock that night an agreement was reached. Nabokov wrote the documents' titles on separate sheets of paper: 1) The abdication of His Sovereign Emperor Nicholas II from the Russian throne on behalf of Grand Prince Mikhail Aleksandrovich; and 2) The Grand Prince Mikhail Aleksandrovich's refusal to accept supreme authority and his recognition that supreme power rests with the Provisional Government, formed on the initiative of the State Duma. We should have entitled these documents 'The result of the first six hours of the Provisional Government's activity.' "[25]

The document Mikhail Romanov signed said that "I have decided to accept the supreme power, only if that be the desire of our great people, expressed at a general election of their representatives to the Constituent Assembly, which should determine the form of government and the new fundamental laws of the Russian empire." Mikhail enjoined the citizens of Russia "to subordinate themselves to the Provisional Government, which has been created by and invested with full power by the State Duma, until the earliest possible convocation of a constituent assembly, elected by universal, direct, equal, and secret ballot, which shall form a government in accord with the will of the people."[26] In this manner the continuity of power was established from Nicholas to Mikhail Romanov and from Mikhail Romanov to the Provisional Government.

Guchkov and Miliukov opposed Mikhail's unwillingness to take power and refused posts in the new ministry. To the bourgeois leaders' alarm, the Provisional Government had barely been formed when it began collapsing. Members of the Central Committee of the Kadet party turned to Miliukov to persuade him to retract his resignation. Miliukov agreed to remain in the government, and he convinced Guchkov to do the same. The latter observed that "Miliukov had little hope that events would turn out favorably, and he was the greater optimist." The crisis hanging over the newly formed Provisional Government had been

25   A. A. Bublikov, *Russkaia revoliutsiia*, New York, 1918, p. 70.
26   *Rech'*, March 4, 1917.

averted. The government, as announced to the populace, buckled down to work.

On March 4 tsarist officials cheerfully greeted the new ministers who appeared in the ministry. Shingarev warmly thanked officials in the Ministry of Agriculture for their congratulations and wishes. "We're happy to try," they said, assuring the minister they would serve the government loyally and honestly. The new ministers removed the throne from the Synod and issued instructions that the tsar and members of the imperial family were not to be mentioned in prayers. The very Synod that had defended the autocracy and Rasputin's excesses now promulgated a pastoral message to believers, which began: "God's will is done. Russia has embarked upon a new path of statehood." Miliukov requested directors of departments and divisions in the Ministry of Foreign Affairs to remain at their posts and continue work. Other ministers of the Provisional Government turned with similar appeals to officials in their respective ministries. The tsarist officials replied that they recognized the Provisional Government and were glad to have lived to see this day.

The Provisional Government left the state apparatus it inherited from tsarism almost untouched. It limited itself to abolishing the special people's courts, the police, Okhranka, and gendarmerie. All other tsarist institutions were preserved, and their officials continued fulfilling their former functions. In leaving the top officialdom virtually unscathed, the bourgeoisie intended to use it to strengthen its own authority. The Provisional Government thus relied on the prerevolutionary bourgeois public organizations – zemstvos, city dumas, war industries committees, trade and industrial and financial associations. Activists in the Council of Congresses, representatives of industry and trade, of banking, mining, the metallurgical industry, war industries committees, and other commercial establishments voiced their complete faith in the new government and readiness to continue the war with even greater resolve.

Nonetheless, the bourgeois government lacked the people's support. "Who should one obey?" queried a leaflet put out by the Kadets. It answered, "Our Provisional Government, headed by G. E. L'vov, founded by the State Duma in accord with the Soviet of Workers' Deputies is the only Supreme Authority we have. . . . Absolute power belongs solely to it. Only the Provisional Government has the right to issue orders, equally binding for Russian citizens of all classes, estates, nationalities, and religions."[27] The broad masses of people, though, recognized another authority – the Soviet of Workers' and Soldiers' Deputies.

27   TsGAOR SSSR, f. pechatnykh izdanii, inv. no. 1710.

At their very first meeting on March 2, the Provisional Government's ministers already admitted that in view of present conditions the Provisional Government must take the Soviet's opinion into account, but that the Soviet's interference in the government's affairs amounted to dual power which was unacceptable. Therefore the Provisional Government "must familiarize itself with the Soviet's intentions at its private meetings before examining these questions at official meetings of the Council of Ministers."[28] The Provisional Government could advocate familiarizing itself with the Soviet's intentions, but could not eliminate its interference in governmental affairs.

The second revolutionary wave had not achieved its main goal. The bourgeoisie remained in power, a provisional government had been formed, and the basic demands of the minimum programs of the RSDRP were yet to be realized. Nonetheless, the new revolutionary onslaught did not recede without leaving a trace. It overthrew the tsarist monarchy and strengthened the organ of genuine popular authority – the Soviet of Workers' and Soldiers' Deputies, and this was of paramount importance for the revolution's further development.

What exactly did the Soviet do?

The Soviet's Activities

During its first three days of sessions, the Petrograd Soviet evolved into a powerful force. By March 3 the number of deputies had swelled to thirteen hundred. Because tiny room number 13 located in the left wing of the Tauride Palace could no longer accommodate them, the Soviet moved that day to the palace's White Hall, where the State Duma had met for eleven years. New individuals now occupied the seats so familiar to the Provisional Government's ministers. Showing up in tattered fur and cloth coats and soldiers' greatcoats, the Soviet's deputies and guests packed the auditorium. The reading of the abdication manifesto electrified the audience. A gilded frame still hung over the chairman's desk, but because the tsar's portrait had been removed from it, it gaped vacantly.

Opening the meeting, Chkheidze said: "Let this room where the last State Duma of the Third of June met behold who is assembled here now. . . . Long live our comrades who sat here at one time but who, until

---

28   Ibid., f. 601, op. 1, d. 2103, l. 1. Here I cite the unofficial protocol of the Provisional Government's first meeting. V. Nabokov, who was managing governmental affairs, said that he was not satisfied with this protocol but that he was unable to correct it since he was not present at the government's first meeting. The minutes of this meeting were not included in the published protocols.

today, languished at hard labor." The Soviet's leaders, however, believed the workers' and soldiers' representatives were filling the Duma benches only temporarily. They presumed they were in session to promote a national assembly. "Your very presence," Chkheidze addressed the Soviet's deputies, "portends that within a short while deputies of a national constituent assembly will occupy these seats."[29]

The union between workers and soldiers forged by the revolution was the source of the Soviet's power. Yet efforts to undermine this solidarity continued. That very day, March 3, four hundred soldier representatives, congregated in the Chinizeli Circus, elected a provisional commission and empowered it to create a separate soldiers' organization. Those at the Soviet meeting who supported such a body argued that it would be easier to preserve unity this way. Maksim (Klivanskii), for example, argued that the practical tasks facing workers and soldiers differed. Soldiers have already "discussed forming company committees. Tomorrow we must clarify how to begin training. . . . Although these matters do not interest a single worker, they're extremely important for the revolution. We're speaking of the creation of a revolutionary army. . . . Soldiers must set up their own institution."[30] The majority of deputies, though, opposed election of a separate soldiers' organization. They agreed to keep the Soviet united, but in view of its unwieldy size and of the various issues of specific interest to workers and soldiers, they formed separate workers' and soldiers' sections. The Soviet's plenums were designed to discuss matters of a general political nature and to formulate joint policy.[31]

Relations between soldiers and officers also appeared as a topic on the Soviet's March 3 agenda. Soldiers reported that officers supporting the old order had tried to disarm soldiers, confiscate political literature, etc. "The majority of speakers insisted on the pressing need to take decisive measures to prevent the disarming of soldiers and avert conflicts between the lower ranks and commanders."

The Soviet confirmed the decision made earlier to elect district workers' soviets to organize the population of a given neighborhood, and it favored letting soldiers quartered in the same neighborhoods participate in the soviets with workers. The Petrograd Soviet chose a special organizational commission, and proposed that it "report on the expedient organization of soviets and neighborhood committees."[32] It also discussed establishing an All-Russian Soviet of Workers', Soldiers' and

29   *Izvestiia Petrogradskogo Soveta Rabochikh i soldatskikh deputatov*, March 5, 1917.
30   *Arkhiv Oktiabr'skoi revoliutsii Leningradskoi oblasti*, f. 1000, op. 73, d. 5, l. 17.
31   Ibid., f. 1000, op. 73, d. 5, l. 18.
32   *Izvestiia Petrogradskogo Soveta Rabochikh i soldatskikh deputatov*, March 5, 1917.

Peasants' Deputies. In the meantime the Petrograd Soviet was to fill this function.

That same day, March 3, the Soviet's Executive Committee set up commissions representing all parties in the Soviet to deal with problems of both local and national importance. The Soviet established commissions for food supplies agitation, transportation and communications, literature, publications, finance, automobiles, information, managing the concerns of publishing houses, and others.[33] Within a day new commissions that dealt with other towns and legislative activities appeared.

The Soviet published its daily newspaper, *Izvestiia*, edited by Steklov, on whom the Executive Committee bestowed enormous power. On March 7, 1917, it "granted Steklov the right of discretionary (unconditional) power over all matters concerning publications as an Executive Committee commissar. B. Avilov, I. Gol'denberg (Meshkovskii), V. Bazarov, V. D. Bonch-Bruevich and G. Tsiperovich joined the editorial board.[34] *Izvestiia* enjoyed broad popularity, especially during the first days of the revolution when other papers were not published. It set up shop in the publishing house of the newspaper *Kopeika*, which Bonch-Bruevich had requisitioned for the Soviet. The first issues of the paper were distributed free. Soldiers designated to control the crowds queuing up for *Izvestiia* soon began fulfilling broader functions. According to an editorial board report, "these soldiers on their own initiative began to deal with organizational problems, management, determining the number of copies to be printed, sales, accounts receivable, etc. . . . They eagerly filled each provincial subscription, regardless of whether money accompanied it or not, for they saw it as a way to spread the Soviet's influence."[35]

Workers welcomed *Izvestiia*. M. Koltsov recalled that "on the corner of Liteinyi and Nevskii two excited and ecstatic men ran up to us. 'Take a paper!' With a loud racket, they jumped down and dragged bales of papers from the sidewalk to the car. Tabloid-sized *Izvestiia* was fresh and had a holiday appearance. Chasing after the trucks, people tore the papers from each other's hands, demanded them, and begged for them!"[36]

Izvestiia published exposés of those who supported the tsarist regime, particularly the generals, but on the fundamental question of political power it backed the SR-Menshevik Soviet leadership and defended the

33   *Petrogradskii Sovet rabochikh i soldatskikh deputatov*, p. 10.
34   Ibid., p. 23.
35   TsGAOR SSSR, f. 1244, op. 1, d. 42, l. 2.
36   *Izvestiia tsentral'nogo ispolnitel'nogo komiteta*, March 12, 1927.

policy of supporting the bourgeois Provisional Government "only insofar as" it carried out the people's demands.[37]

The revolution's victory expanded the Soviet's role even further, but its activities were not well planned or organized. In a sense, they reflected the spontaneous character of the revolution that had created the Soviet. The Soviet met almost daily for hours on end, and sometimes the meetings turned into political rallies. It, and especially its Executive Committee, wrestled not only with major issues but also with less important ones. There were so many of the latter that the major questions drowned in the "endless flow" of pressing concerns that many deputies scornfully referred to as "vermicelli." They said dealing with them was like "playing leap-frog." Yet it was the "endless flow" of a major revolutionary cause, without which the people's victory would have been impossible. Discussion of agenda items alternated with that of matters not formally presented, coupled with urgent announcements at the meetings of both the Soviet and Executive Committee. This was natural enough, since the revolution raised questions that could not have been foreseen and included on the agenda.

Several Executive Committee members were dissatisfied with this aspect of the Soviet's work. Sukhanov wrote: "The Soviet greatly exacerbated the overcrowding, noise, disorder, and confusion in the palace of the revolution. This finally became unbearable for the exhausted members of the Executive Committee. Besides this . . . it was necessary 'to get away' from the Soviet and the crowds of thousands who were drawn to the palace, if only for a day."[38] It was impossible to conclude the never-ending sessions. As a product of the revolution, the Soviet drew more and more people into its orbit. Its membership grew continuously as new groups of working people sent representatives to it. Numerous delegations from factories and military units arrived at the Soviet's meetings. Rank-and-file participants in the revolution, not authorized by any group, also showed up. They considered it their obligation to observe the work of their highest governing body

37   Iu. Steklov thought it curious that the SRs and Mensheviks, composing a majority in the Soviet and in its Executive Committee, were not represented on the editorial board of *Izvestiia* and that the newspaper was "edited if not in a definite Bolshevik Spirit then at least in a clearly revolutionary one, which was at variance with the general mood of the Soviet majority (*Zhurnalist*, no. 3 [1927], p. 4). In fact, Steklov, Gol'denberg, Bazarov, and Avilov had been Bolsheviks formerly. During the war and February Revolution they were closer to the Mensheviks and the tone of *Izvestiia* was not at odds with "the general mood of the Soviet majority." Later Gol'denberg and Steklov again joined the Bolshevik party.

38   N. N. Sukhanov, *Zapiski o revoliutsii*, vol. 2, Petrograd, Berlin and Moscow, 1922, p. 48.

carefully and to inform it of the thoughts and aspirations of the working masses.

The Soviet's composition and activities reflected the working people's level of consciousness and organization. The worker and soldier masses' poor understanding of their own class interests and the influence of petit bourgeois elements stirred by the revolution shaped the alignment of forces within the Soviet. The majority of its deputies were under the authority of the Mensheviks and SRs; the Bolsheviks turned out to be in the minority. Many authors maintain the Mensheviks' and SRs' strength within the Soviet was attributable to the unfair norms of representation established by the Executive Committee. Each thousand workers sent one deputy to the Soviet. Workers from enterprises with fewer than one thousand workers jointly elected deputies or participated in elections by profession, according to the same norm of one deputy per one thousand workers. In some instances, though, factories with fewer than five hundred workers independently elected deputies.

Lack of coordination naturally meant there could not be complete conformity in the elections held at large, middle-sized, and smaller enterprises. Nevertheless, it is incorrect to maintain that delegates from the largest factories floundered among those from smaller handicraft enterprises, or that "at the time of the Petrograd Soviet's formation, SRs and Mensheviks granted the large factories and plants of Petrograd, whose indigenous proletariat supported the Bolsheviks, as many places in the Soviet as the small enterprises whose workers sprang from a petit bourgeois milieu."[39] In reality, the majority of workers' deputies in the Soviet represented the capital's large and middle-sized enterprises. The six largest factories in Petrograd alone sent about one hundred deputies to the Soviet.[40] Menshevik and SR influence predominated then even at these enterprises.[41] The majority of Soviet deputies from the Putilov, Pipe, Baltic, Metalworks, and several other of the largest factories supported the Mensheviks and SRs for deep-lying reasons, especially owing to changes in the composition of the working class during the war, when

39   *Istoriia grazhdanskoi voiny v SSSR* (Moscow, 1955), vol. 1, pp. 74–75; S. Murashov, *Kak pobedila Velikaia Oktiabr'skaia sotsialisticheskaia revoliutsiia* (Moscow, 1957), p. 10.

40   S. A. Artem'ev, "Sostav Petrogradskogo Soveta v marte 1917 g.," *Istoriia SSSR*, no. 5 (1964), p. 123.

41   Artem'ev in the article cited above and M. Potekhin in the essay "K voprosu o vozniknovenii i sostave Petrogradskogo Soveta v 1917 g.," *Istoriia SSSR*, no. 5 (1965), pp. 233–35, correctly note this. For example, the gigantic Obukhov Factory did not send a single Bolshevik deputy to the Soviet. M. Rozanov wrote: "The small Bolshevik organization at the factory turned out to be inadequately prepared for the elections. . . . Political trustfulness, political inexperience, and intoxication with the victory over tsarism prevented the Obukhov workers from making sense of the complex situation." See *Bastiony revoliutsii* (Leningrad, 1957), pp. 139–40.

workers from the petite bourgeoisie infiltrated the largest industrial enterprises.

Soldiers made up an even broader base of support for the SRs and Mensheviks. Politically inexperienced and incited by the revolution to active struggle for the first time, they backed the SRs and Mensheviks, and believed their assertions for the need to establish national unity and continue the war to defend the revolution from German militarism. Soldiers were well represented in the Soviet and numerically dominated the workers' deputies. Soldiers elected one deputy to the Soviet from each company, the basic unit of military organization during the revolution (in reserve battalions, which composed a major part of the Petrograd garrison, companies contained one thousand to fifteen hundred soldiers). The principle of representation by company was established not only by the Provisional Executive Committee in the Soviet's address of February 27 but also by the appeal issued that day by the Vyborg Bolsheviks and published within a day as Order No. 1.

Not only companies sent one deputy each to the Soviet but also staff commands, military hospitals, storehouses, and other support groups that included an insignificant number of soldiers. As Zalezhskii noted, "among the smaller units no revolutionary work had been conducted until now and political consciousness was quite low. It therefore is natural that these units elected as deputies 'chatterboxes,' such as clerks, educated persons serving on privileged conditions, officer trainees, and others from the petit bourgeois ranks. These deputies were attracted to the SR and Menshevik parties, which were psychologically more kindred to them."[42] Although Bolshevik influence was greater in the largest military units, petit bourgeois influence also predominated in them with rare exception.

As already noted, another circumstance told on the Soviet's membership. The Bolsheviks struggling on the streets of the capital did not participate actively enough in electing deputies, so many people were elected to the Soviet by chance. "The most progressive, active members," wrote Shliapnikov, "were involved in all sorts of revolutionary work and in the heat of passion ignored the elections."[43] As Bolshevik Putilovite F. Lemeshev put it, "in the first days of the revolution all party members were in the streets . . . not enough attention was given to elections to the Soviet of Workers' Deputies."[44] This explains the petit bourgeois wave that swelled in the aftermath of the workers' uprising, carrying SRs and

---

42   V. N. Zalezhskii, "Pervyi legal'nyi Peka," *Proletarskaia revoliutsiia*, no. 1 (13) (1923), p. 142.

43   A. G. Shliapnikov, *Semnadtsatyi god*, 4 vols, vol. 1, Moscow and Petrograd, 1925, pp. 203–204.

44   F. A. Lemeshev, "Narvskii raionnyi komitet bol'shevikov ot Fevralia k Oktiabriu 1917 goda: Ocherk," *Krasnaia letopis'*, no. 5–6 (1932).

Mensheviks at its crest, and placing them at the leadership of the Soviet. The Soviet's activities reflected SR and Menshevik influence: leaders of the Petrograd Soviet appealed to the proletariat not to drive away the bourgeoisie. Since power had been transferred to the Provisional Government, the Soviet's Executive Committee strove to avoid encroaching upon the government's territory. It advised, asked, sometimes even demanded, but tried not to resolve, order, or instruct. However, it was difficult to hold this line, for the struggle compelled the Soviet to take independent actions. In the revolutionary atmosphere of those days, in which the Soviet was under intense pressure from the masses, the Soviet and its Executive Committee discussed the most diverse problems and often acted as organs of power.[45] They published orders for the garrison, appointed commissars to military units, commandeered printing offices, determined the makeup of the police, prohibited the shipment of Black Hundred literature, carried resolutions to arrest leaders of the old regime, to replace individuals, etc. Without the Soviet's sanction it was impossible to put out newspapers, resume work at factories, reassign military units, and implement an array of other measures.

The Provisional Government was powerless to stop the arrest of leaders of the old regime, for various organizations and groups of workers and soldiers carried them out without authorization. On March 12 the commissar of Petrograd and the Tauride Palace, Duma deputy L. Pushchin, citing the agreement signed by the Provisional Duma Committee, Ministry of Justice, Staff of the Petrograd Military District, and Petrograd Soviet, ordered that directives for the arrest or searching of individuals who had compromised themselves during the revolution and of those who had committed crimes against the people under the old regime could be issued only by "1) the Provisional Committee of the State Duma; 2) the Ministry of Justice; 3) and the Executive Committee of the Soviet of Workers' and Soldiers' Deputies. These orders are to be executed by the chief of staff of the Petrograd Military District. . . . The incarceration of looters and individuals carrying out arbitrary arrests, violence, and disorders will be conducted under instructions from neighborhood police commanders or commanders of military patrols."[46]

Unauthorized searches and arrests, however, continued. Tsarist officials, officers, gendarmes, police, and all sorts of suspicious individuals

---

45   From March 3 the protocols of the Soviet's Executive Committee were published in *Izvestiia*. Unfortunately, these protocols were summarized and therefore do not give a clear notion of what occurred at the Executive Committee's meetings.
46   TsGAOR SSSR, f. 1235, op. 53, d. 40, ll. 26–27.

were locked up. Many of them were directly handed over to the Tauride Palace; they were brought there at all hours, and not only from Petrograd and its environs but also from the more distant towns of Pskov, Nizhnyi Novgorod, Kostroma, and elsewhere. A special commission comprising jurists and members of the State Duma took charge of cases involving the most prominent military and civil officials arrested during the revolution (these cases were then transferred to the procurator of the Petrograd Law Court and the Extraordinary Investigatory Commission of the Provisional Government). Another commission was organized to examine cases involving ordinary officials, namely the city police and Okhranka agents. It hastily interrogated those detained, after which it continued to hold them under arrest or release them: officers were usually placed under the jurisdiction of the Military Commission.

The Provisional Government and the Soviet next examined the matter of resuming publication of newspapers. Because of the general strike in Petrograd not a single newspaper had been published except for *Izvestiia*. Newspaper publishers and editors as well as journalists protested against the strike, saying that the absence of newspapers "would spawn dangerous rumors." In the name of freedom of the press and in order to keep the population informed, they demanded an end to the strike at printing offices and resumption of newspaper publication. Members of the All-Russian Society of Editors of Daily Newspapers hailed the Provisional Duma Committee as "the only authoritative organ" and asked it to take measures "to guarantee the regular appearance of newspapers."[47] But the editors had to discover for themselves that the Duma Committee was not the "only authoritative organ" and that its measures were insufficient to reactivate the silenced press. Not a single paper could be published without the Soviet's permission. It understood that to permit newspapers to resume publication during the strain of revolution would serve to fortify the defenders of the old order and strike a blow at the revolutionary camp. Publishers and editors waxed indignant and protested, but neither they nor the Provisional Government could do anything about it.

The press's fate remained in the Soviet's hands. "No one doubted," wrote Sukhanov, "that the Soviet of Workers' and Soldiers' Deputies should resolve this question (about the resumption of newspaper publication – E.B.), that only it was capable of doing so. No one doubted that this act of defending the revolution was no longer needed. There was no reason to leave it to the discretion of the new government of the right, there was no need to ask its sanction or even inform it. Only the Soviet

47   *Izvestiia Komiteta petrogradskikh zhurnalistov*, no. 5, March 2, 1917.

had real power at its disposal, in particular, the entire army of typographical workers."[48]

Although the most reactionary Black Hundred newspapers had been totally discredited, their editorial offices sacked by the insurgent people, and their employees dispersed, the danger of their revival could not be ruled out. On March 5 the Soviet's Executive Committee passed a decree "to prohibit publication of all Black Hundred publications such as *Zemshchina* (The Populace), *Golos Rusi* (Voice of Rus'), *Kolokol* (The Bell), *Russkoe znamia* (Russian Banner), and others." The extreme reactionary paper *Novoe vremia* went to press without the Executive Committee's permission, so it decided "to shut the paper down until further notice."[49]

The Society of Journalists and Editors challenged the Executive Committee's decision, declaring that it considered "any sort of censorship inadmissible on principle." The Soviet's Executive Committee ignored this protest. The protocol of the March 6 meeting read: "The Executive Committee discussed the press representatives' statement and reconfirmed its previous position on this question, that is, 1) to forbid publication of counterrevolutionary papers and 2) to permit publication of the newspaper *Novoe vremia* and, if technical conditions make it possible, the newspaper *Kopeika*." The committee decided to add representatives of Russian and foreign journalists to the Soviet's publication-printing-office commission.[50] The decision to issue *Novoe vremia* and to open its printing office was made after the owner pledged to the Soviet in writing that he would not publish antirevolutionary literature.

The Soviet's Executive Committee granted permission to publish each paper on an individual basis. Even the newspaper *Pravitel'stvennyi vestnik* (Government Herald) had to turn to the Soviet for permission to publish and circulate. On March 6 the Executive Committee received a memorandum: "Acting in accord with instructions of the Petrograd City Governor to publish the paper *Vestnik Petrogradskogo Obshchestvennogo Gradonachal'stva* (Herald of the Petrograd Public City Governor), your most humble servant requests the Soviet's Executive Committee to permit typesetters, composers, skilled workmen, and others to begin publishing the paper. (Signed) The editor."[51]

At first the Soviet's Executive Committee gave permission to publish newspapers for several days only. On March 10 it decided that "all pub-

48   Sukhanov, *Zapiski o revoliutsii*, vol. 1, p. 111.
49   *Petrogradskii Sovet rabochikh i soldatskikh deputatov*, Moscow and Leningrad, 1925, p. 14.
50   Ibid., p. 18.
51   *Arkhiv Oktiabr'skoi revoliutsii Leningradskoi oblasti*, f. 4000, op. 1, d. 9, l. 6.

lications can henceforward appear without prior sanction of the Executive Committee." The bourgeois press once again began to speak out, but it had to reorient itself thoroughly. All of the newspapers now welcomed the revolution, proclaiming that the sun of freedom had risen over Russia and appealing for the union of all the country's vital forces. *Novoe vremia* fired the most reactionary employees from the editorial staff and tried to convince its readers of its loyalty to the new order. *Russkaia volia* (Russian Will), also purged its staff, formerly from the Kadet paper *Rech'* (Speech), and promoted the slogan "Democratic Republic," printing these words each day on its first page in boldface type. Several bourgeois newspapers, resorting to cheap sensationalism to win popularity, described intimate secrets of the House of Romanov, detailed the tsarina's private life, printed stories about Rasputin's escapades, etc. The bourgeois press gradually began attacking the revolutionary forces. Although the Soviet had rescinded its prohibition on the publication of reactionary papers, bourgeois leaders accused the Soviet of violating "freedom of the press."

The fate of the former tsar and other members of the deposed Romanov dynasty was one of the most serious questions facing the Petrograd Soviet. A member of the Union of Republican Officers, Liubarskii, stated that members of this organization and soldiers had discussed measures that should be taken to prevent the monarchy's restoration. They decided to arrest Nicholas II but not the entire royal family as long as it recognized the new regime. They feared Nicholas would leave for Supreme Headquarters or for the south to suppress the revolution. As a result, detachments of workers and soldiers were dispatched to cut off Nicholas's path to either potential stronghold.

On March 3 the Soviet's Executive Committee discussed the fate of Nicholas II and other members of the imperial family. It resolved

to arrest the Romanov dynasty and to propose to the Provisional Government that it make the arrest together with the Soviet of Workers' and Soldiers' Deputies; to inquire how the Provisional Government would react if the Executive Committee carried out this arrest itself, should the Provisional Government refuse to join it; to arrest Mikhail but formally declare him subject only to the surveillance of the revolutionary army; to summon Nikolai Nikolaevich to Petrograd as a preliminary step and to establish strict surveillance over him en route, in view of the danger of arresting him in the Caucasus; to arrest the women of the house of Romanov when necessary, depending on the role each of them played in the affairs of the old regime.[52]

52 *Petrogradskii Sovet rabochikh i soldatskikh deputatov,* p. 9.

Indecisiveness permeated this Executive Committee ruling. Although the Executive Committee understood the need to take the former tsar and other members of the Romanov dynasty into custody, it did not carry out this important measure independently. Chkheidze and Skobelev informed the Provisional Government of the Executive Committee's decision to arrest Nicholas and waited for a reply from the government. Meanwhile, the deposed tsar contemplated leaving for England for the duration of the war and returning to Russia afterward. Nicholas negotiated this with the Provisional Government through Alekseev. Nicholas Romanov's memorandum said: "I demand the following guarantees from the Provisional Government: 1) unencumbered passage for me and those accompanying me to Tsarskoe Selo; 2) a safe stay in Tsarskoe Selo with those same individuals until my children recover; 3) unencumbered passage to Romanov-on-the-Murman (now the city of Murmansk – E.B.); 4) permission to return to Russia at the end of the war for permanent residence in the Crimea, in Livadiia." Alekseev supported all of Nicholas II's demands except the last. The Provisional Government also agreed to these so-called guarantees. On March 6 L'vov wrote Alekseev that "the Provisional Government is deciding all of these questions affirmatively, and will take all necessary measures to guarantee unimpeded passage to Tsarskoe Selo, a stay there, and passage to Romanov-on-the-Murman."[53]

Judging by this answer, the Provisional Government had decided to send the former tsar to England through the port of Romanov. The government may have intentionally kept this decision from the Soviet because it feared opposition. On March 6, Chkheidze reported to the Soviet's Executive Committee that the government had not yet given a final answer to Nicholas's request to stay at Tsarskoe Selo, received through Alekseev, to which the Provisional Government apparently did not object. After hearing Chkheidze out, the Executive Committee ordered the Military Commission to arrest Nicholas Romanov at once.[54] But measures were not taken this time either. Demands became more and more insistent for the arrest and handing over of Nicholas Romanov to a people's court. The masses were indignant that the former tsar and several members of the House of Romanov were at Supreme Headquarters, in contact with the field army. Suspicions surfaced that the generals, under the aegis of the tsar, were preparing a plot against the revolution.

On March 7 the Soviet Executive Committee received a statement signed by ninety-five individuals.

53   "Fevral'skaia revoliutsiia 1917 goda: Dokumenty Stavki," *Krasnyi arkhiv*, no. 3 (22), pp. 54–55.
54   *Petrogradskii Sovet rabochikh i soldatskikh deputatov*, p. 17.

We the undersigned members of the Soviet of Workers' and Soldiers' Deputies announce that 1) extreme indignation and alarm exist among workers and soldiers who have won freedom for Russia because the deposed Nicholas II the Bloody, his wife who is guilty of betraying Russia, his son Aleksei, his mother Mariia Fedorovna, and also all other members of the House of Romanov remain free, traveling throughout Russia, even at the theater of military operations. This is absolutely intolerable and extremely dangerous for the restoration of law and order in the country and army, and for Russia's successful defense against the foreign foe; 2) We order the Executive Committee to demand at once that the Provisional Government take the most urgent measures to isolate all members of the House of Romanov in a single designated place under the reliable guard of the people's revolutionary army.[55]

Fearing the Soviet would arrest Nicholas and his family on its own, the Provisional Government decided to preempt its actions. On March 7 it finally resolved "to recognize that the deposed Nicholas II and his wife are deprived of freedom and should be delivered to Tsarskoe Selo."[56] The Provisional Government sought to soften the blow as much as possible. It placed Aleksandra Fedorovna under house arrest in Tsarskoe Selo. As for Nicholas, Duma members Bublikov, Vershinin, and Gribkov went to Mogilev without the Soviet's knowledge to deliver the dethroned emperor to Tsarskoe Selo. This was reminiscent of the manner in which Guchkov and Shul'gin had traveled to Pskov unbeknown to the Soviet to secure the tsar's abdication. The Provisional Duma Committee's injunction to Vershinin said he was going "to accompany the deposed Nicholas II the entire way from Mogilev to Tsarskoe Selo."[57]

The Duma deputies arrived at Mogilev at 3:00 P.M. on March 7, but decided not to meet Nicholas. Believing it would be easier for the tsar to learn of his arrest from someone closer to him, they asked Alekseev to tell him. Yet no arrest followed. As usual, the imperial train contained the tsar, his retinue, and servants. The Duma deputies, with soldiers at their disposal, boarded a car attached to the imperial train without having seen the tsar. The train started out for Tsarskoe Selo. The deputies issued instructions about which stops to make and the route to take, examined telegrams received along the way, and apprised the authorities in the capital of the train's progress. As the train approached Tsarskoe Selo Station, Nicholas hopped off, jumped into an automobile, and sped off to the Aleksandr Palace. The tsar's papers had not yet been confiscated, so he now had the opportunity to destroy many of them. "I

55   "Trebovanie naroda o zakliuchenii Nikolaia Romanova v krepost'," *Krasnyi arkhiv*, no. 81 (2) (1937), pp. 122–23.
56   TsGAOR SSSR, f. 6, op. 2, d. 3, l. 15.
57   Ibid., f. 1278, op. 10, d. 6, l. 22.

continued to burn letters and papers," Nicholas II wrote in his diary on March 11, 1917.[58]

After permitting the former tsar to take up residence in the Aleksandr Palace, the Provisional Government negotiated with the British government to send Nicholas Romanov and his family to England. In his memoirs, George Buchanan said that on March 8, when the former tsar was still at headquarters, he asked Miliukov whether Nicholas II had been arrested. "I therefore reminded him," wrote Buchanan,

> that the Emperor was the King's near relative and intimate friend, adding that I should be glad to receive an assurance that precaution would be taken for his safety. Miliukoff gave me this assurance. He was not, he said, in favor of the Emperor proceeding to the Crimea, as His Majesty had originally suggested, and would prefer that he should remain at Tsarskoe until his children had sufficiently recovered from the measles for the Imperial family to travel to England. He then asked whether we were making any arrangements for their reception. On my replying in the negative, he said that he was most anxious that the Emperor should leave Russia at once. He would, therefore, be grateful if His Majesty's Government would offer him asylum in England, and if they would accompany this offer with an assurance that the Emperor would not be allowed to leave England during the war.[59]

Within a day Buchanan informed Miliukov that the king and government of England would be pleased to honor the Provisional Government's request and offer Nicholas II and his family asylum in England. "In the event of this offer being accepted, the Russian government would naturally, I added, have to make suitable provision for their maintenance. While assuring me that a liberal allowance would be made them, Miliukoff begged that the fact that the Provisional Government had taken the initiative in the matter should not be published. I subsequently expressed the hope that no time would be lost in arranging for Their Majesties' journey to Port Romanoff."[60]

On March 8 the Soviet's Executive Committee carried another resolution more categorical than the first. The Soviet's protocols read: "On the arrest of Nicholas II and his family. It was decided to arrest the entire family, to confiscate their property, and deprive them of their civil rights immediately. [The Soviet resolved] to send its envoy with the delegation that would conduct the arrest."[61] It was impossible to delay implementation of this decision. On the night of March 8–9 the Soviet's leaders

---

58   Sergeev, "Dnevnik Nikolaia Romanova," p. 138.
59   Sir George Buchanan, *My Mission to Russia*, II, Boston, 1923, p. 104.
60   Ibid., p. 105.
61   *Petrogradskii Sovet rabochikh i soldatskikh deputatov*, p. 28.

learned of the tsar's proposed flight abroad, which posed a serious threat to the revolution. An *Izvestiia* report on March 10 said: "The Soviet Executive Committee considered it disastrous for the Russian revolution to permit Nicholas II to remain free or to depart abroad where he, disposing of colossal sums stashed away for a rainy day in foreign banks, would be able to hatch conspiracies against the new regime, fund Black Hundred intrigues, send hired assassins, etc."

The Soviet Executive Committee finally took independent steps to render the former tsar harmless, prevent his departure abroad, and arrest him. The Executive Committee ordered units loyal to the Soviet to occupy all stations in the capital. The Soviet sent commissars to Tsarskoe Selo, Tosno, and Zvanka. In the name of the Soviet's Executive Committee a radio message was broadcast to all railroads, communication centers, commissars, local committees, and military units, which said: "Herein be informed that Nicholas II is intending to flee abroad. Tell your agents and committees along the entire track that the Executive Committee of the Petrograd Soviet of Workers' and Soldiers' Deputies orders the arrest of the former tsar. Report immediately to the Executive Committee at the Tauride Palace for further instructions."[62]

At a meeting on March 9 the Soviet Executive Committee resolved "to inform the Provisional Government at once of the Executive Committee's determination to prevent Nicholas Romanov's departure for England and to arrest him. It has been decided to confine Nicholas Romanov in the Trubetskoi Ravelin of the Peter-Paul Fortress, changing its commander for this purpose. It has been decided to give top priority to arresting Nicholas Romanov, even at the risk of severing relations with the Provisional Government."[63] As soon as the Soviet's Executive Committee learned that the former tsar's train had arrived at Tsarskoe Selo, it dispatched there Colonel S. Maslovskii, Second Lieutenant A. Tarasov-Rodionov, and a detachment of soldiers. Why? Skobelev maintained that "we wanted to see for ourselves whether the tsar was guarded closely enough."[64] The detachment's real purpose was actually quite different. The text of the March 9 order to Colonel Maslovskii has been preserved: "Upon receipt of this you are instructed to leave for Tsarskoe Selo as a special commissar of the Executive Committee of the Soviet of Workers' and Soldiers' Deputies and to assume all administrative and military power in Tsarskoe Selo. The Tsarskoe Selo garrison is enjoined to obey Colonel Maslovskii's orders in carrying out the important political task given him. [Signed] Chairman of the Executive

---

62   *Tsentral'nyi gosudarstvennyi muzei revoliutsii SSSR*, f. listovok, inv. no. 23316/21.
63   *Petrogradskii Sovet rabochikh i soldatskikh deputatov*, p. 29.
64   Personal archive of M. Polievktov. *Materialy Komissii oprosov. Beseda s M. I. Skobelevym.*

Committee of the Soviet Chkheidze. Secretary Kapelinskii."[65] The text of the order to form a detachment of 250 soldiers "at the disposal of Second Lieutenant Tarasov-Rodionov, acting under the authorization of the Executive Committee," is also available.[66]

It is difficult to believe such a large contingent of soldiers was sent to Tsarskoe Selo merely to ascertain "whether the tsar was guarded closely enough." Tarasov-Rodionov told how they went there to prevent the former tsar's departure for England, to arrest and imprison him in the Peter-Paul Fortress, "to seize Nicholas Romanov and escort him to Petrograd dead or alive."[67] Nonetheless, the Soviet's orders were not carried out. Maslovskii arrived at Tsarskoe Selo, negotiated with the garrison commander and with the commander of the Aleksandr Palace and other superiors, demanding they hand over Nicholas Romanov. They refused Maslovskii and declared that, in accordance with the instructions of the commander of the military district, they could not release the former tsar to anyone. The matter ended when Maslovskii was shown Nicholas alive and well and was convinced that the deposed monarch was under reliable guard. "I saw the tsar," Maslovskii reported to Tarasov-Rodionov. "I insisted that they show him to me. And that was enough. . . . Why, they ask, do you want to remove him from here? I spoke with the soldiers . . . and they've sworn not to release Nicholas."[68] Maslovskii telephoned the Executive Committee and received approval for his actions. His mission was considered accomplished.

Both the Provisional Government and the Soviet made concessions. The Soviet no longer demanded the last tsar's imprisonment in the Peter-Paul Fortress and the government rejected (evidently temporarily) plans to send Nicholas Romanov to England, especially since it did not seem possible to carry this out, for workers and soldiers controlled all of the stations and roads. The government promised not to make any decisions in regard to Nicholas II and his family without the Soviet's approval.

Chkheidze reported at a Soviet Executive Committee meeting on March 9: "Pressured by the Executive Committee, the Provisional Government has rejected the idea of permitting Nicholas Romanov to leave for England without the Executive Committee's special approval. He has been left temporarily at Tsarskoe Selo. The Provisional Government and Minister of Justice Kerensky guarantee he will not go anywhere. The Provisional Government agrees that the Executive Committee should appoint a commissar to Tsarskoe Selo to make sure Nicholas II does not

65   *Tsentral'nyi gosudarstvennyi muzei revoliutsii SSSR*, f. listovok, inv. no. 12/200.
66   Ibid., inv. no. 12/429.
67   A. Tarasov-Rodionov, *Fevral'*, Moscow, 1931, p. 315.
68   Ibid., p. 322.

flee."[69] That same day, Maslovskii and Tarasov-Rodionov informed the Executive Committee that "revolutionary troops are responsible for guarding the palace. The order has been issued not to let anyone in or out. All telephones and telegraph equipment have been disconnected. Nicholas Romanov is under close guard. There are about 300 soldiers there from the Third Infantry Regiment. . . . All letters and telegrams are delivered to the sentry room. The representative (of the Soviet – E.B.) was inside and personally saw Nicholas Romanov. The regiment asked me to report that it will be on permanent guard and will not release him. . . . Convinced of the guard's reliability, the representatives (of the Soviet – E.B.) believe it possible to leave Nicholas as is." One Executive Committee member asked the Soviet's representatives: "Why didn't you transfer him to the Peter-Paul Fortress?" When no one else picked up on this suggestion the matter was dropped. After discussing the report the Soviet Executive Committee "dispatched S. D. Maslovskii as commissar of the Executive Committee to supervise the guard and organize the entire affair."

Although the revolutionary workers and soldiers had prevented Nicholas Romanov's flight abroad, it was not ruled out that this might occur later. At a Soviet meeting on March 10 Sokolov admitted the possibility. He therefore proposed to settle the question of Nicholas's property, personal estate, and large financial deposits in English and other foreign banks in the interests of the people. "Before doing this it does not make sense to release him abroad." Thus the door abroad for the former tsar had not been slammed shut. But it was recognized that "the question of Nicholas II's departure and that of other members of the imperial family can be resolved only by an agreement between the Provisional Government and the Soviet of Workers' and Soldiers' Deputies."[70]

The Soviet's opposition prevented the Russian and English bourgeoisie from carrying out their plans for Nicholas. "There was nothing more that we could do," wrote Buchanan.

We offered the Emperor an asylum, in compliance with the request of the Provisional Government; but as the opposition of the Soviet, which they were vainly hoping to overcome, grew stronger, they did not venture to assume the responsibility for the Emperor's departure, and receded from their original position. . . . It would, moreover, have been useless for us to insist on the Emperor being allowed to come to England, seeing that the workmen had threatened to pull up the rails in front of his train. We could take no steps to protect him on his journey to Port Romanoff. The duty

69   *Petrogradskii Sovet rabochikh i soldatskikh deputatov*, p. 30.
70   *Izvestiia Petrogradskogo Soveta rabochikh i soldatskikh deputatov*, March 10, 1917.

devolved on the Provisional Government. But, as they were not masters in their own house, the whole project eventually fell through.[71]

Even though the Soviet remained in control of the situation after the formation of the Provisional Government, the bourgeoisie strove to concentrate all power in its own hands. Several bourgeois and petit bourgeois leaders recognized the Soviet's role in the past, and wanted to limit its influence in the present. The Kadet V. Kuz'min-Karavaev later wrote: "It (the Soviet – E.B.) was a legacy of the Revolution of 1905. For twelve years the revolution was considered to have been under no leadership other than its. It was formed with the first rifle shot. . . . Let it play a historical role in the past. It played – and then should have been spent as a fighting organization, as an organization for struggle. The Soviet is not meant for creative work, let alone for state building." After handing over power to the bourgeoisie the Soviet could not disband, and the bourgeoisie, no matter how hard it tried, could not do away with it. It was this that created the political instability so characteristic of dual power.

Although Popular Socialist V. Miakotin recognized the Petrograd Soviet's services in overthrowing tsarism, he censured it for trying to act as a government, for addressing direct orders and instructions such as Order No. 1 to the population.[72] Political realities had pushed the Soviet to take such actions. Dual power reflected the true alignment of forces that had taken shape as a result of the overthrow of the autocracy. The Soviet voluntarily had abdicated power on behalf of the bourgeoisie, but the interests of the proletariat and bourgeoisie were so contradictory that, with the support of the armed forces and the trust of the people, the Soviet in reality remained the country's unofficial government.

Thus the February Revolution resolved the main question, that of political power, in a contradictory and inconsistent manner. Other questions touching the vital interests of the toiling people also went unanswered. Only the revolution's further deepening, its transition to a new, socialist stage could guarantee their resolution.

Glossary

Alekseev, M. V.   Chief of staff of the Imperial Army, Alekseev served both Nicholas II and the Provisional Government.

Aleksandra Fedorovna   Empress of Russia, wife of Nicholas II.

Avilov, B.   Member of the editorial board of *Izvestiia*, put out by the Petrograd Soviet.

71   Buchanan, *My Mission to Russia*, II, pp. 105–6.
72   V. Miakotin, *Velikii perevorot i zadachi momenta* (Petrograd, 1917), p. 7.

Bazarov, V.   Same as Avilov.

Bednyi, Dem'ian   Pseudonym of E. A. Pridmorov, Bolshevik poet.

Black Hundred   Reactionary political force.

Bonch-Bruevich, V. D.   A Bolshevik since 1903, Bonch-Bruevich co-founded several Bolshevik newspapers after 1905. In March 1917 he became a member of the editorial board of *Izvestiia*.

Bublikov, A. A.   Progressist, appointed by the Provisional Duma Committee as its commissar at the Ministry of Communications. One of the most active Duma commissars.

Buchanan, George   British ambassador to Imperial Russia and author of an important memoir of his time there.

Chkheidze, N. S.   Led Menshevik faction in State Duma. Elected chairman of the Petrograd Soviet in March 1917.

Guchkov, A. I.   Octobrist, headed Central War Industries Committee.

Gurko, V. I.   General in the Imperial army, commander of Special Army.

Ivanov, General N. I.   Petrograd military district commander in February, 1917.

Kapelinskii, N. Iu.   Member of the Petrograd Soviet's first Executive Committee.

Karaulov, M. A.   Progressist and Duma deputy.

Kuz'min-Karavaev, V.   Member of the Kadet party.

Lemeshev, F.   Bolshevik worker (Putilovite).

Liubarskii, [initials unknown]   Member of the Union of Republican Officers.

L'vov, Prince G. E.   Chair of the Council of Ministers.

Maslovskii, S. D.   Colonel in the tsarist imperial army, then commissar of Petrograd Soviet.

Lieutenant Colonel Mstislavskii   Author of a memoir on the Revolution.

Miakotin, V.   Popular Socialist Party member.

Mikhail Aleksandrovich Romanov   Grand Duke, younger brother of Nicholas II.

Miliukov, P.   Liberal Kadet party leader and Foreign Minister of Provisional Government.

Nabokov, V. D.   Chargé d'affaires in London and later secretary of the Provisional Government.

Nicholas II   (Nicholas Aleksandrovich Romanov), tsar and emperor of Russia.

Nikolai Nikolaevich Romanov   Grand Prince.

Nol'de, B. E., Baron   Jurist and historian.

Pushchin, L.   Duma deputy, commissar of Petrograd and of Tauride Palace.

Rodzianko, M. V.   Chairman of State Duma.

Romanov Aleksei Nikolaevich, Son of Nicholas II, heir apparent (tsarevich).

Ruzskii, General N. D.   Commissar of Northern Front.

Shingarev, A. I.   A leader of the Progressive Bloc.

Shliapnikov, A. G.   Petersburg worker and Bolshevik since 1901; co-opted into party's Central Committee in 1915; became commissar of labor after October Revolution and later during the Civil War became one of the leaders of the Workers' Opposition.

Shul'gin, V. V.   Leader of Progressive Nationalists.

Skobelev, M. I.   Menshevik in State Duma.

Steklov, Iu.   Editor of the Soviet newspaper, *Izvestiia*, and historian; member of Executive Committee of Petrograd Soviet.

Sukhanov, N. N.   (Gimmer) Noted economist and populist turned Menshevik; key figure in the Petrograd Soviet's Executive Committee and author of noted memoir of the revolution.

Synod   Holy Synod, the highest Orthodox religious board in the Imperial government.

Tarasov-Rodionov, A.   Second Lieutenant in the tsarist imperial army.

Tereshchenko, M. I.   Finance Minister of the Provisional Government.

Tsiperovich, G.   Member of editorial board of *Izvestiia*.

Vishniakov, N.   Moscow city Duma deputy.

Zalezhskii, V. N.   Working-class party member who joined the Petersburg Bolsheviks during the war.

Further Reading: The February Revolution and the Provisional Government

R. Abraham, *Alexander Kerensky: The First Love of the Revolution* (Columbia University Press, 1987).

R. P. Browder and A. F. Kerensky, *The Russian Provisional Government, 1917: Documents*, 3 vols. (Stanford University Press, 1961).

M. Ferro, *The Russian Revolution of February 1917*, trans. by Norman Stone (Routledge and Kegan Paul, 1980).

T. Hosegowa, *The February Revolution: Petrograd, 1971* (University of Washington Press, 1981).

M. Steinberg and V. Khrustalev, *The Fall of the Romanovs. Political Dreams and Struggles in a Time of Revolution* (Yale University Press, 1995) [archival documents].

3

The Russian Revolution of 1917 and its Language in the Village

Orlando Figes

Originally appeared as Orlando Figes, "The Russian Revolution of 1917 and its Language in the Village," *Russian Review*, 56 (July 1997): 323–45.

Editor's Introduction

Orlando Figes has written numerous books and articles on aspects of Russian history. One of his recent works, *A People's Tragedy*, is a comprehensive analysis of the entire era of the Russian revolution, from 1891 to Lenin's death in 1924, and has surpassed many previous studies on the subject in its mastery of the complex source materials and its judicious evaluations. One of Figes's primary interests is the Russian peasantry, a neglected subject especially in most studies of the revolution.

The reasons for this are not difficult to find. With few exceptions, earlier generations of historians were largely concerned with the educated elites and often ignored the peasantry, except for those instances where the intelligentsia turned its attention to rural Russia. For the last two decades or so, social historians have brought the problems of the peasantry to the forefront of Russian historiography, but primarily through their participation in radical movements or the local economy of the village. Moreover, because most peasants were illiterate, historians of all persuasions could not easily represent them from their own perspective without written sources.

Beginning with his first book, *Peasant Russia, Civil War: The Volga Countryside in Revolution (1917–1921)*, Figes has been concerned not only with the political and economic aspects of peasant Russia, but also with its cultural and symbolic components. In the following article, Figes provides a luminous portrait of the Russian peasantry during the revolutionary year of 1917 under the Provisional Government. He has unearthed a wealth of previously unpublished archival documents which permit him to probe deeply into the peasant mentality. It is important to keep in mind that within the short span of three generations (roughly from the 1860s to the Revolution), the majority of the Russian peasantry moved from the servility, passivity and exclusion of serfdom to the liberating status of free citizenship in a republic. The source materials Figes has made use of allow him to interpret the deeper meaning of this transformative experience.

For Figes, the key to understanding the peasantry and its relationship to the Revolution lies in the role of language. We have long been aware of the gulf that separated the educated sector of Russian society (*obshchestvo*) from the oral traditions of the rural peasants (*narod*), but Figes shows us how the peasantry understood the revolution in its own terms. Particularly significant are the peasant conceptions of citizenship and state power, from which they had been excluded for so long. Moreover, peasants remained close to their religious heritage (a factor most members of the radical intelligentsia never grasped in their long search for a link to the people), and still found ways to integrate this belief system rooted in faith with the new discourse and institutions of secularism and revolution.

Students unfamiliar with Russian may find themselves impatient with the plethora of foreign words included in this selection. One useful way to conceptualize this problem, that is quite relevant to the material discussed here, is to imagine how difficult it was for the peasants themselves to understand the language of educated Russians, which was, to a large extent, just as incomprehensible to them as these words may be to you.

The Russian Revolution of 1917 and its Language in the Village

Orlando Figes

The Provisional Government was a government of persuasion. Not having been elected by the people, it depended largely on the power of the word to establish its authority. It was a government of national confidence, self-appointed during the February Revolution with the aim of steering Russia through the war-time crisis toward democracy, and as such its mandate had to a large extent to be created by propaganda, cults, and festivals, fostering consensus and national unity. There was little else the government could do, since it lacked the power to enforce its will by any other means. And yet many of its liberal leaders also saw a virtue in this necessity. They rejected the traditions of the tsarist state, emphasized the need to govern by consent, and, in the words of Prince G. E. Lvov, the prime minister, placed their faith in the "good sense, statesmanship and loyalty of the people" to uphold the new democracy.[1]

Their optimism was based on the assumption that the primary duty of the February Revolution was to educate the people in their civic rights and duties. Like the French revolutionaries of 1789, they understood their task as nothing less than the creation of a *new political nation*. The peasants, above all, who made up more than three-quarters of the population, had to be transformed into active citizens. They had to be brought out of their cultural isolation and integrated into the national political culture. Upon that hung the Revolution's fate – and not just because it depended on the peasants to fulfill their civic duty by supplying foodstuffs and soldiers for the nation, but even more importantly because, as the vast majority of the electorate, it required them to vote as citizens, free from the domination of their former masters (landowners, priests, and monarchist officials), in the elections to the Constituent Assembly and the other institutions of the nascent democracy.

The "darkness" of the peasants – and its inherent dangers for the Revolution – was the constant refrain of democratic agitators in the countryside during 1917. "The peasants do not understand anything about politics," wrote one soldier from Penza Province to the Petrograd Soviet

---

1   *The Kerensky Memoirs: Russia and History's Turning Point* (London, 1965), 228.

on 25 April. "Although there were deputies [that is, Soviet agitators], the peasants soon forgot what they had told them about freedom, a republic, and a monarchy."[2] As one provincial propagandist concluded:

> The peasant is still very easily deceived by monarchist officials and other dark forces in his midst. He has never been acquainted with the most elementary political questions, he has never received the education of a citizen. But the peasants, whose votes will decide the political and socioeconomic structure of the Russian state, have to become citizens, with an understanding of the different forms of rule and an ability to make rational choices between different political points of view, immediately![3]

Language was the key to this cultural integration of the peasantry. The dissemination of the Revolution's rhetoric to the countryside – the development of a national discourse of civic rights and duties – would create the new political nation dreamed of by the leaders of democracy. Here again there were clear parallels with France. For just as in France there was an enormous gulf between the French written culture of the Revolution and the patois oral culture of the peasantry, so in Russia there was an equal divide between the political language of the towns and the terms in which the peasants couched their own moral and political concepts.

The terminology of the Revolution was a foreign language to most of the peasants (as indeed it was to a large proportion of the uneducated workers) in most parts of Russia.[4] Of course, there were important variations. The younger, richer, and better educated peasants tended to be more politically aware, as did those living closest to the towns or in regions with a well-developed network of party and peasant organization (in parts of the North, the middle Volga, or western Siberia, for example).[5] But in general the peasants and their spokesmen in 1917 were painfully aware of the linguistic gulf that separated them from the Revolution in the towns. "We can't understand many of your words," complained one peasant to the SR leaders of the Kurgan' peasant congress during a debate on the structure of the state – "you have to speak in Russian."[6] Imported words ("republic," "constitution," "federation,"

2 Tsentral'nyi gosudarstvennyi arkhiv Sankt-Peterburga (TsGASP), f. 7384, op. 9, d. 209, l. 17.

3 E. N. Medynskii, *Revoliutsiia i vneshkol'noe obrazovanie: S prilozheniem konspektov besed s krest'ianami nad temami sviazannymi s revoliutsiei* (Moscow, 1917), 4–5.

4 In Ukraine, the Baltic lands, and the Caucasus, where the urban elites were ethnically different from the native peasantry, it was literally a foreign language. But my concern here is exclusively with Russia.

5 For a discussion of these variations see my *A People's Tragedy: The Russian Revolution, 1891–1924* (London, 1996), 92–95, 182–84.

6 *Pervyi kurganskii krest'ianskii s"ezd (8–9 aprelia 1917 g.)* (Kurgan', 1917), 3.

"democracy," "regime," "annexation," and even "revolution") were misunderstood and mispronounced by peasants. Thus the word "republic" (*respublika*) appeared as *despublika* and *razbublika* in various peasant letters; "regime" (*rezhim*) became *prizhim*; "constituent" (*uchreditel'noe*) was transformed into *chereditel'noe* (on the basis that the Constituent Assembly would decide everything "in its turn," or *cheredom*); "revolution" (*revoliutsiia*) was pronounced and written as *revutsia, levoliutsiia,* and *levorutsia*; the "Bolsheviks" (*bol'sheviki*) were confused with a party of *bol'shaki* (peasant elders) and of *bol'shie* (big people); while "annexation" (*anneksiia*) was thought by many peasant soldiers to be a small Balkan kingdom neighboring *kontributsiia* (the Russian word for "indemnity") and at least on one occasion was confused with a woman called "Aksinia." "Who is this Aksinia?" one peasant asked another who had heard about her from an "oratater" (*oratel'* instead of *orator*). "God knows who she is. They say that because of her there will be a great harm, and that if there is Aksinia there will be another war against us after we have made peace with the Germans." "Ooh she must be bad: over one woman there is war again!" (*Ish' ved' kakaia vrednaia: ot odnoi baby i opiat' voina!*).[7]

Equally, the new institutions of the state appeared strange and alien to many of the peasants. For example, a group of wounded peasant soldiers in a Petrograd hospital wrote through a scribe a series of petitions to the Tauride Palace in September. Each one started with the clumsy words: "I have the honor humbly to ask the Tauride Palace not to refuse me an extraordinary pension as a wounded veteran of the war." None of the petitions was addressed to an official body – indeed the palace was empty by this time, the Duma having closed its offices and the Soviet having moved to the Smolny – and it seems the soldiers had no idea of who was in the building. The Tauride Palace – perhaps because of the connotations of the word "palace" or perhaps because it had become a symbol of the Revolution (which frequently appeared in propaganda posters) – simply meant to them the seat of power.[8]

Such misunderstandings were a major hindrance to the democratic cause in the countryside. Its propaganda had to cross a huge linguistic gulf to communicate with the peasantry. The first pamphlets for the

7   TsGASP, f. 7384, op. 7, d. 11, l. 57, op. 9, d. 254, l. 217, and f. 1000, op. 74, d. 13, l. 147; A. M. Selishchev, *Iazyk revoliutsionnoi epokhi: Iz nabliudenii nad russkim iazykom poslednikh let (1917–1926)* (Moscow, 1928), 215; A. Okninskii, *Dva goda sredi krest'ian': Vidennoe slyshannoe, perezhitoe v Tambovskoi gubernii s noiabria 1918 goda do noiabria 1920 goda* (Riga, 1936), 32; Rossiiskii gosudarstvennyi voenno-istoricheskii arkhiv (RGVIA), f. 162, op. 2, d. 18, l. 12; *Volia naroda* (26 May 1917): 2.
8   Rossiiskii gosudarstvennyi istoricheskii arkhiv (RGIA), f. 1278, op. 10, d. 18, ll. 206, 209, 211, 213, 215, 217, 219, 222, 224, 226, 228, 229, and so on.

rural population were mostly reprints of editions written during the 1905 Revolution. According to a valuable report by the Temporary Committee of the Duma during May, they had been written "in a language which the people do not speak. . . . They needed translators." The report concluded that "it played a major role in the rapid alienation of the peasantry from the intelligentsia."[9]

A related problem was the peasants' inclination to believe naively in every printed word. Long starved of an open press, they were hungry for *any* printed news, especially about the war and the latest events in the capital, and as a result they tended to believe that whatever was printed must be true. The Duma report thought that, as a rule,

> The less literate a peasant is, the more he believes in the written word. He has a conviction that if something is printed in a book then it is the truth. He reads one newspaper – and that is one truth; then he reads another – where there is another, even if it is directly contrary to the first. He sits there and tries to work it out "freely" – until his head begins to spin.[10]

Such credulity could make the peasant vulnerable to demagogues, as Kerensky warned in his famous "rebellious slaves" speech to the soldiers' delegates at the end of April, when he spoke of those who "even now take every printed word for truth."[11] One may well ask in this context whether there was any extra persuasive power in the newspaper of the Bolsheviks because it was called *Pravda?*

Oral forms of propaganda had the same problems. Too many agitators spoke in terms the peasants could not understand, especially in the early months before they had been trained for their rural trips. Too many talked *at them* in long and boring speeches rather than engaging them in lively conversations. The educative purpose of the peasant congresses was similarly lost, especially in the early months, because of the tendency of the congress leaders, most of whom were SR *intelligenty*, to speak in abstract terms far above the heads of the peasant delegates. At the Kurgan' peasant congress during April, for example, the SR leaders of the congress became embroiled in a long debate about the relative merits of various federative principles. The peasant delegates became restless, and at last one intervened: "I have been listening for two hours

9   RGIA, f. 1278, op. 10, d. 4, ll. 257–58. The report was compiled from information provided by local correspondents in more than a dozen provinces for the period between the start of March and the end of April. Some thirty pages long, it is an important, yet hitherto neglected, source on the February Revolution in the provinces.

10   RGIA, f. 1278, op. 10, d. 4, l. 257.

11   R. P. Browder and A. F. Kerensky, eds., *The Russian Provisional Government, 1917: Documents*, 3 vols. (Stanford, 1961), 2:915.

and can't understand: is this an assembly for peasants or for speech-making. If this is a peasant assembly, then the peasants ought to speak." There was a general hum of approval so that, while insisting on the need to discuss such important questions, the SR leaders felt obliged to explain the meaning of a federation to the delegates in terms that were more comprehensible to them. They chose to compare the federal division of the state to the division of the communal land. But this merely gave rise to more misunderstandings. One group of delegates said they did not want to "divide Russia," while another suggested "taking away the land of the nobles and dividing it between the peasants" – only to be told, "that is not the question."[12] The all-too-frequent consequence of such abstract debates was that the peasant delegates forgot what had been said. As the Duma report put it:

> There are occasions when a deputy returning from Petrograd, where he has been deluged by noisy rhetoric and the storm of party arguments and debates, replies to the question about what he had heard there: "I have forgotten! I've forgotten everything I heard. I heard so much that in the end I could remember nothing." He has become confused and forgotten all. And his fellow-villagers put him into jail because they have paid him to travel to the city and he has told them nothing.[13]

Bridging the Linguistic Gulf?

The democratic intelligentsia set out with the passion of civic missionaries to break down these linguistic barriers and communicate the gospel of their revolution to the peasantry. It was like another "Going to the people" – the propaganda mission of the Populists in the 1870s – only now the government was on their side. Dictionaries were published to explain the Revolution's strange vocabulary.[14] And there was a whole new range of pamphlets for the peasants telling them what they should know to become citizens.[15] The new rural press also took upon itself the

12   *Pervyi kurganskii krest'ianskii s"ezd*, 3.
13   RGIA, f. 1278, op. 10, d. 4, l. 249.
14   See, for example, *Tolkovnik politicheskikh slov* (Petrograd, 1917); *Karmannyi slovar' revoliutsionera* (Petrograd, 1917); and N. G. Berezin, *Novyi sotsial'no-politicheskii slovar': Sputnik svobodnogo grazhdanina* (Odessa, 1917). Over a dozen such dictionaries were published, with a total print-run of half a million copies, between March and October.
15   See, for example, N. Petrovich, *Chto nuzhno znat' krest'ianinu* (Kiev, 1917); idem, *Krest'ianskaia pamiatka* (Moscow, 1917); S. Zaiats', *Kak muzhiki ostalis' bez nachal'stva* (Moscow, 1917); I. Shadrin, *Blizhaishchie zadachi (krest'ianinu-grazhdaninu)* (Kazan', 1917); and A. Os'minin, *Chto dolzhno dat' narodu uchreditel'noe sobranie* (Petrograd, 1917).

political education of its peasant readers. Many papers had a column such as "Letters from the Village," or "Answers to Your Questions," in which issues raised by peasants were explained. Most of these were technical concerns to do with the land and property, yet they often touched on politics as well. Many of the SR papers, in particular, also published so-called letters "From a Soldier" which were thinly disguised propaganda. The "soldier" (a party activist in the ranks) would call on his peasant "brothers" to help in the defense of their freedom and their farms by giving up their harvest surplus to the government. Such appeals were often couched in religious terms: "Your conscience says it's sinful to think about yourself while your brothers spill their blood. . . . Make a sacrifice, as we soldiers are doing to defend you. We are just to say this."[16]

There was also a small number of newspapers specifically intended for the political education of the peasants, such as the tabloid *Narodnaia gazeta* put out twice a week in the Kerenskii district of Penza Province between May and September. "The aim of our newspaper," its editors declared, "is to help the people understand the events of the war, national and local political life, and to enable every citizen to play a conscious role in the construction of a new life." It printed explanations of political terms and articles with titles such as "What is freedom and why has it been given to us?" or "What is socialism and will it arrive soon?"[17]

The supply of this literature could not keep up with demand. Of course, there were places where the peasants were indifferent to politics, and where any propaganda was torn up by them for cigarette paper. But in general there was a huge demand for news and explanatory literature. The war had opened up the peasants' world and made them more aware that their own daily lives were closely connected with national and international affairs. The publications of the peasant unions and provincial peasant assemblies often had to be reprinted several times. Hand-printed and mimeographed copies were also distributed in huge quantities. A second stenographic edition of the 1905 All-Russian Peasant Union Congress, published in the spring of 1917, carried on its title page a warning from the Main Committee of the Union that there were so many of these unofficial versions that it could not be held responsible for them.[18] The Petrograd Soviet, in particular, but also the Duma and the Provisional Government received hundreds of peasant appeals for political literature. As the Duma report put it, the phrase "we

16 *Izvestiia vserossiiskogo soveta krest'ianskikh deputatov,* 20, July 1917.
17 *Narodnaia gazeta,* 28 July 1917.
18 *Uchredietel'nyi s"ezd vserossiiskogo krest'ianskogo soiuza* (Moscow, 1917).

are dark people" (*my temnye*), which the peasants had used ironically, now contained a message of "sincere regret: there is so much the peasants want to know but cannot understand." It cited the moving words of one peasant from Pskov: "There are no words to explain the shame and pain that engulf a man when he realizes that even what has been given to him is too hard for him to understand, and is like a stone instead of bread."[19]

In addition to pamphlets and newspapers the peasant leaders appealed for agitators, often specifically to help them counteract the influence of the local priests or monarchist officials, or to help them dispel rumors undermining confidence in the Revolution.[20] The demand for such people was increased by the flight of the rural intelligentsia from the countryside during 1917.[21] Impoverished, demoralized, and threatened by the violence of the peasant revolution, many teachers, vets, and doctors fled to the towns. Yet these were the very people who in former years had read the newspapers to the peasants, explained to them the meaning of the news, interpreted decrees, and acted as their scribes to the authorities.

A wide range of public bodies – from working-class organizations to sailors' and soldiers' delegations – dispatched agitators to the countryside. Teachers' bodies were particularly active.[22] One of their main professional journals carried a regular article entitled "For the aid of teachers in their conversations with the population on current affairs," in which they were advised on how best to engage the attention of their peasant audience.[23] Many of the provincial peasant congresses, and even some of the district ones, organized their own teams of rural propagandists to acquaint the peasants with their resolutions or to counteract the influence of local monarchists.[24] In Perm, Nizhegorod, Vladimir, Saratov, and Viatka the provincial zemstvos and public committees trained and paid for "lectors" and "translators" (*perevodchiki*) from the local intelligentsia to go to the peasants and explain to them the main issues of the day.[25]

In Moscow, Petrograd, and Kaluga there was a religiously oriented group called the Union for the Free Person which set up lecture and

19 RGIA, f. 1278, op. 10, d. 4, l. 258.
20 See, for example, TsGASP, f. 7384, op. 9, d. 176, l. 184. and d. 209, l. 10.
21 On this see my *Peasant Russia, Civil War: The Volga Countryside in Revolution, 1917–1921* (Oxford, 1989), 35, 147–51.
22 See N. N. Smirnov, *Na perelome: Rossiiskoe uchitel'stvo nakanune i v dni revoliutsii 1917 goda* (St. Peterburg, 1994), 243–50.
23 *Dlia narodnogo uchitelia*, 1917, no. 8:29–32, no. 10:29–31, and so on.
24 See, for example, TsGASP, f. 1950, op. 1, dd. 10, 13.
25 RGIA, f. 1278, op. 10, d. 4, l. 257.

discussion circles for the peasantry.[26] Democratic priests and seminarians also doubled up as propagandists, the priests often using the church service to preach about the "Christian mission of the revolution" to their peasant worshipers. For example, the chaplain of the 105th Orenburg Regiment gave a speech in the church of Slipki village on Trinity Sunday (21 May) in which he compared the revolutionaries to Jesus Christ, the "liberator of the poor and oppressed peasants and the proletariat" from their "enslavement" to the "Roman tsars."[27] Finally, there was a Society for the Political Education of the Army and Wide Sections of the Population, set up by the zemstvos and cooperatives in several provinces, which trained volunteers (mainly teachers and students) for propaganda work among the peasantry and sent them out to the villages and army units to explain to them the duties of a citizen.[28]

All these missionaries faced the same problem: how to talk to the peasants about politics so that they would listen and understand. It was an old problem, going back at least to the 1870s and the "Going to the people," but it was now more urgent since upon it hung the fate of the democracy.

Many books and articles were published on this problem during 1917. E. N. Medynskii's *How to Conduct Conversations on Political Issues* was perhaps the best known of these manuals, selling fifty thousand copies in its first edition, and up to forty thousand more in two further editions of 1917.[29] But close behind came his *The Revolution and Education Out of School*, which sold up to seventy thousand copies in its two editions of the same year.[30] Both gave advice on how to talk with peasants on political issues. The agitator should speak in the language of the peasants and avoid using foreign words. It was important not to give a "dry and official speech" but to have a "conversation" with the audience and to ask them questions from time to time. The agitator was to illustrate his arguments with examples drawn from peasant daily life. The war, for example, might be compared with a village fight, in which one side (Russia) fights fairly and the other (Germany) unfairly. To explain the advantages of a republic over a monarchy the speaker might say:

26 *Otchet deiatel'nosti soiuza vospitaniia svobodnogo cheloveka za 1917–18 (pervyi) god* (Petrograd, 1918).
27 RGIA, f. 806, op. 5, d. 10313, l. 131.
28 *Biulleten' obshchestva politicheskogo prosveshcheniia armii i shirokikh sloev naseleniia*, 1917, no. 1:1–3, no. 2:1–4.
29 E. N. Medynskii, *Kak vesti besedy po politicheskim voprosam: Metodicheskie ukazaniia, konspekty i spiski literatury dlia lektorov, uchietelei i pr.* (Moscow, 1917). Medynskii (1885–1957) later became a well-known Soviet educationalist.
30 Medynskii, *Revoliutsiia i vneshkol'noe obrazovanie*.

Would it be good if you could not judge the chairman of your co-operative or your volost elder? If he spends your money, or loses it, or rules the volost badly – he is always right. You can not replace him or take him to court. "Do not dare to touch me, to judge me is a sin," he says to you. The same happens with a monarchy. The tsar, however bad, is always right.[31]

One can detect the same philosophy in the rhetoric of the democratic leaders. They made a conscious effort to explain the abstract concepts of democracy in simple concrete terms for the peasantry. The February Revolution was often portrayed as an enormous *physical* effort – comparable to the peasants' own back-breaking toil. "The Russian people has pulled itself free . . . [and] thrown off the heavy chains of tsarist slavery."[32] Notions of statehood and civic duty were couched in metaphors from peasant daily life. The postrevolutionary state was depicted as a "beautiful new house" whose construction, like a village house, required the participation of all its inhabitants.[33] The purpose of the Constituent Assembly was explained by analogy with the coopera-tives, which were normally organized at a "constituent assembly" of their members where the administration was elected and the rules of the society defined.[34] Where there were no cooperatives, and the word "con-stituent" was foreign to the peasants, agitators used the word *narodnoe* ("people's") instead, since this was familiar. Thus one peasant leader in Olonets Province ended a speech with the rallying cry: "Long live Land and Freedom and the People's Assembly! (*narodnoe sobranie*)"[35] The word *narodnyi* was also substituted for other foreign words (for example, "democratic" and "national").[36] Similarly, the "nationalization" of the land was frequently explained as the transfer of the land to the "people's" property.[37]

Family metaphors for society – which were a staple of the political rhetoric of the nineteenth-century revolutionaries – featured promi-nently in the language of the democratic leaders for the peasantry. "The Russian people wants to be and must be a single family of brother-laborers," wrote the peasant propagandist Alexander Os'minin in his

---

31 Ibid., 23; Medynskii, *Kak vesti besedy*, 4, 7.
32 G. Korelin, *Gotovtes' k uchreditel'nomu sobraniiu* (Kerch, 1917), 2.
33 See, for example, the speeches of Uspenskii and Nabatov in *Zhurnal shatskogo uezdnogo s"ezda krest'ianskikh deputatov, 23–25 iiulia 1917 goda*, 2, 5.
34 Shadrin, *Blizhaishchie zadachi*, 7.
35 TsGASP, f. 446. op. 1, d. 15, l. 26.
36 *Tikhvinskii uezdnyi krest'ianskii s"ezd 29–30 aprelia 1917 g.* (Tikhvin, 1917), 6.
37 S. P. Rudnev, *Pri vechernikh ogniakh: Vospominaniia* (Kharbin, 1928), 96–99.

brochure for the first-time rural voter.[38] Two fundamental ideas of democracy were contained in this metaphor: that the people's victory as a brotherhood was incompatible with their domination by patriarchal figures like the "father tsar"; and that its success depended on the expression of that brotherhood as a sense of duty to the nation as a whole. The peasants' obligation to supply the army was often couched in these familial terms of national unity. "If the village does not give its harvest," declared the *Izvestiia* of the Peasant Soviet, "then the ones to suffer will be the poor people and the soldiers, the brothers of the peasantry by blood and destiny."[39] The need for the officers and soldiers to unite was similarly described in familial terms – as in this telegram to the Soviet: "The soldiers and the officer-citizens of the 16th Irkutsk Hussar Regiment, united in a single compact family, send their heart-felt greetings to the Soviet of Workers' and Soldiers' Deputies in celebration of 1 May."[40] Last but not least, the democratic leaders also used the metaphor of the family to assert their status as "the best sons of the nation" because they had "sat in tsarist jails and suffered for their brothers, the peasantry."[41]

How effective was this rhetoric? How far, and in what forms, did the peasants understand the political concepts of the democratic revolution in the towns? It is always difficult to know what peasants think. They may speak in one language to each other, address outsiders in another, and, as far as they are able, write or dictate petitions to the authorities in a third "official" language.[42] Peasants often adopt the language of a politically dominant urban culture without necessarily believing in its values – indeed they may do so to dissimulate conformity to it, to legitimate their own aims and actions, or to ridicule and subvert it. In short, behind the public discourse of any peasantry there may be (and often

38   Os'minin, *Chto dolzhno dat' narodu*, 15. Os'minin is a fascinating figure in the history of the February Revolution. A peasant from Osvishi village in Tver Province, he fought at the Front for thirty months and rose to the rank of a sergeant. On 7 March 1917 he was sent by his village to the capital with a gift of bread and salt and sixty rubles for Rodzianko, chairman of the Duma, in gratitude for "the blessing of the people's victory" (RGIA, f. 1278, op. 10, d. 11, l. 332). There he became involved in politics – figures of his type were in high demand. He wrote for the newspapers *Trud i volia* and *Soldatskaia mysl'* before becoming editor of *Soldatskoe slovo*, a paper oriented toward peasant soldiers like himself. It is thought that he joined the SRs and became a leader of the soldiers' veteran organization. I am grateful to Boris Kolonitskii for this information.
39   *Izvestiia vserossiiskogo soveta krest'ianskikh deputatov*, 22 August 1917.
40   TsGASP, f. 7384, op. 9, d. 158, l. 29.
41   Shadrin, *Blizhaishchie zadachi*, 10–11.
42   See M. Bakhtin, *The Dialogic Imagination* (Austin, 1981), 295–96.

is) what J. C. Scott has called a "hidden transcript," carried through the language of village songs and jokes, rumor and gossip, largely impenetrable to the outside world.[43] In 1917 the peasants would write humble petitions to the Provisional Government, prefacing them with stock phrases of religious thanks, deferential greetings and heart-felt declarations of loyalty – and then go on to demand the release of their sons from the army or the right to confiscate the landowners' land. Or they would pretend that "we are dark people" – echoing the urban myth about the peasantry – to explain and justify their own neglect or contravention of the law. But it would be mistaken to conclude from this that the peasants were indifferent to – and remained untouched by – the new democratic political culture spreading down toward them from the towns. The peasants had their own forms of politicization, their own *prise de conscience politique*, in which certain aspects of the public discourse might be adopted to articulate their own political ideals and traditions, while other aspects of it might be consciously ignored because they could not be "peasantized."

The remainder of this article shall attempt to sketch the political worldview of the peasants – their construction of the state and the nation, their ideas of citizenship and equality – insofar as these may be inferred from their village resolutions and petitions, their private letters and recorded conversations, and the statements of peasant delegates at provincial assemblies. Of course, the reader should bear in mind that sometimes these records have come down to us through nonpeasant intermediaries – scribes, officials, schoolteachers, and other spokesmen for the peasants – and hence may be couched in a language that reflects the intelligentsia's construction of the peasantry ("dark," "dependent," "pious," and so on) rather than the discourse of the peasantry itself. But in the absence of any other sources, and with the proviso that those used below are approached critically, it seems appropriate to proceed.

Peasant Monarchical Attitudes

The idea that the peasant was at heart a monarchist remains one of the most enduring myths of Russian history.[44] Yet throughout Russia in 1917 the peasantry rejected the monarchy. As the Duma report wittily concluded:

43   J. C. Scott, *Domination and the Arts of Resistance: Hidden Transcripts* (New Haven, 1990).
44   The most recent statement of the view is in R. Pipes, *The Russian Revolution, 1899–1919* (London, 1990), 118–19.

The widespread myth that the Russian peasant is devoted to the tsar and that he "cannot live" without him has been destroyed by the universal joy and relief felt by the peasants upon discovering that in reality they *can* live without the tsar, without whom they were told they "could not live." The scandal of Rasputin, which is known in even the remotest villages, has helped to destroy the status of the tsar. Now the peasants say: "The tsar brought himself down and brought us to ruin."[45]

Of course, not all the peasants were equally decided. Many were afraid to speak their minds until the land captains and police were removed – which in some provinces (Mogilev and Kazan, for instance) was not completed until April – and even then they were hesitant in case the Revolution was reversed.[46] Many of the older peasants were confused by the downfall of the tsar.[47] "The church was full of crying peasants," one witness recalled. " 'What will become of us?' they constantly repeated – 'They have taken the tsar away from us.' "[48] Some of these older peasants had venerated the tsar as a god on earth (they crossed themselves whenever his name was mentioned) and saw his removal as an attack on religion – a fact exploited by many priests and monarchist officials in their counterrevolutionary propaganda. Even among the more rural workers the tsar's removal could give rise to religious doubts. The American Frank Golder talked with one such worker, "an old muzhik," in mid-March, who "said it was a sin to overthrow the emperor, since God had placed him in power. It may be that the new regime will help people on this earth, but they will surely pay for it in the world to come."[49] The patrimonial conception of the tsar – as the "master (*khoziain*) of the Russian land" – also found expression in these fears. "How can Russia survive without its master?" one old Tambov peasant asked.[50]

But generally the news of the tsar's abdication was welcomed joyously. "Our village," wrote one peasant, "burst into life with celebrations. Everyone felt enormous relief, as if a heavy rock had suddenly been lifted from our shoulders." Another wrote: "People kissed each other from joy and said that life from now on would be good. Everyone

45   RGIA, f. 1278, op. 10, d. 4, ll. 241–42.
46   Ibid., l. 241.
47   Many propagandists commented on this generational divide. See, for example, TsGASP, f. 1950. op. 1, d. 10, ll. 7–8, f. 7384, op. 9, d. 176, ll. 177–80, and d. 209, l. 5; and Tsentral'nyi gosudarstvennyi arkhiv istoriko-politicheskikh dokumentov (TsGAIPD), St. Petersburg, f. 1, op. 1, d. 228, l. 46.
48   F. Iusupov, *Pered izgnaniem, 1887–1919* (Moscow, 1993), 187.
49   T. Emmons and B. Patenaude, eds., *War, Revolution, and Peace in Russia: The Passages of Frank Golder, 1914–1927* (Stanford, 1992), 50.
50   Okninskii, *Dva goda*, 28.

dressed in their best costumes, as they do on a big holiday. The festivities lasted three days."[51] Many villages held religious processions to thank the Lord for their newly won freedoms, offering up prayers for the new government. The Revolution thus attained the status of a religious cult, while those who had died fighting for freedom (*bortsy za svobodu*) were venerated as modern saints. The villagers of Bol'she-Dvorskaia volost in Tikhvinsk district, for example, held a "service of thanksgiving for the divine gift of the people's victory and the eternal memory of those holy men who fell in the struggle for freedom."[52] To reciprocate this sacrifice many villages sent donations of money, often amounting to several hundred rubles, to the authorities in Petrograd for the benefit of those who had suffered losses in the February Days.

What is striking here is the extent to which the peasantry identified itself with the ideas and the symbols of the republic. There was of course a precedent here. The establishment of a republic had been a basic demand of the peasant unions and the rural socialists ever since the 1905 Revolution. And events since then ("Bloody Sunday" and the suppression of the peasant disorders during 1905–7; the gross mismanagement of the war campaign and its criminal wastage of human life; the scandal of Rasputin and the rumors of treason at the court) had already shaken many of the peasants from their old belief in the tsar's benevolence and the sacred sources of his power. Nonetheless, it is still remarkable how far and how fast the idea of the republic took root among certain sections of the peasantry. The most educated peasants and those living closest to the towns readily adopted the rhetoric and metaphors of the new republican propaganda in their petitions to the authorities. The form of the republic was heatedly debated at most provincial peasant congresses. Hundreds of villages passed formal resolutions in favor of a republic and sent them to the authorities. Some of them took part in the "Festivals of Freedom" and the "Peasant Days," sponsored respectively by the Provisional Government and the Peasant Soviet, where the symbols and the public rituals of the nineteenth-century republican tradition (planting "Trees of Liberty," singing the "Marseillaise," and constructing memorials to those who had died in the struggle against the monarchy) played a major role in the celebrations.[53]

For many peasants, however, the idea of the republic remained confused with the idea of the monarchy. The British ambassador, George Buchanan, was told by one peasant soldier in the spring: "Yes, we need

51   *1917 god v derevne: Vospominaniia krest'ian* (Moscow-Leningrad, 1929), 40, 64.
52   TsGASP, f. 8558, op. 1, d. 5, l. 30.
53   RGIA, f. 794, op. 1, d. 17, l. 23, and f. 1278, op. 10, d. 4. l. 83; *Izvestiia vserossiiskogo soveta krest'ianskikh deputatov*, 14 and 15 March 1917.

a republic, but at its head there should be a good tsar."[54] Similarly, Frank Golder noted during March: "Stories are being told of soldiers who say they wish a republic like England, or a republic with a tsar. One soldier said he wanted to elect a president and when asked. 'Whom would you elect?' he replied. 'The tsar.'"[55] Many soldiers' letters voiced the same confusion. "We want a democratic republic and a *tsar'-batiushka* for three years," declared one regiment. "It would be good if we had a republic with a wise tsar," concluded another.[56] It seems that the peasants found it difficult to distinguish between the person of the sovereign (*gosudar'*) and the abstract institutions of the state (*gosudarstvo*): Hence many peasant soldiers were confused by the new oath of allegiance to the Provisional Government, with some even refusing to swear it because it contained the word *gosudarstvo*. "We are not for a *gosudarstvo*," the soldiers reasoned, "we are for a republic."[57] They conceived of the state as embodied in a monarch, and projected their ideals onto a "peasant king" or some other authoritarian liberator, come to deliver their cherished land and freedom. Here, at least in part, were the popular roots of the cults of Kerensky, the "people's champion," and of Lenin, too. Both were attempts to fill the space left by the myth of the tsar-deliverer. Indeed, at times it seemed that almost anyone could perform the role of the peasants' king, such was their demand for outside leadership. A few weeks after the February Revolution a Menshevik deputy of the Moscow Soviet went to agitate at a regimental meeting near Vladimir. He spoke of the need for peace, of the need for the land to be given to the peasants, and of the advantages of a republic over monarchy. The peasant soldiers cheered loudly and one of them called out. "We want to elect you as tsar," whereupon the other soldiers burst into applause. "I refused the Romanov crown," recalled the Menshevik, "and went away with a heavy feeling of how easy it would be for any adventurer or demagogue to become the master of this simple and naive people."[58]

This monarchical republicanism mirrored in some ways the philosophy and practice of the village assembly, where there was a strange mix between the principles of democratic self-rule by open debate and patriarchal rule by the village elders. During 1917 it was reflected in the way

54 G. Buchanan. *My Mission to Russia and Other Diplomatic Memories*, 2 vols. (London, 1923), 2:86, 114.
55 *War, Revolution and Peace*. 46.
56 RGIA, f. 1278, op. 10, d. 4, 1:243.
57 D. Os'kin, *Zapiski praporshchika* (Moscow, 1931), 110–11. See further A. Wildman. *The End of the Russian Imperial Army: The Old Army and the Soldiers' Revolt (March-April 1917)* (Princeton, 1980), 241–42.
58 "Moskovskii sovet rabochikh deputatov (1917–1922)," p. 10, George Katkov Papers, Russian Centre, St. Antony's College, Oxford University, England.

that many peasants believed the new democratic institutions ought to operate. Thus it was common for the peasants to declare that the Constituent Assembly should "take complete power in its hands" or "become the master (*khoziain*) of the Russian land" in the manner of an autocrat.[59] Two old peasants were heard in conversation in a railway carriage during the autumn, and although this version, printed in the press, may have been exaggerated to amuse the reader, it conveys the spirit of their words:

> *First peasant.* The Constituent Assembly, brother, will be the master; and because we the peasants will be voting, it will be a peasant one (*budet muzhitskim*). The peasant can not stand disorder. Our business is a serious business: we feed everyone. And for our work we need peace and order. We have not had that. There have been too many changes . . .
>
> *Second peasant.* Too many! We don't like changes! Under the tsar everything was normal, but now it is hard to keep up with the changes.
>
> *First peasant.* Our rulers today – they have thought of everything, but they don't have any real strength. They are unable to rule the people strictly as they ought to do. But the Constituent Assembly – that, my friend, will be the real master. It will put everyone in their place. Do not disobey! Do not shout! Wait for us to give you your land and freedom! Great deeds cannot be achieved in a single day. The peasantry has waited a long time for their land and freedom. It has to be done properly – not just for us but also for our children and grandchildren – and for that we need a master's hand (*khoziaiskaia ruka*).[60]

The need for a "master's hand" to maintain order and defend their interests was a frequent theme in the peasants' statements on politics. This authoritarianism was, at least in their view, quite compatible with the democratic goals of the Revolution. So much for the notion of most historians that the Russian peasant was at heart an "anarchist" and rejected the need for a strong authority. On the contrary, many peasant resolutions spoke out in support of a "firm power" (*tverdaia vlast'*) to end the disorder in the country and force the other classes to accept their revolution on the land.[61] The sociologist S. S. Maslov, paraphrasing what the peasants had told him during 1917, claimed that they distinguished between the need for a strong government at the national level and the right of self-rule in the localities:

59 *Tret'ii s"ezd vserossiiskogo krest'ianskogo soiuza v Moskve*, 11; *Gubernskii s"ezd krest'ianskikh deputatov tomskoi gubernii, sostoiavshchiisia v g. Tomske 14–22 sentiabria 1917 g.* (Tomsk, 1917), 27.
60 *Delo derevni*, 3 November 1917.
61 *Sel'skii vestnik*, 5 July 1917.

There can be no order without a stable power. A stable power needs a single person in whose hands are concentrated force and many rights. Such a person ought to be a president but under no circumstances a tsar. A president is elected by the people, he is temporary and can be supervised, but a tsar is like a volost elder who would rule the volost all his life and on his death would pass on his power to his children. With such an elder one could not live. The Russian state should be unified, but it must not oppress the people – let everyone think, believe and speak as they wish, as their mother and father taught them. Local matters must not be left to bureaucrats from Moscow or Petrograd. The people should be given complete freedom to organize their own local affairs.[62]

But some peasants also advocated running local government on the same authoritarian lines as it had been run under the tsarist regime, albeit now in the revolutionary interests of the people. At the Tambov provincial peasant congress in mid-September one delegate argued:

The Soviets do not need the sort of power which the Bolsheviks are foisting upon them – the power to appoint and mix ministers: that is not power but powerlessness. No, give them the power to make people listen, as they once listened to the [provincial] governors. Surely if we are not fully organized for power and cannot use it, then it will be the cause of our downfall. Our enemies will say – they are good for nothing!

Another peasant took up the same theme: "What was the strength of the old regime? It had autocrats at every level – Nicholas, the governor, and the policeman. Let us arrange things so that today there is a people's autocracy (*samoderzhavie narodnoe*)!"[63]

Peasant Notions of Citizenship

During the course of 1917 the word *grazhdane* spread throughout the countryside as a term of peasant self-identity. Village resolutions and petitions tended increasingly to begin with the words, "We the citizens" (*My grazhdane*) of such and such a village, rather than the old phrase, "We the peasants" (*My krest'iane*).[64] Delegates to peasant congresses referred to each other as "citizens" during the debates. This new self-identification was no doubt a source of pride for many peasants. It was

---

62   S. S. Maslov, *Rossiia posle chetyrekh let revoliutsii* (Paris, 1922), 149.
63   *Delo derevni*, 20 September 1917. The phrase *samoderzhavie narodnoe* was sometimes used in propaganda – and so may have been picked up by him in this way.
64   Sometimes a vilage resolution might begin: "We the citizens of peasant origin" (*My grazhdane iz krest'ianskikh proiskhozhdenii*).

a badge of equality with the other classes of society, a society from which they had always been excluded by a comprehensive range of legal discriminations against them. The abolition of the old class system of legal estates (*sosloviia*), a legacy from serfdom which guaranteed the privileged position of the landed nobles, had long been a demand of the peasant movement. The announcement of the Provisional Government's plans to abolish the *sosloviia* ("on the principle of equal rights for all citizens")[65] was hailed by many peasants – and especially by those in the army, where the privileges of the noble officers was still a source of bitter resentment among the peasant soldiers – as a new emancipation. As one soldiers' resolution put it (with a rhetorical flourish that gave expression to their euphoria), the abolition of the estate system "will bring our freedom to full liberation (*raskreposhcheniia*) from the heavy yoke of slavery, from the eternal prison, and the shameful servitude in which we have lived."[66]

But within the village what did "citizenship" mean? Clearly, it did not mean equal rights for everyone: the peasant revolution was itself class-based and directed *against* groups outside "peasant society" (landed nobles, townsmen, the intelligentsia, and so on). The peasants' language of citizenship was thus clearly different from that of other classes." One noble officer understood this well when he wrote to his father on 11 March:

> Between us and the soldiers there is an abyss that one cannot cross. Whatever they might think of us as individuals, we in their eyes remain no more than *barins* (masters). When we talk of "the people" (*narod*) we have in mind the nation as a whole, but they mean only the common people (*demokraticheskie nizy*). In their view what has taken place is not a political but a social revolution, of which we are the losers and they are the winners. They think that things should get better for them and that they should get worse for us. They do not believe us when we talk of our devotion to the soldiers. They say, that we were the *barins* in the past, and that now it is their turn to be the *barins* over us. It is their revenge for the long centuries of servitude.[67]

One way to review this question is in terms of who was given land and voting rights within the village community (*mir*). Generally, the peasants drew up their own circle of "insiders" and assigned a certain set of rights and duties to each subgroup of the community according to their perceived social value. Peasants who farmed with their own

65 *Izvestiia*, 12 March 1917.
66 TsGASP, f. 7384, op. 7, d. 11, l. 32.
67 "Iz ofitserskikh pisem c fronta v 1917 g.," *Krasnyi arkhiv*, 50, no. 1 (1932): 200.

family labor – and former landowners who turned themselves into "peasants" by doing the same – were assigned an equal share of the communal land and full voting rights at the village assembly (*skhod*). The younger peasants, in particular, gained a larger influence at the assembly – partly because the astronomic rate of household partitioning in 1917 created a large number of young household heads (with rights to attend the assembly), and partly because the prestige of the younger peasants increased as a result of their service in the army and the growing need for literate village leaders after the collapse of the old regime and the flight of the rural intelligentsia. Peasant women, too, gained rights at the *skhod*, often as the heads of households in the absence of their husbands on military service. But it was not just the peasants who were given land or rights at the assembly. Nonfarming groups deemed of value to the village (for example, craftsmen who manufactured goods demanded by the peasants, democratic priests and teachers, agronomists and vets, and sometimes landless laborers) were also deemed to be citizens, with a right to share in the benefits of the community. On the other hand, those who were a burden on the village's resources (such as migrants and townspeople without relatives in it) might be given temporary aid "as human beings" but were rarely given land or rights at the *skhod* as "village citizens."[68]

It was common for the peasants to define their own tightly knit community in familial terms. The "peasant family" (*krest'ianskaia sem'ia*) was a stock phrase in their rhetoric, and within the village they addressed each other as if they were kin. A child, for example, would call the men "uncle" or 'grandfather." and all the women "auntie" or "grandmother," whether they were related or not. At one level, then, the familial metaphor for society used by the democratic leadership found an echo in the traditional language of the peasantry. But it would be mistaken to conclude from this that the official usage of the metaphor – to define a nation of civic rights and duties – was also adopted by the peasantry. On the contrary, the peasants used the family metaphor to reinterpret these rights and duties so that they would not undermine the traditions and interests of the village.

Take, for example, the question of elections, where the peasants were to exercise their civic rights. The peasants did not vote as individuals but as families or whole communities (that is, the household or village elders decided how to vote and the rest of the peasants followed suit, or, alternatively, the household or the village decided collectively how to vote).

68   See my "Peasant Farmers and the Minority Groups of Rural Society: Peasant Egalitarianism and Village Social Relations during the Russian Revolution (1917–1921)," in *Peasant Economy, Culture and Politics of European Russia, 1800–1921*, ed. E. Kingston-Mann and T. Mixter (Princeton, 1991), 378–401.

This sort of "herd voting," to adopt the phrase of O. H. Radkey, was widely noted in the three main elections of 1917: to the volost zemstvos, the volost soviets, and the Constituent Assembly.[69] There were obvious reasons to vote in this way. It was very hard, if not impossible, to arrange a secret ballot in the Russian village, where voting had always been done in the open (either by shouting or standing in sides) and where, in any case, everybody knew how everybody else was intending to cast their vote. In this context it was more important for the villagers (or household members) to maintain their unity by voting together than it was for them to exercise their voting rights as individual citizens and yet run the risk of becoming divided on party lines. Unity had always been the main priority at the village assembly – its resolutions were by custom passed unanimously – and it was enforced by the patriarchs. Equally, most peasants were quick to condemn the fighting between the socialist parties, which, to extend the familial metaphor, they blamed for the "war of brothers" (*bratoubiistvennaia voina*), the peasant term for the Civil War.[70]

On the issue of taxation, where they were to exercise their civic duties, the family concept of society was similarly interpreted by the peasants to suit their own best interests. Nearly all the peasants recognized the need to give food to the army, where their sons and brothers were fighting for the defense of the motherland, but very few agreed with the need to give food to the workers in the towns. Despite the efforts of the urban propagandists, they felt no kinship with the workers, whose strikes and eight-hour days they held responsible for the problems of the army and the growing shortages of manufactured goods.[71]

Peasant Constructions of Power and the State

"For hundreds of years the Russian peasant has dreamt of a state with no right to influence the will of the individual and his freedom of action, a state without power over man." Thus wrote Maxim Gorky in 1927.[72] His view of the peasantry as anarchists has been shared by many his-

69   RGIA, f. 1278, op. 10, d. 4, ll. 247–48; *Sel'skii vestnik*, 23 and 30 September 1917; Rudnev, *Pri vechernikh ogniakh*, 83–85; Figes, *Peasant Russia*, 64–66; *Delo naroda*, 19 December 1917; O. H. Radkey, *Russia Goes to the Polls: The Election to the All-Russian Constituent Assembly, 1917* (Ithaca, 1989), 65–71.
70   Figes, *Peasant Russia*, 175–76, 309.
71   RGIA, f. 1278, op. 10, d. 4, l. 255; TsGASP, f. 446, op. 1, d. 1, ll. 11–12; *Sel'skii vestnik*, 9. July, 1917.
72   M. Gorky, "On the Russian Peasantry," in *The Russian Peasantry 1920 and 1984*, ed. R. E. F. Smith (London, 1977), 12.

torians since. Indeed the idea that the peasants wanted nothing to do with the state, that their only aim was to free themselves completely from its influence and to rule themselves in their own villages, has become the dominant conception of the rural revolution in the Western historiography of 1917.

It is, of course, true that among the peasantry there was a marked preference for localist solutions to the social problems of 1917 (land and food distribution above all), and that this formed part of a general peasant drive toward autonomy from the state.[73] But this does not mean that the peasants were indifferent to the structures of the state or that they did not want a state at all. The peasant idea of autonomy was not the same thing as anarchy: it was a demand for a state in their own image, one that would enforce their own agenda of the Revolution and compel the other classes to submit to it. Judging from the fat files of their letters and petitions lying in the archives from 1917, the peasants had a lot to say about the power question. The First World War had politicized the village – literally so during 1917 as the peasant soldiers, revolutionized by their military service, returned home. Thousands of villages passed formal resolutions on the future structure of the state. Many of these mandates were imbued with a solemn rhetoric, such was the seriousness with which they were viewed, and nearly all contained a long list of political demands. The villagers of Vyshgorodetsk in Pskov Province, for example, singed a petition to the Soviet entitled "Our Demands," in which they called for the establishment of a democratic republic, universal suffrage, more rights of local self-government, school education in the local tongue, equal rights for women and all national groups, court reforms, progressive taxes, and the prohibition of all vodka sales.[74] Such resolutions hardly suggest a parochial peasantry, one with its back to the outside world and preoccupied with its own village affairs, as so often depicted in the literature on 1917. Nor could one conclude this from the long and heated debates about the power question which so often dominated peasant congresses, and even less from the high turnout of peasant voters in the elections to the Constituent Assembly. This was not a peasantry indifferent to the state but, on the contrary, one that, for the first time in its history, was becoming aware of its power to reshape it.

Following the February Revolution the Provisional Government and the Petrograd Soviet received hundreds of peasant greetings and declarations of support. Many of these were couched in religious terms. The villagers of Tetrin in Arkhangel'sk Province wrote to express their

73   On this see my *Peasant Russia*, chaps. 2 and 3.
74   TsGASP, f. 7384, op. 9, d. 255, l. 11.

"devout gratitude" to the Provisional Government for Russia's liberation from "the sinful tsarist regime" and to "pray to it to lead Russia onto the just path of salvation and truth."[75] A group of peasant soldiers from XI Army was even more explicit in its religious greeting to the leaders of the Soviet: "You have been blessed by Jesus our Savior and are leading us to the dawn of a new and holy fraternal life. May the Lord help you!"[76] Many peasants saw the February Revolution in religious terms, or at least gave that impression in their correspondence with its official bodies. They described the old regime as sinful and corrupt praised the revolutionary "freedom fighters" as Christ-like saviors of the people, and projected their religious hopes and ideals onto the new government. The words *pravda* ("truth" or "justice") and *pravitel'stvo* ("government") are – uniquely to the Russian language – derived from the same root. These two religious concepts were intimately linked in the Russian peasant mind: the only true form of government (and the only one the peasants recognized) was the administration of *pravda* (meaning it gave land and freedom to the peasantry). By embracing it in these religious terms the peasants sought to imbue the new order with their own ideals of government. As the peasant propagandist Os'minin concluded: "We are standing for the people to become the masters of their own lives, for our country to become a single family of brother laborers, without rich or poor – in short for the Kingdom of God to come to our land."[77]

The peasantry projected its own religious ideals of social justice onto the new order – and in this way they inverted (or perhaps subverted) the whole state structure to suit peasant goals. Thus in the peasants' view any public body sanctioning their revolution on the land was to have the status of an organ of the state with the power to pass its own "laws"; whereas the laws of any other body, including the Provisional Government, that opposed their revolution were not to be recognized at all. This is neatly illustrated by the All-Russian Peasant Congress during May, and the peasant assemblies convened in most central Russian provinces during the spring.[78] Despite the warnings of the Provisional Government, which had pledged to protect the gentry's property rights until the convocation of the Constituent Assembly, most of these assemblies gave what the peasants took to be a legal sanction for their confiscation of the gentry's land. The peasant delegates, in the words of one observer at the All-Russian Congress, "did not clearly understand the difference, firstly, between a declaration of some principle and the implementation

75 RGIA, f. 1278, op. 10, d. 4, ll. 192–93.
76 TsGASP, f. 7384, op. 9, d. 255, l. 24.
77 Os'minin, *Chto dolzhno dat' narodu*, 15.
78 On the peasant assemblies in the Volga provinces see my *Peasant Russia*, 40–46.

of it as a law, or, secondly, between a resolution by the congress, expressing its opinion, and a law by the government, which has a binding force."[79] The peasants seemed to believe that their own assemblies resolutions already carried the status of "laws," and that in order to "socialize" the land it was enough for a large peasant assembly to pass a resolution to that effect. Their expectations transformed their assemblies into pseudogovernments promulgating "laws" by simple declaration – "laws" that then took precedence over the statutes of the Provisional Government. As one of the government's provincial commissars complained, "The peasantry has got a fixed opinion that all civil laws have lost their force, and that all legal relations ought now to be regulated by peasant organizations."[80]

It was precisely in this sense that the peasants came to see their local soviets as sovereign state organs, implementing and legitimizing their own revolution on the land, as the Bolsheviks encouraged them to do through the slogan "All power to the soviets!" In the peasant view their soviets were the only legitimate organs of state power in the countryside, and if they resolved to seize the gentry's land against the orders of the Provisional Government, they did so with the idea that they were acting with the sanction of a national state authority (the All-Russian Soviet Assembly) and as such their actions were "legal." A strong soviet, with the coercive means to enforce this peasant revolution and compel the other classes to submit to it, was thus seen by the peasants as a necessity, both at the local and the national levels. Nearly all the peasant soviets had their own Red Guard or armed detachment, not to mention police and judicial institutions, precisely for this purpose.

Similarly, the peasants tended to regard the Constituent Assembly as a national body giving legal force to their own revolution on the land. They saw it as "the spokesman of the peasants' will," as the "deliverer of land and freedom," which, by "getting all the people to agree" to it, would make their revolution binding and irreversible.[81] At times the peasants expressed the naive belief that as long as the assembly had a wise old peasant at its head, like some elder at a giant "people's *skhod*," or that as long as it contained enough peasants who were known and

79   V. Ia. Gurevich. "Vserossiiskii krest'ianskii s"ezd i pervaia koalitsiia," *Letopis' revoliutsii*, 1923, no. 1:191. See similarly the Duma report in RGIA. f. 1278, op. 10, d. 4, l. 248 ("the peasants take as a law any resolution in the newspaper. . . . And usually they take to be 'the most corect law' those parts of the parties' resolutions . . . in which their own ancient ideals are expressed").
80   L. Trotsky, *The History of the Russian Revolution* (London, 1977), 882.
81   TsGASP, f. 446, op. 1, d. 1, ll. 2, 5, 8, and f. 7384, op. 9, d. 255, l. 11.

trusted by their fellow villagers, then it could not fail to bring them land and freedom.[82]

Finally, to finish with this theme of the peasants' reconstruction and inversion of the state, it was common for them to propose remedies to national problems that they might have applied in their own village. So, in April 1918 the peasants of Trost'ian volost in Samara Province suggested resolving the industrial crisis by a repartition of all town property, just as the repartition of the land had "resolved' the crisis in agriculture.[83] Similarly, many peasants believed that the war with Germany could and should be resolved like a village brawl. A group of mainly peasant soldiers in II Army appealed to the Petrograd Soviet in April: "Once the German people and their Social Democrats have overthrown their Terrible Wilhelm we should hold out to them a brotherly hand and firmly conclude a people's peace (*narodnyi mir*)."[84] And in the same month a peasant from Samara Province wrote to a newspaper: "We should talk things over with the German people: let them overthrow their Wilhelm, as we overthrew the tsar, and then we will hold out a hand to them, and we will all go back to our homes."[85]

The Peasants and the Language of Socialism

There were four aspects of the "Russian peasant ideology" that could loosely be described as "socialist" in content; the belief that all the land should be held collectively and that every person had a right to work it using his own labor; the custom of the land commune (in most parts of Russia) of redistributing the plots of land in accordance with household size; the welfarism of the village (for example, provision for widows and orphans); and the not infrequent custom of collective labor for communal ends (building irrigation schemes or harvesting communal grain stores, for instance). Yet this does not mean that the peasantry was ripe for "socialism" in the usual understanding of that term. The peasants may have assimilated some of the ideas of the socialist movement in the towns, but they added to them a traditional peasant gloss, informed by the egalitarian values of their own political culture, and the result was a strange hybrid creation, in part peasant and in part socialist.

The socialists in Russia had always found it hard to get across their abstract ideas to the peasantry. As one Populist concluded from the

---

82   See, for example. TsGASP, f. 8558, op. 1, d. 5, l. 24; *Zhurnal shatskogo uezdnogo s"ezda*, 7; and *Gubernskii s"ezd krest'ianskikh deputatov Tomskoi gubernii*, 25.

83   Gosudarstvennyi arkhiv Kuibyshevskoi oblasti, f. 81, op. 1, d. 119a, l. 171.

84   TsGASP, f. 7384, op. 7, d. 11, l. 33.

85   *Sel'skii vestnik*, 13 April 1917.

failure of the "Going to the people" in the 1870s, the peasants "were left cold by socialism, and yet they debated heatedly those questions that affected their immediate concerns and which did not go beyond their customary ideas of a better peasant life."[86] Most of the peasants were easily confused by the abstract jargon of the socialists – all their talk of "classes," of successive "stages of development," and their "ism" this and their "ism" that. At the Shatsk district peasant congress in July 1917 one muddled peasant, obviously outraged by the exploitation of the capitalist system, argued that no socialist should be elected to the Constituent Assembly "because socialism grew from capitalism."[87] Even those peasants who had learned to speak this "scientific" language, mostly in the army, and who liked to speak it as a sign of "education," sometimes betrayed a ridiculous confusion about the meaning of its words. The memoirist Okninskii, in his remarkable account of rural life in Tambov Province during the Civil War, recalls the visit of some Soviet propagandists in the summer of 1920. Among them was a young local peasant from the Red Army who, to the delight of the villagers, also gave a speech, from which Okninskii quotes:

> Comrades! Can you tell in diameters what you know of the internal size of our victorious Red Army? I am sure that diametrically-perpendicularly you can not say anything about its internal size. Our victorious Red Army on a scale always beats our enemies in parallel. To understand the axiom, you ought to think not in straight lines, like women, but perpendicularly like men. Then two radiuses will be equal to a diameter.

As the peasant spoke, his fellow villagers were increasingly amazed: "See how clever he has become! All those words! Where did he learn them! He is completely educated!"[88]

The socialists' theoretical language of class was almost entirely alien to the peasants – and was soon transformed by their use of it. The word *burzhooi* – which was roughly synonymous with "bourgeois" in the propaganda of the socialists, yet, as Boris Kolonitskii has so brilliantly shown, had no set class connotations for the urban masses and was used by them as a general form of abuse for virtually *any* perceived social enemy – became in the language of the village a term for all forces hostile to the peasantry.[89] Many peasants used it to describe all townsmen, thought to be hoarding the manufactured goods so badly needed

86 O. V. Aptekman, *Obshchestvo "zemlia i volia" 70-kh gg.* (Petrograd, 1924), 178.
87 *Zhurnal shatskogo uezdnogo s"ezda*, 7.
88 Okninskii, *Dva goda*, 247–48.
89 B. Kolonitskii, "Antibourgeois Propaganda and Anti-'Burzhui' Consciousness in 1917," *Russian Review* 53 (April 1994): 183–96.

in the countryside. Some confused the word *burzhooi* with *barzhui* (the owners of a barge) and *birzhve* (from the word *birzh* for the Stock Exchange) – perhaps on account of this association with the towns.[90] But by far the most common peasant understanding of the term *burzhooi*, at least during 1917, was that he was a supporter of the monarchy and was perhaps plotting for its restoration, along with the power of the gentry on the land. For example, two peasants from Viatka Province wrote in May to the Peasant Soviet claiming that in their district "no new laws have been introduced because all the *burzhooi* support the old regime and do not permit our village committees."[91] In Penza Province the word *borzhuki* (a misspelling of *burzhooi*) was used by the peasants "for all monarchists," who they said had committees called *khameteti* – a compound of *komitety* (committees) and *khamy* (hooligans).[92]

Later, in the summer of 1918, when the Bolsheviks attempted to divide the "rural poor" against the "kulaks" or the "rural bourgeoisie," this language of class was equally rejected by the peasantry. The Committees of the Rural Poor (*kombedy*), which were supposed to ignite this class war in the village, spectacularly failed to get any of the peasants, let alone the poorest, to think of themselves as "proletarians" or of their richer neighbors as a "bourgeoisie." In most villages the peasants thought of themselves as a community or "family" of farmers (*krest'ian-skaia sem'ia*), tied together by their common links to the village and its land, and the notion of a separate body for the village poor, especially when the whole village was united behind the soviet, seemed both strange and unnecessary. The villagers of Kiselevo-Chemizovka in the Atkarsk district of Saratov, for example, resolved that a *kombed* was not needed, "since the peasants are almost equal, and the poor ones are already elected to the Soviet . . . so that the organization of separate committees for the poor peasants would only lead to unnecessary tensions between the citizens of the same commune."[93] Most villages either refused to elect a *kombed*, thus leaving it to outside agitators, or established one which every peasant joined on the grounds that all of them were equally poor. The following resolution, from the Serdobsk district of Saratov Province, was typical of this linguistic subversion: "We the peasants of Commune No. 4 welcome the committees of the rural poor,

90   I. Nazhivin, *Zapiski o revoliutsii* (Vienna, 1921), 15; Gosudarstvennyi arkhiv Rossiiskoi Federatsii (GARF), f. 551, op. 1, d. 108, l. 2; TsGASP, f. 7384, op. 9, d. 255, l. 25.
91   *Izvestiia vserossiiskogo soveta krest'ianskikh deputatov*, 20 May 1917.
92   Ibid., 20 October 1917.
93   Cited in G. A. Gerasimenko and F. A. Rashitov, *Sovety nizhnego povolzh'ia v Oktiabr'skoi revoliutsii* (Saratov, 1972), 266.

for in our commune no one speculates and no one is rich. We are all middle peasants and poor peasants and we will do all we can to help the poor peasants."[94]

"Socialism," recalled Ivan Nazhivin, a Tolstoyan peasant from Vladimir Province, in his entertaining *Notes on the Revolution*, "appeared to us as some mystical method – mystical because it was unclear to us and we could not imagine what it might consist of in practical terms – of dividing all the property and money of the rich; according to our village tailor, this would mean that every peasant household would be given 200,000 rubles. This, it seems, was the biggest number he could think of."[95] Nazhivin meant this as a condemnation of the socialists, and of the naive peasants who believed them. Yet there is no doubt that the propaganda of socialism was most effective when communicated, if not explicitly in religious terms, then at least in terms of the peasantry's traditional community values, which they saw as "just" and "willed by God." If socialism became the dominant political language of 1917, then it was largely because it provided the peasants with an idiom in which to formulate their own revolutionary ideals. The old peasant conception of the "toiling people" (*trudovoi narod*) gave the socialist parties an ideological *point d'appui* for the dissemination of a class-based rhetoric of politics – a rhetoric that increasingly undermined the language of democratic citizenship promoted by the Provisional Government as this came to be seen by the peasantry to signify the defense of the gentry's landed rights.

It was a well-established practice of the socialists to couch their propaganda in religious and peasant terms. The populists of the 1870s had often used the ideas of Christian brotherhood to preach socialism to the peasantry. And the same theme was taken up by the socialist parties in 1917. Pamphlets for the peasants presented socialism as a sort of religious utopia: "Want and hunger will disappear and pleasure will be equally accessible to all. Thieving and robbery will come to an end. In place of compulsion and coercion there will be a kingdom of freedom and fraternity."[96]

It was the Bolsheviks, however, who made the most political capital out of socialism's religious resonance. S. G. Strumilin, in a pamphlet for the rural poor, compared socialism to the work of Christ and claimed that it would create a "terrestrial kingdom of fraternity, equality and freedom."[97] The cult of Lenin, which took off in August 1918 after he

94   GARF, f. 393, op. 3, d. 340, l. 70.
95   Nazhivin, *Zapiski*, 14.
96   *Chto takoe sotsializm?* (Minusinsk, 1917), 9.
97   S. Petrashkevich (Strumilin), *Pro zemliu i sotsializm: Slovo sotsialdemokrata k derevenskoi bednote* (Petrograd, 1917), 1–2.

had been wounded in an assassination attempt, carried explicit religious overtones. Lenin was depicted as a Christ-like figure, ready to die for the people's cause, and, because the bullets had not killed him, blessed by miraculous powers.[98] Even the Red Star, the emblem of the Red Army, had religious connotations deeply rooted in peasant folklore. A Red Army leaflet of 1918 explained to the servicemen why the Red Star appeared on the Soviet flag and their uniforms. There was once a beautiful maiden named Pravda (Truth) who had a burning red star on her forehead which lit up the whole world and brought it truth, justice, and happiness. One day the red star was stolen by Krivda (Falsehood) who wanted to bring darkness and evil to the world. Thus began the rule of Krivda. Meanwhile, Pravda called on the people to retrieve her star and "return the light of truth to the world." A good youth conquered Krivda and her forces and returned the red star to Pravda, whereupon the evil forces ran away from the light "like owls and bats," and "once again the people lived by truth." The leaflet made the parable clear: "So the Red Star of the Red Army is the star of Pravda. And the Red Army servicemen are the brave lads who are fighting Krivda and her evil supporters so that truth should rule the world and so that all those oppressed and wronged by Krivda, all the poor peasants and workers, should live well and in freedom."[99]

The democratic revolution in the towns spoke a foreign language to the peasantry. Its leaders were acutely aware of the problem – many even though that the whole success of their democratic mission would depend on finding a common discourse with the peasantry – and they went to great lengths to explain their ideas in terms they thought the peasants might understand. To some extent they succeeded with that small section of the literate peasantry, among whom the urban culture of democracy was most developed. But in their communication with the peasant masses these ideas were soon translated (almost beyond recognition) into specific peasant forms. The idea of the Republic became in the village a monarchical idea, a demand for order and a "master's hand" to direct the Revolution, shaped less by the democratic culture of the towns than by the patriarchal culture of the peasantry. The new language of citizenship was reinterpreted to suit the peasants' own revolutionary and social needs. The idea of the state and its coercive power, far from being negated by the peasants, was reconstructed and inverted by

---

98   See N. Tumarkin, *Lenin Lives! The Lenin Cult in Soviet Russia* (Cambridge, 1983), 82–95.
99   R. Stites, *Revolutionary Dreams: Utopian Vision and Experimental Life in the Russian Revolution* (Oxford, 1989), 110; and Tumarkin, *Lenin Lives!* 71–72.

them to serve their own interests and religious ideals of social justice. Finally, the language of socialism was similarly understood in these religious terms.

Language, then, was still a fundamental problem for the democratic mission in the village, even after eight months of trying to construct a national political culture. The leaders of the February Revolution had initiated a public discourse of democracy, to which the peasants had been exposed through newspapers, pamphlets, and oral propaganda, but the peasants' "hidden transcripts" of this public discourse gave a different meaning to many of its terms. Whereas the main purpose of this discourse had been to break down class distinctions, resolve social conflicts, and create a nation of citizens, the way it had been received by the peasantry merely served to reinforce these social divisions. Language, more than ever, defined the peasants' self-identity and united them against the educated classes of the towns.

Glossary

Gorky, Maxim   One of the most prominent Soviet writers in the postrevolutionary era.

intelligenty   Members of the intelligentsia.

Izvestiia   "News" (Bolshevik newspaper).

Kerensky, Alexander   Prime Minister of the Provisional Government in 1917.

Narodnaia gazeta   "The People's Newspaper."

Pravda   "Truth" (Bolshevik newspaper).

prise de conscience politique   Hold on political consciousness.

SR   Socialist-Revolutionary Party.

tsar'-batiushka   Affectionate peasant term for the emperor meaning "tsar-the little father."

Wilhelm   A reference to the German emperor until 1918, Wilhelm II.

Further Reading: The Peasantry during the Revolution

O. Figes, *Peasant Russia, Civil War: The Volga Countryside in Revolution, 1917–1921* (Oxford University Press, 1989).
Esther Kingston-Mann and Timothy Mixter (eds.), *Peasant Economy, Culture and Politics of European Russia, 1800–1921* (Princeton University Press, 1991).

T. Shanin, *The Awkward Class: Political Sociology of the Peasantry in a Developing Society: Russia, 1910–1925* (Oxford University Press 1972).

Two earlier foundational books in this subfield are:

J. Blum, *Lord and Peasant in Russia from the Ninth to the Nineteenth Century* (Princeton University Press, 1961).

G. T. Robinson, *Rural Russia under the Old Regime* (Columbia University Press, 1932).

4

The Bolsheviks Come to Power

Alexander Rabinowitch

Originally appeared as Alexander Rabinowitch, "The Bolsheviks Come to Power," *The Bolsheviks Come to Power: The Revolution of 1917 in Petrograd* (NY: Norton, 1978): 273–304.

Editor's Introduction

Alexander Rabinowitch is the author of one of the most detailed and thoroughly researched histories of the process by which the Bolsheviks came to power in October 1917. When the book from which the following chapter is taken first appeared, it opened up a whole new area of inquiry for scholars to pursue. Prior to his book, October had been a minefield of contentious dispute. On one side, Soviet historians argued essentially that Lenin's path to national authority was both an inevitable consequence of the contradictions of capitalism and a beneficent event in which, for the first time in history, a state was created in the interests of the exploited, the excluded and the injured. On the other side, Western historians took the position that October was either a spontaneous accident of history or the result of a ruthless minority willing to go to any lengths to achieve power, leading to, in either case, a state prepared to exercise greater control over its citizenry than anything the tsars had imagined.

Given this context, one can appreciate Rabinowitch's contribution more clearly. In rejecting the binary opposition between heroism and tragedy, he went back to the materials, both published and archival, to fashion a narrative of the events which is both objective and engaging in its portrayal. In the original text, he also included facsimiles of contemporary documents (translated for the English language reader) and documentary photographs, which added to the richness and veracity of his description of the events.

Noteworthy also are the personalities who, as Rabinowitch shows so effectively, try desperately to control a situation that is always one short step from suddenly shifting beyond everyone's grasp. In addition to describing the major and more familiar figures, who were moving rapidly in contrasting trajectories (Kerensky, as head of the Provisional Government, on the way out, and Lenin and Trotsky, the Bolshevik leaders, on the way in), Rabinowitch brings out the confusion and excitement of the situation as experienced by ordinary workers, soldiers, and peasants. The moment of truth for the opposition Mensheviks is also detailed by the author as he explains their reluctance to join "the conspiracy," thereby making themselves vulnerable to charges of being antirevolutionary at a time when such positions would help establish the criteria for loyalty to the new political legitimacy of socialism.

In his virtual hour-by-hour account of the dramatic events of October 24–5, 1917, Rabinowitch shows exactly how the Bolsheviks overthrew the Provisional Government and transferred political power to the Congress of Soviets. Readers of this chapter may well ponder the following question: a coup d'état had certainly taken place, but was this the revolution?

The Bolsheviks Come to Power

Alexander Rabinowitch

At the main bases of the Baltic fleet, activity began long before dawn on the morning of Wednesday, October 25. The first of three large echelons of armed sailors, bound for the capital at the behest of the Military Revolutionary Committee, departed Helsingfors by train along the Finnish railway at 3:00 A.M.; a second echelon got underway at 5:00 A.M., and a third left around midmorning. About the same time, a hastily assembled naval flotilla, consisting of a patrol boat – the *Iastrev* – and five destroyers – the *Metki, Zabiiaka, Moshchny, Deiatelny,* and *Samson* – started off at full steam for the roughly two hundred-mile trip to Petrograd, with the *Samson* in the lead flying a large banner emblazoned with the slogans "Down with the Coalition!" "Long Live the All-Russian Congress of Soviets!" and "All Power to the Soviets!"[1]

Activity of a similar kind was taking place at Kronstadt. Describing the night of October 24–25 in that center of revolutionary radicalism, Flerovsky was later to recall:

> It is doubtful whether anyone in Kronstadt closed his eyes that night. The Naval Club was jammed with sailors, soldiers, and workers. . . . The revolutionary staff drew up a detailed operations plan, designated participating units, made an inventory of available supplies, and issued instructions. . . . When the planning was finished . . . I went into the street. Everywhere there was heavy, but muffled traffic. Groups of soldiers and sailors were making their way to the naval dockyard. By the light of the torches we could see just the first ranks of serious determined faces. . . . Only the rumble of the automobiles, moving supplies from the fortress warehouses to the ships, disturbed the silence of the night.[2]

Shortly after 9:00 A.M. the sailors, clad in black pea jackets, with rifles slung over their shoulders and cartridge pouches on their belts, finished boarding the available vessels: two mine layers, the *Amur* and the *Khopor*; the former yacht of the fort commandant, the *Zarnitsa*, fitted out as a hospital ship; a training vessel, the *Verny*; a battleship, the *Zaria svobody*, so old that it was popularly referred to as the "flatiron" of the

1 *Oktiabr'skoe vooruzhennoe vosstanie v Petrograde: Dokumenty i materialy,* pp. 348–50; "Baltflot v dni kerenshichiny i krasnogo oktiabria," pp. 123–24.
2 I. P. Flerovskii "Kronshtadt v oktiabr'skoi revoliutsii," *PR [Proletarskaia revoliutsiia,* hereafter *PR*], 1922, no. 10, pp. 136–37.

Baltic Fleet and had to be helped along by four tugs; and a host of smaller paddle-wheel passenger boats and barges. As the morning wore on these vessels raised anchor, one after the other, and steamed off in the direction of the capital.[3]

At Smolny at this time, the leaders of the Military Revolutionary Committee and commissars from key locations about the city were completing plans for the capture of the Winter Palace and the arrest of the government. Podvoisky, Antonov-Ovseenko, Konstantin Eremeev, Georgii Blagonravov, Chudnovsky, and Sadovsky are known to have participated in these consultations. According to the blueprint which they worked out, insurrectionary forces were to seize the Mariinsky Palace and disperse the Preparliament; after this the Winter Palace was to be surrounded. The government was to be offered the opportunity of surrendering peacefully. If it refused to do so, the Winter Palace was to be shelled from the *Aurora* and the Peter and Paul Fortress, after which it was to be stormed. The main forces designated to take part in these operations were the Pavlovsky Regiment; Red Guard detachments from the Vyborg, Petrograd, and Vasilevsky Island districts; the Keksgolmsky Regiment; the naval elements arriving from Kronstadt and Helsingfors; and sailors from the Petrograd-based Second Baltic Fleet Detachment. Command posts were to be set up in the barracks of the Pavlovsky Regiment and the Second Baltic Fleet Detachment, the former to be directed by Eremeev and the latter by Chudnovsky. A field headquarters for overall direction of the attacking military forces, to be commanded by Antonov-Ovseenko, was to be established in the Peter and Paul Fortress.[4]

Even as these preparations for the seizure of the last bastions of the Provisional Government in Petrograd were being completed, Lenin, elsewhere at Smolny, was nervously watching the clock, by all indications most anxious to insure that the Kerensky regime would be totally eliminated before the start of the Congress of Soviets, now just a scant few hours away. At about 10:00 A.M. he drafted a manifesto "To the Citizens of Russia," proclaiming the transfer of political power from the Kerensky government to the Military Revolutionary Committee:

25 October 1917

To the Citizens of Russia!

The Provisional Government has been overthrown. State power has passed into the hands of the organ of the Petrograd Soviet of Workers'

3   *Baltiiskie moriaki*, p. 270.
4   *Oktiabr'skoe vooruzhennoe vosstanie*, vol. 2, p. 330, K. Eremeev, "Osada zimnego," *Bakinskii rabochii*, November 7, 1927, p. 9. See also Dzenis, "Kak my brali 25 okt.

and Soldiers' Deputies, the Military Revolutionary Committee, which stands at the head of the Petrograd proletariat and garrison.

The cause for which the people have struggled – the immediate proposal of a democratic peace, the elimination of landlord estates, workers' control over production, the creation of a soviet government – the triumph of this cause has been assured.

Long live the workers', soldiers', and peasants' revolution!

The Military Revolutionary Committee
of the Petrograd Soviet
of Workers' and Soldiers' Deputies[5]

The seminal importance Lenin attached to congress delegates being faced, from the very start, with a *fait accompli* as regards the creation of a soviet government is clearly illustrated by the fact that this proclamation was printed and already going out over the wires to the entire country even before the Military Revolutionary Committee strategy meeting described above had ended.

If October 25 began as a day of energetic activity and hope for the left, the same cannot be said for supporters of the old government. In the Winter Palace, Kerensky by now had completed arrangements to meet troops heading for the capital from the northern front. A striking indication of the isolation and helplessness of the Provisional Government at this point is the fact that the Military Revolutionary committee's control of all rail terminals precluded travel outside of Petrograd by train, while for some time the General Staff was unable to provide the prime minister with even one automobile suitable for an extended trip. Finally, military officials managed to round up an open Pierce Arrow and a Renault, the latter borrowed from the American embassy. At 11:00 A.M., almost precisely the moment when Lenin's manifesto proclaiming the overthrow of the government began circulating, the Renault, flying an American flag, tailed by the aristocratic Pierce Arrow, roared through the main arch of the General Staff building, barreled past Military Revolutionary Committee pickets already forming around the Winter Palace, and sped southwestward out of the capital. Huddled in the back seat of the Pierce Arrow were the assistant to the commander of the Petrograd Military District, Kuzmin; two staff officers; and a pale and haggard Kerensky, on his way to begin a desperate hunt for loyal troops from the front, a mission that was to end in abject failure less than a week later.[6]

zimnii dvorets," p. 7, and G. I. Blagonravov, "Oktiabr'skie dni v petropavlovskoi kreposti," *PR*, 1922, no. 4, p. 33.

5   Lenin, *PSS* [*Polnoe Sobranie Sochinenii*. (Moscow, 1958–1965, 55 vols, hereafter *PSS*)], vol. 35, p. 1.

6   V. I. Startsev, "Begstvo Kerenskogo," *Voprosy istorii*, 1966, no. 11, pp. 204–5; for Kerensky's version of this episode, see *Russia and History's Turning Point*, pp. 437–39.

As Kerensky's entourage streaked by the Mariinsky Palace, the relatively few deputies to the Preparliament assembled there were exchanging news of the latest political developments, awaiting the start of the day's session. Within an hour, a large contingent of armed soldiers and sailors, under Chudnovsky's command, began sealing off adjacent streets and posting guards at all palace entrances and exits. The armored car *Oleg*, flying a red flag, clattered up and took a position at the western corner of the palace.

When these preparations were completed, an unidentified Military Revolutionary Committee commissar entered the palace, searched out Avksentiev, and handed him a directive from the Military Revolutionary Committee ordering that the Mariinsky Palace be cleared without delay. Meanwhile, some soldiers and sailors burst into the building, brandishing their rifles, and posted themselves along the palace's grand main staircase. While many of the frightened deputies dashed for their coats and prepared to brave the phalanx of armed soldiers and sailors, Avksentiev had the presence of mind to collect part of the Preparliament steering committee. These deputies hurriedly agreed to formally protest the Military Revolutionary Committee's attack, but to make no attempt to resist it. They also instructed Avksentiev to reconvene the Preparliament at the earliest practicable moment. Before they were permitted to leave the palace, the identity of each of the deputies was carefully checked, but no one was detained. For the time being, the Military Revolutionary Committee forces were apparently under instructions to limit arrests to members of the government.[7]

Elsewhere by this time, insurgent ranks had been bolstered by the liberation from the Crosses Prison of the remaining Bolsheviks imprisoned there since the July days. A Military Revolutionary Committee commissar simply appeared at the ancient prison on the morning of October 25 with a small detachment of Red Guards and an order for the release of all political prisoners; among others, the Bolsheviks Semion Roshal, Sakharov, Tolkachev, and Khaustov were immediately set free.[8] At 2:00 P.M. the forces at the disposal of the Military Revolutionary Committee were increased still further by the arrival of the armada from Kronstadt. One of the more than a thousand sailors crammed on the deck of the *Amur*, I. Pavlov, subsequently recalled the waters outside Petrograd at midday, October 25:

What did the Gulf of Finland around Kronstadt and Petrograd look like then? This is conveyed well by a song that was popular at the time [sung

7   *Rech'*, October 26, p. 2; *Novaia zhizn'*, October 26, p. 2; *Izvestiia*, October 26, pp. 3–4.
8   Riabinskii, *Khronika sobytii*, vol. 5, p. 177.

to the melody of the familiar folk tune *Stenka Razin*]: "Iz za ostrova Kronshtadta na prostor reki Nevy, vyplyvaiut mnogo lodok, v nikh sidiat bol'sheviki!" [From the island of Kronstadt toward the River Neva broad, there are many boats a-sailing – they have Bolsheviks on board.] If these words do not describe the Gulf of Finland exactly, it's only because "boats" are mentioned. Substitute contemporary ships and you will have a fully accurate picture of the Gulf of Finland a few hours before the October battle.[9]

At the entrance to the harbor canal the *Zaria svobody*, pulled by the four tugs, dropped anchor; a detachment of sailors swarmed ashore and undertook to occupy the Baltic rail line between Ligovo and Oranienbaum. As the rest of the ships inched through the narrow channel, it occurred to Flerovsky, aboard the *Amur*, that if the government had had the foresight to lay a couple of mines and emplace even a dozen machine guns behind the parapet of the canal embankment, the carefully laid plans of the Kronstadters would have been wrecked. He heaved a sigh of relief as the motley assortment of ships passed through the canal unhindered and entered the Neva, where they were greeted by enthusiastic cheers from crowds of workers gathered on the banks. Flerovsky himself was in the cabin of the *Amur* ship's committee below decks, discussing where to cast anchor, when a mighty, jubilant hurrah rent the air. Flerovsky ran up on deck just in time to see the *Aurora* execute a turn in the middle of the river, angling for a better view of the Winter Palace.[10]

As the men on the *Aurora* and the ships from Kronstadt spotted each other, cheers and shouts of greeting rang out, the round caps of the sailors filled the sky, and the *Aurora*'s band broke into a triumphant march. The *Amur* dropped anchor close by the *Aurora*, while some of the smaller boats continued on as far as the Admiralty. Moments later Antonov-Ovseenko went out to the *Amur* to give instructions to leaders of the Kronstadt detachment. Then, as students and professors at St. Petersburg University gawked from classroom windows on the embankment, the sailors, totaling around three thousand, disembarked, large numbers of them to join the forces preparing to besiege the Winter Palace. A member of this contingent later remembered that upon encountering garrison soldiers, some of the sailors berated them for their cowardliness during the July days. He recalled with satisfaction that the soldiers were now ready to repent their errors.[11]

9   I. Pavlov, "Avral'naia rabota 25-go oktiabria 1917 goda," *Krasnyi flot*, 1926, nos. 10–11, p. 25.
10   Flerovskii, "Kronshtadt v oktiabr'skoi revoliutsii," p. 139.
11   Ibid., pp. 139–40; Pavlov, "Avral'naia rabota 25-go oktiabria 1917 goda," p. 25.

Important developments were occurring in the meantime at Smolny. The great main hall there was packed to the rafters with Petrograd Soviet deputies and representatives from provincial soviets anxious for news of the latest events when Trotsky opened an emergency session of the Petrograd Soviet at 2:35 P.M.[12] The fundamental transformation in the party's tactics that had occurred during the night became apparent from the outset of this meeting, perhaps the most momentous in the history of the Petrograd Soviet. It will be recalled that less than twenty-four hours earlier, at another session of the Petrograd Soviet, Trotsky had insisted that an armed conflict "today or tomorrow, on the eve of the congress, is not in our plans." Now, stepping up to the speaker's platform, he immediately pronounced the Provisional Government's obituary. "On behalf of the Military Revolutionary Committee," he shouted, "I declare that the Provisional Government no longer exists!" To a storm of applause and shouts of "Long live the Military Revolutionary Committee!" he announced, in rapid order, that the Preparliament had been dispersed, that individual government ministers had been arrested, and that the rail stations, the post office, the central telegraph, the Petrograd Telegraph Agency, and the state bank had been occupied by forces of the Military Revolutionary Committee. "The Winter Palace has not been taken," he reported, "but its fate will be decided momentarily. . . . In the history of the revolutionary movement I know of no other examples in which such huge masses were involved and which developed so bloodlessly. The power of the Provisional Government, headed by Kerensky, was dead and awaited the blow of the broom of history which had to sweep it away. . . . The population slept peacefully and did not know that at this time one power was replaced by another."

In the midst of Trotsky's speech, Lenin appeared in the hall. Catching sight of him, the audience rose to its feet, delivering a thundering ovation. With the greeting, "Long live Comrade Lenin, back with us again," Trotsky turned the platform over to his comrade. Side by side, Lenin and Trotsky acknowledged the cheers of the crowd. "Comrades!" declared Lenin, over the din:

> The workers' and peasants' revolution, the necessity of which has been talked about continuously by the Bolsheviks, has occurred. What is the significance of this workers' and peasants' revolution? First of all, the significance of this revolution is that we shall have a soviet government, our own organ of power without the participation of any bourgeois. The oppressed masses will form a government themselves. . . . This is the beginning of a new period in the history of Russia; and the present, third

---

12   Riabinskii, *Khronika sobytii*, vol. 5, pp. 179–80; *Izvestiia*, October 26, p. 7; October 27, pp. 4–5.

Russian revolution must ultimately lead to the victory of socialism. One of our immediate tasks is the necessity of ending the war at once.

We shall win the confidence of the peasantry by one decree, which will abolish landlord estates. The peasants will understand that their only salvation lies in an alliance with the workers. We will institute real workers' control over production.

You have now learned how to work together in harmony, as evidenced by the revolution that has just occurred. We now possess the strength of a mass organization, which will triumph over everything and which will lead the proletariat to world revolution.

In Russia we must now devote ourselves to the construction of a proletarian socialist state.

Long live the world socialist revolution.

Lenin's remarks were brief; yet it is perhaps not surprising that on this occasion most of his listeners did not trouble themselves with the question of how a workers' government would survive in backward Russia and a hostile world. After Lenin's remarks, Trotsky proposed that special commissars be dispatched to the front and throughout the country at once to inform the broad masses everywhere of the successful uprising in Petrograd. At this someone shouted, "You are anticipating the will of the Second Congress of Soviets," to which Trotsky immediately retorted: "The will of the Second Congress of Soviets has already been predetermined by the fact of the workers' and soldiers' uprising. Now we have only to develop this triumph."

The relatively few Mensheviks in attendance formally absolved themselves of responsibility for what they called "the tragic consequences of the conspiracy underway" and withdrew from the executive organs of the Petrograd Soviet. But most of the audience listened patiently to greetings by Lunacharsky and Zinoviev, the latter, like Lenin, making his first public appearance since July. The deputies shouted enthusiastic approval for a political statement drafted by Lenin and introduced by Volodarsky. Hailing the overthrow of the Provisional Government, the statement appealed to workers and soldiers everywhere to support the revolution; it also contained an expression of confidence that the Western European proletariat would help bring the cause of socialism to a full and stable victory.[13] The deputies then dispersed, either to factories and barracks to spread the glad tidings, or, like Sukhanov, to grab a bite to eat before the opening session of the All-Russian Congress.

Dusk was nearing, and the Winter Palace was still not in Bolshevik hands. As early as 1:00 P.M. a detachment of sailors commanded by

13   Ibid.

Ivan Sladkov had occupied the Admiralty, a few steps from the Winter Palace, and arrested the naval high command. At the same time, elements of the Pavlovsky Regiment had occupied the area around the Winter Palace, bounded by Millionnaia, Moshkov, and Bolshaia Koniushennaia streets, and Nevsky Prospect from the Ekaterinsky Canal to the Moika. Pickets, manned with armored cars and anti-aircraft guns, were set up on bridges over the Ekaterinsky Canal and the Moika, and on Morskaia Street. Later in the afternoon, Red Guard detachments from the Petrograd District and the Vyborg side joined the Pavlovsky soldiers, and troops from the Keksgolmsky Regiment occupied the area north of the Moika to the Admiralty, closing the ring of insurrectionary forces around the Palace Square. "The Provisional Government," Dashkevich would subsequently recall, "was as good as in a mousetrap."[14]

Noon had been the original deadline for the seizure of the Winter Palace. This was subsequently postponed to 3:00 and then 6:00 P.M., after which, to quote Podvoisky, the Military Revolutionary Committee "no longer bothered to set deadlines."[15] The agreed-upon ultimatum to the government was not dispatched; instead, loyalist forces gained time to strengthen their defenses. Thus in the late afternoon, insurgent troops watched impatiently while cadets on the Palace Square erected massive barricades and machine gun emplacements of firewood brought from the General Staff building.

By 6:00 P.M. it was dark, drizzly, and cold, and many of the soldiers deployed in the area around the palace hours earlier were growing hungry and restless. Occasionally, one of them would lose patience and open fire at the cadets, only to be rebuked with the stern command, "Comrades, don't shoot without orders." On the Petrograd side, the Bolshevik Military Organization leader Tarasov-Rodionov, for one, was beside himself worrying about what was happening in the center of the city. "I had the urge," he later wrote, "to drop everything – to rush to them [the Military Revolutionary Committee] to speed up this idiotically prolonged assault on the Winter Palace." During these hours, Lenin sent Podvoisky, Antonov, and Chudnovsky dozens of notes in which he fumed that their procrastination was delaying the opening of the congress and needlessly stimulating anxiety among congress deputies.[16]

14 P. V. Dashkevich, "Oktiabr'skie dni," *Lcningradskaia pravda*, November 7, 1924, p. 11.
15 "Vospominaniia ob oktiabr'skom perevorote," *PR*, 1922, no. 10, pp. 84–85.
16 A. Tarasov-Rodionov, "Pervaia operatsiia," *Voennyi vestnik*, 1924, no. 42, p. 12; "Vospominaniia ob oktiabr'skom perevorote," *PR*, 1922, no. 10, pp. 78–79.

Antonov implies in his memoirs that unexpected delays in the mobilization of insurgent soldiers, faulty organization, and other problems of a minor yet troublesome nature were the main reasons it took so long to launch the culminating offensive on the government.[17] In support of this view, there are indications that, for one reason or another, last-minute snags developed in connection with mobilizing some elements of the Preobrazhensky and Semenovsky regiments for the attack. More important, most of the sailor detachments from Helsingfors that the Military Revolutionary Committee was counting on for its assault did not arrive until late evening or even the following day. (In one case, a trainload of armed sailors was delayed in an open field outside Vyborg for many hours after the locomotive had burst its pipes; the Vyborg stationmaster, sympathetic to the government, had purposely provided the sailors with the least reliable locomotive available.[18])

The Military Revolutionary Committee did indeed encounter a number of minor difficulties which prompted concern at the time, but which in retrospect appear almost comical. When Blagonravov began checking out the cannon at the Peter and Paul Fortress in preparation for shelling the Winter Palace, he found that the six-inch guns on the walls of the fortress facing the palace had not been used or cleaned for months. Artillery officers persuaded him that they were not serviceable. Blagonravov then made soldiers in the fortress drag heavy three-inch training cannon some distance to where they could be brought into action, only to find that all of these weapons had parts missing or were genuinely defective. He also discovered that shells of the proper caliber were not immediately available. After the loss of considerable time, it was ascertained that making the six-inch guns work was not impossible after all.[19] Even more bizarre, by prior arrangement a lighted red lantern hoisted to the top of the fortress flagpole was to signal the start of the final push against the Winter Palace, yet when the moment for action arrived, no red lantern could be found. Recalls Blagonravov, "After a long search a suitable lamp was located, but then it proved extremely difficult to fix it on the flagpole so it could be seen."[20]

17   V. A. Antonov-Ovseenko, "Baltflot v dni kerenshchiny i krasnogo oktiabria," pp. 124–29; Antonov-Ovseenko, "Revoliutsiia pobedila," *Krasnaia gazeta*, November 7, 1923, p. 3.
18   Kostiukov, "Kak my opozdali ko vziatiu zimnego dvortsa," *Krasnyi balteets*, 1920, no. 6, p. 36.
19   *Oktiabr'skoe vooruzhennoe vosstanie*, vol. 2, p. 346.
20   Blagonravov, "The Fortress of Peter and Paul, October 1917," in *Petrograd October 1917* (Moscow, 1957), p. 206.

Podvoiksy, in his later writings, tended to attribute continuing delays in mounting an attack on the Winter Palace to the Military Revolutionary Committee's hope, for the most part realized, of avoiding a bloody battle. As Podvoisky later recalled: "Already assured of victory, we awaited the humiliating end of the Provisional Government. We strove to insure that it would surrender in the face of the revolutionary strength which we then enjoyed. We did not open artillery fire, giving our strongest weapon, the class struggle, an opportunity to operate within the walls of the palace."[21] This consideration appears to have had some validity as well. There was little food for the almost three thousand officers, cadets, cossacks, and women soldiers in the Winter Palace on October 25. In the early afternoon the ubiquitous American journalist John Reed somehow wangled his way into the palace, wandered through one of the rooms where these troops were billeted, and took note of the dismal surroundings: "On both sides of the parqueted floor lay rows of dirty mattresses and blankets, upon which occasional soldiers were stretched out; everywhere was a litter of cigarette-butts, bits of bread, cloth, and empty bottles with expensive French labels. More and more soldiers, with the red shoulder-straps of the Yunker-schools, moved about in a stale atmosphere of tobacco smoke and unwashed humanity. . . . The place was a huge barrack, and evidently had been for weeks, from the look of the floor and walls."[22]

As time passed and promised provisions and reinforcements from the front did not arrive, the government defenders became more and more demoralized, a circumstance known to the attackers. At 6:15 P.M. a large contingent of cadets from the Mikhailovsky Artillery School departed, taking with them four of the six heavy guns in the palace. Around 8:00 P.M. the two hundred cossacks on guard also returned to their barracks.

Representatives of the Military Revolutionary Committee participated in at least two attempts to convince other elements defending the government to leave peacefully. In the early evening, a representative of the Oranienbaum cadets persuaded Chudnovsky to accompany him to the palace to help arrange the peaceful withdrawal of his men. The cadets guaranteed Chudnovsky's safe conduct and kept their word. But Petr Palchinsky, an engineer and deputy minister of trade and industry who was helping to direct the defense of the government, insisted that Chudnovsky be arrested. The cadets protested, however, and forced Chudnovsky's release. Dashkevich had also slipped into the palace to try

21   "Vospominaniia ob oktiabr'skom perevorote," PR, 1922, no. 10, p. 79.
22   John Reed, Ten Days That Shook the World (New York, 1960), p. 116.

to win over some of the cadets; like Chudnovsky, he was detained and then allowed to leave. Partly as a result of the efforts of Chudnovsky and Dashkevich, more than half of the cadets guarding the Winter Palace left there at around 10:00 P.M.[23]

Whatever obstacles confronted the Military Revolutionary Committee in its assault on the Winter Palace on October 25 pale by comparison with the difficulties facing members of the Provisional Government, gathered in the grand Malachite Hall on the second floor of the palace. Here Konovalov convened a cabinet session at noon, an hour after Kerensky's hurried departure for the front. Present were all of the ministers except Kerensky and the minister of food supply, a distinguished economist, Sergei Prokopovich, who, having been temporarily detained by an insurgent patrol in the morning, was unable to reach the Winter Palace before it was completely sealed off in the afternoon. Fortunately for the historian, several of the participants in this ill-fated last meeting of Kerensky's cabinet penned detailed recollections of their final hours together; these tortured accounts bear witness to the almost complete isolation of the Provisional Government at this time, and to the ministers' resulting confusion and ever-increasing paralysis of will.[24]

Konovalov opened the meeting with a report on the political situation in the capital. He informed the ministers of the Military Revolutionary Committee's virtually unhampered success the previous night, of Polkovnikov's shattering early-morning status report, and of Kerensky's decision to rush to the front. For the first time, the full impact of the Petrograd Military District command's utter helplessness in dealing with the insurrection underway, and indeed of its inability even to furnish personal protection for the ministers, was felt by the cabinet as a whole. Responding to Konovalov's assessment, Admiral Verderevsky, the naval minister, observed coldly: "I don't know why this session was called. . . . We have no tangible military force and conse-

23   G. Chudnovskii, "V zimnem dvortse pered sdachei," *Pravda*, November 21, 1917, p. 2; P. V. Dashkevich, "Oktiabr'skie dni," *Leningradskaia pravda*, November 7, p. 11.

24   See, in particular, Liverovskii, "Poslednie chasy Vremmenogo pravitel'stva"; P. N. Maliantovich, "V zimnem dvortse 25–26 obtiabria 1917 goda," *Byloe*, 1918, no. 12, pp. 111–41; P. N. Pal'chinskii, "Dnevnik," *Krasnyi arkhiv*, 1933, no. 56, pp. 136–38; A. M. Nikitin, "Rasskaz A. M. Nikitina," *Rabochaia gazeta*, October 28, p. 2; "Kak zaniali zimnii dvorets," *Delo naroda*, October 29, pp. 1–2; A. Sinegub, "Zashchita zimnego dvortsa," *Arkhiv russkoi revoliutsii*, 1922, no. 4, pp. 121–97. The most useful secondary source on the final hours of the Provisional Government is V. I. Startsev, "Poslednii den' Vremennogo pravitel'stva," in *Iz istorii velikoi oktiabr'skoi sotsialisticheskoi revoliutsii i sotsialisticheskogo stroitel'stva v SSSR* (Leningrad, 1967), pp. 99–115.

quently are incapable of taking any action whatever."[25] He suggested it would have been wiser to have convened a joint session with the Preparliament, an idea that became moot moments later, when news was received of the latter's dispersal. At the start of their deliberations, however, most of the ministers did not fully share Verderevsky's pessimism. Tending, no doubt wishfully, to place most of the blame for the government's plight on Polkovnikov, they agreed to replace him with a "dictator" who would be given unlimited power to restore order and resolved that the cabinet would remain in continuous session in the Winter Palace for the duration of the emergency.

With periodic interruptions while Konovalov attempted unsuccessfully to bring more cossacks to the Winter Palace grounds, and while other ministers received disjointed reports on late-breaking developments and issued frantic appeals for help over the few phones still in operation to contacts elsewhere in the capital and over the direct wire to the front, the cabinet spent the better part of the next two hours engaged in a disorganized, meandering discussion of possible candidates for the post of "dictator." Ultimately, they displayed their insensitivity to the prevailing popular mood by settling on the minister of welfare, Kishkin. A physician by profession and a Muscovite, Kishkin had no prestige in Petrograd. Worst of all, he was a Kadet. Indeed, the selection of Kishkin was exactly the opposite of the more conciliatory course urged on Kerensky the preceding day by the Preparliament – a blatant provocation to democratic circles and an unexpected boon to the extreme left.

Kishkin formally assumed his new position as governor-general shortly after 4:00 P.M. After naming as his assistants Palchinsky and Petr Rutenberg, an assistant to the commander of the Petrograd Military District, he rushed off to military headquarters to direct the struggle against the insurrection. There Kishkin immediately sacked Polkovnikov, replacing him with the chief of staff, General Bagratuni. As nearly as one can tell, the main effect of this reshuffling of personnel was to increase significantly the chaos reigning at headquarters. For in protest to the treatment accorded Polkovnikov, all of his closest associates, including the quartermaster, General Nikolai Paradelov, immediately resigned in a huff. Some of these individuals packed off and went home. Others simply stopped work; from time to time, they could be seen peering out of the windows of the General Staff building at the clusters of insurgent soldiers, sailors, and workers advancing along the banks of the Moika and up Millionnaia Street.[26]

25 Liverovskii, "Poslednie chasy Vremennogo pravitel'stva," pp. 42–43.
26 Startsev, "Poslednii den' Vremennogo pravitel'stva," p. 101.

Meanwhile, in the Winter Palace, the rest of the cabinet occupied itself in preparing an appeal for support to be printed up for mass circulation. At 6:15 P.M. the ministers were informed of the departure of the cadets from the Mikhailovsky Artillery School; fifteen minutes later, they adjourned to Kerensky's third-floor private dining room, where a supper of borshch, fish, and artichokes – and more painful blows – awaited them.

By now, at the Peter and Paul Fortress, Blagonravov, under continual prodding from Smolny, had decided that the final stage of the attack on the government could be delayed no longer, this despite the fact that difficulties with the cannon and the signal lantern had not yet been fully surmounted. At 6:30 P.M. he dispatched two cyclists to the General Staff building, and in twenty minutes they arrived there armed with the following ultimatum:[27]

> By order of the Military Revolutionary Committee of the Petrograd Soviet, the Provisional Government is declared overthrown. All power is transferred to the Petrograd Soviet of Workers' and Soldiers' Deputies. The Winter Palace is surrounded by revolutionary forces. Cannon at the Peter and Paul Fortress and on the ships *Aurora* and *Amur* are aimed at the Winter Palace and the General Staff building. In the name of the Military Revolutionary Committee we propose that the Provisional Government and the troops loyal to it capitulate. . . . You have twenty minutes to answer. Your response should be given to our messenger. This ultimatum expires at 7:10, after which we will immediately open fire. . . .
>
> Chairman of the Military Revolutionary Committee Antonov
> Commissar of the Peter and Paul Fortress G. B.

At the General Staff building when this message was delivered were, among others, Kishkin, General Bagratuni, General Paradelov, and Palchinsky and Rutenberg. They persuaded one of the cyclists to return to the fortress with a request for a ten-minute extension. Leaving Paradelov behind to receive the government's response by phone and pass it on to the remaining cyclist, Kishkin, Bagratuni, and the others rushed to the Winter Palace to consult with the cabinet.[28]

Along with the news of the Military Revolutionary Committee's ultimatum, the ministers also learned that large numbers of previously wavering cadets from Oranienbaum and Peterhof now intended to leave the palace. Besides, the original deadline set by Antonov was already close to expiration. The ministers hurried back to the Malachite Hall at

27   The text of this ultimatum is contained in Liverovskii, "Poslednie chasy Vremennogo pravitel'stva," p. 45.
28   *Edinstvo*, October 27, p. 3.

once to consider the question of whether or not to surrender. Looking out at the crowded Neva and the Peter and Paul Fortress, one member of the cabinet wondered aloud, "What will happen to the palace if the *Aurora* opens fire?" "It will be turned into a heap of ruins," replied Admiral Verderevsky, adding sanguinely: "Her turrets are higher than the bridges. She can demolish the place without damaging any other building."[29]

Still, all the ministers, including Verderevsky, were agreed that surrender in the prevailing circumstances was unthinkable. They resolved simply to ignore the ultimatum, and Kishkin, Gvozdev, and Konovalov immediately rushed off to coax the cadets to remain at their posts. In his diary, Minister of Justice Pavel Maliantovich attempted to explain the cabinet's decision. He suggested that although at this point the ministers had lost hope of holding out until the arrival of outside help, they believed strongly that legally the Provisional Government could hand over its authority only to the Constituent Assembly. They felt a solemn obligation to resist until the very last moment so that it would be clear beyond doubt that they had yielded only to absolutely overwhelming force. That moment had not yet come, Maliantovich affirmed, hence the cabinet's decision to give no reply to the Military Revolutionary Committee and to continue resistance.[30]

Ironically, at precisely the moment that the Military Revolutionary Committee's ultimatum was delivered to General Staff headquarters, General Cheremisov, in Pskov, was conferring on the direct wire with General Bagratuni. At the start of the communication, Cheremisov had asked for a report on the condition of the capital. Specifically, he inquired as to the whereabouts of the government, the status of the Winter Palace, whether order was being maintained in the city, and whether or not units dispatched from the front had reached Petrograd. Bagratuni was answering these questions, as best he could, when he was called away to receive the ultimatum. General Paradelov then got on the Petrograd end of the direct wire and passed on to Cheremisov his misgivings about Kishkin's appointment and behavior, stating quite directly his belief that the Provisional Government was doomed. Cheremisov, in turn, requested Paradelov to call the Winter Palace to obtain more information about the situation there.[31] Paradelov went off to do this but was interrupted by Bagratuni, just then leaving for the Winter Palace with the ultimatum. Paradelov was instructed to stand by the receive the

29   Maliantovich, "V zimnem dvortse," p. 120.
30   Ibid., p. 121.
31   *Oktiabr'skoe vooruzhennoe vosstanie v Petrograde: Dokumenty i materialy*, pp. 407–8.

government's telephoned response. As Paradelov waited for the message from the Winter Palace, insurgent soldiers and workers suddenly flooded the building; resistance was impossible.[32] Meanwhile, Cheremisov, still at the other end of the direct wire, inquired impatiently, "Where is Paradelov, and will he give me an answer soon?" In response, a military telegrapher barely managed to tap out: "We will find him. . . . The headquarters has been occupied by Military Revolutionary Committee forces. I am quitting work and getting out of here!"[33]

Word of the capture of the General Staff building reached General Bagratuni and the cabinet in the second-floor office of one of Kerensky's assistants, facing the palace courtyard, to which they had moved from the more vulnerable Malachite Hall. Bagratuni responded to the loss of his staff and headquarters by tendering his resignation. Soon after departing the palace, he was pulled from a cab and arrested by an insurgent patrol.

For their part, the ministers now dispatched the following radio-telegram to the Russian people:

To All, All, All!

The Petrograd Soviet has declared the Provisional Government overthrown, and demands that power be yielded to it under threat of shelling the Winter Palace from cannon in the Peter and Paul Fortress and aboard the cruiser *Aurora*, anchored on the Neva. The government can yield power only to the Constituent Assembly; because of this we have decided not to surrender and to put ourselves under the protection of the people and the army. In this regard a telegram was sent to Stavka. Stavka answered with word that a detachment had been dispatched. Let the country and the people respond to the mad attempt of the Bolsheviks to stimulate an uprising in the rear of the fighting army.[34]

32 *Edinstvo*, October 27, p. 3.
33 *Oktiabr'skoe vooruzhennoe vosstanie*, vol. 2, p. 343; *Oktiabr'skoe vooruzhennoe vosstanie v Petrograde: Dokumenty i materialy*, pp. 395–96, 407–8. For Cheremisov, this conversation was apparently the last straw, helping to confirm his conviction that the Provisional Government was totally bankrupt. Much more than most other top military leaders, Cheremisov had been sensitive and responsive to revolutionary sentiment in the army throughout 1917. Initially antagonized by Kerensky in late July at the time of Kornilov's appointment as chief of staff, during the first weeks of October Cheremisov gave only reluctant and half-hearted support to Kerensky's attempts to involve front-line forces in support of the Provisional Government. Now, on the night of October 25, learning firsthand of Kishkin's appointment, of the military shakeup in Petrograd, and of the occupation of General Staff headquarters, he issued an order immediately halting the movement of troops to Petrograd, significantly undercutting Kerensky's hopes of mobilizing help at the front.
34 *Oktiabr'skoe vooruzhennoe vosstanie v Petrograde: Dokumenty i materialy*, pp. 414–15.

The ministers also managed to establish telephone contact with the mayor of Petrograd, Shreider, in the City Duma building. They informed him that the Winter Palace was about to be shelled from the *Aurora* and the Peter and Paul Fortress, and appealed to him to help mobilize support for the government. The previous day, deeply concerned by the actions of the Military Revolutionary Committee, the City Duma, in which the SRs and Kadets still had a majority, had dispatched a fact-finding mission to Smolny; subsequently, in spite of fierce opposition from its Bolshevik members, the Duma, like the Preparliament, had initiated steps to form a Committee of Public Safety to help maintain order in the city and to protect the population. Now, upon receipt of the Provisional Government's appeal, Shreider immediately convened the City Duma in emergency session. Announcing at the outset that "in a few minutes the cannon will begin to thunder . . . [and] the Provisional Government of the Russian Republic will perish in the ruins of the Winter Palace," he called upon the Duma to help the government by all means possible. Inasmuch as the deputies had no military forces at their disposal, they agreed to dispatch emissaries to the *Aurora*, to Smolny, and to the Winter Palace immediately in an effort to halt the siege of the Winter Palace and to mediate differences between the government and the Military Revolutionary Committee.[35]

Meanwhile, at the Peter and Paul Fortress, cannon and signal-lantern difficulties having been overcome at last, Blagonravov and Antonov were preparing to commence the shelling of the Winter Palace. One further delay occurred when they received what turned out to be an erroneous report, evidently sparked by the surrender of General Staff headquarters, that the Winter Palace had capitulated. Blagonravov and Antonov drove across the Neva to check out the rumor themselves. At 9:40 P.M. Blagonravov finally returned to the fortress and signaled the *Aurora* to open fire. The *Aurora* responded by firing one blank round from its bow gun. The blast of a cannon shooting blanks is significantly greater than if it were using combat ammunition, and the ear-splitting reverberations of the *Aurora*'s first shot were felt throughout the capital. The blast impelled gawking spectators lined up on the Neva embankments to flop to the ground and crawl away in panic, and it contributed to the further thinning out of military forces inside the Winter Palace. (Many cadets finally abandoned their posts at this point and were followed shortly afterward by a number of the women soldiers.) Contrary

35   Erykalov, *Oktiabr'skoe vooruzhennoe vosstanie v Petrograde*, pp. 314–17 and 444, drawing upon the journals of the Petrograd City Duma and the stenographic accounts of its proceedings, August 20, 1917, convocation; see also I. Milchik, "Petrogradskaia tsentral'naia gorodskaia duma v fevrale–oktiabre 1917 goda," *KL* [*Krasnaia letopis'*, hereafter *KL*], 1927, no. 2 (23), p. 201.

to legend and to Verderevsky's prediction, the *Aurora*'s shot did no physical damage.

After the *Aurora*'s action the artillerists at the Peter and Paul Fortress allowed time for those forces who wished to do so to leave the palace. During this interim, the officer of the watch on the *Amur* spotted a string of lights at the mouth of the Neva and sounded the alarm: "Ships approaching!" As their silhouettes came into view, old deck hands on the *Amur* triumphantly identified the arriving vessels as the destroyers *Samson* and *Zabiiaka*, accompanied by some of the other ships from Helsingfors.[36]

At around 11:00 P.M. Blagonravov gave the order to commence shooting in earnest. Most of the shells subsequently fired exploded spectacularly but harmlessly over the Neva, but one shattered a cornice on the palace and another smashed a third-floor corner window, exploding just above the room in which the government was meeting. The blast unnerved the ministers and influenced at least a few of them to have second thoughts about the wisdom of further resistance. Meanwhile, from the walls of the Peter and Paul Fortress, Tarasov-Rodionov watched the spectacular fireworks, whose tremors momentarily drowned out the sound of the rifle and machine gun fire and the droning of lighted streetcars crawling single file across the Troitsky and Palace bridges, and wondered at the incredibility of it all, of "the workers' soviet overthrowing the bourgeois government while the peaceful life of the city continued uninterrupted."[37]

To City Duma deputies, it was by this time patently clear that their hopes of interceding between the Military Revolutionary Committee and the embattled ministers in the Winter Palace would not be realized. A Military Revolutionary Committee commissar refused to permit the representatives of the City Duma to go anywhere near the *Aurora*. The delegation sent to the Winter Palace was halted several times by the besiegers and, in the end, forced to scurry back to the City Duma building after being fired upon from upper-story windows of the Winter Palace. ("The cadets probably didn't see our white flag," a member of the delegation later said.) The City Duma emissaries who went to Smolny, Mayor Shreider among them, fared somewhat better. They managed to have a few minutes with Kamenev, who helped arranger for Molotov to accompany them to the Winter Palace. But this delegation, too, was unable to make it through the narrow strip of no man's land which now separated the tight ring of insurrectionary forces from the barricades set up by defenders of the government.[38]

36   Flerovskii, "Kronshtadt v oktiabr'skoi revoliutsii," pp. 141–42.
37   Tarasov-Rodionov, "Pervaia operatsiia," p. 13.
38   Erykalov, *Oktiabr'skoe vooruzhennoe vosstanie v Petrograde*, pp. 445–46; V. M. Molotov, "Smolnyi i zimnii," *Pravda*, November 7, 1924, p. 9.

About the time the City Duma was informed of these setbacks it also received a bitter telephone message from Semion Maslov, the minister of agriculture, and a right SR. The call was taken by Naum Bykhovsky, also an SR, who immediately relayed Maslov's words to a hushed Duma. "We here in the Winter Palace have been abandoned and left to ourselves," declared Maslov, as quoted by Bykhovsky. "The democracy sent us into the Provisional Government; we didn't want the appointments, but we went. Yet now, when tragedy has struck, when we are being shot, we are not supported by anyone. Of course we will die. But my final words will be: 'Contempt and damnation to the democracy which knew how to appoint us but was unable to defend us!'"[39]

Bykhovsky at once proposed that the entire Duma march in a body to the Winter Palace "to die along with our representatives." "Let our comrades know," he proclaimed, "that we have not abandoned them, let them know we will die with them." This idea struck a responsive chord with just about everyone, except the Bolsheviks. Reporters present noted that most deputies stood and cheered for several minutes. Before the proposal was actually voted upon, the City Duma received a request from a representative of the All-Russian Executive Committee of Peasant Soviets that the leadership of the peasant soviets be permitted to "go out and die with the Duma." It also heard from the minister of food supply, Prokopovich, who tearfully pleaded to be allowed to join the procession to the Winter Palace, "so that he could at least share the fate of his comrades." Not to be outdone, Countess Sofia Panina, a prominent Kadet, volunteered "to stand in front of the cannon," adding that "the Bolsheviks can fire at the Provisional Government over our dead bodies." The start of the march to the Winter Palace was delayed a bit because someone demanded a roll call vote on Bykhovsky's motion. During the roll call, most of the deputies insisted on individually declaring their readiness to "die with the government," before voting "Yes" – whereupon each Bolshevik solemnly proclaimed that he would "go to the Soviet," before registering an emphatic "No!"[40]

While all this was going on, Lenin remained at Smolny, raging at every delay in the seizure of the Winter Palace and still anxious that the All-Russian Congress not get underway until the members of the Provisional Government were securely behind bars. Andrei Bubnov later recorded that "the night of October 25 . . . Ilich hurried with the capture of the Winter Palace, putting extreme pressure on everyone and everybody when there was no news of how the attack was going."[41]

39 Erykalov, *Oktiabr'skoe vooruzhennoe vosstanie v Petrograde*, pp. 450–51.
40 *Rech'*, October 26, p. 3; Milchik, "Petrogradskaia tsentral'naia gorodskaia duma v fevrale-oktiabre 1917 goda," p. 202.
41 Bubnov, "Lenin v oktiabr'skie dni," *Bakinskii rabochii*, November 7, 1927, p. 3.

Similarly, Podvoisky later remembered that Lenin now "paced around a small room at Smolny like a lion in a cage. He needed the Winter Palace at any cost: it remained the last gate on the road to workers' power. V. I. scolded . . . he screamed . . . he was ready to shoot us."[42]

Still, the start of the congress had been scheduled for 2:00 P.M. By late evening, the delegates had been milling around for hours; it was impossible to hold them back much longer, regardless of Lenin's predilections. Finally, at 10:40 P.M., Dan rang the chairman's bell, formally calling the congress into session. "The Central Executive Committee considers our customary opening political address superfluous," he announced at the outset. "Even now, our comrades who are selflessly fulfilling the obligations we placed on them are under fire at the Winter Palace."[43]

John Reed, who had pushed his way through a clamorous mob at the door of the hall, subsequently described the scene in Smolny's white assembly hall as the congress opened:

> In the rows of seats, under the white chandeliers, packed immovably in the aisles and on the sides, perched on every windowsill, and even the edge of the platform, the representatives of the workers and soldiers of all Russia awaited in anxious silence or wild exultation the ringing of the chairman's bell. There was no heat in the hall but the stifling heat of unwashed human bodies. A foul blue cloud of cigarette smoke rose from the mass and hung in the thick air. Occasionally someone in authority mounted the tribune and asked the comrades not to smoke; then everybody, smokers and all, took up the cry "Don't smoke, comrades!" and went on smoking. . . .
>
> On the platform sat the leaders of the old Tsay-ee-kah [Central Executive Committee] . . . Dan was ringing the bell. Silence fell sharply intense, broken by the scuffling and disputing of the people at the door. . . .[44]

According to a preliminary report by the Credentials Committee, 300 of the 670 delegates assembled in Petrograd for the congress were Bolsheviks, 193 were SRs (of whom more than half were Left SRs), 68 were Mensheviks, 14 were Menshevik-Internationalists, and the remainder either were affiliated with one of a number of smaller political groups or did not belong to any formal organization.[45] The dramatic rise in support for the Bolsheviks that had occurred in the previous several

42 "Vospominaniia ob oktiabr'skom perevorote," *PR*, 1922, no. 10, p. 79.
43 *Vtoroi vserossiiskii s"ezd sovetov*, p. 33.
44 Reed, *Ten Days That Shook the World*, p. 124.
45 *Oktiabr'skoe vooruzhennoe vosstanie*, vol. 2, p. 353. Figures published in the press on the total size and composition of the congress vary somewhat; those cited here appeared in *Pravda* on October 29.

months was reflected in the fact that the party's fraction was three times greater than it had been at the First All-Russian Congress of Soviets in June; the Bolsheviks were now far and away the largest single party represented at the congress. Yet it is essential to bear in mind that, despite this success, at the opening of the congress the Bolsheviks did not have an absolute majority without significant help from the Left SRs.

Because delegates, upon arrival at Smolny, were asked to fill out detailed personal questionnaires, we can ascertain not only the political affiliation of most of them, but also the character of each of the 402 local soviets represented at the congress and its official position on the construction of a new national government. Tabulation of these questionnaires reveals the striking fact that an overwhelming number of delegates, some 505 of them, came to Petrograd committed in principle to supporting the transfer of "all power to the soviets," that is, the creation of a soviet government presumably reflective of the party composition of the congress. Eighty-six delegates were loosely bound to vote for "all power to the democracy," meaning a homogeneous democratic government including representatives of peasant soviets, trade unions, cooperatives, etc., while twenty-one delegates were committed to support of a coalition democratic government in which some propertied elements, but not the Kadets, would be represented. Only fifty-five delegates, that is, significantly less than 10 percent, represented constituencies still favoring continuation of the Soviet's former policy of coalition with the Kadets.[46]

As a result of the breakdown in relative voting strength, moments after the congress opened fourteen Bolsheviks took seats in the congress Presidium alongside seven Left SRs (the Mensheviks, allotted three seats in the Presidium, declined to fill them; the Menshevik-Internationalists did not fill the one seat allotted to them but reserved the right to do so). Dan, Lieber, Broido, Gots, Bogdanov, and Vasilii Filipovsky, who had directed the work of the Soviet since March, now vacated the seats at the head of the hall reserved for the top Soviet leadership; amid thunderous applause their places were immediately occupied by Trotsky, Kollontai, Lunacharsky, Nogin, Zinoviev, Kamkov, Maria Spiridonova, Mstislavsky, and other prominent Bolsheviks and Left SRs.[47]

As if punctuating this momentous changeover, an ominous sound was heard in the distance – the deep, pounding boom of exploding cannon. Rising to make an emergency announcement, Martov, in a

---

46   *Vtoroi vserossiiskii s"ezd sovetov*, pp. 144–53; A. F. Butenko and D. A. Chugaev, eds., *Vtoroi vserossiiskii s"ezd sovetov rabochikh i soldatskikh deputatov: Sbornik dokumentov* (Moscow, 1957), pp. 386–98.
47   *Vtoroi vserossiiskii s"ezd sovetov*, pp. 2–3, 33.

shrill, trembling voice, demanded that, before anything else, the congress agree to seek a peaceful solution to the existing political crisis; in his view, the only way out of the emergency was first to stop the fighting and then to start negotiations for the creation of a united, democratic government acceptable to the entire democracy. With this in mind, he recommended selection of a special delegation to initiate discussions with other political parties and organizations aimed at bringing to an immediate end the clash which had erupted in the streets.

Speaking for the Left SRs, Mstislavsky immediately endorsed Martov's proposal; more significantly, it was also apparently well received by many Bolsheviks. Glancing around the hall, Sukhanov, for one, noted that "Martov's speech was greeted with a tumult of applause from a very large section of the meeting." Observed a *Delo naroda* reporter, "Martov's appeal was showered with torrents of applause by a majority in the hall." Bearing in mind that most of the congress delegates had mandates to support the creation by the congress of a coalition government of parties represented in the Soviet and since Martov's motion was directed toward that very end, there is no reason to doubt these observations. The published congress proceedings indicate that, on behalf of the Bolsheviks, Lunacharsky responded to Martov's speech with the declaration that "the Bolshevik fraction has absolutely nothing against the proposal made by Martov." The congress documents indicate as well that Martov's proposal was quickly passed by unanimous vote.[48]

No sooner had the congress endorsed the creation of a democratic coalition government by negotiation, however, than a succession of speakers, all representatives of the formerly dominant moderate socialist bloc, rose to denounce the Bolsheviks. These speakers declared their intention of immediately walking out of the congress as a means of protesting and opposing the actions of the Bolsheviks. The first to express himself in this vein was Iakov Kharash, a Menshevik army officer and delegate from the Twelfth Army Committee. Proclaimed Kharash: "A criminal political venture has been going on behind the back of the All-Russian Congress, thanks to the political hypocrisy of the Bolshevik Party. The Mensheviks and SRs consider it necessary to disassociate themselves from everything that is going on here and to mobilize the public for defense against attempts to seize power." Added Georgii Kuchin, also an officer and prominent Menshevik, speaking for a bloc of moderately inclined delegates from army committees at the front: "The congress was called primarily to discuss the question of forming a new government, and yet what do we see? We find that an

48   Ibid., pp. 4, 34–35; Sukhanov, *Zapiski o revoliutsii*, vol. 7, p. 199; *Delo naroda*, October 27, p. 2.

irresponsible seizure of power has already occurred and that the will of the congress has been decided beforehand. . . . We must save the revolution from this mad venture. In the cause of rescuing the revolution we intend to mobilize all of the revolutionary elements in the army and the country. . . . [We] reject any responsibility for the consequences of this reckless venture and are withdrawing from this congress."[49]

These blunt statements triggered a storm of protest and cries of "Kornilovites!" and "Who in the hell do you represent?" from a large portion of the assembled delegates. Yet after Kamenev restored a semblance of order, Lev Khinchuk, from the Moscow Soviet, and Mikhail Gendelman, a lawyer and member of the SR Central Committee, read similarly bitter and militantly hostile declarations on behalf of the Mensheviks and SRs respectively. "The only possible peaceful solution to the present crisis continues to lie in negotiations with the Provisional Government on the formation of a government representing all elements of the democracy," Khinchuk insisted. At this, according to Sukhanov "a terrible din filled the hall; it was not only the Bolsheviks who were indignant, and for a long time the speaker wasn't allowed to continue." "We leave the present congress," Khinchuk finally shouted, "and invite all other fractions similarly unwilling to accept responsibility for the actions of the Bolsheviks to assemble together to discuss the situation." "Deserters," came shouts from the hall. Echoed Gendelman: "Anticipating that an outburst of popular indignation will follow the inevitable discovery of the bankruptcy of Bolshevik promises . . . the Socialist Revolutionary fraction is calling upon the revolutionary forces of the country to organize themselves and to stand guard over the revolution. . . . Taking cognizance of the seizure of power by the Bolsheviks. . . . holding them fully responsible for the consequences of this insane and criminal action, and consequently finding it impossible to collaborate with them, the Socialist Revolutionary fraction is leaving the congress!"[50]

Tempers in the hall now skyrocketed; there erupted a fierce squall of foot-stamping, whistling, and cursing. In response to the uprising now openly proclaimed by the Military Revolutionary Committee, the Mensheviks and SRs had moved rightward, and the gulf separating them from the extreme left had suddenly grown wider than ever. When one recalls that less than twenty-four hours earlier the Menshevik and SR congress fractions, uniting broad segments of both parties, appeared on the verge of at long last breaking with the bourgeois parties and endorsing the creation of a homogeneous socialist government pledged

---

49   *Vtoroi vserossiiskii s"ezd sovetov*, pp. 34–35.
50   Ibid., pp. 37–38; Sukhanov, *Zapiski o revoliutsii*, vol. 7, p. 200.

to a program of peace and reform, the profound impact of the events of October 24–25 becomes clear. One can certainly understand why the Mensheviks and SRs reacted as they did. At the same time, it is difficult to escape the conclusion that by totally repudiating the actions of the Bolsheviks and of the workers and soldiers who willingly followed them, and, even more, by pulling out of the congress, the moderate socialists undercut efforts at compromise by the Menshevik-Internationalists, the Left SRs, and the Bolshevik moderates. In so doing, they played directly into Lenin's hands, abruptly paving the way for the creation of a government which had never been publicly broached before – that is, an exclusively Bolshevik regime. In his memoir-history of the revolution, Sukhanov acknowledged the potentially immense historical significance of the Menshevik-SR walkout. He wrote that in leaving the congress "we completely untied the Bolsheviks' hands, making them masters of the entire situation and yielding to them the whole arena of the revolution. A struggle at the congress for a united democratic front *might* have had some success. . . . By quitting the congress, we ourselves gave the Bolsheviks a monopoly of the Soviet, of the masses, and of the revolution. By our own irrational decision, we ensured the victory of Lenin's whole 'line'!"[51]

All this is doubtless more apparent in retrospect that it was at the time. At any rate, following the declarations of Kharash, Kuchin, Khinchuk, and Gendelman, several radically inclined soldier-delegates took the floor to assert that the views of Kharash and Kuchin in no way represented the thinking of the average solider. "Let them go – the army is not with them," burst out a young, lean-faced soldier named Karl Peterson, representing the Latvian Rifle Regiment; his observation would soon be only too evident to all. At this the hall rocked with wild cheering. "Kuchin refers to the mobilization of forces," shouted Frants Gzhelshchak, a Bolshevik soldier from the Second Army at the front, as soon as he could make himself heard. "Against whom – against the workers and soldiers who have come out to defend the revolution?" he asked. "Whom will he organize? Clearly not the workers and soldiers against whom he himself is determined to wage war." Declared Fedor Lukianov, a soldier from the Third Army, also a Bolshevik, "The thinking of Kuchin is that of the top army organizations which we elected way back in April and which have long since failed to reflect the views and mood of the broad masses of the army."[52]

---

51   Sukhanov, *Zapiski o revoliutsii*, vol. 7, pp. 219–20; on this point see Leonard Schapiro, *Origins of the Communist Autocracy* (New York, 1965), pp. 66–68.
52   *Vtoroi vserossiiskii s"ezd sovetov*, pp. 38–39.

At this point Genrikh Erlikh, a representative of the Bund (the Jewish social democratic organization), interrupted to inform the congress of the decision of a majority of City Duma deputies, taken moments earlier, to march en masse to the Winter Palace. Erlikh added that the Menshevik and SR fractions in the Executive Committee of the All-Russian Soviet of Peasant Deputies had decided to join the Duma deputies in protesting the application of violence against the provisional Government, and invited all congress delegates "who did not wish a bloodbath" to participate in the march. It was at this point that the Mensheviks, SRs, Bundists, and members of the "front group" – deluged by shouts of "Deserters!" "Lackeys of the bourgeoisie!" and "Good riddance!" – rose from their places and made their way out of the hall.

Soon after the departure of the main bloc of Mensheviks and SRs, Martov, still intent most of all on facilitating a peaceful compromise between the moderate socialists and the radical left, took the floor to present a resolution on behalf of the Menshevik-Internationalists. His resolution condemned the Bolsheviks for organizing a coup d'état before the opening of the congress and called for creation of a broadly based democratic government to replace the Provisional Government. It read in part:

> Taking into consideration that this coup d'état threatens to bring about bloodshed, civil war, and the triumph of a counterrevolution . . . [and] that the only way out of this situation which could still prevent the development of a civil war might be an agreement between insurgent elements and the rest of the democratic organizations on the formation of a democratic government which is recognized by the entire revolutionary democracy and to which the Provisional Government could painlessly surrender its power, the Menshevik [Internationalist] fraction proposes that the congress pass a resolution on the necessity of a peaceful settlement of the present crisis by the formation of an all-democratic government . . . that the congress appoint a delegation for the purpose of entering into negotiations with other democratic organs and all the socialist parties . . . [and] that it discontinue its work pending the disclosure of the results of this delegation's efforts.[53]

It is easy to see that from Lenin's point of view, passage of Martov's resolution would have been a disaster; on the other hand, the departure of the moderates offered an opportunity which could now be exploited to consolidate the break with them. Not long after Martov resumed his seat, congress delegates rose and cheered the surprise appearance of the

53   Ibid., pp. 41–42.

Bolshevik City Duma fraction, members of which, pushing their way into the crowded hall, announced that they had come "to triumph or die with the All-Russian Congress!" Then Trotsky, universally recognized as the Bolsheviks' most forceful orator, took the platform to declare:

> A rising of the masses of the people requires no justification. What has happened is an insurrection, and not a conspiracy. We hardened the revolutionary energy of the Petersburg workers and soldiers. We openly forged the will of the masses for an insurrection, and not a conspiracy. The masses of the people followed our banner and our insurrection was victorious. And now we are told: Renounce your victory, make concessions, compromise. With whom? I ask: With whom ought we to compromise? With those wretched groups who have left us or who are making this proposal? But after all we've had a full view of them. No one in Russia is with them any longer. A compromise is supposed to be made, as between two equal sides, by the millions of workers and peasants represented in this congress, whom they are ready, not for the first time or the last, to barter away as the bourgeoisie sees fit. No, here no compromise is possible. To those who have left and to those who tell us to do this we must say: You are miserable bankrupts, your role is played out; go where you ought to go: into the dustbin of history!

Amid stormy applause, Martov shouted in warning, "Then we'll leave!" And Trotsky, without a pause, read a resolution condemning the departure of Menshevik and SR delegates from the congress as "a weak and treacherous attempt to break up the legally constituted all-Russian representative assembly of the worker and soldier masses at precisely the moment when their avant-garde, with arms in hand, is defending the congress and the revolution from the onslaught of the counterrevolution." The resolution endorsed the insurrection against the Provisional Government and concluded: "The departure of the compromisers does not weaken the soviets. Inasmuch as it purges the worker and peasant revolution of counterrevolutionary influences, it strengthens them. Having listened to the declarations of the SRs and Mensheviks, the Second All-Russian Congress continues its work, the tasks of which have been predetermined by the will of the laboring people and their insurrection of October 24 and 25. Down with the compromisers! Down with the servants of the bourgeoisie! Long live the triumphant uprising of soldiers, workers, and peasants!"[54]

This bitter denunciation of the Mensheviks and SRs and blanket endorsement of the armed insurrection in Petrograd was, of course, as

54   Ibid., pp. 43–44.

difficult for the Left SRs, left Mensheviks, and Bolshevik moderates to swallow as Martov's resolution was for the Leninists. Kamkov, in a report to the First Left SR Congress in November, when these events were still very fresh in mind, attempted to explain the thinking of the Left SRs at this moment, when the gulf dividing Russian socialists widened, when in spite of Left SR efforts the Military Revolutionary Committee had been transformed into an insurrectionary organ and had overthrown the Provisional Government, and when the moderate socialists had repudiated and moved to combat this development:

> As political leaders in a moment of decisive historical significance for the fate of not only the Russian but also the world revolution, we, least of all, could occupy ourselves with moralizing. As people concerned with the defense of the revolution we had first of all to ask ourselves what we should do today, when the uprising was a reality . . . and for us it was clear that for a revolutionary party in that phase of the Russian revolution that had developed . . . our place was with the revolution. . . . We decided not only to stay at Smolny but to play the most energetic role possible. . . . We believed we should direct all of our energies toward the creation of a new government, one which would be supported, if not by the entire revolutionary democracy, then at least by a majority of it. Despite the hostility engendered by the insurrection in Petrograd . . . knowing that included within the right was a large mass of honest revolutionaries who simply misunderstood the Russian revolution, we believed our task to be that of not contributing to exacerbating relations within the democracy. . . . We saw our task, the task of the Left SRs, as that of mending the broken links uniting the two fronts of the Russian democracy. . . . We were convinced that they [the moderates] would with some delay accept that platform which is not the platform of any one fraction or party, but the program of history, and that they would ultimately take part in the creation of a new government.[55]

At the Second Congress of Soviets session the night of October 25–26, loud cheers erupted when Kamkov, following Trotsky to the platform, made the ringing declaration: "The right SRs left the congress but we, the Left SRs, have stayed." After the applause subsided, however, tactfully but forcefully, Kamkov spoke out against Trotsky's course, arguing that the step Trotsky proposed was untimely "because counterrevolutionary efforts are continuing." He added that the Bolsheviks did not have the support of the peasantry, "the infantry of the revolution without which the revolution would be destroyed."[56] With this in

55 *Protokoly pervago s"ezda partii levykh sotsialistov-revoliutsionerov (internatsional-istov)*, pp. 41–43.
56 *Delo naroda*, October 27, p. 2.

mind, he insisted that "the left ought not isolate itself from moderate democratic elements, but, to the contrary, should seek agreement with them."

It is perhaps not without significance that the more temperate Lunacharsky, rather than Trotsky, rose to answer Kamkov:

> Heavy tasks have fallen on us, of that there is no doubt. For the effective fulfillment of these tasks the unity of all the various genuinely revolutionary elements of the democracy is neccessary. Kamkov's criticism of us is unfounded. If starting this session we had initiated any steps whatever to reject or remove other elements, then Kamkov would be right. But all of us unanimously accepted Martov's proposal to discuss peaceful ways of solving the crisis. And we were deluged by a hail of declarations. A systematic attack was conducted against us. . . . Without hearing us out, not even bothering to discuss their own proposal, they [the Mensheviks and SRs] immediately sought to fence themselves off from us. . . . In our resolution we simply wanted to say, precisely, honestly, and openly, that despite their treachery we will continue our efforts, we will lead the proletariat and the army to struggle and victory.[57]

The quarrel over the fundamentally differing views of Martov and Trotsky dragged on into the night. Finally, a representative of the Left SRs demanded a break for fractional discussions, threatening an immediate Left SR walkout if a recess were not called. The question was put to a vote and passed at 2:40 A.M., Kamenev warning that the congress would resume its deliberations in half an hour.[58]

By this time, the march of City Duma deputies to the Winter Palace had ended in a soggy fiasco. At around midnight Duma deputies, members of the Executive Committee of the Peasants' Soviets, and deputies from the congress who had just walked out of Smolny (together numbering close to three hundred people), assembled outside the Duma building, on Nevsky Prospect, where a cold rain had now begun to fall. Led by Shreider and Prokopovich (the latter carrying an umbrella in one hand and a lantern in the other), marching four abreast and singing the "Marseillaise," armed only with packages of bread and sausages "for the ministers," the motley procession set out in the direction of the Admiralty. At the Kazan Square, less than a block away, the delegation was halted by a detachment of sailors and dissuaded from attempting to proceed further. John Reed, who was standing by, described the scene:

57   *Vtoroi vserossiiskii s"ezd sovetov*, pp. 45–46.
58   *Rech'*, October 26, p. 3; see also *Izvestiia*, October 26, p. 6.

... Just at the corner of the Ekaterina Canal, under an arc-light, a cordon of armed sailors was drawn across the Nevsky, blocking the way to a crowd of people in column of fours. There were about three or four hundred of them, men in frock coats, well-dressed women, officers ... and at the head white-bearded old Shreider, mayor of Petrograd, and Prokopovich, minister of supplies in the Provisional Government, arrested that morning and released. I caught sight of Malkin, reporter for the *Russian Daily News*. "Going to die in the Winter Palace," he shouted cheerfully. The procession stood still, but from the front of it came loud argument. Shreider and Prokopovich were bellowing at the big sailor who seemed in command. "We demand to pass!" ... "We can't let you pass" [the sailor responded]. ... Another sailor came up, very much irritated. "We will spank you!" he cried, energetically. "And if necessary we will shoot you too. Go home now, and leave us in peace!"

At this there was a great clamor of anger and resentment. Prokopovich had mounted some sort of box, and, waving his umbrella, he made a speech:

"Comrades and citizens!" he said. "Force is being used against us! We cannot have our innocent blood upon the hands of these ignorant men! ... Let us return to the Duma and discuss the best means of saving the country and the Revolution!"

Whereupon, in dignified silence the procession marched around and back up the Nevsky, always in column of fours.[59]

It was now well after midnight, and the situation of the cabinet in the Winter Palace was growing more desperate by the minute. The steady dwindling of loyalist forces had by this time left portions of the east wing almost completely unprotected. Through windows in this section of the building, insurgents, in increasing numbers, were able to infiltrate the palace. In their second-floor meeting-room, many of the ministers now slouched spiritlessly in easy chairs or, like Maliantovich, stretched out on divans, awaiting the end. Konovalov, smoking one cigarette after another, nervously paced the room, disappearing next door from time to time to use the one phone still in service. The ministers could hear shouts, muffled explosions, and rifle and machine gun fire as the officers and cadets who had remained loyal to them fought futilely to fend off revolutionary forces. Their moments of greatest apprehension occurred when the artillery shell from the Peter and Paul Fortress burst in the room above and, somewhat later, when two grenades thrown by infiltrating sailors from an upper gallery exploded in a downstairs hall. Two cadets injured in the latter incident were carried to Kishkin for first aid.

59   Reed, *Ten Days That Shook the World*, pp. 136–37; See also Sukhanov, *Zapiski o revoliutsii*, vol. 7, p. 208.

Every so often Palchinsky popped in to try to calm the ministers, each time assuring them that the insurgents worming their way into the palace were being apprehended, and that the situation was still under control. Maliantovich recorded one of these moments: "Around one o'clock at night, or perhaps it was later, we learned that the procession from the Duma had set out. We let the guard know. . . . Again noise. . . . By this time we were accustomed to it. Most probably the Bolsheviks had broken into the palace once more, and, of course, had again been disarmed. . . . Palchinsky walked in. Of course, this was the case. Again they had let themselves be disarmed without resistance. Again, there were many of them. . . . How many of them are in the palace? Who is actually holding the palace now: we or the Bolsheviks?"[60]

Contrary to most accounts written in the Soviet Union, the Winter Palace was not captured by storm. Antonov himself subsequently recounted that by late evening "the attack on the palace had a completely disorganized character. . . . Finally, when we were able to ascertain that not many cadets remained, Chudnovsky and I led the attackers into the palace. By the time we entered, the cadets were offering no resistance."[61] This must have occurred at close to 2:00 A.M., for at that time Konovalov phoned Mayor Shreider to report: "The Military Revolutionary Committee has burst in. . . . All we have is a small force of cadets. . . . Our arrest is imminent." Moments later, when Shreider called the Winter Palace back, a gruff voice replied: "What do you want? From where are you calling?" – to which Shreider responded, "I am calling from the city administration; what is going on there?" "I am the sentry," answered the unfamiliar voice at the other end of the phone. "There is nothing going on here."[62]

In the intervening moments, the sounds outside the room occupied by the Provisional Government had suddenly become more ominous. "A noise flared up and began to rise, spread, and draw nearer," recalled Maliantovich. "Its varying sounds merged into one wave and at once something unusual, unlike the previous noises, resounded, something final. It was clear instantly that this was the end. . . . Those sitting or lying down jumped up and grabbed their overcoats. The tumult rose swiftly and its wave rolled up to us. . . . All this happened within a few minutes. From the entrance to the room of our guard came the shrill, excited shouts of a mass of voices, some single shots, the trampling of feet, thuds, shuffling, merging into one chaos of sounds and ever-mounting alarm."[63]

60 Maliantovich, "V zimnem dvortse," p. 129.
61 Antonov-Oveseenko, "Oktiabr'skaia buria," p. 104.
62 Erykalov, *Oktiabr'skoe vooruzhennoe vosstanie v Petrograde*, p. 456.
63 Maliantovich, "V zimnem dvortse," pp. 129.

Maliantovich adds that even then the small group of cadets outside the room where the ministers sat seemed ready to continue resistance; however, it was now apparent to everyone that "defense was useless and sacrifices aimless" – that the moment for surrender had finally arrived. Kishkin ordered the commander of the guard to announce the government's readiness to yield. Then the ministers sat down around the table and watched numbly as the door was flung open and, as Maliantovich described it, "a little man flew into the room, like a chip tossed by a wave, under the pressure of the mob which poured in and spread at once, like water, filling all corners of the room." The little man was Antonov. "The Provisional Government is here – what do you want?" Konovalov asked. "You are all under arrest," Antonov replied, as Chudnovsky began taking down the names of the officials present and preparing a formal protocol. The realization that Kerensky, the prize they sought most of all, was not in the room, drove many of the attackers into a frenzy. "Bayonet all the sons of bitches on the spot!" someone yelled. Maliantovich records that it was Antonov who somehow managed to prevent the cabinet from being lynched, insisting firmly that "the members of the Provisional Government are under arrest. They will be confined to the Peter and Paul Fortress. I will not allow any violence against them."[64]

The ministers were accompanied from the Winter Palace and through the Palace Square by a selected convoy of armed sailors and Red Guards and a swearing, mocking, first-shaking mob. Because no cars were available, they were forced to travel to their place of detention on foot. As the procession neared the Troitsky Bridge, the crowd surrounding the ministers once again became ugly, demanding that they be beheaded and thrown into the Neva. This time, the members of the government were saved by the apparently random firing of a machine gun from an approaching car. At the sounds of the shots, machine gunners at the Peter and Paul Fortress, believing themselves under attack, also opened fire. Ministers, escorts, and onlookers scattered for cover. In the ensuing confusion, the prisoners were rushed across the bridge to the safety of the fortress.[65]

The ministers were led into a small garrison club-room, lighted only by a smoky kerosene lamp. At the front of the room they found Antonov, seated at a small table, completing the protocol which Chudnovsky had begun preparing at the Winter Palace. Antonov read the document aloud, calling the roll of arrested officials and inviting each to sign it. Thereupon, the ministers were led to dank cells in the ancient Trubetskoi

---

64   Ibid., p. 130.
65   "Rasskaz K. A. Gvozdeva ob ego areste," and "Rasskaz A. M. Kishkina," in *Rabochaia gazeta*, October 28, p. 2.

Bastion not far from where former tsarist officials had been incarcerated since February. Along the way Konovalov suddenly realized he was without cigarettes. Gingerly, he asked the sailor accompanying him for one and was relieved when the sailor not only offered him shag and paper but, seeing his confusion about what to do with them, rolled him a smoke.[66] Just before the door of his cell banged shut, Nikitin found in his pocket a half-forgotten telegram from the Ukrainian Rada to the Ministry of Interior. Handing it to Antonov, he observed matter of factly: "I received this yesterday – now it's your problem."[67]

At Smolny, meanwhile, the Congress of Soviets session had by now resumed. Ironically, it fell to Kamenev, who had fought tooth and nail against an insurrection for a month and a half, to announce the Provisional Government's demise. "The leaders of the counterrevolution ensconced in the Winter Palace have been seized by the revolutionary garrison," he barely managed to declare before complete pandemonium broke out in the hall. Kamenev went on to read the roll of former officials now incarcerated – at the mention of Tereshchenko, a name synonymous with the continuation of the hated war, the delegates erupted in wild shouts and applause once more.

As if to assure the congress that there was no immediate threat to the revolution, Kamenev also announced that the Third Cycle Battalion, called to Petrograd from the front by Kerensky, had come over to the side of the revolution. Shortly after this encouraging news, the Military Revolutionary Committee's commissar from the garrison at Tsarskoe Selo rushed forward to declare that troops located there had pledged to protect the approaches to Petrograd. "Learning of the approach of the cyclists from the front," he reported, "we prepared to rebuff them, but our concern proved unfounded since it turned out that among the comrade cyclists there were no enemies of the All-Russian Congress [the protocols record that this comment triggered another extended burst of enthusiastic applause]. When we sent our commissars to them it became clear that they also wanted the transfer of all power to the soviets, the immediate transfer of land to the peasants, and the institution of workers' control over industry."[68]

No sooner had the commissars from the Tsarskoe Selo garrison finished speaking than a representative of the Third Cycle Battalion itself demanded to be heard. He explained the attitude of his unit in these terms:

66   I. Kolbin, "Storming the Winter Palace," in *Petrograd 1917*, p. 321.
67   Antonov-Ovseenko, "Oktiabr'skaia buria," p. 104.
68   *Vtoroi vserossiiskii s"ezd sovetov*, pp. 47–50.

Until just recently, we served on the southwestern front. But a few days ago, upon receipt of orders by telephonogram, we were moved north-ward. In the telephonogram it was indicated that we were being moved to defend Petrograd, but from whom – this was not known to us. We were marching on the people blindfolded; we didn't know where we were being sent but we generally guessed what was up. Along the way we were both-ered by the questions: Where? Why? At the station of Peredolsk we held a short meeting in association with the Fifth Cycle Battalion in order to clarify the situation. At this meeting it turned out that among all of the cyclists there could not be found one person who would agree to act against brothers and spill their blood. And we decided that we would not obey the Provisional Government. They, we said, are people who do not want to defend our interests but send us against our brothers. I declare to you concretely: No, we will not give power to a government at the head of which stand bourgeois and landowners!

A bit later, the unwillingness of front soldiers to defend the Provisional Government was further confirmed by Krylenko, who informed the congress of late reports from the northern front. A Military Revolu-tionary Committee had been formed there to counter attempts to send military forces supporting the old government to the capital. Krylenko also announced that General Cheremisov had already recognized the authority of this committee; that Kerensky's commissar on the northern front, Woytinsky, had resigned; and that, one after the other, delegations from those units already in transit to the capital were reporting to the Military Revolutionary Committee to announce their solidarity with the Petrograd garrison.[69]

Apparently at this point at least a portion of the Menshevik-Internationalist fraction reentered the hall, and its spokesman, Kapelin-sky, tried to turn the delegates' attention to Martov's idea of recessing the congress while a delegation was sent to sound out all socialist orga-nizations about the creation of a representative democratic government. Before long, many of the delegates who now either ignored or booed Kapelinsky would regain interest in seeking an accommodation with moderate groups. But for the moment, in their initial ecstasy over the apparently painless triumph over the Kerensky regime, they were in no mood to do so. For the Bolsheviks, Kamenev summarily dismissed Kapelinsky's plea with the claim that the moderate socialists had only themselves to blame for the fact that Martov's proposal to search for peaceful ways of dealing with the crisis had not been implemented. At the same time, he proposed that Trotsky's resolution condemning the Mensheviks and SRs be tabled, thus leaving the door partly open for the resumption of relations with them.

69   Ibid., p. 52.

As the Menshevik-Internationalists again walked out of the hall, Lunacharsky rose to present, for the congress' immediate adoption, a manifesto written by Lenin "To All Workers, Soldiers, and Peasants," endorsing the Petrograd uprising; decreeing the transfer of supreme political authority into the hands of the congress and of local soviets everywhere in Russia; and, in the most general terms, outlining the immediate plan of the new soviet regime. This historic proclamation, ultimately the source of Soviet political authority, read:

To All Workers, Soldiers, and Peasants:

The Second All-Russian Congress of Soviets of Workers' and Soldiers' Deputies has opened. It represents the great majority of the soviets, including a number of deputies of peasant soviets. The prerogatives of the Central Executive Committee of the compromisers are ended.

Supported by an overwhelming majority of the workers, soldiers, and peasants, and basing itself on the victorious insurrection of the workers and the garrison of Petrograd, the congress hereby resolves to take governmental power into its own hands.

The Provisional Government is deposed and most of its members are under arrest.

The Soviet authority will at once propose a democratic peace to all nations and an immediate armistice on all fronts. It will safeguard the transfer without compensation of all land – landlord, imperial, and monastery – to the peasant committees; it will defend the soldiers' rights, introducing a complete democratization of the army; it will establish workers' control over industry; it will insure the convocation of the Constituent Assembly on the date set; it will supply the cities with bread and the villages with articles of first necessity; and it will secure to all nationalities inhabiting Russia the right of self-determination.

The congress resolves that all local authority shall be transferred to the soviets of workers', soldiers', and peasants' deputies, which are charged with the task of enforcing revolutionary order.

The congress calls upon the soldiers in the trenches to be watchful and steadfast. The Congress of Soviets is confident that the revolutionary army will know how to defend the revolution against all imperialistic attempts until the new government has concluded a democratic peace which it is proposing directly to all nations.

The new government will take every measure to provide the revolutionary army with all necessities, by means of a determined policy of requisition from and taxation of the propertied classes. Care will be taken to improve the position of the soldiers' families.

The Kornilovites – Kerensky, Kaledin, and others – are endeavoring to lead troops against Petrograd. Several regiments, deceived by Kerensky, have already joined the insurgents.

Soldiers! Resist Kerensky, who is a Kornilovite! Be on guard!

Railwaymen! Stop all echelons sent by Kerensky against Petrograd!

Soldiers, Workers, Employees! The fate of the revolution and democratic peace is in your hands!
Long live the Revolution!

> The All-Russian Congress of Soviets
> of Workers' and Soldiers' Deputies
> Delegates from the Peasants' Soviets[70]

The reading of this historic manifesto was interrupted again and again by thundering waves of delirious cheers. After Lunacharsky had finished and a semblance of order was restored, Kamkov announced that, with a minor change, the Left SRs would support its adoption. The change was immediately accepted. A spokesman for the tiny Menshevik-United Internationalist fraction declared that if the proclamation would be amended to provide for the immediate organization of a government based on the broadest possible elements of the population, he would vote for it as well; however, when this suggestion was ignored, he announced that his followers would abstain. Finally, at 5:00 A.M., October 26, the manifesto legitimizing the creation of a revolutionary government was voted on and passed by an overwhelming margin, only two deputies voting against and twelve abstaining. A misty gray dawn, typical of Petrograd in late fall, was breaking as congress delegates drifted slowly out of Smolny. Upstairs, exhausted Military Revolutionary Committee leaders stretched out on the floor of their crowded command post to catch some sleep, many of them for the first time in several days. Lenin had gone off to the nearby apartment of Bonch-Bruevich to rest and draft a decree on land reform for adoption at the next session of the congress. The Bolsheviks had come to power in Petrograd, and a new era in the history of Russia and of the world had begun.

Bibliography

1   Chronologies

Riabinskii, K. *Revoliutsiia 1917 goda: Khronika sobytii*. Vol. 5, *Oktiabr'*. Moscow: Gosizdat, 1926.

2   Documentary Materials

Akademiia nauk SSSR, Institut istorii, et al. *Baltiiskie moriaki v podgotovke i provedenii velikoi oktiabr'skoi sotsialisticheskoi revoliutsii*. Edited by P. N. Mordvinov. Moscow and Leningrad: Izdatel'stvo Akademii nauk SSSR, 1957.

---

70   *Vtoroi vserossiiskii s"ezd sovetov*, pp. 53–54; translation from Browder and Kerensky, *The Russian Provisional Government*, vol. 3, pp. 1797–98.

Browder, Robert P., and Kerensky, Alexander F., eds. *The Russian Provisional Government 1917: Documents*. 3 vols. Stanford: Stanford University Press, 1961.

Butenko, A. F., and Chugaev, D. A., eds. *Vtoroi vserossiiskii s"ezd sovetov rabochikh i soldatskikh deputatov: Sbornik dokumentov*. Moscow: Gospolitizdat, 1957.

Liverovskii, A. V. "Poslednie chasy Vremennogo pravitel'stva: Dnevnik ministra Liverovskogo." *Istoricheskii arkhiv*, 1960, no. 6, pp. 38–48.

Protokoly pervago s"ezda partii levykh sotsialistov-revoliutsionerov (internatsionalistov). Moscow: Revoliutsionnyi sotsializm, 1918.

3 Memoirs and Other Works by Bolsheviks

Antonov-Ovseenko, V. A. "Baltflot v dni kerenshchiny i krasnogo oktiabria." *Proletarskaia revoliutsiia*, 1922, no. 10, pp. 118–29.

——. "Oktiabr'skaia buria." *Pervyi narodnyi kalendar' na 1919 g*. Petrograd: Izdatel'stvo Soiuza kommunistov severnoi oblasti, 1919.

——. "Revoliutsiia pobedila." *Krasnaia gazeta*, November 7, 1923, p. 3.

Blagonravov, G. I. "Oktiabr'skie dni v petropavlovskoi kreposti." *Proletarskaia revoliutsiia*, 1922, no. 4, pp. 24–52.

Dzenis, O. P. "Kak my brali 25 okt. zimnii dvorets." *Pravda*, November 6–7, 1921, p. 7.

Flerovskii, I. P. "Kronshtadt v oktiabr'skoi revoliutsii," *Proletarskaia revoliutsiia*, 1992, no. 10, pp. 130–50.

Lenin, V. I. *Polnoe sobranie sochinenii*. 55 vols. 5th ed. Moscow: Gospolitizdat, 1958–1965.

Tarasov-Rodionov, A. "Pervaia operatsiia," *Voennyi vestnik*, 1924, no. 42, pp. 10–13.

4 Non-Bolshevik Memoirs

Kerensky, A. F. *Russia and History's Turning Point*. New York: Duell, Sloan & Pearce, 1965.

Maliantovich, P. N. "V zimnem dvortse 25–26 oktiabria 1917 goda." *Byloe*, 1918, no. 12, pp. 111–41.

Reed, John. *Ten Days That Shook the World*. New York: Vintage Books, 1960.

Sukhanov, N. N. *Zapiski o revoliutsii*. 7 vols. Berlin, Petersburg, Moscow: Z. I. Grzhebin, 1922–1923.

5 Soviet Secondary Sources

Akademiia nauk SSSR, Institut istorii, Leningradskoe otdelenie. *Oktiabr'skoe vooruzhennoe vosstanie*. Edited by S. N. Valk, et al. 2 vols. Leningrad: Nauka, 1967.

Erykalov, E. F. *Oktiabr'skoe vooruzhennoe vosstanie v Petrograde.* Leningrad: Lenizdat, 1966.

Milchik, I. "Petrogradskaia tsentral'naia gorodskaia duma v fevrale–oktiabre 1917 goda." *Krasnaia letopis'*, 1927, no. 2 (23), pp. 189–218.

Startsev, V. I. "Poslednii den' Vremennogo pravitel'stva." In *Iz istorii velikoi oktiabr'skoi sotsialisticheskoi revoliutsii i sotsialisticheskogo stroitel'stva v SSSR*, pp. 99–115. Leningrad: Izdatel'stvo Leningradskogo universiteta, 1967.

Glossary

Antonov-Ovseenko, V. A. Bolshevik, member of Military Revolutionary Committee; led capture of Provisional Government in Winter Palace.

Avksentiev, N. D. Socialist Revolutionary; member of Executive Committee of Petrograd Soviet; Minister of Internal Affairs in Provisional Government, July–August 1917; President of Preparliament in October.

Bagratuni, General I. Chief of Staff of the Petrograd Military District. Helped lead unsuccessful defense of the Provisional Government during the October days.

Blagonravov, G. I. Bolshevik; officer in Petrograd garrison; member of Bolshevik Military Organization and of the leadership of the Military Revolutionary Committee in October.

Bogdanov, V. O. Menshevik; one of the founders of the Petrograd Soviet and a leader of its Executive Committee as well as of the moderate socialist bloc in the All-Russian Central Executive Committee. Delegate to the Second All-Russian Congress of Soviets.

Broido, M. I. Menshevik; member of the Executive Committee of the Petrograd Soviet and of the All-Russian Central Executive Committee.

Bubnov, A. S. Bolshevik; member of party Central Committee and of the Military Revolutionary Committee.

Bykhovsky, N. Socialist Revolutionary; an official of the Petrograd City Duma who initiated its abortive march to the Winter Palace the night of 25 October.

Cheremisov, General A. V. Progressive military reformer who commanded Russian forces on the Northern front during the October days.

Chudnovsky, G. I. Bolshevik; prominent in Bolshevik Military Organization and in the Military Revolutionary Committee.

Dan, F. I. Menshevik; a highly influential member of the Executive Committee of the Petrograd Soviet and of the moderate socialist leadership in the All-Russian Central Executive Committee; one of the "defensists'" chief theoreticians and policy makers throughout 1917.

Dashkevich, P. V.   Bolshevik; helped found the party Military Organization and prominent figure in the Military Revolutionary Committee during the capture of the Winter Palace in October.

Eremeev, K.   Bolshevik; member of party's Military Organization and Military Revolutionary Committee.

Erlikh, G.   Bundist (the Bund was the Jewish social democratic organization); delegate to the Second All-Russian Congress of Soviets where he sharply criticized Bolshevik policies.

Filipovsky, V. N.   An SR officer. Official in the Petrograd Soviet and the All-Russian Central Executive Committee.

Flerovsky, I. P.   Prominent Kronstadt Bolshevik; a member of both the Petrograd Soviet and Executive Committee of the Kronstadt Soviet.

Gendelman, M.   Socialist Revolutionary; member of the Central Committee and delegate to the Second All-Russian Congress of Soviets. Opposed Bolsheviks at the Congress.

Gots, A. R.   Socialist Revolutionary; key moderate socialist leader in the Petrograd Soviet and in the Central Executive Committee.

Gzel'shchak, F.   A Bolshevik delegate to the Second All-Russian Congress of Soviets from the Secondary Army.

Kamenev, L. B.   Bolshevik; member of party Central Committee; enormously influential in developing popular Bolshevik political program in 1917; opposed Lenin's call for the independent seizure of power in October.

Kamkov, B. D.   Left SR; one of the founders of the Left SR party and its most prominent spokesman in the Preparliament.

Kaledin, General A. M.   Supporter of General Lavr Kornilov at the Moscow State Conference. Among political and military leaders most fiercely committed to traditional Russian national goals, including vigorous pursuit of the failed war effort; therefore, he was a dyed-in-the-wool opponent of both moderate and radical socialists.

Kapelinsky, N. Iu.   Menshevik-Internationalist; advocated suspending the Second All-Russian Congress of Soviets in order to build support for the formation of a broad socialist coalition government.

Kharash, Ia. Ia.   Menshevik; army officer and delegate from the Twelfth Army to the Second All-Russian Congress of Soviets.

Khaustov, F. P.   Bolshevik; a radical officer and party organizer in the Twelfth Army; radical member of the Bolshevik Military Organization; arrested in Petrograd in mid-summer 1917 and liberated from prison during the October days.

Khinchuk, L. M. Menshevik; moderately inclined member of party Central Committee; leader in Moscow Soviet; delegate to Second All-Russian Congress of Soviets.

Kollontai, A. M. Bolshevik; a member of the party Central Committee and one of the most prominent and independent-minded women Bolsheviks; arrested after the July days; participant in party meetings leading to the October revolution; participant in Second All-Russian Congress of Soviets.

Konovalov, A. I. Kadet; Minister of Trade and Industry in Provisional Government, March–May, September–October 1917.

Krylenko, N. I. Bolshevik; key member of the Bolshevik Military Organization and of the Military Revolutionary Committee. In trumvirate heading the Commissariat for the Army and Navy in the first Soviet government.

Kuchin, G. D. Menshevik; representative of Northern front Army Committee at the Second All-Russian Congress of Soviets, where he vehemently criticized the Bolsheviks.

Kuzmin, A. A. Assisant to the commander of the Petrograd Military District; participated in the crackdown on the Bolsheviks following the July uprising.

Liber, M. A prominent Bundist and right Menshevik in 1917; harsh critic of the Bolsheviks in the Petrograd Soviet.

Lukianov, F. Bolshevik; a delegate from the Third Army to the Second All-Russian Congress of Soviets.

Lunacharsky, A. Bolshevik; influential Bolshevik moderate; powerful revolutionary orator; first People's Commissar for Education; prominent party spokesman in the Second-All-Russian Congress of Soviets.

Maliantovich, P. N. Memoirist and Minister of Justice in the Provisional Government; captured in the Winter Palace.

Martov, Iu. O. A leader of Menshevism from its beginnings in 1903; a Menshevik-Internationalist throughout 1917. Strongly opposed coalition with liberals but led the Menshevik-Internationalists in walking out of the Second All-Russian Congress of Soviets to protest Bolshevik violence.

Molotov, V. M. Bolshevik; member of party's Petersburg Committee in 1917 and of the Military Revolutionary Committee during the October days.

Mstislavsky, S. D. Left SR; leader of the group's delegation at the Second All-Russian Congress of Soviets.

Nogin, V. Bolshevik; moderate member of the party Central Committee. Elected chairman of the Moscow Soviet in September 1917 and took part in the October revolution in Moscow. Delegate from Moscow at the Second All-Russian Congress of Soviets.

Palchinsky, P. I. An engineer and Deputy Minister of Trade and Industry in the Provisional Government. Helped coordinate defense of the Provisional Government during the October days.

Prokopovich, S. N. Menshevik; a distinguished economist and Minister of Food Supply in the last Provisional Government. Participated in the Petrograd City Duma's abortive march to the Winter Palace the night of 25 October.

Roshal, S. G. Radical Bolshevik organizer in Kronstadt; arrested after the July uprising.

Rutenberg, P. M. Socialist Revolutionary; an assistant to the commander of the Petrograd Military District during the October revolution in Petrograd.

Sadovsky, A. Bolshevik; army officer; leader in the Bolshevik Military Organization and chairman of the Military Section of the Petrograd Soviet in fall 1917; also a member of the All-Russian Central Executive Committee and the Military Revolutionary Committee.

Sakharov, V. V. Bolshevik; a party Military Organization leader from the Petrograd garrison; arrested following the July uprising. Liberated during the October days.

Tarasov-Rodionov, A. Bolshevik; member of the party's military organization from the Infantry Officers' Academy in Oranienbaum; active participant in the July uprising.

Tolkachev, A. Bolshevik; officer in the Petrograd garrison and member of the Bolshevik Military Organization; participated in the July uprising, after which he was arrested; liberated from prison during the October days.

Verderevsky, Rear Admiral D. N. Minister of the Navy in the Provisional Government, September–October 1917.

Volodarsky, V. Bolshevik; especially effective party agitator and influential leader in the Bolshevik Petersburg Committee.

Woytinsky, V. S. Menshevik; chief editor of the Petrograd Soviet's newspaper, *Izvestiia*, and a leading spokesman for revolutionary defensism; Soviet commissar in the Twelfth Army and opponent of transfer of government power to the Soviets in 1917.

Zinoviev, G. E. Bolshevik; member of party Central Committee; opposed independent seizure of power in fall 1917.

Further Reading: October, 1917

General works

O. Anweiler, *The Soviets: The Russian Workers', Peasants' and Soldiers' Councils, 1905–1921*, trans. by Ruth Hein (Pantheon, 1974).

A. Gleason, P. Kenez and R. Stites (eds.), *Bolshevik Culture: Experimentation and Order in the Russian Revolution* (Indiana University Press, 1985) [documents].

O. Figes, *A People's Tragedy: The Russian Revolution, 1891–1924* (Jonathan Cape, 1996).

S. Fitzpatrick, *The Russian Revolution*, 2nd. edn. (Oxford University Press, 1994).

J. L. H. Keep, *The Russian Revolution: A Study in Mass Mobilization* (Norton, 1976).

M. McCauley (ed.), *The Russian Revolution and the Soviet State, 1917–1921: Documents* (Macmillan, 1975, revised, 1980).

R. Medvedev, *The October Revolution* (Norton, 1979) [a dissident Soviet perspective].

R. Pipes, *The Russian Revolution, 1899–1919* (Knopf, 1990).

C. Read, *From Tsar to Soviets: The Russian People and their Revolution, 1917–1921* (UCL Press, 1996).

R. Wade, *Red Guards and Workers' Militias in the Russian Revolution* (Stanford University Press, 1984).

Accounts of participants

T. Dan, *The Origins of Bolshevism*, trans. and ed. by Joel Carmichael (Harper and Row, 1964).

P. Miliukov, *Political Memoirs, 1905–1917* (University of Michigan Press, 1967).

N. N. Sukhanov, *The Russian Revolution*, trans. and ed. by Joel Carmichael (Harper and Row, 1955).

L. Trotsky, *The History of the Russian Revolution* (1933; reprinted by Pathfinder Press, 1977).

Leadership personalities

S. Baron, *Plekhanov, Father of Russian Marxism* (Stanford University Press, 1963).

S. Cohen, *Bukharin and the Bolshevik Revolution: A Political Biography, 1888–1938* (Knopf, 1973).

I. Getzler, *Martov: A Political Biography of a Russian Social Democrat* (Cambridge University Press, 1967).

M. Miller, *Kropotkin* (University of Chicago Press, 1976).

R. Service, *Lenin: A Political Life*, 3 vols. (Indiana University Press, 1985–1995).

D. Volkogonov, *Trotsky: The Eternal Revolutionary*, trans. by H. Shukman (Free Press, 1996) [based on unpublished archival materials].

Political parties

P. Avrich, *The Russian Anarchists* (Princeton University Press, 1967).

J. Burbank, *Intelligentsia and Revolution: Russian Views of Bolshevism, 1917–1922* (Oxford University Press, 1986) [opposition parties and leaders vs. Bolshevism].

Z. Galili, *The Mensheviks in the Russian Revolution* (Princeton University Press, 1989).

M. Melancon, *The Socialist Revolutionaries and the Russian Anti-War Movement, 1914–1917* (Ohio State University Press, 1990).

M. Perrie, *The Agrarian Policy of the Russian Socialist Revolutionary Party* (Cambridge University Press, 1976).

O. Radkey, *The Agrarian Foes of Bolshevism* (Columbia University Press, 1958) [Socialist Revolutionary Party].

O. Radkey, *The Sickle under the Hammer: The Russian Socialist Revolutionaries in the Early Months of Soviet Rule* (Columbia University Press, 1963).

W. Rosenberg, *Liberals in the Russian Revolution: The Constitutional Democratic Party, 1917–1921* (Princeton University Press, 1974).

A. Ulam, *The Bolsheviks: The Intellectual and Political History of the Triumph of Communism in Russia* (Macmillan, 1965).

Part III
Issues of Class, Gender, and Ethnicity in the Revolution

5

Russian Labor and Bolshevik Power: Social Dimensions of Protest after October

William Rosenberg

Originally appeared as introduction to William G. Rosenberg, "Russian Labor and Bolshevik Power: Social Dimensions of Protest in Petrograd after October," in Daniel H. Kaiser (ed.), *The Workers' Revolution in Russia, 1917: The View from Below* (Cambridge: Cambridge University Press, 1987), 98–131.

Editor's Introduction

Having begun his career with what is still regarded as the definitive history of the Russian liberal movement during the revolutionary era, William Rosenberg has in recent decades become one of the premier historians of the Russian working class. Social historians have made seminal contributions over the years to a subject which, in this case, had already been the object of enormous attention among Soviet and Russian historians. Most students of the topic agree that the opening to a less ideological approach to the subject began with Leopold Haimson's now classic articles in the *Slavic Review* in 1964–5. Haimson conceptualized the notion of social polarization in Russia as a crucial process in the prerevolutionary period which affected both the intelligentsia and the lower classes of workers and peasants. This was a critical turn in the historiography of the revolutionary era in that attention was directed to the workers as a distinct object of study set apart from Soviet methodology.

Rosenberg's article, which extends Haimson's original analysis into new areas, is one of the clearest explanations of the problems confronting the working class in Russia during and immediately after the October seizure of power (described by Rabinowitch in the previous reading). Rosenberg begins by questioning the received wisdom of many prominent historians concerning the assumed political opposition of workers to the Bolshevik party which, after all, was dedicated ideologically precisely to their interests.

For Rosenberg, October must be understood neither as an inevitable political outcome nor simply in terms of Lenin's passion for dictatorial state control. It was, rather, "part of a vast social upheaval over which [the Bolsheviks] had, in fact, very little control," especially with regard to the working class. The complexity and chaos of a deteriorating economic situation amidst continuing sacrifices in an unpopular world war formed a significant context for Lenin to inaugurate his programs. More specifically, this crisis made workers more susceptible, if not vulnerable, to the appeals of the Bolsheviks. Once under Soviet power after October, workers continued to function with a rising sense of class consciousness as they moved to take control of sectors of the economy through local soviets and factory committees. However, worker discontent revived early in 1918 as social and economic conditions did not improve and labor disruptions spread throughout the country. Rosenberg cogently analyzes the consequences of this upheaval, and simultaneously demonstrates the thesis he posed at the start.

Russian Labor and Bolshevik Power: Social Dimensions of Protest in Petrograd after October

William G. Rosenberg

The relationship between Russian labor and Bolshevik power in the months immediately following October remains a central and contentious issue of early Soviet history. Bolshevik political legitimacy turns in large measure on the degree to which the party was able in this period to retain the support of workers whose activism in 1917 had brought the Bolsheviks to power; and the nature and extent of workers' opposition to the new regime in these early months is fundamental to our understanding of its dictatorial structure. These issues, central to the work of E. H. Carr, Leonard Schapiro, and others, have recently reemerged in the literature, both implicitly and explicitly. Whereas new books by S. A. Smith, David Mandel, and Diane Koenker on 1917 have examined carefully the social circumstances of Petrograd and Moscow workers, Schapiro's own last volume, *The Russian Revolutions of 1917*, takes sharp issue with historians whose work centers on "social trends, economic theories, or sociological analysis." Roy Medvedev and Vladimir Brovkin have demonstrated how elections to local soviets in the spring of 1918 brought extensive gains for Mensheviks and Socialist Revolutionaries, including popular majorities in all provincial capitals where elections took place;[1] and an important new collection of materials edited by M. S. Bernshtam for Alexander Solzhenitsyn's series on modern Russian history reasserts an old Right Menshevik view, put most forcefully perhaps by Grigorii Aronson, who maintained that the Bolsheviks had been in power scarcely two months before

all sympathy for them had disappeared, and the benevolent neutrality of the weeks preceding [October] gave way to a committed opposition. . . . After [Brest Litovsk], the convocation of the Constituent Assembly again

This essay first appeared in *Slavic Review* 44(1985):213–38, and is here slightly revised. Readers are referred to the original version for full documentation.

1 Vladimir Brovkin, "The Mensheviks' Political Comeback: The Elections to the Provincial City Soviets in Spring 1918," *Russian Review* 42(1983):1–50, esp. 37–8; Roy Medvedev, *The October Revolution* (New York: W. W. Norton, 1979), esp. chap. 12, "The Masses Turn Away From the Bolsheviks."

became a popular watchword. The need for a democratic state power qualified to speak in the name of the entire country was felt more and more. And in the workers' quarters, sympathies for the Mensheviks and SRs revived, after having abated. Thanks to the actions of these groups in the soviets and bolshevized trade unions, and the ideological influence they exercised, the opposition gained the upper hand.[2]

Suppressing the opposition, and "regaining the upper hand" thus became, for Aronson and others, the first requirement of early Bolshevik politics and the cornerstone of "communist autocracy."

The importance of these issues to our understanding of early Soviet history has prompted me to raise them again here, and to examine in particular the validity of conceptualizing labor opposition to the Bolsheviks between October 1917 and July 1918 in essentially political terms. I hope to do this by focusing on several longer-term patterns that I think proved of great importance in these months; by looking closely at certain social characteristics of the opposition movement in Petrograd that may have had a greater bearing on events than we have recognized; and by attempting, finally, to relate these characteristics to the opposition's failure in the capital to "gain the upper hand." It might then be possible to frame a broader argument by way of conclusion about the failure of labor protest generally in this period, and to gain a somewhat fuller understanding of the complex processes involved in the Bolsheviks' consolidation of power.

Long-term Patterns

At the risk of emphasizing the obvious, let me stress, first, the importance of remembering that whereas the Bolsheviks came to power reflecting politically the perceived interests and will of a great number of Russia's fifteen to eighteen million workers,[3] they did so only as part of a vast social upheaval over which they had, in fact, very little control. Theirs was, to be sure, a critical part, vital of course to the *political* outcome of 1917; but equally important is the way in which the overthrow of the old order involved, simultaneously, a massive, and ulti-

---

2   G. Aronson, "Ouvriers russes contre le Bolchevisme," *Le Contrat social* 10(1966):202.
3   The number (and definition) of "workers" in Russia at this time is the subject of much dispute. See L. S. Gaponenko, *Rabochii klass Rossii v 1917 godu* (Moscow, 1970), 33–75, who gives 15 million as the figure for all hired labor in industry, including transport, construction, and agricultural workers, and 18.5 million for all hired labor in general (p. 75).

mately for the Bolsheviks, problematic assault on a wide array of social relationships and values that reflected Russia's political institutions. Authority based on traditional social hierarchies in the workplace weakened dramatically, as it did in the army and elsewhere, as the Provisional Government's political power itself began to decline. What emerged from this assault was social polarization and the civil war mentality used by Lenin and his comrades to such great political advantage. Ordinary workers and peasants developed a new understanding of the nature of "democratic Russia" that reflected elemental notions of social dominance – *vlast'* – rather than the relatively rarefied (and nonRussian) concepts of a rule of law and universal civil liberties. For our purposes, however, what needs to be stressed in this regard is not the Bolsheviks' obvious relative political strength by the fall of 1917, or their skillful arrogation of mass "democratic" commitments to further mobilize workers, but rather the party's *weakness* in facing the monumental tasks of Russia's social and economic reconstruction.

Crucial to the emergence of Lenin's new order, moreover, was a familiar range of new or newly reestablished mass organizations – factory committees, trade unions, workers' control organizations, and the like – that not only reflected workers' ideas about democracy and social change, but also represented workers' solutions to acute socioeconomic problems. Although the Bolsheviks increasingly identified with these mass organizations as the revolution unfolded, they were not primarily of the party's making, any more than was the overthrow of the tsarist regime. On the contrary, it remained quite unclear to Lenin and others in the party leadership, whose sights were focused on securing political power, exactly how these organizations or the values they reflected corresponded to the requirements of a communist order. The party's support for institutions such as factory committees was conditioned in large measure by the desire to destroy bourgeois Russia, and by the fact that many in the committee movement became Bolsheviks themselves. The further social upheaval needed to complete the assault on Russia's "bourgeois order" was, in fact, also clearly an impediment to the party's need to create the stable socioeconomic conditions required for social welfare, as well as for socialism.

At the same time, the Russian workers' movement of 1917 was itself a product of longer processes of change, including the uneven and dependent nature of Russian industrial development during the war, and the differential impact of the war itself on various industrial and social groups. Even though the period between July 1914 and the spring of 1915 brought some dislocation almost everywhere, the needs of the war soon began to have a strengthening effect on some industries. By the late spring of 1915, as state resources were mobilized to support defense production, and deferments and exemptions were introduced for skilled workers, a complex process of industrial segregation began to unfold, separating "favored" industries from those the state was unable or unwilling to protect, on the one hand, and identifying particular branches of production and particular plants for special consideration, on the other.

The broadest patterns of segregation are visible in output data. Total industrial production grew some 21.5 percent between 1913 and 1916, but this was almost entirely the result of increased output in only two sectors, metals and chemicals. In Russia's two most populous industrial branches, food processing and cotton textiles, output fell 22 percent and 18 percent, respectively, between 1913 and 1916.[4] These differential rates were at least partly attributable to the nature of government intervention. State resources began to pour into weapons and armament production, especially in Petrograd, and into the production of gunpowder and explosives, soon the major product of chemical plants. These sectors also gained priority in fuel and resource allocations, and were the beneficiaries of new machine tool imports, financed at state expense, which helped output per worker increase some 40 percent in metals and some 30 percent in chemicals between 1915 and 1917. By contrast, output per worker fell from between 15 percent and 20 percent in almost all other sectors, and more than 30 percent in lumber mills and factories making wood products. Textiles were particularly affected.

At the same time, the state bestowed the largest and most lucrative military contracts on a relatively small number of major producers. As late as February 1917, demand for military goods from Petrograd metalworking plants was still some 16 percent greater than their production capacity, a ratio that, among other things, allowed Petrograd metalworkers the luxury of striking without great fear of massive retaliation. In chemicals, the state's demand was even higher.

These developments had important social consequences, some of which are well known: The number of metalworkers in Petrograd increased by some 400 percent between 1914 and 1917, and the number of chemical workers by 250 percent. These enormous increases, however, were accompanied by, and in part engendered, a deep instability in the workplace, even in chemicals and metals. At the Putilov works, for example, some 9,000 employees left their jobs in 1915 alone, some to the army, some to higher paying jobs elsewhere. At

---

4   Of the other major industrial sectors, only leather, linen, hemp and jute, and some clothing branches (including shoes) showed any increase whatsoever, and accounted for only 8.3 percent of new output. Wood production fell 38 percent, and the production of paper some 20 percent.

the Treugol'nik rubber plant in the nearby Narvskii district, the number of workers replaced in 1915 may have exceeded 10,000. If we lack precise figures on these changes, their dynamics are still clear and quite extraordinary. In Russia as a whole, at least one-third of all workers employed in January 1914 had left their jobs by 1917, and the actual figure was probably much higher. In Moscow alone more than 300,000 filed through the labor exchange during the first nine months of its operation in 1915–16.

Many newcomers to the industrial labor force were women, and their employment helped effect a decline in real wages in all industrial sectors. More important for our purposes, however, is the likelihood that these changes contributed to the erosion of the relative security of skilled workers, both in terms of real wages, and as a result of the introduction of new machinery, new factory discipline, and the further rationalization of work processes.[5] These developments took place against a background of rising living costs, growing shortages of food and other essentials, and increasing labor militancy, particularly in Petrograd. Manufacturers and the government responded in many places with arrests, dismissals, fines, and such tactics as compulsory overtimes, which added greatly to the burdens of maintaining some semblance of family stability or welfare.

It is important, finally, to emphasize even in bare outline some of the ways in which all of these processes related to Russia's revolutionary development in 1917, and helped define the problems that Lenin and his comrades might be said to have inherited as they came to power in October. Not least among these is the way in which many workers heralded February as the opportunity, at long last, to establish some degree of stability and order in the workplace, in part by ending arbitrary and repressive behavior of managers and foremen, in part by assuring steady and orderly production with adequate wages and secure jobs. Undoubtedly skilled workers and artisans felt strongly the desire for security, hoping to maintain the traditional perquisites of their crafts; but semiskilled machine operators and even unskilled workers, who must have looked with some envy at their better paid and more secure comrades, clearly felt the same desire. In any event, the important points are that the quest for security was very broadly based; that it accompanied more familiar expectations for an improvement in material welfare in 1917 (reflected, for example, in the wage and hour demands of strikers in the spring); and that both sets of aspirations

5   See the discussion in Heather Hogan, "Industrial Rationalization and the Roots of Labor Militance in the St. Petersburg Metalworking Industry, 1901–1914," *Russian Review* 42(1983):163–90.

accompanied from the start more politicized hopes for the creation of a democratic order.

Yet one of the most salient aspects of 1917 was the inability of the Provisional Government not only to stem the processes of economic deterioration throughout the country as a whole, but even to prevent its spread into "favored" industrial sectors. Most important, defense production itself fell by as much as 10 percent between February and July; and output from all metalworking and machine plants declined by almost a third from 1916. Coal production in the Donbas, which had been as much as 172 million puds [1 pud = 36 lb.] as late as November 1916 and which was crucial to iron and steel production, fell to less than 110 million puds by the end of the summer. Reserves awaiting shipment at mine heads were only one-fifth of what they had been in 1916. By early 1917, many plants, like the Parviainen works in Petrograd, had less than a single day's reserve of coal. Putilov, which used some 10 percent of all industrial coal deliveries in the capital, by mid-August was receiving only one-quarter of what it needed.

If by late summer 1917, therefore, "crisis" had become a common noun in all Russian public discourse, one must especially appreciate the ways in which the country's threatened economic collapse now raised the specter of massive hardship and ruination even for "privileged" workers in the Petrograd metal plants. Russia's economy seemed threatened with systemic collapse. Central financial institutions like the stock exchanges began to weaken, along with the various regulatory agencies governing commodity exchange. The normative processes of capitalist finance – investments, loans, issuing stocks and bonds, collecting receivables, the repayment of debt – were all seriously disrupted by the summer of 1917. Risks increased drastically. The state banking apparatus came under tremendous pressure.

What must be emphasized is that these circumstances seemed to many to require energetic state intervention at precisely the moment the Provisional Government itself was under increasing attack from all sides, and mortally weak. It is important conceptually, as it was important tactically for Lenin and other activists at the time, to distinguish "state" and "government" in this regard. The government, clearly, was ineffective. Increasingly, this seemed due to the ways that it reflected "bourgeois" interests. The state apparatus itself, however, still seemed to afford workers at least the *possibility* of economic and social relief, especially with the formation of the first coalition in May, and then again, after July, when the Soviet's declaration of July 8 became, in effect, the platform of the second coalition. Countless workers' delegations besieged state offices throughout this period demanding assistance, even as the "bourgeois" ministers themselves came under increasing attack. And if from the standpoint of democratic politics one can understand the Provisional Government's reluctance to have the state intervene further in the economy, one can also understand why growing numbers of workers came to see the Provisional regime as reflecting, above all, the failures and insecurities of "bourgeois capitalism."

It is against the background of these broader processes that one must appreciate the enormous impact of more immediate changes, both before and after October, and understand important aspects of the workers' own response. And here one must note not only the problems associated with the formation of factory committees and other autonomous workers' organizations, but the related emergence of two broad tendencies among workers that also had a bearing on events, and that were, in important ways, contradictory. There emerged on the one hand, as S. A. Smith has argued convincingly,[6] a forceful and increasingly strident sense of proletarian class identity – a generalized class consciousness that reflected broad patterns of social polarization – that was of crucial political importance, and served so vital a role in the Bolsheviks coming to power. On the other hand, however, there also emerged a somewhat less familiar but equally important concurrent tendency toward what one might call "localism," in which traditionally unifying national loyalties and commitments gave way to concerns bounded by factory gates. The developing characteristics of proletarian and peasant social hegemony increasingly were defined in terms of particularistic (rather than class) interests and needs. Localism was at once a natural result of the need workers felt to find immediate "solutions" in 1917 to the problems of their own plants and factories, and the result of longer-term social influences – craft identities and consciousness, common backgrounds (*zemliachestvo*), and the like.[7]

As Russia's crisis deepened and class-conscious workers increasingly took local matters into their own hands, the defensive (and particularistic) functions of factory committees took on increasing importance. Moreover, and especially important to events after October, the strongest and most active factory committees emerged in Russia's favored and most protected industrial branches and plants. More than half the delegates at the first conference of factory committees in Petrograd in late May and early June, for example, were from the capital's metalworking

6   S. A. Smith, "Craft Consciousness, Class Consciousness: Petrograd 1917," *History Workshop Journal* 11(Spring 1981):33–58. See also William G. Rosenberg, "Workers and Workers' Control in the Russian Revolution," *History Workshop Journal* 5(Spring 1978):89–97.
7   See, for example, James D. White, "The Sormovo-Nikolaev zemlyachestvo in the February Revolution," *Soviet Studies* 31(1979):475–504.

plants. They represented more than 230,000 workers in 134 enterprises, and as an industrial group constituted a delegation eight times larger than both the printers (the next most heavily represented branch) and the textile workers. By August 1917, at the second Petrograd conference, chemical workers constituted the second largest delegation, and by now had almost three times as many representatives as the printers.

It is important to emphasize the obvious political aspects of this process. As Smith demonstrates in *Red Petrograd*, factory committees played out within an enterprise the broader struggle for control over resources and the distribution of power. At the same time, both moderate Soviet leaders and Provisional Government figures could not fail to incur workers' animosity as they tried to restrain the committees' growing influence. When socialist Minister of Labor M. I. Skobelev tried late in the summer to set limits on committee power, workers responded by saying, "Precisely now, when disruption of the economy is reaching new heights, when firings have become massive and factories all over the place are being closed and evacuated, the intensive, unrestricted and most diverse work of factory committees and their central organs is absolutely necessary." In fact, of course, not only were all such workers' groups powerless to stem the systemic disintegration of Russia's state capitalist economy in 1917, but indeed they made matters worse. More important in terms of developments after October, they also increased by their actions an overall dependency on state, as opposed to market, economic mechanisms.

It is at least partly against this background that the Bolsheviks soon appeared so attractive to many Russian workers in 1917, especially in Petrograd. Lenin and his comrades offered both an explanation for Russia's crisis, and the simultaneous hope that complete disaster could be avoided if government authorities used the country's seemingly vast state resources in the workers' own interests. Thus the Bolsheviks' own arguments about the relationship between the war and capitalism generally, their insistence that Russia's threatened economic collapse could be attributed largely to industrialists "sabotaging" the revolution in order to preserve social and political hegemony, and above all, their emphasis on seizing state power and using it to "smash the capitalist order" all seemed both to explain Russia's crisis and to promise effective, permanent solutions – all the more, in fact, because they involved at least some elements of truth. Russia's particular form of capitalism *was* failing, as a system of finance, commodity exchange, social relations, and industrial production; indeed, it had already begun to fail before February, a process at once the cause and consequence of political weakness, social upheaval, and the carnage of war. Little wonder thousands of workers with varying degrees of political consciousness regarded so enthusiastically the "overthrow of capitalism and the end of the bourgeois order," and anticipated so hopefully an end to the insecurities of liberal democracy.

Social Characteristics of the Opposition Movement

One of the most salient features of revolutionary Russia in the eight months or so after October 1917 is that nothing seemed to have changed for the better. This realization, and the even more precarious, uncertain conditions that soon emerged, disturbed and angered broad groups of workers. By the early summer there were widespread anti-Bolshevik protests. Armed clashes occurred in the factory districts of Petrograd and other industrial centers. Under the aegis of the Conference of Factory and Plant Representatives (*Sobranie Upolnomochennykh Fabrik i Zavodov Petrograda*), a general strike was set for July 2.

In October most celebrating workers did not suspect that this would be the short-term outcome of one of the most momentous changes in Russian history. For a few short weeks, while capitalist management began to disappear from their factories, workers seemed to believe that they themselves could find at least temporary solutions to the problems besetting their plants, and that Bolshevik rule would assist these efforts, both by using the state apparatus in their support, especially in the area of banking and finance, and by restoring some semblance of economic control. By early December, encouraged by the Bolsheviks' draft decree promising the "legal" extension of workers' control in all enterprises with more than five employees, workers had organized committees in more than 2,100 major enterprises, including some 68 percent of all plants with more than 200 workers. Scores of plants and major railroads were "nationalized" from below in the expectation that this would finally guarantee effective state assistance. "What had begun to happen before the October Revolution now happened more frequently and more openly," E. H. Carr writes of this process. "For the moment, nothing would have dammed the tide of revolt."[8]

But it is doubtful that the principal force behind the "tide of revolt" after October was essentially a political one, and even unlikely that many Bolsheviks were primarily concerned with workers' control in order "to secure the allegiance of the working masses," as Paul Avrich has suggested.[9] The consolidation of power was clearly the central concern of Lenin and his comrades, and the factory committee move-

8 E. H. Carr, *The Bolshevik Revolution, 1917–1923*, 3 vols. (New York: Macmillan, 1950–3), 2:69.
9 Paul H. Avrich, "The Bolshevik Revolution and Workers' Control in Russian Industry," *Slavic Review* 22 (1963): 48.

ment was obviously of political importance, but what occurred in November and early December was not so much revolt (or perhaps, more precisely, not only revolt) as an effort by workers to stave off total economic disaster on a local level by securing a dominant role in plant affairs. In political terms, the revolt was largely over. State power, such as it was, belonged to workers' parties, even if not yet to the Bolsheviks alone. The enormously difficult and frightening task now was to cope with production problems and survive, a task that workers simply could no longer leave to others, and for which now, more than ever, they needed state support.

The very necessity of this process further strengthened the defensive characteristics of factory committees in these weeks. November and December 1917 were months in which factory committees desperately sought new orders for goods, had to procure scarce materials and supplies, turn up funds to pay workers, and resolve their own difficulties with technicians and other experienced administrators in order to keep plants running. In many places managers and workers' representatives signed papers together in order to receive funds (especially from private banks) or procure goods. Elsewhere, seats on factory committees were given to technicians to prevent their departure and assure their help. Collegial administration emerged as a common form of management, in other words, because it seemed the most effective way to get things done. Meanwhile, committees explained their actions at frequent meetings and sought popular confirmation for their policies through "plant democracy."

Moreover, for a period perhaps no longer than six to eight weeks, many in the factories must have thought these efforts were working. Taking control of production in many enterprises gave committees immediate access to financial reserves and other resources remaining in the commercial "pipeline." Some new funds thus became available for the moment for pay increases, procuring materials, even settling outstanding obligations in cases where suppliers demanded immediate payment. Private wealth, of course, was also confiscated, and in many places redistributed to workers along with space in apartments and other sequestered living quarters. Workers entered their plants in early November with a new sense of commitment and enthusiasm, convinced their insecurity and dislocation would soon come to an end. Russian workers were buoyed by a political triumph that wrested state power from the bourgeoisie, confident in their own ability to manage affairs, and elated by the reality of their new social dominance. Workers could hardly fail to expect that conditions would improve as their leaders and comrades within the Bolshevik party now began to employ the full resources of the state in support of their own class interests.

Irreversible forces were already working to pulverize these hopes, of course, and to destroy even a semblance of economic order. The very process of draining the pipeline for immediate gain made ultimate disaster inevitable unless the flow of goods could be increased at their source. Solving this problem required the total reconstruction of Russia's economic infrastructure, a task difficult enough in any circumstance, but now almost impossible in the time required to maintain the supply of goods and materials needed to keep most plants in operation. It also became clear that little effective assistance would be forthcoming from various state agencies, even for nationalized plants. Despite taking over state banks and other agencies, the Bolsheviks were simply not able to provide the relief workers expected, and whose promise was implicit in the party coming to power.

Quite to the contrary, in fact. The very seizure of state power contributed enormously – if indirectly – to undermining workers' material well-being by precipitating one of the most rapid and least controlled military demobilizations in history, a process that had begun before October, of course, but that now erupted without restraint. The more familiar side of demobilization involved the breakup of the old army: Within weeks hundreds of thousands had left their units, armed, impatient, often angry. But demobilization meant as well the reorientation of industry from war to peacetime needs, an overwhelming task even in conditions of relative political stability. In Petrograd more than 70 percent of all Russian industrial production was directed toward military needs; some 80 percent of the industrial workforce was in defense-related occupations. As late as September 1917 there were also some seven million men still in uniform. As the Bolsheviks pursued their peace plans and the army dissolved, most state procurements ceased. In some places, manufacturers stopped production in mid-stream. Elsewhere, payments were not made when goods were ready in early November.

Delegations of anxious workers pressured Soviet and state of ficials alike for relief as difficulties mounted, but the magnitude of the problem was simply overwhelming. The Council of People's Commissars of the new soviet regime itself may have made matters worse by decreeing in December that strictly military production should cease entirely ("for example, work on artillery shells"), an order that sent shock waves through plants like the Petrograd Trubochnyi works, Russia's largest producer in 1917 of shell casings. Factory committees and unions were simply to "take the most decisive measures to find work" for displaced workers, "sending delegations to the Urals, to the north and so forth, in order to work out necessary arrangements."

Late December and early January thus saw a transition in proletarian Russia from relative enthusiasm and even some limited material improvement to extremely rapid economic decline, deepening insecurity, and in some places outright panic. Petrograd, the very center of proletarian power, with its heavy concentration of armament and other defense industries, suffered most. Between January and April 1918, the supply of goods coming into the capital dropped precipitously in almost every category.[10] Almost 60 percent of the industrial workforce here was forced into the streets.

Aggregate figures are less important for our purposes, however, than the distribution of unemployed workers by industrial branch in Petrograd. And what is most striking is not simply the extent of the crisis, but its unevenness and the singular concentration of unemployed workers in what had been Russia's most favored industries and plants. The greatest declines by far were in chemicals (including rubber) and metals, 79 percent and 74 percent, respectively, in April 1918, relative to January 1917. These two branches, moreover, had employed by far the greatest number of workers in Petrograd before October, some 250,000 (more than 70 percent), excluding those in service occupations. Hence the spring of 1918 saw the emergence of an extraordinary concentration of unemployed workers in what had been the city's best paid, most numerous, and most secure section of the workforce, employed in the largest and most productive plants.

In contrast, Petrograd textile workers, who had suffered severe dislocation during the first years of the war, as we have seen, now suffered only a 15 percent decline (21 percent if one includes the 5,000 or so workers who had been employed in cotton cloth manufacturing, and where production was now further curtailed because cotton imports were shut off). Leather workers declined 31 percent; food workers, 23 percent; and paper manufacturing, 22 percent.

The Bolsheviks' decision to evacuate Petrograd clearly contributed to the crisis. Information here is obviously incomplete, and the process itself was chaotic. Even so, it seems clear that the largest group of outmigrants was not, as one might suspect, skilled workers being transferred to industrial centers elsewhere in the country, but unskilled labor and recent in-migrants. Even allowing for errors in the records, it seems likely that a very large proportion of unemployed workers remaining in the capital were skilled and semiskilled metalworkers and defense

---

10   Carloads of cattle, meat, and fowl dropped more than 85 percent; eggs by 90 percent; sugar and salt by more than 70 percent; similarly with fuel oil, peat, and coal. From an average of some 4.8 million puds of coal per month in 1917, a figure that was already only half of what it had been in 1916, Petrograd received an average of only 0.9 million puds a month in early 1918, and only 0.5 million puds of oil, one-quarter of the city's monthly average for 1917. The declines in other goods were comparable.

workers – the very social group who had enjoyed such relative prosperity before February and had constituted one of the Bolsheviks' strongest bases of support in the capital throughout 1917, and whose revolutionary expectations had been raised the highest.

While the magnitude of the crisis in both objective and subjective terms is hard to measure, it is also difficult to underestimate. So is the suddenness with which the crisis undercut workers' hopes. February and March 1918 were months of precarious uncertainty. Factories that stayed open were unable to get new orders for goods, supplies and materials dwindled, funds dried up, pilfering and theft were common, and decrees from the center were "almost totally ignored." Productivity, of course, fell precipitously. The more mechanized a plant (and thus the higher its complement of skilled and semiskilled workers), the greater the problems of maintaining production, given the lack of fuel and spare parts.[11] It is hardly surprising in these circumstances that some workers sold off machinery and equipment, acts ridiculed by observers as brainless anarchism.

What is important for our purposes, however, is not so much the magnitude of this disaster in statistical terms as the ways in which it may have acted quickly to undermine workers' confidence and sense of unity, and given new impetus to centrifugal tendencies that had largely been overcome in the fall. Questions of worker unity and the broad issues of power were now largely past, partly because many activists were themselves siphoned away from the factories, partly because, as one Bolshevik observer put it, political questions per se were no longer urgent with workers and Bolsheviks in power. What mattered instead was how to get help "from above," and how to manage individual factories, a situation that put enormous pressure on workers' committees. It was now the committees' responsibility alone, for example, even in plants still under private ownership, to decide what to do with demobilized soldiers appearing at their gates and demanding their old jobs back; and it was logically the committees who now assumed responsibility for regulating wages and imposing plant discipline – or, as V. Maiskii put it in April, for finding "disciplinary measures . . . which appeal not to the best, but to the worst side of human nature, not to revolutionary enthusiasm, but to direct self-interest." One historian has described committee activities at this time as "bringing Russia to the brink of economic collapse."[12] But

11   Peat production in the Central Industrial Region, for example, accounting for some 70 percent of the country's total output, fell to near zero precisely because less than 3 percent was still produced by hand, and workers were unable to keep equipment running.
12   Avrich, "Bolshevik Revolution," 58.

more to the point is the way in which committees were forced to assume extensive new responsibilities and powers at precisely the moment they could least effectively meet them, and when any action whatsoever on their part was bound to create dissension. In contrast to 1917, moreover, the "bourgeoisie" was now a much less ready target for worker dissidence. The familiar cry of 1917 that the government was defending "capitalist" interests could no longer explain the lack of effective state intervention.

Particularly heavy tasks fell on committees in plants formerly tied to military production; and where a shift had been made to natural wages, committees could never satisfy demand.[13] Frequently delivery of wages required the use of armed force, although there were many other reasons as well why committees built their militias in these weeks. Goods needed protection, committee meetings were often disrupted, and attacks on warehouses, storage sheds, even rail lines began to occur almost daily. Clashes between groups from different factories also became more frequent as conditions deteriorated. Even dormitories were invaded; and as factory militias tightened their control at plant gates, employment documents came to matter as much as ration cards.

In these circumstances the reemergence of both craft consciousness and factory particularism was inevitable. If maintaining a job in a particular shop or factory became one's primary source of security, local commitments naturally had to increase. The tasks that now seemed most urgent in personal and practical terms were simply not conducive to sustaining broader allegiances, especially since the principal goal for which workers had mobilized in 1917 – the overthrow of capitalism and the creation of a "workers' state" – had now been achieved. In the spring of 1918 one's occupation again came to matter significantly *for workers as well as for others*, and in ways hardly conducive to harmonious social relations even within factory gates.

Evidence is skimpy, and one can only hypothesize about the degree of real conflict that emerged on these grounds, but both the available evidence and the logic of events themselves press in this direction. Facing impossible tasks, unable to meet workers' needs and demands, and now in some places working closely with technical personnel or even former factory administrators, the committees themselves increasingly became the objects of workers' anger, even as (and in fact, precisely because)

13   With the publication of the decree on demobilization the Erikson telephone factory suddenly found all its outstanding military orders canceled outright, and had to ask for "voluntary resignations" until new buyers could be found. Workers responded by demanding six weeks' terminal wages, and in the face of their anger the factory committee yielded, even though this meant all work would soon have to stop.

their powers were increasing. Workers at the Nobel factory (chemicals), Old Lessner (metal processing), and the Okhtenskii powder works (chemicals) turned sharply against their own factory committees in late January and February for "excessive discipline" and "inadequate administration": Those "privileged" to sit on committees were now acting "too much like factory administrators," even "carrying out their orders" and "defending employer interests, not ours." "Comrades elect their factory committee and within a week the grumbling begins." New factory meetings are called, new instructions issued from the workers, and soon "the cycle begins again." Such antagonism, moreover, logically ran both ways, since from the committee members' viewpoint, rank-and-file hostility was hardly fair. It was also a genuine threat to plant operations and led to new demands for discipline, often accompanied by charges of laziness and irresponsibility. Events were coming full circle, back to the very issues of concern and protest that had surfaced in the spring of 1917, except that now they occurred under Bolshevik rule and were thus necessarily focused on the workers' own representatives.

One must emphasize the contradictory nature of these pressures in the late winter of 1918, and appreciate as well the manner in which they simultaneously reinforced a commitment to collegiality and democracy within many enterprises, a desire for autonomy, and at the same time, reinforced social tensions and demands for effective state intervention. Autonomy was necessary because factories everywhere needed to protect themselves from the "paroxysm of requisitioning taking hold of all official agencies," as leather workers expressed it. Effective state intervention remained necessary because of the overwhelming need for orders, goods, and essential supplies. Plant democracy, finally, was essential not only because of workers' own political commitments and values, but also because factory committees themselves recognized that "rank-and-file confidence" was critical to sustaining production, as the chairman of the Nikolaev railroad committee put it, and that complex production problems simply were not amenable to any other form of management on a local level. The trust and cooperation of those they represented, in fact, were the committees' best hope for maintaining any production whatsoever.

Bolsheviks and Workers after October

Lenin's approach to these issues is familiar: Economic chaos was fundamentally the consequence of prerevolutionary circumstances; the factory committee movement reflected dangerous anarchistic and syndicalistic tendencies, as it had even in 1917, despite its importance as a political base for the party; factory administration had to come under the centralizing and coordinating control of trade unions, which themselves had to be integrated into the Bolsheviks' state and party apparatus. Almost without exception, spokesmen for the various chief committees and commissions set up within the new structure of the Council of People's Commissars condemned the autonomy and independence of factory or railroad committees and assailed workers for lack of discipline. "There are no collegial administrations anywhere in the world like ours," a prominent Bolshevik authority on the railroads complained, "where the majority of members are switchmen, engineers, and other rank-and-file employees." N. Osinskii (V. V. Obolenskii), head of the Supreme Economic Council, described workers' control as a form of "disintegrative syndicalism"; trade unionists like A. Lozovskii demanded that committees be restrained. On March 23 the Council of People's Commissars issued a decree "On the Centralization of Railroad Administration," placing "dictatorial power" in the hands of a single person in each administrative center, and thereby making clear its future plans for industrial management everywhere.

Yet it was just this confidence in the efficacy of one-man management that startled committee members themselves. From below, it simply did not seem that most plants and enterprises could be managed in this way. "If it were only the case that a dictatorship would improve matters," workers discussing the March 23 decree insisted, "the question of what to do would be clear. But . . . we've heard these songs sung for years. In the past, these 'iron hands' brought nothing but trouble."

Indeed, it seems apparent that many workers themselves, particularly in Petrograd, had now come to believe, just as earlier, that confusion and anarchy *at the top* were the major causes of their difficulties, and with some justification. The fact was that Bolshevik administration was chaotic. An endless series of miscalculations occurred in these weeks. Scores of competitive and conflicting Bolshevik and Soviet authorities issued contradictory orders, often brought to factories by armed Chekists. The Supreme Economic Council itself operated from Osinskii's suite in the Astoria hotel, issuing dozens of orders and passing countless directives with virtually no real knowledge of affairs. Scores of technicians were dismissed *from above* in this way, despite the insistence of workers' committees that the technicians' skills were crucial to operations, and the view of some officials, like the Commissar of Transport, that this was "absolutely wrong." Demobilization, as we have seen, was unplanned; the evacuation of Petrograd was chaotic. The greater the authority of the center in these weeks, the more factories like the Parviainen works found their own supplies requisitioned.[14] "Accusations of 'anarcho-syndicalism' have always come in Russia from anti-worker, right-wing elements," one railroad committee spokesman put it; "how very strange that representatives of Bolshevik power now join in similar denunciations."

Thus, after the initial weeks of "triumph" and the period of traumatic demobilization and rapid socioeconomic decline in the winter, a third stage began to unfold in the evolution of Bolshevik labor relations after October, one that soon led to open conflict, repression, and the consolidation of Bolshevik dictatorship over the proletariat in place of proletarian dictatorship itself. Brest Litovsk was clearly a turning point, in Petrograd and elsewhere. If we can judge from newspapers like *Petrogradskoe Ekho*, a reasonably objective nonparty evening daily, even to state workers at the Tula armament works the peace treaty seemed "treasonous, . . . destructive to the international proletarian movement, and deeply harmful to the interests of Russian workers, the revolution, and the Russian economy in general." There were also feelings of panic in the capital that the peace would not hold, and that Germans would soon enter the city. Groups of Putilov workers demanded immediate payment of one-and-one-half months' wages, insisting that soviet power was *their* power, and the demands of the lower orders had to be met.

It is hardly surprising that worker opposition to the Bolsheviks also became much more visible in these weeks, partly organized around the Conference of Factory and Plant Representatives in Petrograd and Moscow. A major outbreak of worker protest in Petrograd occurred around the closing of the Constituent Assembly, when a number of demonstrators were killed and wounded. Thousands had gathered at the Obukhov works in the southeastern district of the city and at nearby plants in the Nevskii district, including the important Aleksandrovsk locomotive works. There were also protests at several plants in the Vyborg district, and at the Trubochnyi works on Vasil'evskii Island.[15]

Undoubtedly Socialist Revolutionary and Menshevik activists stirred up some of this protest. The Obukhov works was known as an SR stronghold, and there was clearly still considerable support for both parties, particularly their left faction, throughout the city. Yet in some ways,

14 The Treugol'nik works, for example, shut its doors after a special delegation sent to Rostov brought back forty tank cars of fuel, only to have them requisitioned by the Council of People's Commissars.
15 According to Bolshevik accounts some twenty-one persons were killed, but the number was undoubtedly higher.

these protests seemed more to mark the diffusion and even irrelevance of organized party politics at this juncture. Speakers denounced the shootings, attacking the Council of People's Commissars and the Petrograd Soviet, and expressed outrage at the closing of the Assembly. But the greatest shock seemed to be over the brutality with which Bolshevik forces had turned "on their own." The protests also centered in major state enterprises engaged in war production and directly affected by demobilization. Thus the deteriorating social circumstances of "favored" workers in proletarian Petrograd may well have begun to eclipse the issues of politics per se, while the Bolsheviks' own condemnation of the shootings and their courage in addressing angry workers (particularly at Obukhov, which had suffered a major share of the casualties) tended to depoliticize workers' anger. In any event, in the aftermath of the Assembly's closing, many in Petrograd seem to have become genuinely indifferent to the struggles and fate of other parties as political organizations, as if they belonged to the days before October.

It is largely in this context that one needs to understand the emergence of the Conference of Factory and Plant Representatives as a center of worker dissidence. In mid-January a meeting described in the press as a "Workers' Conference of the Union to Defend the Constituent Assembly" took place in Petrograd, organized in the main, apparently, by self-described "Right" Mensheviks disaffected from their Central Committee over the question of cooperation with the Bolsheviks. They were determined to build a new, representative movement "from below," shedding formal party affiliations. Workers from a number of plants soon joined them in forming the conference as a broad-based assembly, hoping among other things to counter what one observer lamented as the Petrograd workers' new "passivity and indifference." The first "extraordinary" meeting of the conference convened in Petrograd on March 13 in the midst of new protests over the evacuation, which occurred most intensely just before Brest Litovsk when it seemed the city might fall under German control.[16]

Delegates attended from at least fifteen major metalworking plants, including the Obukhov, Trubochnyi, and Aleksandrovsk mechanical plants, which were scenes of protest in January, and a number of print shops, which were, of course, Menshevik strongholds. The delegates' mood was angry, and focused directly on those seemingly responsible for

16   At Putilov anxious workers demanded information from the Metalworkers' Union about evacuation plans. Union leaders had no satisfactory answers, but castigated workers in turn for meeting during working hours. At the Westinghouse plant workers sent an angry delegation to the city soviet with similar questions. To the question "Where do we go?" soviet spokesmen are reported to have told them, "wherever you like," suggesting that they take "whatever they like" with them!

the "chaos of evacuation," shortages of food and other goods, and the arbitrary exercise of authority, but the delegates were also confused and desperate. "The workers are lost," a spokesman from the Rechkin plant declared; "it seems to them that everything is falling apart."

Reports of the March 13 conference appeared in Social Democratic newspapers as well as in what remained of the nonparty press. On April 7 the Menshevik Central Committee officially endorsed the conference, yielding to the Right Menshevik conception of "appealing broadly to workers' gatherings in order to facilitate the formation of working-class consciousness and reconstructing labor unity," or, as M. I. Liber put it at a Moscow committee plenum one week later, allowing workers to feel "the strength of their class position." By this time there were apparently representatives in more than forty Petrograd enterprises, officially "representing," if that is the proper term, some 55,000 or more workers. Five meetings were reportedly held between March 13 and the end of the month. According to an account published in Den', 33 of the 110 participants at the March 13 meeting were Socialist Revolutionaries, 35 were Social Democrats (Unityists), one was a Popular Socialist, and 42 were non-party. On April 3 a second "extraordinary" meeting took place where the Bolsheviks were attacked directly for "assaulting the workers' movement with tsarist methods."

What is important in all this, however, is not only the weakening of Bolshevik support, but also the powerful, contradictory pressures building from below in the spring of 1918 for solutions to problems that, at the time, were essentially insoluble. What seems most striking about the disaffection that the conference demonstrated is the focus on the breakdown of order, disillusionment with revolutionary politics generally (party affiliations notwithstanding), and the insistence on a greater degree of local plant autonomy, despite overt hostility toward plant administrators and the delegates' own factory committees. Conference delegates attacked not only the Bolsheviks, but also the soviets "which have ceased to be the political representatives of the proletariat and are little more than judicial or police institutions." They condemned the Red Guards for their brutality, but demanded more protection for their dormitories and factories, and asserted their own right to use force. They demanded freer trade regulations, following their Menshevik and Socialist Revolutionary leaders, an end to restrictions on movement, and also insisted on the right to manage their own affairs, while bitterly attacking trade unions and their own factory committees for "not fulfilling their obligations to the workers":

The war has ended but our misfortunes are only beginning. There is little work; a senseless, disorderly evacuation has virtually destroyed industry.

Workers are being thrown out on the streets by the tens of thousands. It is impossible to go anywhere, and there is nowhere to go. Our last coins are being spent. A hungry summer is coming. We cannot expect help from anyone. Are the trade unions doing much for the unemployed? They aren't concerned with the unemployed, and aren't even concerned with the employed. The unions organize the economy, not the workers. Factory committees organize commissions to fire workers, organize bureaucratic organs which don't need our trust and have long lost it. And they don't help us.

There were strong overtones here as well of rank-and-file hostility to the more privileged workers who now may have controlled many factory committees, and whose factory positions, in any event, were more secure. In the view of many, an "irresponsible technical apparatus" was now in charge of many factories, falsely representing rank-and-file interest: "[Our committees] ought immediately to refuse to do the things that are not properly their real tasks, sever their links with the government, and become organs of the free will of the working class, organs of its struggle." "We state honestly and openly that we have lost all faith in those above us." These views, moreover, were no less strident for the fact that those "above" them, in committees and unions, were also struggling with authorities in almost precisely the same terms, as we have seen, and being condemned in return for anarchism and acts "contrary to proletarian state interests."

Obviously the generalized (and to some extent, internally contradictory) protest was partly the result of the efforts of Socialist Revolutionary and Menshevik activists. But evidence on the social composition of conference delegates indicates that the protest was also related more acutely to Petrograd's critical socio-economic circumstances. In effect, only two major industrial branches – printing and metalworking – were represented in conference meetings, and the largest number of "delegates" (the nature of actual representation remains an open question) was from twenty-six metalworking plants formerly engaged in defense production, including seven that had been entirely shut down. Otherwise, the only other significant representation came from some sixteen typographers and print shops, strongholds of Menshevism. Only three of the city's food processing plants sent delegates, all from the Rozhdestvenskii district, and only two delegates represented workers in wood crafts or manufacturing. Most striking is the almost complete absence of textile workers. The one exception was the Tornton (Thornton) plant in the Vyborg district, where approximately one-third of all the factories "represented" in the conference were located.

Employment statistics help explain the textile workers' absence. For the twenty-eight factories with delegates in the conference for which we have data, the average unemployment rate on April 1, 1918 (contrasted with January 1, 1917) was 50.5 percent. In contrast, the average unemployment rate for some thirty-six major nonparticipating factories for which we have data was only 21.6 percent. The Skorokhod leather works, for example, which did not send delegates to the conference, had almost the same number of workers employed in April 1918 as it had had in January 1917 (4,900). The Bodganov works (11,669) had a similar experience, and the Laferm tobacco works actually showed an employment increase from 2,363 to 2,507. Most importantly, the relatively small employment declines we have noted among Petrograd textile workers affected primarily those working in smaller shops; employment in larger plants, which had experienced their "shake out" many months earlier, held rather steady. Thus, the Nevskii cotton plant continued to employ more than 1,700 workers in April 1918, compared to 2,056 in January 1917; the Kersten plant in Vyborg, 1,070 compared to 2,252; and the Sampsonievskaia works, also in Vyborg, 1,618 compared to 1,592 in January 1917. Although other factors also undoubtedly affected workers' connections with the Conference of Factory and Plant Representatives, the importance of social circumstances seems to have been paramount.

It is possible, albeit deductively, to get an additional fix on conference participants by taking into account the patterns of evacuation from Petrograd, and the general content of discussions at conference meetings. The animosity shown toward factory committees makes it unlikely that conference leaders were closely tied to workers' control organizations or the unions. Also, most of the skeleton crews that continued to work even at plants that had closed, tended to be, in the main, skilled workers and technical personnel. Finally, as we have noted, the least skilled laborers in the metal plants constituted the largest group of evacuees, whereas the most recent arrivals to the city, those with the closest ties to the countryside, were also the largest category of workers to leave voluntarily. We can thus deduce that the largest group of conference supporters were most probably semiskilled workers who had moved into important jobs with the great increase in military production during the war, but who now found their hopes for security and advancement crushed by an economic collapse that left them vulnerable and expendable.

The only other significant group of conference delegates, the printers, undoubtedly came in part because of their close association with the Mensheviks, but also, in all likelihood, because of the specific threat Bolshevism represented to the livelihood of what had become in 1917 one of the city's most rapidly growing industrial sectors. Thus they may well have been pushed toward the conference by social circumstances they shared, or felt they were about to share, with the metalworkers, as well as by political convictions.

By April 1918 a range of dissidence had thus emerged in Petrograd, reinforced by – and doubtlessly also reinforcing – the various forms of craft and factory particularism that had become so important in conditions of social dislocation and economic disaster. All dissident elements, from the overworked and harassed factory committees to the idle and anxious unemployed, demanded effective state intervention, particularly in Petrograd in the matter of evacuation, but elsewhere as well. Among many there was also an abhorrence of Bolshevik political repression and arbitrariness, as well as varying degrees of sympathy for the oppositional parties. The question for conference leaders was whether these various strains could be effectively mobilized.

On May 9, 1918 at the town of Kolpino near Petrograd, armed guards opened fire on an angry group of workers protesting at the local soviet over shortages of jobs and food. Word of the shooting spread quickly, and while the incident was hardly the first of its kind, it triggered a massive wave of indignation.[17] The Conference of Factory and Plant Representatives met to demand "the complete liquidation of the current regime." Work temporarily stopped at a number of plants.

Popular outrage spread rapidly. Like the Lena shootings in 1912, Kolpino quickly emerged as a focal point for more generalized anger and frustration. In Moscow, Tula, Kolomna, Nizhnii-Novgorod, Rybinsk, Orel, Tver', and elsewhere, workers gathered to issue new protests, in some cases identifying themselves openly with the conference. "The suffering of the masses has reached an extreme limit," one group insisted; "to live like this any longer is absolutely impossible." In Petrograd, textile workers went on strike for increased food rations, and a wave of demonstrations spread in response to still more Bolshevik arrests until, at the end of May, a long meeting of the conference asked workers to postpone further protests "until a more favorable moment," when better organization and coordination could lead to a citywide, and perhaps nationwide, general strike.

It is possible to trace quickly this first major wave of labor protest through to its climax in early July, and to understand, finally, its various dimensions. Contemporary newspapers and journals document more than seventy different incidents in Petrograd between Kolpino and the beginning of July, including strikes, demonstrations, and anti-Bolshevik

17 Protests centered at Putilov, Siemens-Schuckert, Rechkin, and especially Obukhov, which sent a delegation to visit additional factories and mobilize further protests. On May 11 and 12 thousands gathered at meetings in the Narvskii and Nevskii districts and on Vasil'evskii Island. Some twenty-one factories sent delegations to attend the victims' funeral.

factory meetings. Some of these were meetings convened in conjunction with Petrograd soviet elections held at the end of June. Others were less focused, sometimes addressed by speakers from various oppositional parties, sometimes not. Of the latter sort, the greatest number by far were protests against some form of Bolshevik repression: shootings, incidents of "terroristic activities," and arrests. In some forty incidents workers' protests focused on these issues, and the data surely understate the actual number by a wide margin. There were as well some eighteen separate strikes or other work stoppages with an explicitly anti-Bolshevik character.

Many of the protests included calls for democratic political reforms. Seven large gatherings in May passed resolutions demanding that the Constituent Assembly be reconvened, following the program of the conference. There were an additional four meetings, only one of which seems to have been attended primarily by printers, where workers specifically demanded freedom of the press. Very few protests, in fact, appear directly related to essentially social issues: unemployment, the cost of living, and wages. Of these, most were strikes and protests over food shortages of the sort that triggered the Kolpino incident, particularly on the part of Petrograd textile workers, a contingent that was largely female and whose factories were still running.

Thus, on the surface at least, workers' protests seemed to be assuming a new and stronger political content, and one can readily understand in examining them why hopeful observers like Aronson became convinced that by June 1918 "a committed opposition . . . [had] gained the upper hand." Political values and affiliations seemed to lie at the heart of these protests; indeed, one can hardly deny their political character or import. Such protests, moreover, were not limited to Petrograd;[18] and in many places, elections to local soviets began to return large numbers of Menshevik and Socialist Revolutionary deputies, even majorities.[19]

On closer examination, the broader social dimensions of protest are also apparent, and in ways that suggest that social issues continued to

18   In Moscow, Tula, Iaroslavl', Briansk, and other places, gatherings like those in Petrograd took place in plants like the Tula armament works and the huge Sormovo complex in Nizhnii, formerly one of the country's major defense producers. In Moscow a gathering of more than four thousand railroaders in the Aleksandrovsk shops endorsed the conference's demand for civil liberties and an end to Bolshevik rule.

19   See the discussion by Vladimir Brovkin, "The Mensheviks' Political Comeback." On elections to the Petrograd Soviet in July, which returned a comfortable Bolshevik majority, see David Mandel. *Petrograd Workers and the Soviet Seizure of Power*, 403–9.

be as important as politics, despite the political effect of almost every demonstration and work stoppage. As before, the overwhelming preponderance of protests came from displaced metalworkers. More than 75 percent of all incidents I have been able to catalog in Petrograd between the end of March and early July 1918 involved this group.

The largest number of incidents by far continued to center around such plants as the Patronnyi works and the Arsenal in the Vyborg district, the Obukhov works in the Nevskii district (where some 2,500 workers, with close ties in the past to the Socialist Revolutionaries, continued to struggle to fill state orders for locomotives), and Putilov – all of which had been devastated by the chaos of demobilization and evacuation. Only a handful of protests, largely short strikes over food rations, came from the city's textile plants, despite reports that workers here felt "things are worse now than under the tsar."

Although the evidence is incomplete, the patterns still seem evident. They correlate with what we have been able to surmise about the social composition of the conference delegates. Further corroborating evidence comes from the geographical distribution of the protests, which shows a heavy concentration in two districts – the Nevskii (Obukhov, Nevskii shipbuilding, and the Aleksandrovsk mechanical shops) and Vyborg (Arsenal, Old Lessner, the Old Baranovskii works, and the Patronnyi plant). There were also a number of protests in the Narvskii district, but on examination these seem almost entirely connected to Putilov. Other districts, including Vasil'evskii, were relatively quiet. Even in rough outline, this configuration reinforces the conclusion that protests came overwhelmingly from the ranks of displaced, semiskilled metalworkers who were, of course, geographically concentrated in the Nevskii and Vyborg districts.[20]

Finally, we can also see further indication in these weeks of continued conflict between factory committee personnel and their rank and file; between higher paid skilled workers and their less well off, less skilled

20   We know, moreover, that residence patterns in the Vyborg district before 1918 had been relatively stable. This district, and to a lesser extent the Nevskii region, had a much smaller annual influx of migrants than the Vasil'evskii district and other outlying neighborhoods. While Vyborg district's population had increased over the past two decades, it also retained a large core of long-term, established city residents. Given the concentration of protests here in May and June 1918, it is reasonable to assume that the protesters were themselves largely long-term residents. Even though we lack direct evidence, this pattern is at least consistent with what we know about the evacuation during which the greatest number of departures were from the ranks of the unskilled and recent migrants. See James H. Bater, *St. Petersburg: Industrialization and Change* (London: Edward Arnold, 1976), esp. Chap. 4 and pp. 165–8, 250, 375.

comrades, and, of course, between virtually everyone still struggling with the tasks of production at the factory level and those attempting to impose discipline from above. At Siemens-Schuckert and Obukhov, for example, there were incidents of violence as unemployed workers attempted to prevent others from entering the plant; at Putilov, shop committees openly refused to implement the directives of the factory committee and demanded a citywide meeting to discuss inequalities in wages. At a meeting of Vyborg district factory committees in mid-June, organized by the metalworkers' union, representatives stressed how negligent and hostile attitudes toward the committees greatly hindered production.

Throughout, strong anti-Bolshevik feelings remained evident. When meetings began in mid-June in connection with the Petrograd Soviet elections, in many plants prominent Bolsheviks had real difficulties making themselves heard.[21] But the importance of political commitments must be set in social context; the way the political drama was played out in Petrograd at the end of June makes clear that issues such as the Constituent Assembly and democratic government faded.

On June 20 V. Volodarskii, a popular and talented Bolshevik publicist and member of the Soviet Executive Committee, was killed on his way to an election meeting. This time reprisals were particularly swift. Large numbers of people were arrested, apparently including many workers. Again, angry meetings took place in factories around the city. At the Obukhov works a large delegation of sailors joined workers in issuing an appeal to the Conference of Factory and Plant Representatives to declare a one-day strike of protest on June 25. The Bolsheviks responded by "invading" the whole Nevskii district with troops and shutting down Obukhov completely. Meetings everywhere were forbidden.[22]

This time, however, workers were not so readily pacified. In scores of additional factories and shops protests mounted and rapidly spread along the railroads. On the evening of June 26, the conference met in another "extraordinary session." Reports estimated that out of 146,000 workers still in Petrograd, as many as 100,000 supported the conference's goals. As a result, a general strike was declared for Tuesday July 2.

It is not really necessary to describe subsequent events in any detail, or to examine the organization and ultimate failure of the July 2 general

21   Zinoviev, Lunacharskii, and Volodarskii seem to have been treated with special rudeness, perhaps because they were all experienced and familiar orators whose style now angered their listeners.
22   The Nevskii district was placed under "martial law," which, according to one report, produced an effect "like an exploding bomb."

strike. Zinoviev and others took quick counteraction, particularly on the railroads. Any sign of sympathy for the strike was declared a criminal act. More arrests were made. In Moscow, Bolsheviks raided the Aleksandrovsk railroad shops, not without bloodshed. Dissidence spread, particularly on the Nikolaev, Moscow-Kazan', and Mosow-Kursk railroads.

After meeting all night on June 28, the Council of People's Commissars issued its famous decree nationalizing all major branches of industry. As we know, the measure had long been contemplated, but resisted in part because it meant that the state would formally assume, at least indirectly, the responsibilities and unmanageable tasks of administration in nationalized plants. But it also meant, of course, a greater degree of state control. The irony was that the decree finally implemented what many workers had long demanded, even before October; but it was now the *party's* need for security, rather than the workers', that had become paramount. On July 1, as if to emphasize the point, machine guns were set up at main points throughout the Petrograd and Moscow railroad junctions, and elsewhere in both cities as well. Controls were tightened in factories. Meetings were forcefully dispersed.

All of this proved sufficient for Lenin's government to maintain order. When the morning of July 2 arrived, most trains were running. By evening it was clear that striking workers and the Conference of Factory and Plant Representatives both had failed, and that proletarian Russia had reached another important turning point.

The End of Proletarian Independence

The events of late June signaled a crisis that extended through the assassinations of Mirbach and Uritskii, additional strikes, the attempt on Lenin's own life, and the unleashing in force of Red terror as the summer came to an end. Scores of additional arrests decimated the Conference of Factory and Plant Representatives. There was soon little question that the era of workers' control was over, supplanted now by the programs of War Communism and by a party dictatorship determined to enforce its own view of proletarian interests on recalcitrants everywhere.

Yet the history of proletarian Russia in the important first months of Bolshevik power indicates the weakness of seeing the consolidation of party rule in political terms alone, and the limits of explaining the workers' failure to maintain their own independence primarily in terms of Bolshevik repression. Without discounting the importance of force, one must recognize too that the failure of July 2 was evidence of

Petrograd workers' inability to mobilize effectively in defense of their own self-defined interests and goals, as they had in 1917, particularly in Petrograd.

It is now possible to understand this failure, and to consider briefly what it suggests about the workers' movement and party–labor relations more broadly in the immediate post-October period. The first point to be emphasized is that in contrast to 1917 the promise of personal security and material betterment implicit in earlier labor activism was singularly absent in the spring of 1918; and unlike the Bolsheviks, neither the Conference of Factory and Plant Representatives nor other oppositional groups had either a compelling explanation for the new disasters besetting Russian workers, nor a clear and convincing vision of a viable alternative social order. The conference called for a general strike in the name of the Constituent Assembly, civil liberties, a single indivisible republic, and an end to repression, but these had little to do with solving the problems of food supply, unemployment, or production, or otherwise constructing an effective state economic apparatus. Indeed, the disaster was beyond short-term relief. This was true as well before October, and one might argue that the promises of 1917 were false and illusory. But they nonetheless had political force, whereas in the aftermath of October, no promises of betterment were persuasive.

Important here, in my judgment, is that workers themselves had largely completed the "expropriation" of Russia's bourgeoisie by the spring of 1918, and "capitalists" could no longer be identified as the primary cause of privation and want. Mobilization in the course of 1917 involved a discernible social enemy. Bolshevik strength grew not only because of the party's relative organizational strength, but also because of the explanatory content of party views and programs, and because workers were compelled by economic circumstances to organize both offensively and defensively against the "bourgeoisie." The complementary tasks of proletarian social and Bolshevik political revolution thus coalesced; so too did workers and party "professionals" in a period of increasing economic privation and social polarization, when Bolsheviks (and others) could provide most workers with seemingly clear ideas of an alternative, socialist, mode of production.

The destruction of Russia's "bourgeois order" complicated Lenin's own task of maintaining a high degree of political consciousness among workers after October, but it made those of the conference virtually impossible. The distinction drawn earlier between a Russian state and a bourgeois government no longer served to galvanize political resistance. Even as workers demonstrated against Bolshevik officials, the party remained a workers' party. Many voting in the soviet elections for Mensheviks and especially Left Socialist Revolutionaries were seeking, in effect, "better" Bolsheviks. Efforts to build a more politically democratic order thus had little foundation in the broader patterns of social dissidence; party politics themselves seemed irrelevant.

Even more important, and for reasons that should now be clear, the Petrograd labor movement in 1918 was very narrowly based in social terms. It may well have been, as delegates to conference meetings believed in late June, that the overwhelming majority of workers in the city "supported" conference goals. But those most active in the movement seem to have been preponderantly semiskilled metalworkers, who, despite their strong protests in the spring of 1918, had long been closely tied to the Bolsheviks. Probably their political loyalties still lay in that direction. Their dissidence seems to have been directed more toward obtaining effective relief than in support of Mensheviks or other oppositioal parties; and votes of protest are never the same as a commitment to the opposition. In any event, their concerns were primarily with issues of social security and well-being, something no political group could effectively meet in the first months after October.

Part of the opposition's difficulty also turned on problems associated with the workers' own local organizations, particularly factory committees. It is conceivable that in somewhat better economic circumstances, the Conference of Factory and Plant Representatives might have effectively allied with committee leaders in support of a more democratic political and economic administration. Yet not only were factory committees relatively powerless to protect worker interests in the spring of 1918; they clearly became themselves focal points of worker dissidence, partly as a result of hierarchy and social stratification within the workplace, partly because their tasks now were necessarily so onerous, especially in Petrograd metal plants. Paradoxically, proletarian dictatorship itself helped break elements of worker solidarity after October.

One can similarly understand from this perspective why even many opposition figures within the party had trouble accepting democratic organizations as an institutional basis for Bolshevik administration, and why many factory committees themselves came to repress democracy in their plants. The pressures for authority developed strongly, in other words, under conditions of labor conflict, particularism, and devastating economic privation. The deeper Russia's economic crisis, in fact, the more desperate the need for effective state control, something which in the end must have left even dissident metalworkers in Petrograd hoping that in the longer run Bolshevik power would still represent their interests.

In the spring and early summer of 1918 most Bolsheviks understood that conflicts among workers and the danger of anarchy posed real threats and jeopardized any socialist order whatsoever. Broader class consciousness and a muting of particularism also remained essential to any effective defense against the Whites and foreign intervention. In this respect the protests of May and June and the attempted general strike of July 2 may only have further impressed party leaders with the dangers of depoliticization and worker passivity, and the need to strengthen class consciousness as in 1917. These events also undoubtedly strengthened tendencies toward identifying and attacking "class enemies," and made new forms of repression more acceptable. In this sense, in the end, the ensuing civil war may have been as much an instrument of ultimate Bolshevik repression as it was simultaneously a danger and further threat; in any event, it marked as much the end of proletarian independence as the foundation of a new workers' state.

Glossary

Cheka   Bolshevik national security force designed to combat anti-Bolshevik resistance.

Lunacharsky, A   Prominent Bolshevik party member, later Soviet Commissar of Education.

Mirbach, Count Wilhelm   German ambassador to Moscow; assassinated by Left SRs in 1918.

Uritsky, Mikhail   Bolshevik head of the Petrograd Cheka assassinated by Left SRs in 1918.

Zinoviev, G   Prominent Bolshevik party leader.

Further Reading: The Working Class

D. H. Kaiser (ed.), *The Workers' Revolution in Russia, 1917: The View from Below* (Cambridge University Press, 1987).

D. Koenker, *Moscow Workers and the 1917 Revolution* (Princeton University Press 1981).

D. Koenker and W. Rosenberg, *Strikes and Revolution in Russia, 1917* (Princeton University, 1989).

D. Mandel, *The Petrograd Workers and the Soviet Seizure of Power* (Macmillan, 1984).

S. Smith, *Red Petrograd: Revolution in the Factories, 1917–1918* (Cambridge University Press, 1983).

6

Bolshevik Women

Barbara Evans Clements

Originally appeared as Barbara Evans Clements, "The Revolution," *Bolshevik Women* (Cambridge: Cambridge University Press, 1997): 120 – 42.

Editor's Introduction

As was the case in so many fields, the role of women in the history of the Russian revolution was largely ignored until recent decades. Most scholars agree that the incorporation of women into the historiography of the revolution begins with the pathbreaking work of Robert McNeal, *Bride of the Revolution: Krupskaya and Lenin* (University of Michigan Press, 1972), Richard Stites, *The Women's Liberation Movement in Russia: Feminism, Nihilism and Bolshevism, 1860–1930* (Princeton University Press, 1978), Barbara Evans Clements, *Bolshevik Feminist: The Life of Alexandra Kollontai* (Indiana University Press, 1979), and Barbara A. Engel, *Mothers and Daughters: Women of the Intelligentsia in Nineteenth Century Russia* (Cambridge University Press, 1983). Since that time, much important work has also been done on Russian women in the rural agricultural economy and in the urban workplace.

Barbara Clements has been at the forefront of this scholarship for years. Expanding upon her earlier biography of Alexandra Kollontai, Clements has now written the definitive history of female activists in the Bolshevik party – before, during and after the 1917 revolution. Her book is a model of the kind of work that still needs to be done on non-Bolshevik women, from the radicals of the Menshevik, Socialist Revolutionary and Anarchist parties, to the aristocratic supporters of the opposition to Bolshevism and the less politically visible women whether in professional positions (teachers, etc.) or in the labor force.

In the chapter of her book on Bolshevik women which is included below, Clements describes in rich detail the varied paths to revolutionary activism chosen by the *Bolshevichki* (Bolshevik women). She begins with the situation on the streets of the capital (St. Petersburg, renamed Petrograd at the outset of the First World War and renamed Leningrad after the death of the Soviet leader in 1924), where an International Women's day demonstration combined with crowds of working class women to inaugurate the chaos that led to the abdication of Nicholas II. Discussing the rest of 1917, Clements details the involvement of Elena Stasova and Evgeniia Bosh as well as of Kollontai and Krupskaya as they made their way toward positions of leadership in the party. In their dedication to radicalizing women in support of the Bolshevik cause, they and other colleagues established a separate section of the party, from which they were able to mobilize and coordinate a variety of activities, including publishing the widely read women's magazine, *Rabotnitsa*.

The women tirelessly devoted themselves to public forums and political organizing with surprisingly successful results, as Clements shows. Not all their efforts succeeded, however. Barriers remained in place, including the patriarchal tradition of maintaining the top party positions for men and the continuation of the tendency to rely on authoritarian rather than democratic means of deciding certain policy issues. Nevertheless, Clements has made a decisive claim for the role of women in the Bolshevik party that should become an integral part of all future discussions of the revolution.

Bolshevik Women

Barbara Evans Clements

The Revolution

By February 1917 outrage over worsening economic conditions and despair at continuing losses in the endless war extended from the top to the bottom of Russian society. In December 1916, cousins of the tsar murdered his favorite, Grigorii Rasputin, the disreputable Siberian faith-healer who had come to symbolize the moral bankruptcy of the government. During the early weeks of 1917, as strikes rumbled through the capital's grimy factory districts, liberal Duma delegates talked in tones of rising desperation about forcing the blockheaded monarch to share power. At the same time, poor women stood in long lines on the frozen streets, waiting to buy bread. Frustrated, angry, and cold, they shouted their complaints to one another as they trudged home. Occasionally someone picked up rocks off the street and threw them at shop windows. A prescient tsarist police official reported to his superiors in late January that these women, "mothers of families, who are exhausted by the endless standing in line at the stores," were "a store of combustible material." "One spark," he predicted, "will be enough for a conflagration to blaze up."[1]

That conflagration began on 23 February (8 March by the Western calendar), International Women's Day. Four years after Samoilova's peaceful meeting at the stock exchange, working-class women streamed out of their workplaces and homes, shouting for bread and an end to the war. They marched through the industrial neighborhoods of the city, and as they passed factories and tenements they called on the people inside to join them. The swelling crowds then headed toward Nevskii Prospekt, the broad boulevard that ran through the heart of Petrograd. Police blocked the bridges that led to the city center, so the women slid down embankments along the river and walked across the ice. Crowds of tens of thousands ebbed and flowed through the downtown all morning and afternoon. When the springlike warmth of the day faded with sunset, the demonstrators went home, but the next morning even more people gathered to protest the government's incompetence and the hardships of the war. Over several days of disturbances,

1   Quoted in Z. Igumnova, *Zhenshchiny Moskvy v gody grazhdanskoi voiny* (Moscow, 1958), 11.

troops sent out to control the marchers mutinied. Liberal and socialist leaders began to organize a new government. Even the military high command turned against the emperor. On 3 March 1917 Nicholas II abdicated the throne at the request of his generals. The Romanov dynasty was dead and the Russian Revolution had begun, sparked by a Woman's Day march.

Elena Stasova heard the noise of the demonstrations from a prison cell. She had been back in Petrograd since the autumn of 1916, there on a furlough from exile that her father had arranged so that she could recuperate once again from tuberculosis. Stasova had spent the fall and winter with her parents, away from illegal activities. "I'm living completely properly here," she wrote to Krupskaia in November.[2] The Okhrana was watching her day and night, and she did not want to betray anyone else to them or give them an excuse to send her back to Minusinsk.

The day after the Woman's Day demonstrations, 24 February, Stasova went with her father to a meeting of Petrograd attorneys hastily called to discuss the rising tide of protest. There she heard a rousing speech by Alexander Kerensky, soon to be the minister of justice in the Provisional Government. Later that night, the police came banging on the Stasovs' door. They searched Elena's room and found nothing incriminating, but arrested her anyway. They intended to make sure that as many known revolutionaries as they could find would sit out the uprising in jail.

Stasova thus spent the early days of the February Revolution locked up in a women's prison. She could hear shots echoing from the nearby streets, but news of what they signified did not penetrate the stone walls. For two days she speculated on events with her cellmates, also revolutionaries picked up in the police sweep. Then, on 27 February, the streets fell silent. After some hours, footsteps rang along the prison's stone floors, the door opened, and several guards, all men, ordered the women to come with them. Stasova's cellmates gathered around her, waiting for her, the prison veteran, to decide what to do. Stasova hesitated; the solemn men standing in the hall gave no sign of their intentions. Perhaps they were Black Hundreds, the anti-Semitic thugs who had preyed on revolutionaries in the past, with the government's blessings. Perhaps they would lead the women to some darker corner of the prison and assault them. And yet, Stasova thought, it was pointless to stay in the cell. Maybe if they came out, they could manage to escape. She told the others to get their things. Then they all followed the taciturn guards down the corridor. The men opened the first door they came to and

2   E. D. Stasova, *Vospominaniia* (Moscow, 1969), 130.

stepped aside. Stasova feared that an ambush awaited them on the other side, but she saw no point in turning back. She remembered feeling like a mother hen leading her chicks as she went through the door, down another empty hallway, and through yet another door. The guards did not follow. Now the women were standing in a courtyard, across which they could see another group of men. For a moment they hesitated in fear. The men turned, caught sight of them, threw up their hands in a happy salute, and began shouting, "Hurrah, freedom!" They were, it turned out, a harmless lot, the prison fire brigade. Only now did Stasova and her charges realize that they were being released. Within twenty-four hours she had located the Bolshevik city committee and resumed her old place as its secretary.[3]

Other Bolshevichki came back to political life in less dramatic ways. Those who were abroad hurried to arrange passage home. Bosh and Kollontai returned from Scandinavia in March, Inessa and Krupskaia from Switzerland in April. By April, Samoilova was also back from Moscow, where she had been in hiding, and Bosh's sister, Elena Rozmirovich, had made her way from exile in Siberia. The Petrograd veterans, Kollontai, Stasova, Krupskaia, Samoilova, and Rozmirovich, stayed on to work in the capital city. Inessa soon went home to Moscow, where Zemliachka was just coming out of retirement. Bosh set off for Kiev.

All the Bolsheviks, male and female, emerged from the underground euphoric, but also confused and dazed by the chaotic liberation going on around them. Alexandra Rodionova, a tram conductor in Petrograd, later remembered the moment: "It seemed so recently that I had walked with the demonstrators around the city. I yelled 'Down with the tsar!' and it seemed to me that I had lost touch with solid ground and flew in giddy uncertainty. Yes, I had participated in many strikes and demonstrations. But this had happened secretly; I had never taken a clear political position. And suddenly, all at once, the unknown future became real." Giddiness also beset T. F. Liudvinskaia, a seamstress living in Paris, when she heard of the revolution. "We Bolsheviks felt as though we had grown wings," she wrote many years later. "We ran to meetings, got together, argued, quarreled, and made up, argued again tirelessly."[4] The arguments arose out of their attempts to understand what the events in Petrograd meant and how they should deal with them. Revolutionaries who had contemplated revolution as a distant possibility now had to cope with the reality.

3   Ibid., 132.
4   *Zhenshchiny goroda Lenina* (Leningrad, 1963), 89; T. F. Liudvinskaia, *Nas Leninskaia partiia vela. Vospominaniia* (Moscow, 1976), 102.

Bolshevichki respond to the revolution

There was much to delight the Bolshevichki in the events of the spring and summer of 1917. As the old regime collapsed, it took with it the structure of authority throughout Russia, creating enormous social instability that was frightening but at the same time exhilarating.

Never had the working class in the cities been more energetic. Demonstrations were a daily event, and, just as significant from the Bolshevik point of view, the representation of the poor by socialist parties was institutionalized in soviets, popular, elected assemblies that sprang up in all the major cities. Trade unions became assertive in their negotiations with suddenly weakened industrial managements. Women's organizations found their voice as well: the feminists spoke out (to the irritation of the Bolshevichki), but so too did female trade unionists and the wives of soldiers. By mid-summer the Russian military, still at war with Germany and Austria, had begun to disintegrate and the peasants in the countryside were seizing control of the nobility's land.

People with political ambitions experienced some difficulty in orienting themselves amid this sea of change. The liberal Constitutional-Democratic Party, the radical SRs and SDs, and a host of other alliances and organizations agreed on the necessity of building a representative, republican government. But they agreed on little else. Each party brought to the revolution its prior experience and beliefs, but, however well developed these were, they could provide only general guidance in the fundamentally changed situation. To respond to Russia's new realities effectively, political actors had to read the shifting popular mood, calculate their options carefully, and act decisively. The Bolsheviks, particularly Lenin and Trotsky, proved the ablest of all the contenders in this dangerous game. By September they had amassed considerable support in the cities, particularly St. Petersburg and Moscow. In October they overthrew the stumbling Provisional Government and seized power in the name of the soviets.

The Bolsheviks arrived at this course of action under Lenin's persistent prodding. In March, most of them had come out of the underground under the assumption that the Provisional Government would be led by liberals, who would cooperate with socialist parties based in the soviets. Their expectations in this regard had been governed by the notion, widespread among Social Democrats of both factions, that Russia must pass through a capitalist stage of development, during which it would be ruled by a liberal parliamentary government. Lenin had rejected this proposition long before 1917 and had adopted instead

Trotsky's conception of "permanent revolution," according to which Russia could move directly from monarchy to rule by the left without any intervening phase of bourgeois supremacy. Once the revolution actually began, Lenin rejected as well any power-sharing arrangement with moderate politicians and became suspicious too of coalitions with Mensheviks and SRs. Boldly he called instead for an immediate transfer of power to the soviets, for an equally immediate withdrawal of Russia from the war, and for a confrontational posture toward all political rivals.

The prominent Bolshevichki followed Lenin enthusiastically. Kollontai and Bosh carried his earliest calls to arms back to Russia in March, before he himself returned. He made peace with Bosh in a series of letters in January and February, in which he never mentioned their earlier disagreements. She then presented his case to the party organization in Petrograd in late March, before heading off to Ukraine to preach his message in Kiev. Kollontai, with whom he had always been on good terms, became Lenin's most ardent and visible supporter in April 1917, when many Bolsheviks were convinced that he was vastly overestimating what they could accomplish. In Moscow, Inessa was an equally convinced disciple, as were Sofia Smidovich and Zemliachka. Stasova seems to have wavered a bit, perhaps because she felt more kindly disposed toward the Mensheviks, but soon she was persuaded as well.[5]

The attitudes of less well-known Bolshevichki are harder to assess, for they are not as fully documented. The majority of Bolsheviks, male and female, appear to have come around to supporting Lenin by May. The crucial issue then became developing the tactics that would win support among the workers and soldiers, and gain elective seats in the soviets. The party sent speakers to all the many public meetings, arranged delegations to march at demonstrations, and published newspapers, flyers, and pamphlets. It put forward slates of candidates for election to the soviets and to the municipal dumas, assemblies that had been part of city government under the old regime. Bolsheviks also devoted

5   On Kollontai, see Barbara Evans Clements, *Bolshevik Feminist: The Life of Aleksandra Kollontai* (Bloomington, Ind., 1979), 103–09. On Bosh, see "Protokoly i rezoliutsii Biuro TsK RSDRP(b), mart 1917 g.," *Voprosy istorii KPSS*, no. 3 (1962): 145–47, 149–51. On Inessa, see R. C. Elwood, *Inessa Armand* (Cambridge, 1992), 206–08. Speeches in April by Inessa and Smidovich are recorded in "Protokoly pervoi (Moskovskoi) oblastnoi konferentsii tsentral'nogo-promyshlennogo raiona RSDRP(b) proiskhodivshei v g. Moskve (2–4 maia) 19–21 aprelia 1917 g.," *Proletarskaia revoliutsiia*, no. 10 (1929): 137–42, 148. On Zemliachka, see *Oktiabr' v Moskve* (Moscow, 1967), 66; and RTsKhIDNI, f. 17, op. 4, d. 180, l. 29. On Stasova, see her *Vospominaniia*, 134–35; and N. N. Sukhanov, *The Russian Revolution*, ed., abridged, and trans. Joel Carmichael (New York, 1955), 405.

a good deal of time to building their own organization, recruiting new members, and expanding and regularizing the party's administrative structure.[6]

Bolshevichki as agitators

The Bolshevichki were engaged in all the activities that prepared the way for their party's seizure of power in October. (See table 1.) They made speeches, wrote newspaper articles, served as soviet and duma delegates, did clerical work, ran committees, and, in the fall, as the party began to plan its coup, built bombs and trained with the pro-Bolshevik militia units, the Red Guards. As they had in the past, Bolshevichki did what was needed, with little regard being given to their gender. Men were more likely to work with the army and navy than were women, but many Bolshevichki also went into the barracks to speak to the troops. The revolution actually intensified the party's long-standing practice of engaging women in all its activities, because it sustained the crisis atmosphere that had nurtured egalitarianism throughout the underground years, and it strengthened the commitment most Bolsheviks professed to women's equality. The revolutionary year 1917 was so filled with general ideas of freedom that in fact it quickly became a special point of official pride with the Bolsheviks that they had so many women working in their organization.

The most invigorating projects for the Bolshevichki were those that took them out among the poor to do what the party came to call "agitation," that is, spreading the party's message. For years these women had struggled to find a sufficient audience, often discovering not only that the police thwarted their efforts but that the workers themselves were unreceptive. With the fall of Nicholas II the situation changed quickly. Now the party had the funds to publish not just one newspaper but several, aimed at different audiences, and printing presses were free to print whatever the party could afford to publish. Still more encouraging was the fact that the Bolshevichki found lots of people willing, even happy, to listen to them. They responded by writing newspaper pieces, pamphlets, and leaflets, cultivating personal contacts with sympathizers in their neighborhoods, training workers and soldiers to spread the party's message among their mates, and speaking at public meetings.

6 On the Bolsheviks in Petrograd in the spring and early summer, see Alexander Rabinowitch, *Prelude to Revolution: The Petrograd Bolsheviks and the July 1917 Uprising* (Bloomington, Ind., 1968).

Table 1   Fields of activity of Bolsheviks, February–October 1917

	Women's activities (%) (N = 159)	Men's activities (%) (N = 685)
Journalism	6.3	9.3
Government[a]	31.4	33.7
Military	8.8	16.9
Party	50.9	33.3
Trade unions	2.5	6.7
Total	99.9	99.9

Note: This table records all types of work by women, including more than one activity per individual in some cases. The column for men records only one activity per individual.
[a] Soviets at all levels, and city dumas.

Public speaking was the one of these activities of which the Bolshevichki possessed the least experience, but it became a major means of communicating with the public in 1917. Dozens, if not hundreds, of Bolshevichki mounted rickety platforms on shop floors or street-corners to issue to milling crowds the party's call to arms. This was not an entirely unprecedented activity for women in Russia. Female radicals had addressed the demonstrations of 1905 and the revolutionaries' secret gatherings throughout the underground years, but the best-known women orators in Russia before 1917 were the feminists, philanthropists, and other social activists who spoke at conferences and other sorts of meetings permitted by the government. These women had been careful to stay within the limits imposed on them by the police. The Bolshevichki were under no such constraints after the fall of the tsar, so they could model themselves on such socialist firebrands as Emma Goldman and Sylvia Pankhurst. Shouting to be heard in an era before microphones, they condemned the Provisional Government and preached revolution to crowds that numbered in the tens of thousands.

Alexandra Kollontai was widely considered to be the party's most accomplished female orator in 1917. Very pretty and always well dressed, Kollontai looked like the noblewoman she was, but when her voice, accented with the tones of the privileged, began to sail out over the crowds, her message was all confrontation. "Where is the people's money going?," Kollontai demanded to know in a speech in the spring of 1917,

To the schools, the hospitals, to housing, to maternity and childcare benefits? Nothing of the sort is happening. The people's money is going to finance bloody skirmishes. The bankers, the factory owners, the landlord-moneybags are responsible for this war. They all belong to one gang of thieves. And the people die! Stand under the red banner of the Bolshevik Party! Swell the ranks of the Bolsheviks, fearless fighters for soviet power, for the workers' and peasants' power, for peace, for freedom, for land![7]

Not all the Bolshevichki who took the podium in 1917 were as eloquent as Kollontai, but many of them seem to have received warm receptions from their audiences. There can be little doubt that the revolution weakened popular resistance to the idea of women speaking in public. Of course there were instances when the Bolshevichki were shouted down, but even the military was willing to listen attentively to female orators with whom they agreed. Kollontai spoke frequently to audiences of soldiers and sailors, as did Liudmila Stal and Elena Rozmirovich. Rozmirovich's sister, Evgeniia Bosh, was so successful in rousing the troops to support her that she even managed to lead a regiment of infantry into battle against the Provisional Government in the fall of 1917.

Bosh circulated among the men of the southwestern front in Ukraine throughout the summer and fall of 1917; historian Allan Wildman has described her as "the flaming evangel" of the Bolshevik organization there.[8] Bosh's public persona was very different from Kollontai's, suggesting that in 1917 there was no one model of the ardent female revolutionary, and no one means to success with crowds. Kollontai, who rejected the notion common among Russian revolutionaries that women should pay little attention to their physical appearance, cultivated her looks. She also wrote about heterosexual relationships and had a series of love affairs. Her reputation as a sexual rebel, her beauty, the ardor of her delivery, and the uncompromising tenor of her speeches intrigued her audiences and made her a celebrity, something she enjoyed immensely. Bosh, although equally pretty, was sober, dour, even puritanical. She wore simple, dark blouses and skirts, and severe hairstyles. She, like Kollontai, persuaded with impassioned words and calls to confrontation, but she also overawed the crowds with her intellect and impressed them with her powerful will. There was nothing alluring about Evgeniia Bosh on the speakers' platform, but her school-teacher

7 Quoted in A. M. Itkina, *Revoliutsioner, tribun, diplomat. Stranitsy zhizni Aleksandry Mikhailovny Kollontai*, 2nd ed. (Moscow, 1970), 143–44. Excerpts of recordings of Kollontai's speeches can be heard in the documentary film *A Wave of Passion*, prod. Kevin M. Mulhern, Kevin M. Mulhern Productions, 1994, videocassette.
8 Allan K. Wildman, *The End of the Russian Imperial Army*, 2 vols. (Princeton, 1980–87), vol. II, 360.

seriousness appears to have been as effective in winning the support of the soldiers as Kollontai's glamor.[9]

Bosh, in her history of the revolution in Ukraine (written in 1924), described with muted pride one of her more successful appearances. It occurred early in October of 1917, after the Keksgolm Regiment of the Second Guards Corps came to the town of Zhmerinka in central Ukraine, on leave from front-line duty. Also known as "The Wild Division," these men were reputed to be little more than a collection of bandits, but Bosh took their unsavory reputation as a sign that they might be favorably disposed toward her anti-war, anti-Provisional Government message. She therefore persuaded their officers to let her speak to the regiment. When she and two bodyguards entered the courtyard of their barracks on the outskirts of Zhmerinka, Bosh had no idea what sort of reception she would receive. These men were armed, she had reason to believe that some of them had been drinking heavily, and no one could tell her exactly where their political sympathies lay or how they would receive a woman speaker.

"The complete quiet of the audience there, more than a thousand strong, the tense attention of those present, the noticeable excitement and fussing of the organizers – all this created the impression of a calm before a storm," Bosh wrote later. For two hours she dissected before them the evils of the Provisional Government and explained the necessity of replacing it with a soviet government representing poor people. The men listened to her quietly and attentively. Then they began to ask her questions. When Bosh finally told the soldiers, some four hours later, that she had to leave, the company's musical band rushed off to find its instruments, and the Wild Division escorted her to her car with hurrahs and music. One month later, on 8 November, the Chief of Staff of Southwestern Front, N. N. Stogov, gruffly testified to Bosh's effectiveness in a report filed with his superiors: "In the majority of units of the [Second Guards] regiment, the unhindered comings and goings of agitators, such as the Jewess [sic] Bosh . . . has contaminated all the units of the regiment."[10]

It is difficult to determine how many Bolshevichki became public speakers in 1917, for the sources often record that a woman was a party agitator without going into greater detail as to her precise activities. "Agitation" was a catch-all term that embraced all the many ways of building support in the working class and the military through public speaking, producing and distributing leaflets and newspapers, and

---

9   There is rare footage of Kollontai speaking at meetings in *A Wave of Passion*.
10   E. B. Bosh, *God bor'by* (Moscow, 1925), 29; L. S. Gaponenko, ed., *Oktiabr'skaia revoliutsiia i armiia. Sbornik dokumentov* (Moscow, 1973), 103.

sending emissaries to talk with the leaders of trade unions and soldiers' and sailors' committees. Most Bolshevichki were involved in agitation in 1917, so it is likely that many of them did some speaking, if only to small gatherings in a neighborhood or workplace.

Bolshevichki also worked to establish the party's political presence in popular organizations, particularly the soviets and the trade unions, and especially those unions with strong female membership. For example, Ekaterina Shalaginova, Anna Sakharova, and Iadviga Netupskaia, factory workers in Petrograd, organized a laundresses' union in their neighborhood in the spring of 1917. At the same time, Kollontai was coordinating the creation of a city-wide laundresses' union. Bolshevichki in Petrograd, Moscow, and several provincial cities competed energetically with feminist organizations to gain support among the *soldatki*, the soldiers' wives who had organized themselves to press for higher military allotments. Liudmila Stal spent most of the year at Kronstadt, the naval base in the Gulf of Finland, winning over the sailors there and paying attention as well to their wives. Other Bolshevichki attempted to recruit female factory workers already in unions, particularly those employed in textile mills and in military-related manufacturing.[11]

Bolshevichki made these efforts because they realized that there were many more women in the factories than there had been in the past, and that among these tens of thousands, hundreds at least were receptive to the party's ideas. The female percentage of the industrial labor force had grown enormously during the war, from 26 percent in 1914 to 43 percent in 1917.[12] The revolution had then opened channels of communication to women which had formerly been blocked by the old regime, and had made political participation the order of the day. Furthermore, the faltering economy was feeding the discontent of the working class throughout 1917. Women angry over miserable working conditions, falling wages, and food shortages, and emboldened by the general spirit of liberation, were indeed, as the Okhrana official had written, "a store of combustible material." Although most of them probably continued to believe that politics was, in the common phrase, "not a woman's business" (*ne zhenskoe delo*), a substantial minority, especially

11   *Leningradki. Vospominaniia, ocherki, dokumenty* ([Leningrad], 1968), 65; Institut istorii partii pri TsK KP Belorussii, Filial instituta Marksizma-Leninizma pri TsK KPSS, *Pod krasnym znamenem oktiabria* (Minsk, 1987), 191–94; N. D. Karpetskaia, *Rabotnitsy i velikii oktiabr'* (Leningrad, 1974), 27–61; *Oktiabriem mobilizovannye. Zhenshchiny-kommunistki v bor'be za pobedu sotsialisticheskoi revoliutsii* (Moscow, 1987), 56–57, 76–77; *Zhenshchiny goroda Lenina*, 77–86.
12   Barbara Evans Clements, *Daughters of Revolution: A History of Women in the USSR* (Arlington Heights, Ill., 1994), 29.

in Petrograd, was becoming involved in demonstrations, meetings, and unions. Bolshevichki did not rush off en masse to seek out the female proletariat; most of them divided their time between a variety of agitational activities aimed at men as well as women. But more Bolshevichki than in the past, in Petrograd, Moscow, and such provincial cities as Saratov, did become engaged at least part-time in "work among women" during the revolutionary year.[13]

The revival of work among women

Before the leaders of the party's earlier efforts among women – Inessa, Samoilova, Krupskaia, and Stal – returned to Petrograd, a Bolshevichka previously unknown to them had already begun setting up an organization to reach out to the female proletariat. She was Vera Slutskaia, a dentist from a merchant family in Minsk who had joined the Social Democrats in 1902. Slutskaia came to Petrograd in March 1917 from the Caucasus and went to work as secretary of the party committee in the working-class neighborhood of Vasileostrovskii raion. Quickly she emerged as a good speaker. Just as quickly she realized that there were poor women in her neighborhood who could be persuaded to support the Bolsheviks. Soon Slutskaia had obtained authorization from the raion party committee to organize a subcommittee specializing in work with women. She then went to the city committee with a proposal for work among women that called for publication of pamphlets and leaflets addressed to the female proletariat, the revival of *Rabotnitsa*, and the creation of a city-wide "bureau" to coordinate activities. The usual opposition arose to what committee member Olga Livshits criticized as "a special women's organization of the party," but after several meetings and some debate, Slutskaia secured authorization and funding for everything she had requested. When Samoilova, Inessa, Krupskaia, and Kollontai arrived in the city, Slutskaia already had a small organization ready to work with them.[14]

The new *Rabotnitsa* (the police had closed the prior one after the war began in August 1914) became the centerpiece of work among women in 1917, the leading voice of the Bolshevichki's agitation aimed at the female proletariat, and the forum in which they worked out an analysis

13   On the efforts in Moscow, see Elwood, *Inessa Armand*, 211–13. On Saratov, see Donald J. Raleigh, *Revolution on the Volga: 1917 in Saratov* (Ithaca, N. Y., 1986), 133.
14   *Slavnye bol'shevichki* (Moscow, 1958), 265–67; *Zhenshchiny goroda Lenina*, 90, 93–94; "Protokoly pervogo legal'nogo Petersburgskogo komiteta bol'shevikov i ispol'nitel'noi komissii za period s 15 marta po 7 aprelia (c 2 po 25 marta) 1917 g.," *Proletarskaia revoliutsiia*, no. 3 (1927): 318, 350–51, 355, 360–61, 382.

of the place of women's issues in the revolution. Edited by Samoilova, Klavdiia Nikolaeva, and Praskovia Kudelli (the last was a teacher and alumna of the Bestuzhevskii courses), *Rabotnitsa* was a lively, engaging, tabloid-sized magazine containing poetry, fiction, news stories on conditions in the factories, articles on the history of the revolutionary movement, and editorials on political events. Samoilova, Nikolaeva, and Kudelli, in addition to editing, wrote many of its articles and managed its publication and distribution. They enlisted Stal, Kollontai, Zlata Lilina, and a few male journalists as contributors and specially commissioned female workers to file reports on political developments in their factories. The magazine soon found a large readership in Petrograd, with occasional copies making their way to the other major cities of the empire and even to places as far away as Barnaul in Siberia.

As they had done in 1914, the editors of *Rabotnitsa* declared their socialist bona fides often. An unsigned editorial in the first issue justified the existence of a newspaper for women by arguing that other periodicals did not cover issues of particular concern to them, such as maternity insurance and child care. Such issues would only be addressed politically, the article asserted, when women joined men in the struggle for socialism. In later articles the editors declared that they did not blame men for women's problems, as feminists did. Instead they emphasized that they considered the old regime to be the enemy, and explained that their purpose was to draw women into a common effort with their working-class brothers to construct a better world for all people.[15]

Despite such diplomatic disavowals, the *Rabotnitsa* of 1917 was actually more feminist than its predecessor, in the sense that it accorded women's emancipation an even higher priority within the revolutionary process. Its editors and contributors denounced the burdens heaped on women by patriarchal traditions and capitalism. They declared women's rights to political and legal equality, to improved wages and working conditions, to a greater voice in the union movement, and to protective labor regulations. They argued that women had now proven their entitlement to those rights. "If a woman is capable of climbing the scaffold and fighting on the barricades," Samoilova wrote, "then she is capable of being an equal in the workers' family and in workers' organizations." Samoilova and other contributors, emphasizing the point that the Bolshevichki had stressed earlier, repeatedly argued that the revolution would not be won without women's participation. "The time has passed when the success of the workers' cause will be decided only by organizing men," an unsigned editorial in the first issue proclaimed.

15   "Rabotnitsa, 1914–1917 goda," *Rabotnitsa*, 10 May 1917, 1–2.

And they called on women to become politically active so as to guarantee their liberation. "Many female comrades say that everything will be done without us," wrote Prokhorova, a *Rabotnitsa* staffer, in a May issue, "but comrades, what is done without us will be dangerous to us!"[16]

The 1917 *Rabotnitsa* was also more critical of the sexist behavior of men, its disclaimers to the contrary notwithstanding. This criticism usually came from female factory workers themselves and was aimed at their male comrades. Correspondents attacked trade-union leaders for discriminating against female workers, called for female representation on factory committees and union boards, and asked male workers to put women's demands on their political agenda. Male factory workers "are all for equal rights in words," wrote M. Boretskaia, who identified herself as a *rabotnitsa* in a June issue, "but when it comes to deeds it turns out that a chicken is not a bird and a *baba* is not a human being."[17] Other contributors supported the principle of equal pay for equal work and criticized proposals floated in various unions to lay off married women. *Rabotnitsa* also published letters and articles publicizing the sexual harassment of women in the workplace. And there was even an occasional suggestion, seemingly aimed more at Lenin and his associates than at female readers, that the Bolshevik Party should increase its efforts to reach out to working-class women.[18]

Rabotnitsa carried these central ideas of Bolshevik feminism to tens of thousands of party members. Samoilova and Kudelli hoped that the newspaper would do more than cultivate the support of working-class women; they hoped its propaganda would also help to allay the fears of male Bolsheviks that female activism would be detrimental to the party's interests. That had been an important goal of the 1914 version as well. But the *Rabotnitsa* of 1917 was not nearly so supplicatory as its predecessor. It contained the usual denunciations of the feminists, particularly in articles by Kudelli, and pledges that its editors were not seeking to divide the revolutionary movement. But far more common in its pages than reassuring words to the skeptical were assertions of women's rights

16   N. Sibiriakova [Samoilova], "Rabotnitsy i professional'nye soiuzy," *Rabotnitsa,* 30 May 1917, 6–7.
17   *Rabotnitsa,* 28 June 1917, 5. *Baba* was a mildly pejorative term for "woman." "A chicken is not a bird and a *baba* is not a human being" is one of the most frequently quoted examples of Russian folk misogyny. It is noteworthy for being wrong in both its propositions.
18   All of the following references are to *Rabotnitsa,* 1917. On layoffs, see 13 August, 11–14. On sexual harassment, see 20 May, 7; 30 May, 11; and 28 June, 13–14. On equal pay for equal work, see 10 May, 12; 14 June, 3, 6–8; 19 July, 8; and 18 October, 12. On the attitudes of trade unionists toward women workers, see 30 May, 1, 6; 19 July, 8; and 1 September, 9–10. On the party paying more attention to women, see 13 August, 1.

and denunciations of their continuing inequality. The developments of 1917 were inspiring Samoilova, Kudelli, and Nikolaeva to demand that women's liberation become a high revolutionary priority, and perhaps were awakening them as well to the possibility it would not be unless women themselves made it so.[19]

Bolshevichki in revolutionary leadership

If power is, as writer Carolyn Heilbrun has observed, "the ability to take one's place in whatever discourse is essential to action and the right to have one's part matter," then many Bolshevichki had power in 1917.[20] They participated in the revolutionary discourse in the pages of *Rabotnitsa* as well as on street-corners and in barracks all over Russia. Bolshevichki also spoke up within the narrower confines of party committees. In fact, in the sample analyzed for this study, more women held party office in the seven months between February and October 1917 than had ever been the case earlier, during the entire period of the underground. Of the Bolshevichki in the sample, 36 percent, had served on city or émigré committees before 1917; 57 percent occupied comparable positions in 1917.

The party proved more hospitable to women than other political institutions of the new Russian democracy. A comparison of all political posts held by Bolsheviks in 1917 reveals that males were more likely to serve as soviet or municipal duma delegates, women as party officials. (See table 2.) These differences probably reflect the party's relative enlightenment; it was easier for a women to become a member of a Bolshevik committee than to be elected to a city soviet's executive committee. Yet it was also true that women's opportunities were, in general, greater in the major cities than in lesser ones, as had been the case before 1917: 60 percent of the women in the sample who held party office in 1917 did so either in Moscow or Petrograd. In less cosmopolitan locations, more Bolshevichki stayed in the rank and file. (See table 3.)

The process of choosing party officials remained as unsystematized in 1917 as it had been in the underground. Some were elected by the local organization as a whole, some by the committee members them-

---

19 On Samoilova's motivation, see Clements, *Bolshevik Feminist*, 111–12; Sibiriakova [Samoilova], "Rabotnitsy i professional'nye soiuzy." For Kudelli's articles against the feminists, see P. F. K., "Ob organizatsiiakh burzhuaznykh zhenshchin," *Rabotnitsa*, 30 May 1917, 10–11; P. F. K., "O respublikanskom soiuze zhenskikh organizatskiiakh pri soiuz ravnopravikh," *Rabotnitsa*, 14 June 1917, 9–10.
20 Carolyn G. Heilbrun, *Writing a Woman's Life* (New York, 1988), 16.

Table 2   Offices held by Bolsheviks, February–October 1917

Office	Women (%) (N = 182)	Men (%) (N = 458)
Duma		
Delegate (raion, city)	4.9	4.1
Executive committee	2.8	0.2
Factory committee member	0.5	2.0
Party		
Local party committee member (raion, city, uezd)	37.3	20.7
Military-revolutionary committee member	4.9	10.9
Provincial party committee member	6.0	6.3
Central Committee member	1.6	3.5
Soviets		
Local soviet delegate (raion, city, guberniia)	30.7	30.3
Local soviet executive committee member	6.5	15.1
Soviet congress delegate	2.2	3.3
Trade unions		
City trade union board member	1.6	2.6
Guberniia trade union council member	0.5	0.6
All-Russian trade union council member	0.5	0.4
Total	100.0	100.0

Note: Only one office held per individual was coded.

Table 3   Levels of party office-holding, February–October 1917

Level of party office	Women (%)	Men (%)
Raion, uezd	41.9 (36)	9.4 (13)
City	36.0 (31)	59.4 (82)
Guberniia	17.4 (15)	21.0 (29)
Central Committee	4.7 (4)	10.1 (14)
Total	100.0 (86)	99.9 (138)

Note: Figures in parentheses are base Ns for the adjacent percentages.

selves, and some were appointed by higher-ranking Bolsheviks. The criteria employed in judging candidates appear to have been equally unstandardized, so it is difficult to determine why some Bolshevichki became party officials while others did not. Of course personal merit and desire to serve were important qualifications. Seniority was not; many of the Bolshevichki who held party office in 1917 had only recently joined the Social Democrats and had not held party office in the past. A primary qualification seems to have been the long-standing one of education. Of the Bolshevichki in the sample who had attended secondary school, 62 percent held party office in 1917, as compared with 32.5 percent of those with less schooling.[21] (See table 4.)

The revolution seems also to have brought some class bias to the process of selecting party officials, for women of noble birth were slightly less likely to hold office than were middle-class women. Yet this bias worked in the other direction too. Women from the peasantry and the working class were decidedly less likely to serve than were their more privileged comrades, a difference that probably resulted in part from their lack of education. It is also probable that working-class and peasant women were impeded by the difficulties that beset all poor women – the necessity of earning an income, family responsibilities, and pressure from the men in their lives. Given the notions about the backwardness of working-class women that prevailed among Bolsheviks themselves, one cannot rule out the possibility of discrimination against them within the party. (See table 5.)

Most Bolshevichki who held office in 1917 did the same sort of work that women had done in the underground, that is, they were party secretaries handling the 1917 equivalent of *tekhnika* in neighborhood committees. They kept records, collected dues, made job assignments, wrote pamphlets and newspaper stories, and organized meetings and demonstrations. The earlier tacit understanding that it was the men's role to set policy and the women's to handle administration continued right through the revolution. Nor did that great upheaval, which led to enormous growth in the size of the party, lead to upward mobility for Bolshevichki. Most of those women who held office both before and during 1917 occupied positions at the same, lower level of the hierarchy (although they rarely did exactly the same jobs). (See table 4.) Thus the upper reaches of the party remained more or less exclusively male preserves. As in the past, the higher the party committee, the lower the number of women to be found on it.

And yet, the relationship between the Bolshevichki and power was not so simple as these generalizations suggest. There was space within which an enterprising woman could maneuver during the revolution. Raion and city committees remained democratic because of the party's

---

21   For a general discussion of the selection process, see Robert Service, *The Bolshevik Party in Revolution: A Study in Organisational Change, 1917–1923* (New York, 1979), 49–51.

Table 4   Patterns in Bolshevichki's party office-holding, February–October 1917

Of the Bolshevichki who held party office between 1898 and 1917:
   27.6% (40) did so both before 1917 and in 1917;
   33.8% (49) did so in 1917 but not before;
   38.6% (56) did so before 1917 but not in 1917.
Of the Bolshevichki holding office both before and during 1917:
   30.0% (12) held a higher-ranking office in 1917 than that held earlier;
   60.0% (24) held an office in 1917 equivalent to that held earlier;
   10.0% (4) held an office in 1917 lower than that held earlier.

Note: The total N = 145 (all women who held a party office at any time between 1898 and November 1917), which constitutes 45.6 percent of all female Old Bolshevichki in the sample.

Table 5   Social origins and party office-holding by Bolshevichki, February–October 1917

Social origins	Held party office (%)	Held no party office (%)	Total (%)
Nobility	40.0 (12)	60.0 (18)	100.0 (30)
Intelligentsia	29.0 (9)	71.0 (22)	100.0 (31)
Sluzhashchie	42.1 (8)	57.9 (11)	100.0 (19)
Meshchanstvo	62.9 (22)	37.1 (13)	100.0 (35)
Workers	31.2 (24)	68.8 (53)	100.0 (77)
Peasants	12.1 (4)	87.9 (29)	100.0 (33)

Note: Figures in parentheses are base Ns for the adjacent percentages. Total N = 225.

egalitarian traditions and the institutional informality that inevitably accompanied such rapidly changing times. This openness made it possible for Bolshevichki to "take [their] place in [the] discourse," to use Heilbrun's phrase, and make their voices heard. Women could also still rise to the very top of the party. Bosh, Stasova, and Zemliachka became leaders of national stature in 1917, and Kollontai earned appointment as commissar in the first Bolshevik government.[22]

It would also be mistaken to assume that the Bolshevichki measured their standing within the party by criteria such as rank and upward mobility. They would have denounced such calculations as disreputable. The Bolshevichki were, after all, revolutionaries. In 1917 their inten-

22   On the democratic nature of the party in 1917, see ibid., 50–53; Rabinowitch, *Prelude to Revolution*; Alexander Rabinowitch, *The Bolsheviks Come to Power: The Revolution of 1917 in Petrograd* (New York, 1978). Donald J. Raleigh has analyzed similar characteristics outside Petrograd. See his *Revolution on the Volga*, 128–36.

tions were not to aggrandize themselves as individuals, or to build their own regime so as to hand power and privilege around among themselves. They were going to lead Russia to a new plateau of historical society from which power and privilege would be banished. Being a Bolshevik was not yet a career planned with personal advancement in mind; it was a calling, at least in the view of the Bolshevichki. One's position in the party was simply the place from which one made a contribution. In an article in *Rabotnitsa* in June 1917, an anonymous female recruit voiced the devotion to the cause so central to the Bolshevichki's sense of vocation: "With all my soul I want to participate in this life, in this struggle," she wrote, "with all my strength to help it go forward." Such notions of a great popular enterprise to which the individual committed herself as an act of faith and devotion were as old as revolutionary movements themselves, but they had particular appeal to women, for they drew on traditional notions of the feminine duty to serve.[23]

The Bolshevichki had other reasons to think that the grass-roots organizing in which most of them were engaged was as important as the debates of the Central Committee. As Marxists they believed that the great moving mass of the people would carve out Russia's future. Historians today agree, and argue that the Bolsheviks managed to seize power not only because Lenin and Trotsky were audacious, but also because the party had a firm base of support in Petrograd, Moscow, and other major cities by the fall of 1917.[24] That support grew from the success of the rank and file in getting the party's message out, as well as from the radicalizing of public opinion as the revolutionary process continued. If power means taking part in the discourses that matter, then the Bolshevichki who were agitators in 1917 had power, for they believed, with good reason, that the discourses that counted in that revolutionary year were taking place in the streets; and that is where they were, in the streets, handing out leaflets, talking to factory workers, marching in demonstrations, swaying crowds.

There is another element of the Bolshevichki's attitudes toward power that is more difficult to probe, but that is as important as their revolutionary consciousness in shaping their behavior. Their conception of the party as serving a cause, and their contempt for the usual business of politics, were attitudes shared with many male Bolsheviks, but the Bolshevichki could embrace these attitudes with special fervor because they, as women, were more distanced from politics than were

23   *Rabotnitsa*, 14 June 1917, 7. See also 10 May, 3–4; 20 May, 7–8; and 14 June, 15–16.
24   See Rabinowitch, *The Bolsheviks Come to Power*, 83–93; Service, *The Bolshevik Party in Revolution*, 43–45.

male Bolsheviks. Throughout Europe, politics – the discourses that mattered and the distributions of power, status, and wealth that they validated – had long been a male-dominated endeavor to which women gained access only through their male kin. The political marginalization of women was particularly great in the early twentieth century, for the rise of capitalism and parliamentary government had decreased the importance of kinship and had concentrated power instead in public organizations, chiefly government departments and political parties, to which women were denied access. Strangers to the multifarious negotiations and the web of personal obligations that sustained such institutions, even politically active women such as the Bolshevichki tended to regard all politics as alien territory.[25]

Krupskaia and Inessa avoided it altogether. Each was entitled by virtue of her loyal work as Lenin's assistant to claim a role in the top leadership in 1917, but neither chose to do so, preferring instead grass-roots organizing. Krupskaia settled in a neighborhood in Petrograd where she was able, for the first time in decades, to work in her first love, education. As a member of a municipal duma, a neighborhood-level assembly that was part of the city government of St. Petersburg, she labored to keep the schools open. Inessa, for her part, spent the year in Moscow, her home town, as a low-ranking committee member, involving herself also in agitation. She reemerged as a major figure only after the Bolshevik seizure of power. It is instructive by way of contrast to note that Grigorii Zinoviev, the male Bolshevik who had stood closest to Lenin during the prerevolutionary period of the emigration, simply stepped off the train from Switzerland directly into positions on the Petrograd committee as well as the Central Committee.[26]

Neither Krupskaia nor Inessa ever explained her withdrawal from the center of party life in 1917. Stasova wrote later that both women had been nominated for positions as Central Committee secretaries in April 1917, but neither was elected. Robert H. McNeal, Krupskaia's biographer, argues that Krupskaia thought she had been displaced by Stasova, but this seems unlikely. There was ample work and responsibility for all three women, and Krupskaia and Stasova had always been on cordial terms. Krupskaia and Inessa probably wanted to get back in touch with Russia after years as émigrés. Whatever their motives, they sought out

---

25   On the development of political parties and the consequences for women in the United States in the late nineteenth and early twentieth centuries, see Suzanne Lebsock, "Women and American Politics, 1880–1920," in Louise A. Tilly and Patricia Gurin, eds., *Women, Politics, and Change* (New York, 1990), 55–58.

26   On Krupskaia in 1917, see Robert H. McNeal, *Bride of the Revolution: Krupskaia and Lenin* (Ann Arbor, Mich., 1972), 168–82. On Inessa, see Elwood, *Inessa Armand*, 205–14.

political anonymity while male Bolsheviks who had occupied important positions as émigrés continued as the party's top leaders.

Kollontai, for all her prominence in that year of the revolutionary agitator, also remained outside the ranks of the top leadership, even after she was elected to the Central Committee in August 1917 on the strength of her popularity with the crowds. She attended the meetings of the Central Committee in September and October, and participated in its debates over whether to seize power, but there is no evidence that she sought to enter the inner circle, the Politburo. Nor did she establish strong ties to any of the men at the top. Instead, Kollontai focused her attention on becoming preeminent among the Bolshevik feminists and cultivated her relationships with Samoilova, Nikolaeva, and Kudelli, rather than Lenin, Trotsky, or Stalin. She also continued to devote herself to efforts to reach out to working-class women. By identifying herself so completely with "work with women," Kollontai consigned herself to a marginal place in the party leadership.[27]

Stasova, on the other hand, occupied an important position in the leadership. In April she was elected technical secretary of the Central Committee, where she served under Iakov Sverdlov, the organizational secretary. Sverdlov formulated policy regarding party structure and financing and made major personnel assignments; Stasova and a staff of three or four women, including Sverdlov's wife Klavdiia Novgorod-tseva, maintained correspondence with provincial party organizations, assigned workers to various jobs, kept financial records, and distributed some of the party's money.[28]

Stasova was returning to the sort of work she had left when she went to the Caucasus in 1907, but she took it up in much changed circumstances. The party was now legal, it was huge and growing, and she was serving in its national leadership. But Stasova did not seize the opportunities the revolution had created to redefine herself. Rather, she chose to do what she had always done – administration. While Kollontai took to the podium and Krupskaia and Inessa worked among the poor, Stasova stayed in an office, content to hand out assignments and to write memos. She made few public appearances and published no

27   On Kollontai in 1917, see Clements, *Bolshevik Feminist*, 103–21. On her increasing standing among Bolshevichki working with women, see *Rabotnitsa*, especially the coverage of organizational meetings for a woman's conference held in October (18 October, 14–15).

28   V. V. Anikeev, *Deiatel'nost' TsK RSDRP(b)–RKP(b) v 1917–1918 godakh* (Moscow, 1974), 60, 63–64, 72, 83–84, 116, 123, 125, 135; Akademiia nauk SSSR, Institut istorii, *Velikaia oktiabr'skaia sotsialisticheskaia revoliutsiia. Khromika sobytii, 12 sentiabria-5 oktiabria 1917 goda* (Moscow, 1961), 217, 232.

articles. She considered *tekhnika* "most important work,"[29] as indeed it was, but her unwillingness to explore other activities, to mingle with the crowds or to raise her voice to welcome the revolution, seems curious, if not timid, nonetheless.

Nor did Stasova rethink her old idea that she should defer to others in policy-making. As technical secretary she was a voting member of the Central Committee, entitled to speak up in the group's deliberations. She attended the meetings regularly, but, according to the committee's published minutes, rarely said anything. Rather, she acted as a secretary in the clerical sense of that term, listening intently and taking notes, but not participating in discussions. The revolution appears to have changed nothing in her definition of her revolutionary role. She continued to be what she had been in the underground – a good soldier who executed the decisions of others.[30]

Krupskaia, Inessa, Kollontai, and Stasova do not appear to have been told by the men on the Central Committee in 1917, many of whom were their close comrades, that they were not welcome in the top counsels of the party. Instead, they appear to have chosen of their own accord not to assert themselves in those counsels. This is not to say that their choices, and the similar ones made by so many other Bolshevichki in the revolutionary year, were not affected by assumptions about the division of labor between women and men that had been established in the underground among Bolsheviks. Clearly they were. Women at the center of the party and in its rank and file went where they felt capable and accepted, that is, into agitation and administration. But the Bolshevichki were not simply conforming to the collective expectations about them as women. Speaking to demonstrations or running a neighborhood committee also enabled them to live out their vision of the revolution as a great forward movement of the masses, guided by enlightened revolutionaries closely connected to the people. The personal preferences of the Bolshevichki, like the personal preferences of

---

29   Stasova, *Vospominaniia*, 130.
30   For protocols of Central Committee meetings, see "Protokoly pervogo legal'nogo Peterburgskogo komiteta . . . za period s 15 marta po 7 aprelia"; Akademiia nauk SSSR, Institut istorii, *Revoliutsionnoe dvizhenie v Rossii v aprele 1917 g. Aprelskii krizis* (Moscow, 1958), 15–16, 17–24, 30–35, 107, 508; "Protokoly i rezoliutsii Biuro TsK RSDRP(b), mart 1917 g."; "Protokoly Tsentral'nogo komiteta RSDRP(b), avgust–sentiabr' 1917 g.," *Proletarskaia revoliutsiia*, no. 8 (1927): 322–51; "Protokoly Tsentral'nogo komiteta RSDRP(b), noiabr' 1917 g.," *Proletarskaia revoliutsiia*, no. 11 (1927): 202–14; "Protokoly TsK RSDRP(b) perioda Brestskikh peregovorov (fevral' 1918 g.)," *Proletarskaia revoliutsiia*, no. 2 (1928): 132–69.

all human beings, were shaped by the assumptions, experiences, and ideals of the group of which they were members, that is, by the party's collective identity.

That other options did exist, that individual women possessed of more conventionally masculine political ambitions, could seize political power if they so chose, is indicated by the careers of Zemliachka and Bosh. Both became important leaders in 1917, Zemliachka in Moscow, Bosh in Ukraine. Their achievements, particularly Bosh's, reveal the possibilities that the revolution had opened up for a few Bolshevichki to move into the male sphere of policy-making and party politics.

Glossary

Antonov-Ovseenko, Vladimir   Bolshevik leader during the October uprising in Petrograd; later commander during the Civil War.

Armand, Inessa   Bolshevik from Moscow who was one of the architects of the party's policies on women's emancipation; served as head of the Party Woman's Department 1919–20.

Bosh, Evgeniia   Bolshevik from Kiev who had been a leader of the party organization in Ukraine before World War I; served as a military and political officer during the Civil War.

Dzerzhinski, Felix   Head of the Cheka, national security police force founded by the Bolsheviks in 1917.

Goldman, Emma   Russian anarchist and activist deported from the U.S. to Soviet Russia in 1918.

Iakovleva, Varvara   Secretary of the Moscow regional Bolshevik party committee in 1917; later member of various opposition groups within the party.

Kaledin, A. M.   Cossack general who commanded an anti-Bolshevik army in the Ukraine in 1918.

Kolchak, Admiral A. V.   Commander of White Army forces opposing the Red Army during the Civil War.

Kollontai, Alexandra   Founder of Bolshevik feminism, although a Menshevik until 1915; Commissar of Social Welfare, 1917–March 1918; head of the Party Women's Department, 1920–2.

Kudelli, Praskovia   editor of the journal *Rabotnitsa* in 1917.

Krupskaia, Nadezhda   Prominent Bolshevik and wife of Lenin.

Lilina, Zlata   Bolshevik active in the underground before the Revolution and worker in education thereafter; wife of Bolshevik leader Grigorii Zinoviev.

Livshits, Olga Bolshevik party worker in Petrograd in 1917.

Neputskaia, Iadviga Bolshevik party worker and labor-union organizer in Petrograd in 1917.

Novgorodtseva, Klavdiia Central Committee staffer, assistant to Elena Stasova in 1918 and 1919, wife of Bolshevik party secretary Iakov Sverdlov.

Nikolaeva, Klavdiia Printer from Petrograd; one of the founders of Bolshevik efforts to organize women, head of the party Women's Department in Petrograd during the Civil War.

Pankhurst, Sylvia English socialist and feminist; head of the Women's Social and Political Union.

Piatakov, Iurii Bolshevik from Kiev who was a leader of the Ukrainian party organization before the First World War and during the Civil War; later prominent in economic planning and management.

Piatakov, Leonid Brother of Iurii Piatakov and leader of Ukrainian communists during the Civil War.

Prokhorova, A. O. Staff worker in the party Women's Department during the Civil War.

Rozmirovich, Elena Bolshevik from Kiev who served as a judge in Petrograd during the Civil War and later took positions in education; sister of Evgeniia Bosh.

Sakharova, Anna Bolshevik and trade-union organizer in Petrograd in 1917.

Samoilova, Konkordiia Bolshevik from Siberia who was an editor of Pravda, 1912–13 and founder of Bolshevik efforts to emancipate women; editor of *Rabotnitsa* 1917–18; leader of the party Women's Department during the Civil War.

Shalaginova, Ekaterina Bolshevik and trade-union organizer in Petrograd, 1917.

Slutskaia, Vera Bolshevik from Minsk who worked in organizing women in Petrograd in 1917; killed in a skirmish with anti-Bolshevik forces, November 1917.

Smidovich, Sofia Bolshevik active in Moscow; worked in the party Women's Department during the Civil War; head of the Women's Department, 1922–4.

Stal, Liudmila Bolshevik who was a founder of work with women; worked during the Civil War in journalism.

Stasova, Elena Bolshevik from St. Petersburg who had been a party secretary before 1917; Central Committee secretary, 1919–20.

Sverdlov, Iakov Bolshevik party secretary from 1917 until his death in March 1919.

Zemliachka, Rozaliia   a Moscow Bolshevik who was a party secretary in that city both before 1917 and in 1918; became a prominent political officer in the Red Army during the Civil War.

Further Reading: Issues of Women and Gender

B. E. Clements, B. A. Engel and C. D. Worebec (eds.), *Russia's Women: Accommodation, Resistance, Transformation* (University of California Press, 1991).

B. E. Clements, *Bolshevik Feminist: The Life of Alexandra Kollontai* (Indiana University Press, 1979).

L. Edmondson, *Feminism in Russia, 1900–1917* (Standford University Press, 1984).

B. Engel and C. Rosenthal (eds.), *Five Sisters: Women against the Tsar* (Knopf, 1975, rev. edn., Routledge, 1992).

R. C. Elwood, *Inessa Armand* (Cambridge University Press, 1992).

B. Farnsworth and L. Viola (eds.), *Russian Peasant Women* (Oxford University Press, 1992).

W. Goldman, *Women, the State and Revolution: Soviet Family Policy and Social Life, 1917–1936* (Harvard University Press, 1993).

R. Stites, *The Women's Liberation Movement in Russia: Feminism, Nihilism and Bolshevism, 1860–1930* (Princeton University Press, 1978).

7

Ascribing Class: The Construction of Social Identity in Soviet Russia

Sheila Fitzpatrick

Originally appeared as Sheila Fitzpatrick, "Ascribing Class: The Construction of Social Identity in Soviet Russia," *Journal of Modern History*, 65 (December, 1993): 745–770.

Editor's Introduction

Sheila Fitzpatrick has been one of the most distinguished historians of Soviet history since the appearance of her first book, *The Commissar of Enlightenment: Soviet Organization of the Arts under Lunacharsky* (Cambridge University Press, 1970). Fitzpatrick was one of the first Western scholars to gain even limited access to Soviet archives at the height of the Cold War when such requests were routinely rejected by the authorities. In the years since then, she has gone on to produce some of the most innovative studies of the postrevolutionary era, especially the decade of the Stalinist 1930s. In the article which is reprinted below, Fitzpatrick tackles the crucial problem of social class ascription in the revolutionary era. One of the least understood topics of the revolution is the transition that took place in the minds of ordinary people as they shifted from being subjects of the tsar's realm to citizens first (and briefly) of a republic promising democratic elections and, thereafter, of a socialist commonwealth. Fitzpatrick investigates this by focusing on the change that took place as the Bolshevik government sought to abolish the old tsarist legal system of social divisions according to "estates" (*sosloviia*) and replace it with a new order rooted in the Marxist notion of social class distinctions.

The effort was flawed from the start, as Fitzpatrick points out, by the inherent contradiction between legal categories, which can be ascribed, and ideological concepts, according to which, in theory, were not, since class was determined by socioeconomic position. Thus, ascribing class for the Bolshevik regime after 1917 involved labeling sectors of society in a stigmatizing hierarchy and establishing a new order of "class" distinctions on the basis of definitions of loyalty to the state.

This opened the door farther to the emerging tendency in the party leadership toward reclassifying Russian (and Soviet) society on the basis of "class discrimination" which, according to Fitzpatrick, ended up resembling the old "estates" divisions once this was enacted into a communist legal system. In pointing out so many of the problems the Bolsheviks created with this process, Fitzpatrick reveals some of the hidden aspects of social identity formation in the revolutionary era as well as providing signposts that indicate the party's increasing reliance on nomenklatura, the fossilizing hierarchy of privilege in the party elite which did so much damage to the government's credibility and prestige among Soviet citizens.

Ascribing Class: The Construction of Social Identity in Soviet Russia

Sheila Fitzpatrick

To ascribe, according to one of the definitions offered by the *OED*, means "to enroll, register, reckon in a class." But there is no known process of enrollment in Marxist classes. A class in the Marxist sense is something to which a person belongs by virtue of his socioeconomic position and relationship to the means of production (or, in some formulations, the class consciousness engendered by socioeconomic position). In this it differs fundamentally from the kind of class to which one might be ascribed: for example, a social estate (*soslovie*, Russian; *état*, French; *Stand*, German), which is first and foremost a legal category that defines an individual's rights and obligations to the state.

This article is about the peculiar conjunction of two incompatible concepts, ascription and Marxist class, that existed in Soviet Russia in the 1920s and 1930s. This conjunction was the product of a Marxist revolution that occurred in a country where class structure was weak and social identity in crisis. While the Marxist framing of the revolution required that society be properly "classed" in Marxist terms, the society's own disarray prevented it. The outcome was a reinvention of class that involved the ascription of class identities to citizens so that the revolutionary regime (a self-defined "dictatorship of the proletariat") could know its allies from its enemies.

The marriage of ascription and Marxist class produced an offspring: stigma. There were "untouchable" classes in revolutionary Russia, notably the much-vilified kulaks and Nepmen (private entrepreneurs), whose fate it was to be "liquidated as a class" at the end of the 1920s. At the other end of the spectrum, to be sure, were the proletarians, whose favored class status was a guarantee of advancement, at least for all those who were young and ambitious (and preferably male) in the

Previous versions of this article were presented at the University of Chicago, Johns Hopkins University, and the first Midwestern Workshop of Russian Historians in Ann Arbor. Thanks are due to all those who contributed to the discussion on these occasions, especially Jeffrey Brooks and Ronald G. Suny. I am also grateful to Pierre Bourdieu for his comments and encouragement at an earlier stage of the project and to Laura Engelstein, Jean Comaroff, and Steven L. Kaplan, whose careful readings of the manuscript were extremely helpful.

first fifteen years after the revolution. But this aspect of the matter, which is by now relatively familiar, will be less emphasized in this article.[1]

The main thesis of this article is that the process of revolutionary ascription produced social entities that looked like classes in the Marxist sense, and were so described by contemporaries, but might more accurately be described as Soviet *sosloviia*. Whether, in addition to these "*sosloviia*-classes," postrevolutionary Russian society was also in the process of making real Marxist classes is a question that lies outside my scope here. But I would tentatively suggest that processes of class formation in the Marxist sense were much inhibited in Soviet Russia in the 1920s and early 1930s, partly as a result of the ascriptive use of Marxist class categories that is the subject of this article.[2]

Social Identity in Early Twentieth-Century Russia

Russian society was in flux at the turn of the century. The crisis of identity that had long preoccupied educated Russians extended to the basic categories of social structure. At the time of the country's first modern population census in 1897, citizens of the Russian Empire were still officially identified by *soslovie* rather than occupation.[3] *Soslovie* categories (noble, clergy, merchant, townsman, peasant) were ascriptive and usually hereditary; historically, their main function had been to define the rights and obligations of different social groups toward the state. To all educated Russians, the survival of *sosloviia* was an embarrassing anachronism, pointing up the contrast between backward Russia and the progressive West. Liberals asserted that *soslovie* had "lost its practical significance as a social indicator" and even claimed (uncon-

---

1   See Sheila Fitzpatrick, *Education and Social Mobility in the Soviet Union, 1921–1934* (Cambridge, 1979), and "Stalin and the Making of a New Elite, 1928–1939," *Slavic Review* 38 (1979): 377–402, and reprinted in my *The Cultural Front* (Ithaca, N.Y., 1992), pp. 149–82.

2   This applies particularly to those Marxist concepts of class formation (e.g., E. P. Thompson's) that emphasize consciousness. Consider, e.g., the problems of (re)formation of the Russian working class in the early Soviet period, given the Bolsheviks' appropriation for their party of a version of "proletarian consciousness" that actual industrial workers neither wholly accepted nor wholly disowned.

3   Form A of the 1897 population census is reproduced in Vl. Plandovskii, *Narodnaia perepis'* (St. Petersburg, 1898), app. 1. Respondents were required to give their "Social estate, status, or title" (*soslovie, sostoianie, ili zvanie*), as well as the branch of the economy in which they worked (agriculture, industry, mining, trade, and so on).

vincingly) that many Russians had forgotten which *soslovie* they belonged to.[4]

Judging by the entries in the St. Petersburg and Moscow city directories,[5] however, urban citizens of substance remembered their *soslovie* but did not always choose to identify themselves by it. Many directory entries gave a *soslovie* description such as "noble," "merchant of the first guild," and "honored citizen" (or, even more frequently, "widow of," "daughter of"). But those who had a service rank ("privy counsellor," "retired general") or profession ("engineer," "physician") tended to list it, in rare instances adding *soslovie* if that lent weight to the persona ("noble, dentist").

The *soslovie* structure offended educated Russians because it was incompatible with the modern, democratic, meritocratic principles they saw emerging and admired in Western Europe and North America. They assumed – not entirely accurately, as historians have recently pointed out – that the Russian *sosloviia* had no vitality or raison d'être other than tradition and state inertia.[6] Following Kliuchevskii and other liberal historians, it was fashionable in the early years of the twentieth century to condemn the Russian *soslovie* system, past as well as present, as an artificial creation that the tsarist state had foisted on society.[7] (The estates of early modern Europe, by contrast, were seen as "real" social groups whose existence and corporate life were independent of the state's imprimatur.) Dissatisfaction with the *soslovie* system focused particularly on its failure to incorporate the two "modern" social entities that were of particular interest to educated Russians: the intelligentsia and the industrial working class.[8] This was regarded, not without reason, as a reflection of the regime's suspicion and fear of these groups.

---

4   Ibid., p. 339. The only example cited is that of peasant respondents to the 1897 census who were unable to identify their families' pre-1861 status (*razriad*, not *soslovie*) under serfdom, i.e., whether they were manorial serfs, state peasants, and so on.

5   *Vsia Moskva* and *Ves' Peterburg*, published annually or biannually from the turn of the century.

6   For discussion of the general problems of *soslovie*, see Gregory L. Freeze, "The Soslovie (Estate) Paradigm and Russian Social History," *American Historical Review* 91 (1986): 11–36; Leopold H. Haimson, "The Problem of Social Identities in Early Twentieth Century Russia," *Slavic Review* 47 (1988): 1–20; Alfred J. Rieber *Merchants and Entrepreneurs in Imperial Russia* (Chapel Hill, N.C., 1982), pp. ix–xvi, and "The Sedimentary Society" in *Between Tsar and People: Educated Society and the Quest for Public Identity in Late Imperial Russia*, ed. Edith W. Clowes, Samuel D. Kassow, and James L. West (Princeton, N.J., 1991); and Abbott Gleason, "The Terms of Russian Social History," in Clowes, Kassow, and West, eds., pp. 23–27.

7   See V. O. Kliuchevskii, *Istoriia soslovii v Rossii: Kurs, chitannyi v Moskovskom Universitete v 1886 g.* (St. Petersburg, 1913).

8   The intelligentsia emerged out of the nobility in the mid nineteenth century as a distinct group of educated Russians not in (or not committed to) government

It was taken for granted in educated circles at the turn of the century that the *soslovie* system would soon wither entirely, even in backward Russia, and that a modern class society on the Western pattern would emerge. While this reflected the popularity of Marxism among Russia's intellectuals, it was by no means only Marxists who thought that a capitalist bourgeoisie and industrial proletariat were necessary attributes of modernity. The belief was widespread; even Russia's conservative statesmen and publicists shared it, though they had a different value judgment of modernity. Even though Russia was still lacking one of the two great classes of modern society, the notoriously "missing" bourgeoisie, this did not disturb the general assumption of educated Russians that when (as must inevitably happen) classes finally superseded *sosloviia* as the structural underpinning, Russian society would have made the transition from the "artificial" to the "real."[9]

The definitive transition to a class society came – or seemed to come – in 1917. First, the February Revolution created a "dual power" structure that looked like a textbook illustration of Marxist principles: a bourgeois, liberal Provisional Government dependent for its survival upon the goodwill of the proletarian, socialist Petrograd Soviet. Class polarization of urban society and politics proceeded apace in the months that followed: even the Cadet party, traditionally committed to a liberalism that was "above class," found itself inexorably drawn to the defense of property rights and an image of politics as class struggle.[10] In the summer, the landowning nobility fled the countryside as peasants began to seize their estates. In October, the Bolsheviks, self-described "vanguard of the proletariat," drove out the Provisional Government and

service. Its non-noble members, many of whom were sons of clergy, were sometimes given the estate classification of *raznochintsy* (various ranks). As separate professions such as law and medicine became more important in the society in the late nineteenth century, the state showed some inclination to treat them as new *sosloviia* – a development to which Russian intellectuals, already focused on Marxist classes as the necessary "modern" unit of social aggregation, paid little attention. The rapid growth of the urban industrial working class was a result of Russia's pell-mell industrialization under the leadership of Count Witte from the 1890s. Most industrial workers, recent or not-so-recent migrants from the villages, were legally peasants by *soslovie*.

9 On this perception, see Freeze, p. 13. Yet, as Leopold Haimson has pointed out ("The Problem of Social Identities in Early Twentieth Century Russia," pp. 3–4), if *sosloviia* were the state's representation of society, so Marxist classes were essentially an "alternative representation" offered by a quasi-dissident intelligentsia on the basis of observation of Western rather than Russian society.

10 See William G. Rosenberg's comment that "for a brief historical moment, at least, dominant identities allowed the lines of social conflict to be very clearly drawn" ("Identities, Power, and Social Interactions in Revolutionary Russia," *Slavic Review* 47 [1988]: 27) and the data on liberal perceptions of class polarization in his *Liberals in the Russian Revolution* (Princeton, N.J., 1974), esp. pp. 209–12.

proclaimed the creation of a revolutionary workers' state. The centrality of class and the reality of class conflict in Russia could scarcely have
been more spectacularly demonstrated.

Yet the moment of clarity about class was fleeting. No sooner had
word reached the outside world that Russia had experienced a Marxist
class revolution than its newly revealed class structure started to disintegrate. In the first place, the revolution deconstructed its own class
premises by expropriating capitalists and landowners and turning
factory workers into revolutionary cadres. In the second place, the
turmoil attendant upon revolution and civil war led to a breakdown
of industry and flight from the cities that, in one of the great ironies of
revolutionary history, temporarily wiped out the Russian industrial
working class as a coherent social group.[11] The proletarian revolution
had indeed been premature, the Mensheviks crowed; and within the Bolshevik party harsh words were exchanged about the vanishing of the
proletariat. ("Permit me to congratulate you on being the vanguard of
a non-existent class," an opponent taunted the Bolshevik leaders in
1922.)[12] But in a sense the debacle was even worse: in addition to
leading a premature revolution, the Bolsheviks apparently had achieved
a prematurely "classless" society in which the absence of classes had
nothing to do with socialism.

Class Principles

For the Bolsheviks, it was imperative that Russian society be "reclassed"
forthwith. If the class identity of individuals was not known, how was
it possible for the revolution to recognize its friends and enemies? Equality and fraternity were not among the immediate goals of the Marxist
revolutionaries, for in their view members of the former ruling and privileged classes were exploiters who (in the transitional period of "dictatorship of the proletariat") could not be granted full citizenship. Thus,
the immediate political thrust of the new rulers' interest in class was to
find out who should be stigmatized as a bourgeois class enemy, on the
one hand, and who should be trusted and rewarded as a proletarian ally,
on the other.

---

11   On the demographic process, see Diane P. Koenker, "Urbanization and Deurbanization in the Russian Revolution and Civil War," *Journal of Modern History* 57
(1985): 424–50; on its political significance, see Sheila Fitzpatrick, "The Bolsheviks'
Dilemma: Class, Culture and Politics in the Early Soviet Years," *Slavic Review* 47
(1988): 599–613, and reprinted in *The Cultural Front* (n. 1 above), pp. 16–36.
12   *XI syezd RKP(b). Mart-aprel' 1922 g. Stenograficheskii otchet* (Moscow, 1961),
pp. 103–4.

Class rule and the dialectics of class conflict were the key concepts about class that the Bolsheviks derived from Marx and their own revolutionary experience. Every society had a ruling class (they believed), and every ruling class had a potential challenger; as a result of the October Revolution, the proletariat was Russia's new ruling class and its potential challenger was the old ruling class that had been overthrown in October, the counterrevolutionary bourgeoisie. In fact, according to strict Marxist-Leninist analysis, this "bourgeoisie" was actually a composite of capitalist bourgeoisie and feudal aristocracy. But the distinction was really irrelevant, since by the early 1920s neither capitalists nor feudal lords remained in Russia as a result of the expropriations of the revolution and the large-scale emigration from the old upper classes at the end of the Civil War. In their absence, the symbolic mantle of the bourgeoisie fell on the intelligentsia, the most visible survivor from Russia's prerevolutionary elites and the Bolshevik's only serious competitor for moral authority in postrevolutionary society. For this reason, as well as for baser purposes of insult and polemic, the group was commonly referred to by Bolsheviks of the 1920s as "the bourgeois intelligentsia."[13]

The term *bourgeois* was also applied in the 1920s to members of a variety of other social and occupational groups that had little in common with each other or, in most cases, with capitalism. One set of "bourgeois" groups, whose members were collectively known as "former people" (the Russian term, *byvshii*, is comparable with the French Revolution's *ci-devant*), derived its class identity from social or service status under the old regime. It included nobles (both former landowners and former tsarist bureaucrats), former industrialists, members of the old merchant estate, officers of the Imperial and White Armies, former gendarmes, and, somewhat anomalously, priests. A second set, the emerging "new bourgeoisie" of the 1920s, consisted of persons whose class identity was derived from their current social position and occupation under the New Economic Policy (NEP), introduced in 1921, which gave a qualified license to private trading and manufacturing. The urban private entrepreneurs of the 1920s were known as "Nepmen."

On the other side of the equation was the proletariat, defined as the new ruling class in Soviet society. As a socioeconomic class, its main constituent groups were the urban industrial workers and landless agricultural laborers (batraks). As a sociopolitical entity, however, it necessarily included the Bolshevik party, "vanguard of the proletariat."

---

13   The insult was particularly effective because *bourgeois* was as much a term of opprobrium in the lexicon of the Russian intelligentsia as it was in Bolshevik discourse.

Bolsheviks who were not of proletarian origin considered themselves to be "proletarians by conviction."[14]

The peasantry – four-fifths of the total population, poor, still farming by the primitive strip system, and maintaining the traditional communal organization in much of Russia – was difficult to categorize in class terms, but the Bolsheviks did their best, using a tripartite classification according to which peasants were either "poor peasants" (*bedniaki*), "middle peasants" (*seredniaki*), or "kulaks," the last being regarded as exploiters and proto-capitalists. Lenin's 1899 monograph *The Development of Capitalism in Russia* had pointed out early signs of class differentiation in the Russian countryside. The Stolypin agrarian reforms in the years immediately before the First World War furthered the process, but then rural revolution of 1917–18 reversed it. During the Civil War, the Bolsheviks' attempts to stimulate class conflict in the villages and ally themselves with the poor peasants against the kulaks were largely unsuccessful. Nevertheless, the Bolsheviks continued to fear a resurgence of kulak power, and Soviet statisticians and sociologists diligently monitored the "balance of class forces" in the countryside throughout the 1920s.

Large segments of the society that were neither clearly proletarian nor clearly bourgeois were supposed to be drifting between the two poles, capable of responding to the attraction of either. Such groups included urban white-collar workers (usually called "employees" [*sluzhashchie*] in the 1920s and 1930s), middle peasants, and artisans. While one might logically argue that the Bolsheviks should have done their utmost to draw them to the proletarian cause, the opposite was true in practice. The Bolsheviks were much too anxious about the class purity of the proletariat and the validity of their own proletarian credentials to do any such thing. "A distrustful, ironic, and sometimes hostile attitude" toward white-collar workers prevailed in party circles and Soviet public discourse for many years after the revolution.[15] A similar distrust, mingled with patronizing contempt, was often directed toward peasants and artisans, who were perceived as nonmodern (*otstalye*) as well as petit bourgeois.

14   Workers made up about 60 percent of the party's membership in October 1917, but this dropped to around 40 percent in the course of the Civil War (partly as a result of peasant recruitment via the Red Army); moreover, most of the party's leaders came from the intelligentsia. Energetic efforts were made to increase the party's working-class membership in the 1920s. But the process of worker recruitment was matched by an equally intensive process of worker "promotion" to cadre status and administrative jobs. The associated practical and conceptual problems are discussed in Fitzpatrick, "The Bolsheviks' Dilemma."
15   *Pravda* (April 20, 1936), p. 1.

The revolutionary "classing" of Soviet society required a definitive rejection of the old *soslovie* system of social classification. Thus, *sosloviia* were officially abolished, along with titles and service ranks, within a month of the October Revolution.[16] Yet from the very beginning there was a hint of *soslovie* in the Soviet approach to class, as indeed was natural in terms of the society's heritage. The white-collar "employee" class, for example, was anomalous in strict Marxist terms. White-collar workers should by rights have been put in the same "proletarian" category as blue-collar workers (and sometimes were, for purposes of academic Soviet-Marxist analysis);[17] yet popular usage persisted in giving them a separate class status, distinctly nonproletarian in political flavor. The pejorative term *meshchanstvo*, derived from the lower urban *soslovie* of *meshchane* and denoting a petit bourgeois, philistine mentality, was so regularly used by Bolsheviks to describe white-collar office workers as to suggest that the new class of *sluzhashchie* was in effect a Soviet version of the old estate of *meshchane*.

Priests and members of clerical families constituted another anomalous "class" in Soviet popular usage that was clearly a direct descendant of the old clerical *soslovie*.[18] In contrast to the "employee" class, which was merely an object of suspicion and disapproval, priests belonged to a stigmatized class deemed unworthy of full Soviet citizenship. They figured prominently in Soviet thinking about potentially counterrevolutionary "class enemies" in the 1920s, and efforts were made to prevent their children, who were also stigmatized, from getting higher education or "penetrating" (in the terminology of the time) the teaching profession. The assumption that priests were ipso facto class enemies was so strong that large numbers of village priests were "dekulakized" – that is, stripped of their property, evicted from their homes, and arrested or deported along with the kulaks – at the end of the decade.

Structures of Class Discrimination

Class was built into the very constitutional foundations of the new Soviet state. The 1918 Constitution of the Russian Republic extended

16   Decree of TsIK and Sovnarkom (November 11 [24], 1917) signed by Sverdlov and Lenin, "Ob unichtozhenii soslovii i grazhdanskikh chinov," in *Dekrety sovetskoi vlasti* (Moscow, 1957), 1:72.
17   See e.g., the detailed class breakdown of Soviet society, based on census returns, in *Statisticheskii spravochnik SSSR za 1928 g.* (Moscow, 1929), p. 42.
18   In a context of serious social-statistical analysis, however, priests and other religious servitors (*sluzhiteli kul'ta*) were subsumed under the category of "free professionals" (*litsa svobodnykh professii*).

full citizenship and the right to vote only to "toilers." Those who lived parasitically off unearned income or the exploitation of hired labor, including private entrepreneurs and kulaks, were deprived of the right to vote in elections to the soviets, along with priests, former gendarmes and officers of the White Army, and other "socially alien" groups.[19] Although these class-based restrictions on voting rights merely formalized the established (pre-October) practice of the soviets and cannot be regarded as a Bolshevik innovation or even a conscious policy decision, the effect of their incorporation in the constitution of the new Soviet state was to make class a legal category, a situation never envisaged by Marx but nevertheless quite familiar to any Russian brought up under the *soslovie* system.

Virtually all Soviet institutions practiced some kind of class discrimination in the 1920s, giving highest preference to proletarians and lowest to disenfranchised persons and members of various "bourgeois" groups.[20] High schools and universities had class-discriminatory admissions procedures, as did the Communist party and the Komsomol (the Communist youth organization). Purges of "class aliens" from government employment, party membership, and student status in universities occurred from time to time, often as a result of local initiative rather than central instructions. The judicial system operated according to the principles of "class justice," treating proletarian defendants leniently and favoring their claims in civil cases over those of bourgeois plaintiffs. Municipal housing bodies and rationing boards discriminated on the basis of class, and there were special punitive tax rates for social undesirables like kulaks and Nepmen.

In order for this system of class discrimination to work really efficiently, it would have been necessary to have citizens carry internal passports showing their social class (just as they had shown *soslovie* under the old regime), but this was going too far for the Bolsheviks in the 1920s. Internal passports had been abolished with the revolution as a symbol of autocratic repression, and they were not reintroduced until 1932. In the interim, there was no truly effective means of class identification, and discrimination was usually conducted on an ad hoc basis with unpredictable results. Among the types of documentation that could be used were birth and marriage certificates, which recorded class ("social position") in the place where tsarist authorities had registered

---

19   "Konstitutsiia (osnovnoi zakon) RSFSR, priniataia Piatym Vserossiiskim syezdom Sovetov" (July 10, 1918), in *Sobranie uzakonenii i rasporiazhenii rabochego i krest'ianskogo pravitel'stva*, no. 51 (1918), art. 582. Section 4 (pt. 13) of the constitution deals with voting rights.

20   For a detailed discussion of this question, see Elise Kimerling, "Civil Rights and Social Policy in Soviet Russia, 1918–1936," *Russian Review* 41 (1982): 24–46.

soslovie, and letters of attestation from the workplace or rural soviet.[21] Personal testimony about an individual's class origins could also be cited, as could the lists of disenfranchised persons (*lishentsy*) maintained in each soviet electoral district maintained by local electoral commissions.

Since the procedures of class discrimination tended to be haphazard and informal, they were also to some degree negotiable. In judicial practice, for example, one form of appeal by a defendant identified as "bourgeois" or "kulak" (and thus liable to a heavy sentence) was a petition to change the class label: "Relatives, and sometimes the accused themselves, obtain documents after the trial to *change their economic and social position*, and the supervisory committees permit them [to raise] the question of transferring from one [class] category to another."[22]

In the higher educational system, too, class identities were often contested by persons refused admission on class grounds or expelled in the course of social purges. The whole issue of class discrimination in education was a painful one to Bolsheviks old enough to remember the time when, in a policy shift universally condemned by Russian radicals, the tsarist government had sought to restrict the educational access of members of lower *sosloviia* ("children of cooks and washerwomen"). Nobody went so far as to raise the issue of a new Soviet *soslovnost'* (*soslovie* order) explicitly in public debates. But the "quota politics" that developed in education in the 1920s had disconcerting overtones. When, for example, teachers pressed a government spokesman on the issue of "parity of rights with workers" in regard to university admissions, it was almost as if a time warp had plunged Russia back to 1767 and Catherine the Great's Legislative Commission was arguing about *soslovie* privileges.[23]

If Soviet class-discriminatory laws were creating new "*sosloviia*-classes," however, this was an involuntary process that went unnoticed by the Bolsheviks. Russian Marxist intellectuals were deeply committed to the belief that classes and class relations were objective socioeco-

---

21   The 1926–27 registration forms for marriage, birth, divorce, and death are reproduced in V. Z. Drobizhev, *U istokov sovetskoi demografii* (Moscow, 1987), pp. 208–15. The options listed under the heading of "social position" (*sotsial'noe polozhenie*) were worker, employee, proprietor, assisting family member (in a family enterprise such as a peasant farm), free professional, and other.

22   *Sovetskaia iustitsiia*, no. 1 (1932), p. 20; my emphasis.

23   The government spokesman was Lunacharsky, People's Commissar of Education, who was being questioned at a teachers' conference in 1929. (He advised the teachers to rely on the goodwill of the admissions boards rather than pushing their luck by trying to get this enacted into law.) Tsentral'nyi Gosudarstvennyi Arkhiv Oktiabr'skoi Revoliutsii (TsGAOR), f. 5462, op. 11, d. 12, l. 37.

nomic phenomena and that gathering information on them was the only way to gain a scientific understanding of society. It was in this spirit, undoubtedly, that even before the Civil War was over Lenin was pressing for a population census that would provide data on occupations and class relations.[24]

A national population census, designed and analyzed according to impeccable Marxist principles, was conducted in 1926 and published in fifty-six volumes. Its basic socioeconomic categories were wage and salary earners (proletariat), on the one hand, and "proprietors" (*khoziaeva*), urban and rural, on the other. In the latter group, which included the entire peasantry[25] as well as urban artisans and businessmen, those employing hired labor (capitalists!) were rigorously differentiated from those working alone or with the assistance of family members.[26] The census, which was exhaustively analyzed and studied by contemporary demographers, sociologists, journalists, and politicians, constituted a major step in the "classing" of Russian society.[27] Of course it did not and could not create classes in the real world. But it created something that might be called *virtual classes*: a statistical representation that enabled Soviet Marxists (and future generations of historians) to operate on the premise that Russia was a class society.

Class Stigma

There were stigmatized, "untouchable" groups in Soviet society in the 1920s: kulaks, Nepmen, priests, and *ci-devants*. People in all these stigmatized groups were *lishentsy* – that is, they shared the common legal status of disenfranchisement and the civil disadvantages that flowed from it. The "untouchables," however, were not members of a tradi-

24   The failure of the 1897 census to provide such data had been a source of great frustration to Lenin when he was writing *The Development of Capitalism in Russia*. A census was duly taken in 1920, during the last stages of the Civil War, but because of the social turmoil and dislocation of the period its occupational data turned out to be of little value. *Massovye istochniki po sotsial'no-ekonomicheskoi istorii sovetskogo obshchestva* (Moscow, 1979), p. 24; Drobizhev, pp. 47–48, 53.
25   With the exception of agricultural laborers.
26   See *Vsesoiuznaia perepis' naseleniia 17 dekabria 1926 g. Kratkie svodki*, vyp. 10 (Moscow, 1929): *Naselenie Soiuza SSR po polozheniiu v zaniatii i otrasliam narodnogo khoziaistva*.
27   On the general question of the uses of statistics for purposes of social construction and control, see Ian Hacking, *The Taming of Chance* (Cambridge, 1990); and Joan Scott, "Statistical Representation of Work: The Politics of the Chamber of Commerce's *Statistique de l'Industrie à Paris, 1847–48*," in her *Gender and the Politics of History* (New York, 1988).

tionally separate caste, and they could not be distinguished by visible physical characteristics such as skin color or gender. If the kulak left the village or the priest stopped wearing his vestments and became a teacher, who but their old acquaintances would know that they bore the stigmata of class?

Like Russian society as a whole in the first third of the twentieth century, but to an even greater degree, the stigmatized population of the 1920s was unstable and in constant flux. People of all sorts frequently changed occupations, statuses, familial arrangements, and places of residence as part of the general turmoil of war, revolution, civil war, and postwar readjustment. But people who found themselves with class stigmas were even more prone to change, because they hoped that change would rid them of the stigma. For example, a former high-ranking civil servant of noble birth might work as a humble Soviet book-keeper not only because he needed a job but also as a way of shedding the old identity.

The class identity of a very large number of Soviet citizens was both contestable and contested in the 1920s.[28] This was not only because of high geographical, social, and occupational mobility in the previous decade and the evasive strategies of the stigmatized but also because there were no hard-and-fast criteria for class identification or rules about how to resolve ambiguous cases. The three basic indicators of class were generally considered to be current social position, former (prewar or prerevolutionary) social position, and parents' social status. But there was disagreement on the relative importance of these indicators. The most popular method of identification, inside and outside the Bolshevik party, was "genealogical" or *soslovie*-based, especially in the case of stigmatized identities: a priest's son was always "from the clergy," regardless of occupation; a noble was always a noble.[29] But party intellectuals were unhappy about this approach on Marxist theoretical grounds; and the Communist party itself used a much more complicated procedure to determine the class identity of its members, using the two indicators of "social position" (usually defined in this context as an individual's basic occupation in 1917) and current occupation, and disdaining "genealogy."[30]

28 For a more extended discussion, see Sheila Fitzpatrick, "The Problem of Class Identity in NEP Society," in *Russia in the Era of NEP: Explorations in Soviet Society and Culture*, ed. Sheila Fitzpatrick, Alexander Rabinowitch, and Richard Stites (Bloomington, Ind., 1991), pp. 12–33.

29 Communists did not usually apply the "genealogical" approach to the working class. Those workers (a high proportion of the whole) who had been born peasants were still regarded as "proletarian."

30 The two headings were *"po sotsial'nomu polozheniiu"* and *"po zaniatiiu."* See questionnaire for the 1927 party census, reproduced in *Vsesoiuznaia partiinaia*

Avoiding ascription to a stigmatized class was among the basic concerns of many Soviet citizens in the 1920s, as was achieving ascription to the proletariat or the poor peasantry in order (for example) to get into university or secure a paid job in the rural soviet. There were numerous behavioral strategies for avoiding class stigma, and outright fraud, such as the purchase of documents attesting to a false class identity, was not uncommon. But these practices generated their own "dialectical antithesis": the more prevalent became evasion and manipulation of class ascription, the more energetically Communist militants strove to "unmask" the evaders and reveal their true class identity.

The unmasking of class enemies rose to a pitch of hysteria and became a real witch-hunt at the end of the 1920s and beginning of the 1930s. The most remarkable episode of "class war" in this period was the dekulakization campaign whose purpose was to "liquidate kulaks as a class." This involved not only the expropriation of all those ascribed to the kulak class and their "hirelings" (*podkulachniki*) but also the deportation of a substantial part of the group to distant regions of the country.[31] Urban Nepmen were being forced out of business and in many cases arrested at the same period, as the entire urban economy was nationalized. In the Cultural Revolution, "bourgeois specialists" came collectively under attack, and a number of those who had held senior posts in the state bureaucracy were accused of counterrevolutionary wrecking and sabotage.[32]

The "heightened class vigilance" of the Cultural Revolution meant that the situation of *lishentsy* became ever more precarious even as the lists of officially disenfranchised persons grew longer. *Lishentsy* were liable to be fired from their jobs, evicted from housing, and declared ineligible for rations, while their children were unable to enter university and join the Komsomol or even the Young Pioneers (for ages ten to fourteen). A wave of social purging (*chistki*) swept through government offices, schools, universities, Komsomol and party organizations, and even factories in 1929–30. Rural schoolteachers lost their jobs because they were sons of priests; kulaks who had fled the village and found work in industry were denounced; elderly widows of tsarist generals were

perepis' 1927 g., vyp. 3 (Moscow: Statisticheskii otdel TsK VKP[b], 1927), pp. 179–80. On the "genealogical" issue, the Central Committee's statisticians believed that parents' class status was "less characteristic of a party man" and "lays a less bright imprint on his whole spiritual profile" than his own immediate class experience and occupational history: *Sotsial'nyi i natsional'nyi sostav VKP(b). Itogi vsesoiuznoi perepisi 1927 goda* (Moscow, 1928), p. 26.

31 On dekulakization, see R. W. Davies, *The Socialist Offensive: The Collectivisation of Soviet Agriculture, 1929–1930* (Cambridge, mass., 1980), chaps. 4–5.

32 See Kendall E. Bailes, *Technology and Society under Lenin and Stalin* (Princeton, N.J., 1978), chaps. 3–5.

"unmasked" and subjected to various indignities. Neighbors and professional colleagues accused each other of hiding class stigmas. Persons from stigmatized classes sometimes publicly repudiated their parents in a vain effort to wipe out the stain.[33]

Then, as was inevitable, the witch-hunt for class enemies died down. In reaction to its excesses, the institutional structures of class discrimination were largely dismantled in the period 1931–36. Kulaks and their children recovered some (though not all) civil rights; class discrimination in university admissions was abolished; first the Komsomol and then the Communist party changed recruitment rules to make it easier for nonproletarians to join.[34]

It was time to move toward full equality of citizens and abolition of all class restrictions, Molotov said in 1935, since those had merely been "temporary measures" to counteract the "exploiters' attempts to assert or reestablish their privileges."[35] The government had decided that it was important to lift class stigmas, reported a member of the Soviet Control Commission, "in order that a person can forget his social origins. . . . The offspring of a kulak is not to blame for that, since he did not choose his parents. Therefore they are saying now: don't persecute people for their [class] origins."[36] Stalin made the same point with his famous interjection: "A son does not answer for his father." The remark was made at a conference of peasant Stakhanovites in response to the complaint of one delegate about the discrimination he had suffered because his father had been dekulakized.[37]

---

33   See Sheila Fitzpatrick, "Cultural Revolution as Class War," in *Cultural Revolution in Russia, 1928–1931*, ed. Sheila Fitzpatrick (Bloomington, Ind., 1978), pp. 8–40.

34   On restoration of rights to kulaks and their children, see "O poriadke vosstanovleniia v izbiratel'nykh pravakh detei kulakov," *Sobranie zakonov i rasporiazhenii raboche-krest'ianskogo pravitel'stva S.S.S.R.*, no. 21 (1933), art. 117; and "O poriadke vosstanovleniia v grazhdanskikh pravakh byvshikh kulakov," *Sobranie zakonov*, no. 33 (1934), art. 257. On college admissions, see Fitzpatrick, *Education and Social Mobility in the Soviet Union, 1921–1934* (n. 1 above). On party admissions rules, see T. H. Rigby, *Communist Party Membership in the U.S.S.R., 1917–1967* (Princeton, N.J., 1968), pp. 221–26. On changes in the basis of Komsomol enrollment, see speech by Central Committee secretary Andreev at the Tenth Komsomol Congress, *Pravda* (April 21, 1936), p. 2.

35   Molotov, speech to Seventh Congress of Soviets on forthcoming changes in the Soviet Constitution (February 6, 1935), *Komsomol'skaia pravda* (February 8, 1935), p. 2.

36   A. A. Solts, *Sovetskaia iustitsiia*, no. 22 (1936), p. 15.

37   *Komsomol'skaia pravda* (December 2, 1935), p. 2. The delegate, A. G. Tilba, a combine driver from Bashkiriia, claimed that local party officials had tried to prevent him from attending the conference, despite his merits as a Stakhanovite, and he had been able to attend after intervention by the head of the party Central Committee's agriculture department.

The move away from class discrimination and class stigma was completed with the adoption of the new "Stalin" Constitution of the USSR of 1936. The new constitution stated that all citizens of the country had equal rights and that all could vote and hold elective office "regardless of race and nationality, religious creed, . . . social origin, property status, and past activity."[38] This restored voting rights to kulaks, priests, *ci-devants*, and others formerly stigmatized and disenfranchised.

"A Son Does Not Answer for His Father" – or Does He?

Stalin's interjection quickly became part of Soviet folklore.[39] Untypically, however, it was not followed up by approving commentary and elaboration in the press, and it was never republished after the initial press report.[40] This suggests that the conciliatory policy it implied remained controversial – not least, perhaps, in Stalin's own mind. It was a question on which Stalin must surely have had mixed feelings. The kulaks' sons who had become honest toilers might be "innocent" in class terms, but did that mean they were harmless as far as the state was concerned? Stalin himself was not a man to forget an injury done to him or his, and the Soviet regime had undoubtedly injured the kulaks' sons. Might they not be cherishing bitter resentment behind an outward show of loyalty and obedience?

In 1929, on the eve of the great onslaught against class enemies in the countryside that was described as "liquidation of the kulaks as a class," Stalin had predicted that, as the defeat of the class enemy became more certain, his resistance would become all the more vicious and desperate.[41] This introduced a psychological twist to Marxist doctrine on class conflict that discomforted some theoretically minded Communists. All the same, if what Stalin was saying was that "class enemies" become real enemies once you liquidate them as a class, it is hard to disagree

38 "Konstitutsiia (Osnovnoi Zakon) Soiuza Sovetskikh Sotsialisticheskikh Respublik" (1936), in *Istoriia sovetskoi konstitutsii (v dokumentakh) 1917–1956* (Moscow, 1957), p. 726.
39 Note, e.g., its use in Aleksandr Tvardovskii's poem, "Po pravu pamiati," which began to circulate in Soviet samizdat in the 1960s. Tvardovskii's parents and brothers were deported as kulaks at the time he was embarking on a successful career as a people's poet in Smolensk.
40 While most newspapers simply failed to react, the Komsomol paper ran an editorial a few weeks later calling for more revolutionary vigilance against class enemies that sounded like an oblique rebuttal: *Komsomol'skaia pravda* (December 28, 1935), p. 1.
41 "O pravom uklone v VKP(b)," in I. V. Stalin, *Sochineniia* (Moscow, 1952), 12: 34–39.

with him. As he reflected somberly a few years later, destroying a class did not eliminate its (anti-Soviet) consciousness, for the former members of the class remained, "with all their class sympathies, antipathies, traditions, habits, opinions, [and] world views. . . . The class enemy survives . . . in the person of living representatives of those former classes."[42]

It is clear that fear of the (former) class enemy remained very strong in the Communist party through the 1930s and that, even more than the similar fears of the 1920s, it was directly related to the perception that people whose lives had been shattered, either by the original revolution or Stalin's "revolution from above," were likely to remain irredeemably hostile to the Soviet regime. This was particularly frightening because – as a result of Soviet policies liquidating the rural and urban bourgeoisie and discriminating against persons who had once belonged to these classes – many of the enemies were now dispersed and hidden. For every kulak or kulak family member who had been deported or sent to labor camp in the early 1930s, for example, there were several who had fled from the village during collectivization and made new lives elsewhere, usually as urban wage earners. For obvious reasons, such people tried to hide their past from workmates and the authorities because their former identities carried a stigma.

In principle, there was nothing illegal about this, any more than it was illegal for a former noble to work quietly as an accountant without advertising his lineage: after all, it was not only the right but also the obligation of all Soviet citizens to work. In practice, however, the discovery that former kulaks or former Nepmen were employed in the work force always produced alarm, and the most sinister interpretation was put on their attempts to "pass" as normal citizens. Melodrama hinging on the "hand of the hidden class enemy" theme was one of the standard genres of Soviet mass culture in the 1930s. In the film *Party Card* (1936), for example, an unknown youth turns up in a factory town and meets a woman worker, Anna, who falls in love with him. Through her, he gets a job at the plant and is even able to join the party. But he is really a kulak who fled from his native village during collectivization. Anna gets some inkling of this but decides not to tell the party. It turns out that this is a terrible mistake. Not only is he a kulak and a murderer but he is also a spy in the pay of foreign intelligence.[43]

42   Speech by State Prosecutor Nikolai Krylenko, allegedly paraphrasing unpublished remarks by Stalin, delivered to judicial officers in Ufa, March 1934: *Sovetskaia iustitsiia*, no. 9 (1934), p. 2.

43   The plot summary, which may not be strictly accurate, is taken from the film's very favorable review in a local newspaper, *Magnitogorskii rabochii* (Magnitogorsk) (May 5, 1936), p. 3.

Class stigma proved very resilient in Soviet society, despite the sporadic attempts of the party leadership to move away from policies of stigmatization. Both in the leadership and the party's rank and file, there was a basic ambivalence on the class issue throughout the 1930s, interludes of comparative relaxation alternating with fresh outbursts of paranoia right up to the bacchanalia of the Great Purges and its hungover aftermath in the last prewar years. Policies of destigmatization were neither wholeheartedly recommended by party leaders nor systematically implemented by officials at the local level.

In addition, there are indications of considerable grassroots suspicion of destigmatization policies, especially in the now-collectivized villages. At a national conference of kolkhoz activists in 1935, the Central Committee secretary for agriculture floated the idea of allowing deported kulaks to return home, but the proposal received an extremely tepid response and was not pursued further.[44] (Any "return of the dekulakized" obviously would have led to monumental conflicts between peasant households about the houses, cows, and samovars that once had belonged to kulaks but were now in other hands.) In the Smolensk region the next year, two Communist district officials took the new constitution's guarantee of equality of all citizens seriously, ordering that the old stigmatizing lists of kulaks and *lishentsy* be destroyed and that competent former kulaks and traders be employed in places where their skills could be useful – for example, in Soviet trading institutions. These actions were subsequently interpreted as counterrevolutionary sabotage during the Great Purges, in a context that strongly suggests that they offended the local population.[45]

For *Homo sovieticus*, the left and right brain were often at odds on questions involving class and the class enemy: the rational man might accept that class-discriminatory policies had outlived their day and the class enemy was no longer a real threat, but the intuitive man remained dubious and fearful. In each successive political crisis of the 1930s, Communists hastened to round up "the usual suspects," knowing instinctively that the class enemy must be somehow to blame.

This happened during the crisis of the winter of 1932–33, when the introduction of passports was accompanied by a purge of the urban population in which large numbers of disenfranchised persons and other class aliens were refused urban registration cards, summarily

44   See *Vtoroi vsesoiuznyi syezd kolkhoznikov-udarnikov. 11–17 fevralia 1939 g. Stenograficheskii otchet* (Moscow, 1935), pp. 60, 81, 130.
45   See the report of the Sychevka trial – one of many provincial show trials of 1937 in which rural Communist officials were accused of abusive, arbitrary, and repressive behavior toward the local peasant population – in *Rabochii put'* (Smolensk) (October 16, 1937), p. 2.

evicted from their homes, and expelled from the city.[46] It happened again in Leningrad in 1935 after the murder of Kirov, then the number 2 man in the party. In response to the murder (which had no apparent connection with any "class enemies"), the NKVD rounded up many *ci-devants*, including forty-two former princes, thirty-five former capitalists, and more than a hundred former gendarmes and members of the tsarist police.[47]

The Great Purges of 1937–38 marked an apparent change in the pattern. In the first place, the witches in this witch-hunt were called "enemies of the people," not "class enemies." In the second place, as was clearly signaled by Stalin and Molotov in their speeches and reiterated day after day in the press, the prime candidates for the "enemies of the people" title were not the old class enemies but highly placed Communist officials – regional party secretaries, heads of government agencies, industrial managers, Red Army leaders, and the like.

But old habits die hard, and "the usual suspects" often found themselves caught up once again. In Leningrad in the autumn of 1937, Zakovskii, head of the NKVD, identified university students who were sons of kulaks and Nepmen as a particular category of "enemies of the people" who should be exposed and rooted out.[48] The Komsomol organization in Smolensk province expelled dozens and probably hundreds of its members on grounds of alien social origin, connection by marriage with class aliens, concealment of such origins and connections, and so on.[49] In Cheliabinsk (and surely also elsewhere), former class enemies were among those executed as counterrevolutionaries in 1937–38.[50]

Hidden former kulaks who had "wormed their way" into the factories and government institutions were frequent targets of exposure during the Great Purges. In the villages, denunciations of "kulaks" (or "kulak, Trotskyite enemies of the people" – usually kolkhoz chairmen) by other peasants were even more frequent in 1937 than in previous years; and it was not uncommon for the NKVD to arrest as a counterrevolutionary in 1937 someone whose brother or father had been

46 See Sheila Fitzpatrick, "The Great Departure: Rural-Urban Migration, 1929–33," in *Social Dimensions of Soviet Industrialization*, ed. William G. Rosenberg and Lewis Siegelbaum (Bloomington, Ind., 1993), pp. 15–40.
47 *Za industrializatsiiu* (March 20, 1935), p. 2.
48 Reported in *Komsomol'skaia pravda* (October 5, 1937), p. 2.
49 A large number of these victims were formally reinstated in the Komsomol in 1938 after appealing their expulsions. Their rehabilitation hearings are in Smolensk Archive, WKP 416.
50 See data from local NKVD files cited in G. Izhbuldin, "Nazvat' vse imena," *Ogonek*, no. 7 (February 1989), p. 30.

arrested or deported as a kulak earlier in the decade.[51] The newspaper *Krest'ianskaia gazeta*, recipient of many peasant complaints and denunciations, had to rebuke one correspondent for sending in a denunciation that confused the old stigmatized categories and the new: "In giving information about the kolkhoz veterinarian, A. P. Timofeev, you write: 'His brother was arrested by organs of the NKVD as a former Junker.' Obviously you meant to say 'arrested for counter-revolutionary work.' "[52]

Data recently released from NKVD archives indicates that the gulag labor camps took in almost 200,000 prisoners classified as "socially-harmful and socially-dangerous elements" in the Great Purge years (1937–38) – not a negligible quantity even in comparison with the half-million-odd "counter-revolutionaries" flooding into the gulag at the same period, and particularly striking in light of the fact that class enemies were not officially a target in this witch-hunt.[53]

Passports and Stalinist *Soslovnost'*

At the end of 1932, the Soviet government introduced internal passports for the first time since the fall of the old regime. This was a reaction to the immediate threat of a flood of peasant refugees from the famine-stricken countryside overwhelming the towns, which were already drastically overcrowded as a result of the large-scale out-migration associated with collectivization and the rapid expansion of industry under the First Five-Year Plan. But it also turned out to be something of a milestone in the evolution of the new Soviet *soslovie* order (*soslovnost'*). Just as tsarist passports had identified the bearers by *soslovie*, so the new Soviet passports identified them by "social position" – in effect, by class.[54]

---

51   These observations are based on reading archival files of peasant letters of complaint in 1938. The files, which come from the Soviet archive Tsentral'nyi gosudarstvennyi arkhiv narodnogo khoziaistva SSSR (TsGANKh), f. 396, op. 10, are discussed in Sheila Fitzpatrick, *Stalin's Peasants: Resistance and Survival in the Russian Village after Collectivization* (New York and Oxford, 1994), in press, see esp. app. "On Bibliography and Sources."
52   TsGANKh, f. 396, op. 10, d. 121, 1.
53   Figures from N. Dugin, "Otkryvaia arkhivy," *Na boevom postu* (December 27, 1989), p. 3, based on NKVD archival data classifying prisoners on the basis of the articles of the Criminal Code on which they had been convicted.
54   The basic coordinates of personal identity given in the passports of the 1930s were age, sex, social position (*sotsial'noe polozhenie*), and nationality: see resolution of TsIK and Sovnarkom USSR of December 27, 1932, "Ob ustanovlenii edinoi pasportnoi sistemy v SSSR," published in *Pravda* (December 28, 1932), p. 1. "Social position" remained as an entry in Soviet passports until 1974.

Notable features of the new passport system were that the passports were issued to urban inhabitants by the OGPU (forerunner of the NKVD and KGB), along with city residence permits (*propiski*), and that passports were not automatically issued to peasants. As in tsarist times, peasants had to apply to the local authorities for a passport before departing for temporary or permanent work outside the district, and their requests were not always granted. Kolkhoz members also needed permission from the kolkhoz to depart, just as in the old days of *krugovaia poruka*[55] they had needed permission from the mir. It was hard to ignore the *soslovie* overtones, once the peasantry was placed in such a juridically distinct (and, of course, inferior) position. The rules on passports were not significantly changed in the course of the 1930s, despite the equality-of-rights principle that was declared to be a foundation of Soviet law and government by the constitution of 1936.

The normal passport entries under the "social position" heading in the 1930s were worker, employee, kolkhoznik, and, for members of the intelligentsia, a designation of profession, such as doctor, engineer, teacher, or factory director.[56] With the exception of "kolkhoznik," these passport listings seem usually to have been an accurate representation of the individual's basic occupation.[57] No doubt the fact that passports came under NKVD jurisdiction improved their accuracy; but in addition it should be noted that, with the decline of class-discriminatory laws and procedures, there was a corresponding decline in contestation of social identity. No stigma in the old sense attached to any of the class identities given in passports. "Kolkhoznik" and "*edinolichnik*" (noncollectivized peasant) – the two juridical categories of peasant in the 1930s, which replaced the three quasi-legal, quasi-economic categories of the 1920s – were certainly inferior statuses in Soviet society. But neither can be regarded as having the pariah status of the old "kulak."

When the Communist party and Soviet society emerged from the maelstrom of collectivization and cultural revolution in the second quarter of the 1930s, the depth and sincerity of the leaders' commitment to Marxist principles on class had noticeably waned. As has already been noted, the regime started moving away from practices of

55   Collective responsibility for redemption and tax payments of households in the peasant commune in the post-Emancipation era.
56   *McGraw Hill Encyclopedia of Russia and the Soviet Union*, ed. Michael T. Florinsky (New York, 1961), s.v. "passports," p. 412; information from Harvard Refugee Interview Project cited in Alex Inkeles and Raymond A. Bauer, *The Soviet Citizen: Daily Life in a Totalitarian Society* (New York, 1968), pp. 73–74.
57   "Kolkhoznik" falls into a special category because the passport-holding kolkhoznik was almost by definition not occupied full-time in kolkhoz agriculture. As in the tsarist period, this was often the designation of a former peasant who had in practice become an urban worker but had not yet succeeded in changing his legal status.

class stigmatization and class discrimination. If this meant little in the case of the new constitution, real changes in Soviet practice occurred in other areas; for example, educational opportunity and elite recruitment via Komsomol and party membership. The decline of genuine concern about class was also manifest in the abrupt collapse of social statistics, a major research industry in the 1920s – particularly the disappearance of the formerly ubiquitous tables showing the class breakdown of every imaginable population and institution.

All the same, it would be misleading to leave the impression that the Soviet authorities no longer bothered to collect data on social origin and class background. The concerns about hidden enemies discussed in the previous section were reflected in Soviet recordkeeping practices, but this was mainly in the context of personal dossiers. As Malenkov told a national party conference as late as 1941, "When an official is appointed in many party and economic organs, despite the Party's instructions, people spend more time establishing his genealogy, finding out who his grandfather and grandmother were, than studying his personal managerial and political qualities [and] his abilities."[58] The standard questionnaire filled out by all state employees and party members in the 1930s pursued every possible circumstance bearing on social identity, including class origins (former *soslovie* and rank, parents' basic occupation), occupation before entering state employment (or, for party members, occupation before joining the Communist party), year of first job in state employment, and current social status.[59]

One question about class that remained very relevant in the 1930s was that of an individual's social trajectory. It remained extremely important to differentiate between, say, a worker whose father had also been a worker and a worker who had left the village, perhaps fearing dekulakization, in 1930, or between an official who had started off life as a priest's or noble's son and one who had struggled up from village to factory and then in 1929 become a beneficiary of "proletarian promotion." In the comparatively few large-scale social surveys conducted and published in the 1930s, such questions were also central.[60]

---

58   Reported in *Pravda* (February 16, 1941), p. 3.
59   TsGAOR, f. 5457, op. 22, d. 48, ll. 80–81 (personal dossier [*lichnyi listok po uchetu kadrov*] of P. M. Grigorev, member of knitting workers' trade union, 1935).
60   See, e.g., the trade union census of 1932–33, which paid special attention to union members from the village and their former class status there (*Profsoiuznaia perepis' 1932–1933 g.* [Moscow, 1934]); the 1935 census of personnel in state and cooperative trade, which focused on the employment of former Nepmen and employees from the private sector (*Itogi torgovoi perepisi 1935 g.*, pt. 2: *Kadry sovetskoi torgovli* [Moscow, 1936]); and the 1933 survey of the Soviet administrative and professional elite (published in 1936), which distinguished not only those cadres

The population censuses of the 1930s, in contrast to the 1926 census, dealt briskly and briefly with social position. In a sense, this simply reflected changing external circumstances, notably the "liquidation as a class" of kulaks and other private employers of hired labor. But it was also clear that, in an unarticulated reversion to the spirit of the 1897 census, the question about class (identical in the 1937 and 1939 censuses) had suddenly ceased to be complicated and had become almost as straightforward as the old question about *soslovie*. Class position no longer had to be deduced on the basis of painstakingly assembled and analyzed economic data; for a large part of the population, it was conveniently written in the passport and just had to be reported. In the 1937 and 1939 question on social position, respondents were simply required to say which of the following groups they belonged to: "workers, employees, kolkhozniks, *edinolichniki*, craftsmen, free professionals or servants of a religious cult, and non-toiling elements." In addition, in an evocative turn of phrase that would not have displeased Peter the Great, they were asked to identify their present "service" (*sluzhba*) – that is, their branch of employment if they worked for the state.[61]

The term *class* was not used in the census forms, suggesting some uncertainty about its continuing relevance as a category.[62] In the mid-1930s, after all, the Soviet Union had officially reached the stage of socialist construction (*sotsialisticheskoe stroitel'stvo*): it was possible, despite the lack of theoretical clarity about the relationship of socialist construction to socialism, that this implied that the achievement of a classless society was imminent. Stalin, however, confirmed that classes did indeed remain in Soviet society, although they were classes of a special, nonantagonistic kind due to the ending of exploitation and class conflict.[63] He did not bother to justify this assertion with elaborate theorizing. "Can we, as Marxists, evade the question of the class composition of our society in the Constitution?" he asked rhetorically. The laconic answer was, "No, we cannot."[64]

who were of working-class background but also those who had still been "workers at the bench" in 1928 (*Sostav rukovodiashchikh rabotnikov i spetsialistov Soiuza SSSR* [Moscow, 1936]).

61   See census forms for 1937 and 1939 censuses, published in TsUNKhU pri Gosplane SSSR, Vsesoiuznaia perepis' naseleniia 1939 g., *Perepisi naseleniia. Al'bom nagliadnykh posobii* (Moscow, 1938), pp. 25–26. The 1937 census was suppressed and never published because the population total was unacceptably low.

62   Instead, a completely new term was introduced: *social group* (*obshchestvennaia gruppa*).

63   "O proekte konstitutsii Soiuza SSR" (November 25, 1936), in I. V. Stalin, *Sochineniia* I (XIV), ed. Robert H. McNeal (Stanford, Calif., 1967), pp. 142–46.

64   Ibid., p. 169.

In the spirit of Catherine the Great clarifying the principles of *soslovnost'* in the eighteenth century, Stalin laid out the three major groupings of Soviet society: workers, collectivized peasants (*kolkhoznoe krest'ianstvo*), and intelligentsia.[65] This was a reasonable adaptation of Catherine's four basic *sosloviia* divisions to contemporary Soviet circumstances, except for one peculiarity.[66] This was the merging of the old "employees" category with both the intelligentsia and the Communist administrative elite to form a single white-collar conglomerate called "the Soviet intelligentsia."

It would, of course, be an exaggeration to claim that a full-blown *soslovie* system emerged in the Soviet Union in the 1930s. Nevertheless, there were many signs of a tendency toward *soslovnost'* in Soviet social organization at this time, starting with the entry of social position in internal passports discussed above. The peasantry had the most clearly defined *soslovie* characteristics. Unlike the other basic *soslovie* classes, workers and intelligentsia, peasants did not have the automatic right to passports and thus had special restrictions on mobility. They bore a corvée obligation to the state to provide labor and horses for roadwork and logging from which the other *soslovie* classes were exempt. On the positive side of the ledger, peasants were alone in having the collective right to use land,[67] and they also had the right, which was strictly denied to all other Soviet citizens, to engage in individual trade.[68]

More subtle distinctions in the rights and privileges of different social groups also existed in Soviet society in the 1930s. Some of them were enshrined in law: for example, the right of noncollectivized peasant households – in contrast to kolkhoz households and members of urban *sosloviia* – to own a horse and the right of "worker" and "employee" households to the use of village plots or urban allotments of a designated size.[69] Cossacks, one of the traditional minor *sosloviia* under the old regime, recovered quasi-*soslovie* status with regard to military service privileges in 1936, after twenty years in disgrace because of their opposition to Soviet power during the Civil War and collectiviza-

65   Ibid., p. 142. For reasons of doctrinal orthodoxy, Stalin called the first two groups "classes" and the third (which was not defined by relation to the means of production) a "stratum" (*prosloika*). This was sometimes referred to irreverently as the "two-and-a-half" formula.

66   The four divisions were nobility, clergy, urban estates, and peasantry.

67   Noncollectivized peasants had an individual (household) right in their native village, though not elsewhere.

68   This right was limited to certain designated spaces, the "kolkhoz markets" in towns to which individual peasants and kolkhozy brought surplus produce.

69   Note that for most practical purposes, "employees" (*sluzhashchie*) were still treated as a separate estate in the 1930s, despite Stalin's "two-and-a-half" formula.

tion.[70] Kulaks deported at the beginning of the 1930s and other "special settlers" (*spetsposelentsy*) in Siberia and elsewhere must also be regarded as a separate estate, since their rights and restrictions as agriculturalists and industrial workers were carefully spelled out in laws as well as secret instructions.[71]

We can also distinguish at least one "proto-*soslovie*" whose existence was recognized by custom and official statistical classification, if not by law. This was the new Soviet upper class, the administrative and professional elite that constituted the top layer of the general white-collar group that Stalin called "intelligentsia." The formal designation of this elite, used in statistical analyses of the 1930s that were usually unpublished, was "leading cadres and specialists."[72] Members of the group enjoyed a range of special privileges, including access to closed stores, chauffered cars, and government dachas.[73]

In this connection, it should be noted that the whole economy of scarcity and "closed distribution" networks[74] that developed in the 1930s tended to encourage the trend toward *soslovnost'*. This applied not only to the new upper class of "leading cadres and specialists" but also to groups lower in the social hierarchy that also enjoyed access to

70   See the letter from Cossacks of the Don, Kuban, and Terek pledging loyalty to the Soviet regime in *Pravda* (March 18, 1936), p. 1, and the statute on their new status passed by the Central Executive Committee of the Congress of Soviets of the USSR on April 20, 1936, cited in *Bol'shaia sovetskaia entsiklopediia*, 2d ed. (Moscow, 1953), 19:363 (s.v. *Kazachestvo*). It is possible that the new Cossack *soslovie* also received the right to own horses, a much-coveted privilege in the 1930s, but I have so far been unable to determine this.

71   See V. N. Zemskov, "Spetsposelentsy (po dokumentatsii NKVD – MVD SSSR)," *Sotsiologicheskie issledovaniia*, no. 11 (1990), pp. 3–17, and (on the removal of legal restrictions from this group in the 1950s) "Massovoe osvobozhdenie spetsposelentsev i ssyn'nykh (1954–1960 gg.)," *Sotsiologicheskie issledovaniia*, no. 1 (1991), pp. 10–12.

72   *Rukovodiashchie kadry (rabotniki) i spetsialisty.* See *Sostav rukovodiashchikh rabotnikov i spetsialistov Soiuza SSR* (Moscow, 1936); "Iz dokladnoi zapiski TsSU SSSR v Prezidium Gosplana SSSR ob itogakh ucheta rukovodiashchikh kadrov i spetsialistov na 1 ianvaria 1941 g.," in *Industrializatsiia SSSR 1938–1941 gg. Dokumenty i materialy* (Moscow, 1973), pp. 269–76; and other surveys cited in Nicholas de Witt, *Education and Professional Employment in the USSR* (Washington, D.C., 1961), pp. 638–39. In industrial statistics of the 1930s, the category of "ITR" (engineering-technical personnel) was used in the same way: it included administrators as well as professionals, but excluded lower-status office workers, who were put in a separate "employees" category.

73   See Mervyn Matthews, *Privilege in the Soviet Union: A Study of Elite Life-Styles under Communism* (London, 1978), chap. 4.

74   That is, distribution of rationed and scarce consumer goods via workplaces and professional organizations.

privileges of various kinds. At the beginning of the 1930s, for example, the closed distribution and public dining room system in factories often distinguished three categories: managers and engineers (known as ITR), privileged workers,[75] and ordinary workers.[76] Later, with the development of the Stakhanovite movement in the latter part of the decade, Stakhanovites and *udarniki* came to constitute a distinct stratum of workers who received special privileges and rewards for their achievements.[77] In theory, Stakhanovite status was not permanent but was dependent on performance. But it is clear that many workers perceived it as a new "honored worker" status – comparable perhaps with the "honored citizens" *soslovie* of tsarist times? – that, once earned, was bestowed for a lifetime.[78]

Conclusion

I have argued in this article that class became an ascribed category in Russia after the revolution. The main proximate causes were the legal and institutional structures that discriminated on the basis of class and the societal flux and disintegration that made an individual's "real" socioeconomic class elusive and indeterminate. More generally, one can say that the Soviet practice of ascribing class arose out of a combination of Marxist theory and the underdeveloped nature of Russian society.

In a sense, class (in its Soviet form) can be seen as a Bolshevik invention. The Bolsheviks, after all, were the rulers of the new Soviet state and the framers of class-discriminatory legislation, and Marxism was their professed ideology. All the same, it is too simple to give the Bolsheviks all the credit for the Soviet invention of class. This invention also had Russian popular roots: after all, it was the popularly created workers' soviets of 1905 and 1917 whose class-based franchise set the pattern for the restriction of voting rights in the 1918 constitution and

75 That is, "shockworkers" (*udarniki*), so designated in recognition of their high productivity as workers.
76 See Leonard E. Hubbard, *Soviet Trade and Distribution* (London, 1938), pp. 38–39, 238–40.
77 On Stakhanovism, see Lewis H. Siegelbaum, *Stakhanovism and the Politics of Productivity in the USSR, 1935–1941* (Cambridge, 1988).
78 See, e.g., the heartfelt complaint from an illiterate woman worker in the flax industry who wrote (via her literate daughter) to Maria Kaganovich, the national head of her trade union, to complain of the gross injustice committed when she was deprived of Stakhanovite status (and forbidden, therefore, to sit in the front row at the factory club) just because her health declined and she could no longer work as well as she used to. TsGAOR, f. 5457, op. 22, d. 48 (letter of November 1935).

thus indirectly for the whole corpus of class-discriminatory legislation of the early Soviet period. Moreover, the *soslovie* overtones of class in the 1920s – particularly evident with regard to the "class" status of the clergy and the *meshchane*-like category of "employees" – also suggests popular rather than Bolshevik imagination.

Where a specifically Bolshevik (or Marxist intellectual) construction of class was most evident was in the realm of social statistics. Convinced that a scientific analysis of society required class categories, Soviet statisticians of the 1920s painstakingly built such categories into their data, including the volumes of the 1927 population census dealing with occupation. In this article, I have suggested that the great corpus of social statistics of the 1920s was part of the creation of a "virtual class society" – that is, a representation whose purpose was to sustain the illusion of classes. One inference to be drawn is, of course, that historians should be extremely wary of taking these statistics at face value.

In the 1920s, the ascription of stigma was a very important – if not crucial – aspect of the general process of ascribing class. Here we are obviously in the realm of popular revolutionary passion as much as that of Marxist theory or even Bolshevik ideology. Bolshevik intellectuals (including Lenin and other party leaders) were uncomfortable with the stigmatizing and scapegoating implications of their class policies; in particular, they resisted the popular notion that a person's class origins should be the basis of stigma. But these objections went largely unheeded. Class stigmatization reached its height in the outburst of state-incited witch-hunting of the Cultural Revolution.

In the 1930s, after the orgy of collectivization, dekulakization, and Cultural Revolution at the beginning of the decade, many things changed. Revolutionary passions waned; Marxism became routinized and lost its charisma for Communists; and, in 1937–38, Soviet witch-hunting was at least partly diverted away from class channels. Nevertheless, class was still a basic category of identity for Soviet citizens, and this was institutionalized in a new way when internal passports including a "social position" entry were introduced at the end of 1932. This "social position" entry was an almost exact counterpart of the old *soslovie* notation in tsarist identification documents. No longer a matter of contestation or (with the dismantling of legal and institutional structures of class discrimination) of stigma, Soviet "class" increasingly assumed the meaning of Imperial *soslovie*.

The implications of a "Stalinist *soslovnost'* " model of Soviet society obviously cannot be adequately explored here, but it may be useful to suggest a few possible lines of enquiry. In the first place, *soslovnost'* provides a framework within which it becomes immediately comprehensible that the "classes" of Stalinist society should have been defined, like *sosloviia*, in terms of their relationship to the state rather than, like Marxist classes, in terms of their relationship to each other. This gives us a new perspective on the much-remarked "primacy of the state" in the Soviet state-and-society relationship.

In the second place, the *soslovnost'* model helps us deal with the issue of social hierarchy. While it has often been pointed out that an unmistakable social hierarchy emerged in the Stalin period, its nature has remained conceptually blurred. It is easy to agree with Trotsky and Djilas that a new upper class, strongly associated with office holding, emerged in the Stalin period, but it is much more difficult to accept the Marxist proposition that this was a new *ruling* class rather than simply a new privileged one. Within the framework of "Stalinist *soslovnost'*," this class becomes a latterday "service nobility"[79] whose status and functions are as transparent to historians as they were to contemporaries, and other *soslovie*-classes fall into place in the social hierarchy with equal ease.

Finally, it is worth asking whether the same framework might be applied to the study of Soviet nationalities. In Imperial Russia, there were ethnic/national *sosloviia* (e.g., Bashkirs or German colonists) as well as social ones. Nationality, like class, was a category that achieved full legal recognition only with the revolution. Its Soviet construction at first seemed to proceed on very different lines from the Soviet construction of class. In the Stalin period, however, things changed, especially in connection with the deportations of nationalities in the 1940s. There is an intriguing possibility that the shadow of *soslovnost'* hung over the construction of national as well as social identity in the Stalin period.

Glossary

ci-devants   "Those in front", former privileged classes under a monarchy.

Collectivization   Violent assault on the Russian peasantry, and most particularly the kulaks in 1929–30 to end private landholdings.

Cultural Revolution   Doctrinal policy in art and literature established by Stalin in 1930s.

Dekulakization   Destruction of the kulak peasants by collectivization policy.

Kirov, Sergei   Head of the Leningrad Communist party, murdered in 1934.

---

79   For a similar suggestion, see Robert C. Tucker, "Stalinism as Revolution from Above," in *Stalinism: Essays in Historical Interpretation*, ed. Robert C. Tucker (New York, 1977), pp. 99–100.

Kliuchevskii, V. O.   One of the most respected prerevolutionary historians of Russia.

kulaks   Peasants with private holdings; considered as a profit-making rural elite.

Malenkov, G. M.   Leading party member who remained close to Stalin.

Molotov, V. M.   Rising Bolshevik linked with Stalin after the revolution and later national leader.

Nepman   Supporter of the New Economic Policy of limited capitalism introduced in 1921.

Stakhanovite   Term for a worker who overproduced; used as a model for the Soviet proletariat at large.

udarniki   Workers rewarded for their excess commitment to communist labor.

Stolypin, Peter   Minister of the Interior and architect of comprehensive agrarian reform policy, 1906.

Further Reading: Problems of Social Class

S. Fitzpatrick, *Education and Social Mobility in the Soviet Union, 1921–1934*, Cambridge University Press, 1979.

G. Freeze, "The Soslovie (Estate) Paradigm and Russian Social History," *American Historical Review*, 91 (1986): 11–36.

L. Haimson, "The Problem of Social Identities in Early Twentieth Century Russia," *Slavic Review*, 47 (1988): 1–20.

D. P. Koenker, "Urbanization and Deurbanization in the Russian Revolution and Civil War," *Journal of Modern History*, 57 (1985): 424–50.

A. J. Rieber, *Merchants and Entrepeneurs in Imperial Russia* (University of North Carolina Press, 1982).

8

State-Building and Nation-Making: The Soviet Experience

Ronald G. Suny

Originally appeared as Ronald Grigor Suny, "State-Building and Nation-Making: The Soviet Experience," in *The Revenge of the Past: Nationalism, Revolution and the Collapse of the Soviet Union* (Stanford: Stanford University Press, 1993): 84–106.

Editor's Introduction

The study of nationalities in the former Soviet Union has been a concern of scholars for some time, though the linguistic skills necessary for this work has obviously limited the historiography, as did the absence of access to archives in the former republics. Though there has been a long tradition of national histories, such as works on Poland, Ukraine, and the Baltic states, many have either not been translated into English or have suffered from partisan interpretations.

One of the earliest accounts by an historian of the nationality issues related to the consequences of the Russian Revolution was *The Formation of the Soviet Union: Communism and Nationalism, 1917–1923* (Harvard University Press, 1954) by Richard Pipes. Ronald G. Suny later initiated great interest in the study of Soviet nationalities with his book *The Baku Commune, 1917–1918: Class and Nationality in the Russian Revolution* (Princeton University Press, 1972). Suny also was able to make use for the first time of regional and unpublished sources in that volume, and has gone on to a distinguished career as one of the leading historians of Soviet nationalities.

In the selection below, Suny discusses the problems that Lenin and the Bolsheviks faced after taking power in October 1917. As Imperial Russia had been a multinational empire, the new regime inherited a vast territorial space of eleven time zones with numerous ethnicities, stretching from the Baltic in the west, to the Caucasus in the south, to the Siberian

Pacific coast in the east. One of the most complicated issues concerned the conflict between socialist internationalism as proclaimed by the Bolsheviks and the rights of nationalities. Marxists had for decades devoted attention to this interrelationship, and proposed a variety of solutions. In its most extreme form, the spectrum extended from a position of complete autonomy on the basis of nationality to that of the subordination of nationalism to a larger supranational center based on socialist equality. In part, this debate was framed at a time when the reigning assumption argued that bourgeois imperialism was the main oppressive global force, and socialism's appeal was seen as an alternative to this system.

Lenin and his commissar of nationalities, Stalin, were confronted with the reality for the first time in history of applying Marxist theory on nationality to a commonwealth established on the foundation of ideology. Compromises then had to be worked out. As Suny shows, the ethnic and national divisions of the former tsarist empire were accommodated in a plethora of forms, including "involuntary Sovietization" on the one hand, and the sponsorship of native languages and culture on the other. Nevertheless, "the first state in history to be formed of ethnic political units" ended up becoming "the incubator of new nations." The origins of this process are the central concern of Suny's essay.

State-Building and Nation-Making: The Soviet Experience

Ronald G. Suny

In an illuminating chapter, "Revolution over Asia," E. H. Carr notes the assimilation of the "national question" to the "colonial" issue in the Bolshevik discourse. Colonial policy was

> a logical corollary and a natural extension of national policy; the theoretical foundations of both were the same. . . . Soviet policy appealed in one broad sweep to the peoples of Asia as a whole, to the former subjects of the Tsar, to the subjects of other empires and to the nominally independent dependencies of the capitalist world-market.[1]

Already in the appeal "To All Muslim Toilers of Russia and the East," issued just one month after the Bolsheviks came to power, the powerful rhetoric of self-determination, liberation, independence, and anti-imperialism established a unity of the struggle against colonial and national oppression. Since the Red Army was engaged for much of the period of the Russian Civil War in a simultaneous battle against "bourgeois nationalists" and "foreign interventionists," anti-imperialism was not distinguished from the drive to "liberate" the former subject peoples of the Russian empire.

Soviet Russia was conceived not as an ordinary national state but as the first stone in a future multinational socialist edifice. The reach of the Russian Revolution was to be limitless. What its enemies would later build into a potent ideological image of a drive toward world domination was in its incarnation an effort directed primarily against British imperialism. It brought Lenin and his comrades into a series of peculiar alliances with the fallen Turkish leader Enver Pasha, King Amanullah of Afghanistan, the rebel Kuchuk Khan in northern Persia, Kemal Pasha in Anatolia, and other non-socialist nationalists. The empires of the Europeans in Asia, the semicolonial periphery of Persia, China, and Turkey (in Lenin's conceptualization), and the newly independent national states established after the October Revolution, dependent as they were on the presence and support of European power, all were linked in a single understanding as the last props of a moribund capi-

---

1 E. H. Carr, *The Bolshevik Revolution, 1917–1923*, vol. 3 (London: Macmillan, 1953), pp. 234–235.

talism. With a confidence born of recent victories and faith in a Marxist eschatology, and with an opportunism rooted in the limited resources at hand, the Bolsheviks used all the means available to realize their dream of international revolution. For Communists of the civil-war period, internationalism was less the servant of the Soviet state than the Soviet state was the servant of internationalism.

From the very beginning, the pull between nationalism and socialism was a struggle between supporters of the Soviet government and foreign interventionists who hoped to gain allies in the war against the Reds. A pristine nationalism, able to establish a firm base of support in the ethnic population and to hold on to political independence without foreign help, was difficult to find in the peripheries of the Russian empire. Two fiercely antagonistic discourses contended in a battle of rhetoric and violence: nationalists appealed to the West to defend their right to national self-determination against a renewed Russian threat, whereas Communists portrayed the nationalists and their foreign backers as part of an imperialist endeavor to contain or destroy Bolshevism and the coming international revolution.

At the beginning of the twentieth century, when Social Democrats agonized over the emerging "national question," Russian Marxists sought both to win allies among the non-Russian nationalities and to combat the nationalists' attempts to splinter the unitary state. Secure in their faith in Marx's assertions that "national differences and antagonisms between peoples are vanishing gradually from day to day" and that "the supremacy of the proletariat will cause them to vanish still faster," Bolshevik theorists were opposed to political solutions that would divert what they understood to be the flow of history and promote ethnic identity. Lenin, Stalin, Armenian Bolshevik Stepan Shahumian, and others were adamant in their opposition to federalism, to the Austromarxist principle of "extraterritorial national cultural autonomy" (each nationality represented in parliament no matter where its members live), and to the moderate nationalist principle of "territorial national cultural autonomy" (ethnicity defining autonomous territorial political units). Leninists preferred "regional autonomy," in which political units would not have ethnic designations. The "proletarian solution" to the nationality question would preserve the unitary state while allowing for local self-government and guaranteeing complete cultural and linguistic freedom within the socialist state. Although national self-determination for Lenin meant that a nationality could choose to become fully independent, in his pre-1917 formulation nationalities that stayed within the socialist state would have neither the right to an autonomous political territory nor the right to a federative relationship to the center.

The Bolsheviks' prerevolutionary thinking on the national question did not survive the revolution intact. The new Soviet state was both federative, at least in name and theory, and based on ethnic political units. Indeed, for more than a decade following the civil war, nationalities like the Jews and Armenians, and the Ukrainians in Russia, enjoyed extra-territorial privileges, with their own schools and soviets operating in republics of other nationalities. Soviet practice was a compromise with maximal ideological desiderata. And the very expectation that such concessions to the national principle would lead to the consolidation of ethnicity, rather than to its disappearance, proved to be correct for the larger nationalities. Rather than a melting pot, the Soviet Union became the incubator of new nations.

Though many of his comrades consistently favored subordinating nationalism strictly to class considerations, Lenin was both aware of the power of nationalism (even as he hoped to harness it to the proletarian revolution) and ready to concede the need to ally with "bourgeois nationalists." For Lenin, nationalism and separatism were neither natural nor inevitable, but were contingent on the sense of oppression that nationalities experienced from imperialism. He remained convinced that nationalism reflected only the interests of the bourgeoisie, that the proletariat's true interests were supranational, and that the end of colonialism would diminish the power of nationalist sentiments.[2] In contrast to his party comrades on the Left, he refused to oppose the independence of Finland, Poland, and Ukraine. Though he hoped that such separations could be avoided and reserved the option to oppose specific moves toward independence on principle, he abjured the use of force to keep the empire whole. He was unequivocal in his public commitment to "the full right of separation from Russia of all nations and nationalities, oppressed by tsarism, joined by force or held by force within the borders of the state, i.e., annexed." At the same time, he argued that the goal of the proletarian party was the creation of the largest state possible and the rapprochement (*sblizhenie*) and eventual merging (*sliianie*) of nations. Such a goal was to be reached, not through force, but voluntarily, by the will of the workers. Already in early 1917,

---

2   "We say to the Ukrainians: as Ukrainians, you can run your own lives as you wish. But we extend a fraternal hand to the Ukrainian workers and say to them: together with you we will fight against your and our bourgeoisie. Only a socialist alliance of laborers of all countries eliminates any ground for national persecution and fighting." V. I. Lenin, *Polnoe sobranie sochinenii* (henceforth *PSS*) (Moscow: Gosizpolit, 1959–), 116.

Lenin moderated his earlier position and proposed that full regional (and national) autonomy be guaranteed in the new state.[3]

Lenin understood the need for alliances with the peasants and the non-Russians, and he was convinced that the approaching international socialist revolution would make the movements for land and statehood largely irrelevant. Acutely aware that the weakness of the central state gave new potency to movements for autonomy and separation from the empire, as well as the spontaneous resolution of the land question by peasants, Lenin staked out a clear position supporting both processes. In contrast, neither the Provisional Government nor the successive White leaderships were sympathetic to the nationalists.

Immediately after taking power, the Bolsheviks set up the People's Commissariat of Nationalities under Stalin and issued a series of declarations on "the rights of the toiling and exploited peoples," "to all Muslim toilers of Russia and the East," and on the disposition of Turkish Armenia. Most importantly, with little real ability to effect its will in the peripheries, the Soviet government made a strategic shift in response to the growing number of autonomies and accepted by January 1918 the principle of federalism. As they launched an attack on Ukraine, the Bolsheviks announced that they recognized the Central Executive Committee of Soviets of Ukraine as "the supreme authority in Ukraine" and accepted "a federal union with Russia and complete unity in matters of internal and external policy." By the end of the month, the Third Congress of Soviets resolved: "The Soviet Russian Republic is established on the basis of a free union of free nations, as a federation of Soviet national republics." Both federalism and national-territorial autonomy were written into the first Soviet constitution, adopted in July 1918. As Richard Pipes has noted, "Soviet Russia . . . became the first modern state to place the national principle at the base of its federal structure."[4]

In the ferocity of the civil war, many Communists, particularly those in the peripheries or of non-Russian origin, opposed Lenin's principled stand in favor of national self-determination, fearing the dissolution of the unitary state. As early as December 1917, Stalin argued that the freedom of self-determination should be given only to the laboring classes, not to the bourgeoisie. At the Eighth Party Congress in March

3   From the brochure *Zadachi proletariata v nashei revoliutsii (Proekt platformy proletarskoi partii)*, written in April 1917, first published in September. Lenin, *PSS* 31: 167–68.
4   Richard Pipes, *The Formation of the Soviet Union: Communism and Nationalism, 1917–1923* (Cambridge, Mass.: Harvard University Press, 1954; reprinted 1964), p. 11.

1919, Bukharin supported Stalin's position and tried to divide the national from the colonial question. Only in those nations where the proletariat had not defined its interests as separate from the bourgeoisie should the slogan of "self-determination of nations" be employed. Lenin's formula, he claimed, was appropriate only "for Hottentots, Bushmen, Negroes, Indians," whereas Stalin's notion of "self-determination for the laboring classes" corresponded to the period in which the dictatorship of the proletariat was being established.[5]

Lenin answered Bukharin sharply. "There are no Bushmen in Russia; as for the Hottentots, I also have not heard that they have pretensions to an autonomous republic, but we have the Bashkirs, the Kyrgyz, a whole series of other peoples, and in relation to them we cannot refuse recognition." All nations, he reasserted, have the right to self-determination, and Bolshevik support for this principle would aid the self-determination of the laboring classes. The stage of a given nation as it moved from "medieval forms to bourgeois democracy and on to proletarian democracy" should be considered, he stated, but it was difficult to differentiate the interests of the proletariat and the bourgeoisie, which had been sharply defined only in Russia.[6]

The final resolution of the Congress was a compromise between Lenin's tolerance of nationalism and the more militant opposition to it. Maintaining the principle of national self-determination, the resolution went on to say: "As to the question who is the carrier of the nation's will to separation, the RKP stands on the historico-class point-of-view, taking into consideration the level of historical development on which a given nation stands."[7] The Bolsheviks reached no consensus on nationality policy, and the conflict between those who, like Lenin, considered the national agenda of non-Russians and those who, like Stalin, subordinated the national to the "proletarian" continued until the former's death and the latter's consolidation of power within the party. On the ground, Communists decided themselves who was the carrier of the nation's will, and after the initial recognition of independence for Finland, Poland, the Baltic republics, and (for a time) Georgia, few other gestures were made toward "separatists."

Toward the end of 1919, while reflecting on the factors that had led to Bolshevik victory in 1917, Lenin turned to Ukraine to underscore the importance of tolerance in national policy. Reviewing the Constituent Assembly election results, in which Ukrainian SRs and socialists out-

---

5   *Vosmoi s"ezd RKP (b). Mart 1919 goda. Protokoly* (Moscow: Gosizpolit, 1959), pp. 46–48.
6   Ibid., pp. 52–56.
7   Ibid., pp. 397–98.

polled the Russian SRs, he noted: "The division between the Russian and Ukrainian Socialist Revolutionaries as early as 1917 could not have been accidental." Without holding that national sentiments are fixed or permanent, he suggested once again that internationalists must be tolerant of the changing national consciousness of non-Russians, which, he was confident, was part of the petty bourgeois vacillation that had been characteristic of the peasantry throughout the civil war.

> The question whether the Ukraine will be a separate state is far less important [than the fundamental interests of the proletarian dictatorship, the unity of the Red Army, or the leading role of the proletariat in relation to the peasantry]. We must not be in the least surprised, or frightened, even by the prospect of the Ukrainian workers and peasants trying out different systems, and in the course of, say, several years, testing by practice union with the RSFSR, or seceding from the latter and forming an independent Ukrainian SSR, or various forms of their close alliance. . . .
>
> The vacillation of non-proletarian working people on *such* a question is quite natural, even inevitable, but not in the least frightful for the proletariat. It is the duty of the proletarian who is really capable of being an internationalist . . . to leave it to the non-proletarian masses *themselves* to *get rid* of this vacillation as a result of their own experience.[8]

As the strategic situation improved for the Bolsheviks and their allies by the summer of 1920, the "national-colonial question" was put squarely on the agenda. The British were leaving the Russian periphery, and communism had gained its first foothold south of the Caucasus with the relatively easy Sovietization of Azerbaijan in April. The balance of forces in Central Asia and in Transcaucasia, where Georgia and Armenia remained independent, was clearly in favor of the Soviets, and direct links were established between the Soviets and the Kemalist nationalists in Anatolia. On April 26, Kemal sent an official communication to Moscow expressing his appreciation of Moscow's fight against imperialism and his readiness to take upon himself "military operations against the imperialist Armenian government" and to encourage Azerbaijan "to enter the Bolshevik state union."[9] In May, Soviet troops and the Persian revolutionary Kuchuk Khan established the Soviet republic of Gilan on the southern coast of the Caspian Sea, and though the situation in Persia remained extraordinarily fluid, the government at Teheran appeared prepared to distance itself from the British and

8   Lenin, *PSS* 50: 20; idem, *Collected Works* (London: Lawrence and Wishart, 1960–), 30: 271.
9   Richard G. Hovannisian, "Armenia and the Caucasus in the Genesis of the Soviet-Turkish Entente," *International Journal of Middle East Studies* 4 (1973): 147.

open negotiations with the Soviets. With Denikin defeated, Kolchak dead, and the Red Army marching against Pilsudski's Poland, the latter half of 1920 turned out to be a high point of revolutionary enthusiasm and direct Bolshevik promotion of the revolution in the East.

Several themes repeatedly reasserted themselves in the discussions around the national-colonial question in 1920, both at the Second Congress of the Communist International and the Baku Congress of the Peoples of the East. The first was Lenin's leitmotiv, which had haunted his writings since 1914 – the relationship of capitalist imperialism and the revolutionary crisis in both the advanced and the colonial world. Besides the one billion people living in colonial and semicolonial states, and another quarter-billion living in Russia, since the war Germany, Austria, and Bulgaria, he argued, had been relegated to "what amounts to colonial status." The "super-profits of thousands of millions form the economic basis on which opportunism in the labour movement is built."[10] This dependency of the capitalist metropole on the colonial and semicolonial world was recognized by all communists, but some non-European communists, like the Indian M. N. Roy and "many comrades in Turkestan" (referred to by the Iranian delegate Sultan Zade at the Second World Congress), went further and argued that the revolution in Europe required a revolution in the East.

A second theme was the failure of the Second International to address the colonial issue in a revolutionary manner. Lenin, Roy, Sultan Zade, and others portrayed the Social Democrats as Eurocentric reformers, willing to support movements toward self-government in the colonies but reluctant to back revolutionary efforts. Communists, on the other hand, recognized the need for collaboration between revolutionaries in Europe, America, and Asia, and took pride in the multiracial representation in the Comintern meetings.

A third dominant theme was the historic difference between bourgeois democracy, supported by the Social Democrats of Europe, and soviet democracy, and the strong sense that a new historical epoch had opened that had rendered parliamentarianism obsolete.[11] In his "Preliminary Theses on the National-Colonial Question," Lenin began with the distinction between formal bourgeois democracy, which grants juridical equality to all, and "the real meaning of the demand of equality," which requires the abolition of classes.[12] Bourgeois democracy also

10   Ibid., pp. 15, 27.
11   *Second Congress of the Communist International: Minutes of the Proceedings*, 2 vols. (London: New Park, 1977), 1: 11.
12   "Pervonachal'nyi nabrosok tezisov po natsional'nomu i kolonial'nomu voprosam," Lenin, *PSS* 41: 161–68.

disguised the exploitation of weaker nations by the stronger, though the imperialist war of 1914–18 had exposed this hypocrisy. Only a common struggle of all proletarians and laboring people of all nations could overthrow the rule of the landlords and bourgeoisie.

Yet another theme was the nature of the future socialist state, a grand multinational federation not unlike the Russian Socialist Federative Soviet Republic (RSFSR). Federation, Lenin maintained, was the advanced form for the full unity of the toilers of different countries. Federation already had shown its utility in practice, both in the relations of the RSFSR with other soviet republics (Hungarian, Finnish, and Latvian in the past; Azerbaijani and Ukrainian in the present) and, within the RSFSR, in relations with the nationalities that earlier had not had either state existence or autonomy (for example, the Bashkir and Tatar autonomous republics in the RSFSR). It was essential to work for a tighter federative union, both politically and economically, but at the same time, Lenin cautioned, full recognition of the rights of nations and minorities, including the right to separate states, had to be supported.

Differences in tone and direction arose in discussions of appropriate strategies to win over the masses of the East. In his original theses delivered to the Second Comintern Congress, Lenin had argued that "all communist parties must aid the bourgeois-democratic liberation movement" in backward countries with feudal or patriarchal relations. While fighting against clerical reaction and medieval elements, against Pan-Islam and other movements that attempt to unite the liberation movement while strengthening the khans, landlords, mullahs, etc., communists must support the peasant movement against landlords by forming a "provisional alliance" with bourgeois democracy of the colonies and backward countries.

When Lenin submitted his theses to his comrades, he met resistance to his provisional alliance with the national bourgeoisie. Lenin assured the doubters that "the alliance with the peasantry is more strongly underlined for me (and this is not completely equal to the bourgeoisie)."[13] Most vociferously, Roy disputed Lenin's support of the

---

13   In a letter of June 12, 1920, Stalin told Lenin that he ought to include the idea of confederation as the transition step bringing different nations into a single political unit. The Soviet federation (RSFSR) was appropriate for the nationalities that had been part of the old Russia, but not for those which had been independent. He noted that differences between the federative relations within the RSFSR and between the RSFSR and other soviet republics did not exist or were so few that they meant nothing (*net, ili ona tak mala, chto ravniaetsia nuliu*; Lenin, *PSS* 41: 513). This idea was later brought up in Stalin's notion of autonomization. (Stalin's letter is available in an English translation in Xenia Joukoff Eudin and Robert C. North,

national bourgeoisie and argued that Lenin was mistaken to believe that the national liberation movement had the significance of the bourgeois democratic revolution. Though as yet an unproven revolutionary, Roy (as he tells us in his memoirs)

> pointed out that the bourgeoisie even in the most advanced colonial countries, like India, as a class, was not economically and culturally differentiated from the feudal social order: therefore, the nationalist movement was ideologically reactionary in the sense that the triumph would not necessarily mean a bourgeois democratic revolution. The role of Gandhi was the crucial point of difference. Lenin believed that, as the inspirer and leader of a mass movement, he was a revolutionary. I maintained that, as a religious and cultural revivalist, he was bound to be a reactionary socially, however revolutionary he might appear politically.[14]

After several private discussions with Roy and a general debate in the Commission on the National-Colonial Question, Lenin admitted that his views had been changed by Roy's challenge.[15] Roy argued that

> foreign domination constantly obstructs the free development of social life; therefore the revolution's first step must be the removal of this foreign domination. The struggle to overthrow foreign domination in the colonies does not therefore mean underwriting the national aims of the national bourgeoisie but much rather smoothing the path to liberation for the proletariat of the colonies.

Roy distinguished more clearly than Lenin the two opposing movements in the colonial world: "the bourgeois-democratic nationalist movement, which pursues the program of political liberation with the conservation of the capitalist order; [and] the struggle of the propertyless peasants for their liberation from every kind of exploitation."[16] Communists must not allow the former movement to dominate the latter and must ally with and support the latter. Lenin agreed that Communists should support "national-revolutionary" movements but withhold support from reformist movements based on collaboration of the colonial and the metropolitan bourgeoisies. In the absence of a proletariat, as in Turkestan, the Communist party must take over the leading

---

Soviet Russia and the East, 1920–1927: A Documentary Survey [Stanford, Calif.: Stanford University Press, 1957], pp. 67–68.)
14   M. N. Roy, *M. N. Roy's Memoirs* (Bombay: Allied Publishers, 1964), p. 379.
15   Ibid., p. 380.
16   *Second Congress of the Communist International*, 1: 117.

role "in order to awaken independent political thinking and political action."[17]

Though he held on to his principle of national self-determination, Lenin's adjustment to Roy's formulation had a political effect similar to the move by Stalin and Bukharin to consider the stage that a nation had reached. Both undermined the authenticity of the claims of nationalism and removed the restraints that Lenin had previously proposed. These more revolutionary positions pushed the Communists to a leadership in the peripheral and colonial struggles that hardly corresponded to their real power in these regions. In the absence of a significant proletariat, in situations where the only viable revolutionary movement was one that Communists could not bring themselves to support wholly, the party became a surrogate-proletariat. Instead of being engaged in the actual revolution, which was anti-colonial and led by nationalists or ethnosocialists, the party constructed a reading of the political moment that allowed them extraordinary freedom and left them open to precisely the charges of Russian expansionism of which Lenin had warned.

Within a few months, the Armenian republic, facing an invasion by the Kemalist Turks, capitulated to the Bolshevik forces stationed on its border as the lesser evil. In February 1921, the Red Army drove the Mensheviks out of Georgia. Both Transcaucasian "revolutions" were far more artificial and external than had been the collapse of Azerbaijan, where Bolsheviks enjoyed considerable support from Baku workers. Though at first the Armenian Communists agreed to work with the Dashnaks and Lenin preferred some accommodation with the Georgian

17   Ibid., 1: 110–12. Though Roy himself later underlined Lenin's shift toward his position, a comparison of his original draft and his theses as presented at the Congress show a significant adjustment on Roy's part as well. Before the Congress, Roy had taken a more forthright position on the primacy of the extra-European revolution, writing: "The fountainhead from which capitalism draws its main strength is no longer to be found in the industrial countries, but in the colonial possessions and dependencies." The European bourgeoisie, he argued, could sacrifice "the entire surplus value in the home country so long as it continues in the position to gain its huge superprofits in the colonies." Thus, the fate of the West was being determined in the East. In his Supplementary Theses at the Congress, he softened this assertion: "European capitalism draws its strength *in the main* not so much from the industrial countries of Europe as from its colonial possessions" (Sibnarayan Ray, ed., *Selected Works of M. N. Roy, Volume I, 1917–1922* [Delhi and New York: Oxford University Press, 1987], pp. 165–66; *Second Congress of the Communist International*, 1: 116; italics added for emphasis). Or in another translation: "One of the main sources from which European capitalism draws its chief strength is to be found in the colonial possessions and dependencies" (*Selected Works of M. N. Roy, Volume I, 1917–1922*, p. 174).

Mensheviks, in both cases the moderates were quickly eliminated and purely Communist political orders were established. In Transcaucasia, at least, no real attempt was made to implement the more cautious aspect of Comintern strategy, namely, limited cooperation with non-Communist nationalists. Rather, the more militant reading of that strategy, advancing as soon as possible to Communist direction of the movement, was adopted. But in Armenia and Georgia, where there was no significant support for Bolshevism, the party remained an isolated political force until time, inertia, and coercion brought grudging acquiescence from the population.

The first phase of the Comintern's involvement with the peoples of the East was over by late 1921. The revolutionary wave had receded, and the Soviet government began to see itself as one state among many, albeit with a different historical role. The link between the national question within the USSR and the anti-imperialist struggle abroad became more tenuous. Perhaps most ominously, in the light of a resistant reality in which the inevitable movement toward communism appeared stalled, the gap widened between the actual practice of Bolsheviks and the inflated rhetoric that disguised it.

Bolsheviks were a minority party representing a social class that had nearly disappeared in the civil war. With no political or cultural hegemony over the vast peasant masses and with exceptional vulnerability in the non-Russian regions, the Communist parties moderated their own leap into socialism. The years of the New Economic Policy (1921–28) were a period of strategic compromise with the peasantry in both Russia and the national republics, a time of retreat and patience awaiting the delayed international revolution. Lenin continued to advocate caution and sensitivity toward non-Russians, whereas many of his comrades, most notably Stalin and Orjonikidze, were less willing to accommodate even moderate nationalists. In several republics, leaders of defeated parties were quickly removed from power and driven into exile; but other former members of the nationalist or moderate socialist movements were integrated into the Communist parties and state apparatus. The Bolshevik project now involved the building of a new federated state that would both nurture the nations within it and forge new loyalties to the ideals of the socialists.

Nations and States

Though in popular understanding and in nationalists' ideologies the nation is usually thought to exist prior to the state and to be the basis on which the state has been formed, historians have long recognized the importance of states in the creation of nations. A quarter-century ago, Victor Kiernan wrote: "Of the two elements (nation-state) included here, it was the state that came first and fashioned the mould for the nation." The process by which the new state created the conditions for turning "a vague sense of nationality . . . into conscious nationalism" was intimately linked with the new (Renaissance) monarchies' relationship to the constituent social classes and their struggles.[18] Ernest Gellner places the state at the center of his theory of nationalism, along with industrial society, and declares bluntly that "the problem of nationalism does not arise from stateless societies."[19] Likewise, in a recent critique of John Breuilly's work on nationalism and the state, Henry Patterson agrees that "in the transition from some sense of cultural or ethnic identity to full-blown nationalism the development of the state is crucial."[20] He faults Breuilly for neglecting the ways nationalisms build on class coalitions and argues that the very success of nationalist movements, which are always class coalitions with ostensibly classless ideologies, requires an "approach that allows for the crucial role of the framework of state institutions in providing a point for the constitution and focusing of nationalist objectives."[21]

On the empirical level, the centrality of the state in nation formation has been exhaustively elaborated in an influential book by Eugen Weber, *Peasants into Frenchmen*: he shows how for a great number of French peasants a sense of being French overcame more local and particularistic identities only a century after the French Revolution.[22] Here the state was fundamental in establishing a unified school system with a homogeneous French language, mobilizing men into an army that socialized them to new norms, and breaking down the cultural and social isolation of thousands of villages. On the other hand, although it is evident that state policies and interstate warfare create opportunities for consolidating nationality and nation, it is equally clear that the original exemplars of nation-states, England and France, however they may have been formed, had a relatively homogeneous ethnic core around which other ethnic groups consolidated. The ideal for nationalists, which then was read back into the past as if it were "real history," was

18   Victor Kiernan, "State and Nation in Western Europe," *Past and Present* 30–32 (1965): 20.
19   Ernest Gellner, *Nations and Nationalism* (Ithaca, N.Y.: Cornell University Press, 1983), p. 4.
20   Henry Patterson, "Neo-Nationalism and Class," *Social History* 13, 3 (Oct. 1988): 347.
21   Ibid., p. 246.
22   Weber, *Peasants into Frenchmen: The Modernization of Rural France, 1870–1914* (Stanford, Calif.: Stanford University Press, 1976).

the coincidence of state with pre-existing nationality. With the emergence of the democratic discourse of national self-determination, it was only a small step to conclude that the only (or at least, the most) legitimate states were those based on the "natural" affinities offered by ethnicity.

"Making of Nations," Soviet-Style

The making of nationality and the spread of nationalism involved political conjunctures in which people were forced to make less ambiguous choices about their friends and enemies than they had in the past. However artificial the generation of the independent republics that mushroomed in the turned-up soil of the revolution, the very experience of a brief statehood had a profound influence on future developments. The years of independence, the ascendancy of a more nationalist discourse among their intelligentsias, and the involuntary Sovietization all contributed to the growth of secular nationalist sentiments. But the displacement of populations, the forced migration of much of the old nationalist intelligentsia and bourgeoisie, and the vast devastation of the economy, particularly in cities, during the civil war provided a political opportunity for the Bolsheviks, who proposed a program of recovery and limited self-determination.

The experience of independence and intervention differed greatly from nationality to nationality. Among the most successful was the Georgian republic, often cited as a model of a Social Democratic peasant republic by Western enthusiasts; it managed to defend itself against threats from the White forces under Denikin, rebellious local minorities, and Armenian incursions before it succumbed to the invading Red Army. In both Georgia and Armenia, parliamentary systems with representation of oppositional parties were implemented, and in both republics, desperate revolts by Mensheviks and Dashnaks after the establishment of Soviet power testified to continuing support for the anti-Soviet leaderships.

The picture is far less clear elsewhere in the non-Russian peripheries. In Ukraine, the destructiveness of the civil war (in which an estimated one million Ukrainians died), the fragility of each of the established governments, and the ferocity of the terror on both sides left a society devastated and desperate for peaceful recovery. The dearth of social historical research on the revolution in Ukraine prevents firm conclusions about the success of nationalist mobilization. The years of civil war were marked by political fragmentation and localism. Villagers turned inward in both psychological and physical self-defense. Though it is difficult

to follow the extreme conclusion that the "raising of national consciousness of the peasantry, which began in 1917, was completed by
the peasants' experience of the various Soviet regimes, foreign intervention as well as Denikin's occupation of Ukraine," Ukrainian nationalism was far stronger and more widespread at the end of the civil war
than at the beginning.[23] Identification with a territorial nation would
grow even more impressively in the 1920s under Soviet rule.[24]

In the lands inhabited by the Kazakhs, a fierce triangular struggle
pitted urban-based Bolsheviks against local White forces and the Kazakh
Alash Orda autonomous movement. As they fought alongside the
Whites between 1918 and 1919, Alash Orda grew discontented with
Kolchak's resistance to their autonomy and attempted to negotiate with
Moscow. With the defeat of the Whites late in 1919, the Bolsheviks tried
to win over the Kazakhs through a broad amnesty and concessions to
local autonomy. In the absence of alternatives, Kazakhs acquiesced to
Bolshevik rule. They returned to their seminomadic mode of existence
and regenerated their traditional social structures in the new guise of
local soviet power.[25]

For those who ended up outside the Soviet federation, like the Baltic
peoples, the even longer independence period and the brutality with
which it was ended helped to define their representation of nation. The
political and economic power of the Baltic German elites was eliminated
in the early years of independence, and, though minority cultures were
permitted free expression, the dominant nationalities now promoted
their own ethnic cultural and educational institutions. Demographically
the Baltic republics were securely national. In the 1922 census, Estoni-
ans made up 87.6 percent of the republic's population; according to
1935 figures, Latvians comprised 75.5 percent of their state's population; and in 1937, Lithuanians made up 84.2 percent of the population
in their republic.[26] The parliamentary systems established in all three
republics in the revolutionary period succumbed to more dictatorial
forms in the late 1920s and 1930s, and hostility between the Baltic
republics and their Soviet neighbor increased in the years before World
War II. Yet for all their political and economic difficulties, the Baltic

23   Bohdan Krawchenko, *Social Change and National Consciousness in Twentieth-
Century Ukraine* (Edmonton: Canadian Institute of Ukrainian Studies, University of
Alberta, 1987), p. 64.
24   Ibid., pp. 46–47.
25   "Clan, village, and all authorities simply reconstituted themselves as soviets
and governed their population much as before" (Martha Brill Olcott, *The Kazakhs*
[Stanford: Hoover Institution Press, 1987], p. 162).
26   Georg Von Rauch, *The Baltic States, The Years of Independence: Estonia, Latvia,
Lithuania 1917–1940* (Berkeley: University of California Press, 1974), pp. 82, 85.

states demonstrated viability as independent political actors, and the memory of that experience remained for the half-century of Soviet rule after 1940, eventually mobilizing the Baltic peoples in the Gorbachev years.

In the nationalist discourses of the present movements for self-determination in the Soviet Union, the brief period of independence has been transformed into a moment of light to contrast with the long, dark experience with Soviet rule, which in turn is depicted as the destruction of the national. Repression, forced Russification, imposed modernization, the suppression of national traditions, the destruction of the village, even an assault on nature are combined in powerful images that show Soviet power as the enemy of the nation. Lost in this powerful nationalist rhetoric is any sense of the degree to which the long and difficult years of Communist party rule actually continued the "making of nations" of the prerevolutionary period. As the present generation watches the self-destruction of the Soviet Union, the irony is lost that the USSR was the victim not only of its negative effects on the non-Russian peoples but of its own "progressive" contribution to the process of nation-building.

The first state in history to be formed of ethnic political units, the USSR was a pseudofederal state that both eliminated political sovereignty for the nationalities and guaranteed them territorial identity, educational and cultural institutions in their own language, and the promotion of native cadres into positions of power. Though the powerful appeal of nationalism has been a global phenomenon in the twentieth century, its potency in the Soviet Union requires analysis of the peculiar historic formation of coherent, conscious nations in a unique political system that deliberately set out to thwart nationalism. [. . .]

The policy of "nativization" (*korenizatsiia*), encouraged by Lenin and supported by Stalin until the early 1930s, contributed to the consolidation of nationality in three important ways: by supporting the native language, by creating a national intelligentsia and political elite, and by formally institutionalizing ethnicity in the state apparatus.

Already in the years of civil war, the Soviet governments adopted laws establishing the equality of languages in courts and administration, the free choice of language in schooling, and the protection of minority languages. The short-lived Latvian Soviet government adopted such a law as early as January 1918, as did the Ukrainian Soviet authorities in December 1919. In Belorussia, four different languages – Belorussian, Russian, Polish, and Yiddish – were used in signs, in local governments, and in schools. The central state promoted alphabets for peoples who had no writing, opened schools for those who had had none under tsarism, and set up hundreds of national soviets for peoples living outside their national regions. In ways strikingly similar to the work of patriotic intellectuals on behalf of some nationalities in the nineteenth century, Soviet activists set out to create educational systems and literary languages for their peoples by selecting the dialect to be promoted and by systematizing, refining, and "purifying" the lexicon.[27] By 1927, 82 percent of the schools in Ukraine had been Ukrainized, and more than three-quarters of the pupils were attending Ukrainian-language schools.[28]

Russian officials were steadily replaced by national leaders, and since many of the new Bolshevik cadres in the national republics were former members of other parties, like the Ukrainian Left SRs (known as *Borotbisti* [Fighters]), the nativization campaigns created a broad base of support for the common enterprise of ethnic liberation and socialist construction. The formation of new political classes in the national republics, Communist but made up of the local nationality, can be observed from figures for membership in the Communist parties. In 1922, 72 percent of all Communists were Russians; only 15,000 were from traditionally Muslim peoples (6,534 Tatars, 4,964 Kazakhs). Five years later, Russians made up only 65 percent of the RKP(b), and the various national regions of the USSR – union republics, autonomous republics and regions, and national territories – had achieved a level of 46.6 percent native membership (about 180,000 Communists). This trend continued until about 1932, when the native Communist party membership in the national regions reached 53.8 percent (582,000 Communists).[29] Ukrainian membership in the Ukrainian Communist party increased from 24 percent to 59 percent in the decade 1922–32; Belorussians grew from 21 percent to 60 percent of the Belorussian party. In Transcaucasia, meanwhile, the already high native percentages grew at a less spectacular rate: in Georgia, from 62 percent to 66 percent; in Armenia, from 89 percent to 90 percent; in Azerbaijan, from 39 percent to 44 percent. The figures for Central Asia were particularly noteworthy: Kazakh membership in the republican Communist party grew from 8 percent to 53 percent (1924–33), and every party in the region (that reported figures) had a majority of native members.[30]

27   Al'bert Pavlovich Nenarokov, "Iz opyta natsional'noiazykovoi politiki pervykh let sovetskoi vlasti," *Istoriia SSSR* 2 (1990): 3–14.
28   Krawchenko, *Social Change*, p. 89.
29   Gerhard Simon, *Nationalism and Policy Toward the Nationalities in the Soviet Union: From Totalitarian Dictatorship to Post-Stalinist Society* (Boulder, Colo.: Westview, 1991), p. 31.
30   Ibid., p. 48.

A similar trend can be observed in the state apparatuses of the Union republics, though here the representation of the local nationalities was far greater at the *raion* (district) level than at the republic level. In Ukraine in 1929, for example, Ukrainians made up 36 percent of the apparatus at the republic level and 76 percent at the *raion* level. The corresponding figures for Belorussians were 49.5 percent and 73 percent; for Azerbaijanis, 36 percent and 69 percent; for Georgians, 74 percent and 81 percent; for Armenians, 93.5 percent and 94.6 percent; for Turkmen, 8.4 percent and 24 percent; for Uzbeks, 11.5 percent and 41.6 percent; and for Tajiks, 14 percent and 45 percent.[31]

But the policy of nativization was contested by party members suspicious of concessions to nationality and of the inclusion in the party and state of peoples less committed to the rigid vision of the dominant faction in the Communist party. Stalin and his closest comrades were particularly hostile to the growth of "national communisms" in Georgia and Ukraine, and a bitter confrontation over the extent to which autonomy should be allowed in the non-Russian republics cooled relations between Stalin and the ailing Lenin. Once Lenin had been incapacitated by a series of strokes, Stalin used his power to exile to diplomatic posts both the Georgian Bolshevik Budu Mdivani and one of the early leaders of Ukraine, the Bulgarian Khristian Rakovskii.[32] To Stalin, local nationalism appeared to be a greater danger than the Great Russian Chauvinism of which Lenin repeatedly warned.

Despite opposition from strategically located opponents and countervailing tendencies toward political centralization, the nativization policies bore a rich harvest in the 1920s, as works by Zvi Gitelman, Bohdan Krawchenko, James Mace, and George Liber attest.[33] In Armenia, the Communists spoke of the resurrection of Armenia from the ashes of genocide, and although they drove out or arrested the anti-Bolshevik nationalists, they began the rebuilding of an Armenian state to which refugees from other parts of the Soviet Union and the world could migrate. The cosmopolitan capitals of Georgia and Azerbaijan now

31   Ibid., p. 51.
32   The struggle between Lenin and Stalin over the nationality question has been extensively explored. See, for example, Pipes, *Formation*, pp. 271–82; Moshe Lewin, *Lenin's Last Struggle* (New York: Pantheon Books, 1968); R. G. Suny, *The Making of the Georgian Nation* (Bloomington: Indiana University Press, 1988), pp. 208–21.
33   Zvi Y. Gitelman, *Jewish Nationality and Soviet Politics: The Jewish Sections of the CPSU, 1917–1930* (Princeton: Princeton University Press, 1972); Bohdan Krawchenko, Social Change; James E. Mace, *Communism and the Dilemmas of National Liberation: National Communism in Soviet Ukraine, 1918–1933* (Cambridge, Mass.: Harvard Ukrainian Research Institute, 1983); George Liber, "Urban Growth and Ethnic Change in the Ukrainian SSR, 1923–1933," *Soviet Studies* 41, 4 (Oct. 1989): 574–91.

became the seats of power of native Communists, and the infrastructures of national states, complete with national operas, national academies of science, and national film studios, were built up.

In each of the national republics, national identity was both transformed and reinforced in its new form. In Ukraine, for example, where in prerevolutionary times Ukrainian peasants had easily assimilated to a Russified working class, the new political environment and the shifts in national awareness in the 1920s were reflected in the increase in the number of "Ukrainians" in towns. "There were two aspects to this process," writes Bohdan Krawchenko. "The first was the re-absorption into a Ukrainian identity of assimilated Ukrainians. The second was that Russification, if not halted, was certainly reduced to a minimum. This meant that assimilation did not offset whatever gains Ukrainians made by urban immigration."[34] Ukrainians and other non-Russian peoples gained an urban presence they had never enjoyed before, and the dominance of Russians in the cities was compromised. "We will not forcibly Ukrainise the Russian proletariat in Ukraine," said a Ukrainian Communist leader, "but we will ensure that the Ukrainian . . . when he goes to the city will not be Russified . . . and yes, we will repaint the signs in towns."[35]

Even after it was undercut by the Stalinist emphasis on rapid industrialization, the Soviet policy of *korenizatsiia*, which involved the promotion of national languages and national cadres in the governance of national areas, increased the language capabilities and the politicization of the non-Russians in the national republics. The creation of national working classes, newly urbanized populations, national intelligentsias, and ethnic political elites contributed to the more complete elaboration of nationhood.

Yet even as ethnicity was being strengthened in some ways, it was being limited and even undermined in others. Official Soviet doctrine repeated Lenin's prediction of *sblizhenie* (rapprochement) and *sliianie* (merger) of Soviet peoples and of the creation of a single Soviet culture. Mobility, acculturation of political and intellectual elites, the preference for Russian schooling, and the generalized effects of industrialization and urbanization created anxiety about assimilation and loss of culture. A deep contradiction developed: on the one hand, *korenizatsiia* and the "renationalization" of ethnic groups in the Soviet years created strong nationalist pressures; on the other, state policies transformed an agrarian society into an industrial urban one and promoted assimilation to a generalized Soviet culture.

34   Krawchenko, p. 50.
35   Ibid., p. 56.

Glossary

Bukharin, Nikolai   One of the most prominent Bolsheviks at the national level.

Dashnak   Dashnaktsutiun: Armenian nationalist revolutionary group during the World War I era.

Denikin, Anton   One of the leading generals of the White Army in the Russian Civil War.

Kolchak, Admiral A. V.   Commander of the White Army opposing the Bolsheviks.

Orjonikidze, Sergo   Head of party bureau responsible for control of the Caucasus.

Pilsudsky, Marshal Joseph   Head of Poland's government and army at time of Red Army attack.

Further Reading: Nationalities and Regions

N. Davies, *God's Playground: A History of Poland*, 2 vols. (Columbia University Press, 1982).

Z. Y. Gitelman, *Jewish Nationality and Soviet Politics: The Jewish Sections of the Communist Party of the Soviet Union, 1917–1930* (Princeton University Press, 1972).

M. F. Hamm, *Kiev: A Portrait, 1800–1917* (Princeton University Press, 1993).

J. E. Mace, *Communism and the Dilemmas of National Liberation: National Communism in Soviet Ukraine* (Harvard Ukrainian Research Institute, 1983).

G. Massell, *The Surrogate Proletariat: Moslem Women and Revolutionary Strategies in Soviet Central Asia, 1919–1929* (Princeton University Press, 1974).

M. Olcott, *The Kazakhs* (Stanford University Press, 1987).

R. Pipes, *The Formation of the Soviet Union: Communism and Nationalism, 1917–1923* (Harvard University Press, 1954).

D. J. Raleigh, *Revolution on the Volga: 1917 in Saratov* (Cornell University Press, 1986).

Y. Slezkine, *Arctic Mirrors: Russia and the Small Peoples of the North* (Cornell University Press, 1994).

J. J. Stephan, *The Russian Far East: A History* (Stanford University Press, 1994).

R. G. Suny, *The Making of the Georgian Nation* (Indiana University Press, 1988).

Part IV
Conclusions and Prospects

9

Writing the History of the Russian Revolution after the Fall of Communism

Steve Smith

Originally appeared as Steve Smith, "Writing the History of the Russian Revolution after the Fall of Communism," *Europe-Asia Studies*, 46(4), 1994: 563–78.

Editor's Introduction

In this bold essay, Steve Smith, one of the most important social historians of the Russian Revolution, makes an attempt to summarize the main problems that have characterized the general historiography on 1917 to date and then sets forth a potential research agenda for future historians. Using the contemporary methodological paradigm of postmodernism as an analytic signpost for our time, Smith sees the work of earlier generations (their contributions notwithstanding) as being circumscribed by leaning too far either in the direction of cold War "triumphalism" or New Left "political naïveté." The former sought a moral victory over totalitarianism while the latter engaged in "apologetics" for the Soviet system or were attracted to aspects of Soviet culture at the expense of its politics. This, in turn, led to a narrowing of the kinds of questions that historians examined. Above all, Smith recognizes the virtual absence of theory in the scholarship on the Russian Revolution over the decades and the reluctance to make use of the findings in allied disciplines for comparative work.

With the opening of the archives, historians of 1917 no longer suffer from the disadvantage of the inaccessibility of unpublished materials, so crucial and available in most other fields of historical study. Smith urges future researchers to interrogate those sources in order to tackle questions that previous historians have neglected and that postmodernism has opened up for exploration. By abandoning the "grand narrative" and the moral absolutes generated by the superpower competition between the Soviet Union and the West, historians should be able to engage in the necessary work of dealing with a variety of previously buried themes that may reveal a vastly different portrait of the revolutionary era. Smith carefully outlines some of these topics and where the "exciting vistas" of such studies may lead us in the twenty-first century.

Writing the History of the Russian Revolution after the Fall of Communism

Steve Smith

A Chinese proverb speaks of 'hurling a brick in order to attract jade'. The present article is written in that spirit: it presents its arguments boldly in the hope that it will provoke lively and thoughtful reaction. It is an attempt to speculate on the implications of the fall of communism in the former Soviet Union for the writing of the history of the Russian Revolution over the next 20 years. This is self-evidently a foolhardy undertaking, since it is clearly too early to pronounce on the historical significance of the entire Soviet era.

Nevertheless the article is written in the conviction that since 1991 the history of the Russian Revolution has become 'history' in a new sense. First, historians have suddenly gained a sharper perspective on the system that was born in October 1917: it can now be seen to have a beginning, a middle and an (uncertain!) end, and it is appropriate to speculate on what this increased hindsight signifies. Second, up to 1989 the continuance of the Soviet regime and the wider system of super-power rivalry meant that study of the Russian Revolution could never be insulated from the short-term pressures of contemporary politics. That is no longer so. It does not mean that the history of the Russian Revolution has ceased to be the object of political controversy and passion, or that the Russian Revolution is 'over', as François Furet famously pronounced of the French Revolution,[1] but it does allow historians greater scope to determine agendas outside the problematics of sovietology.

The article seeks to suggest what such an agenda might look like by linking the fall of communism to the emergence of that condition of postmodernity which has been a notable feature of advanced capitalist societies during the past 20 years. It is my contention that as historians we cannot escape this condition, and that we should seek to utilise what

The author would like to thank Linda Edmondson. Chris Ward and all the participants in the discussion at the 20th annual conference of the Study Group of the Russian Revolution in January 1994 for their critical comments on this article.

1   F. Furet, *Reinterpreting the French Revolution* (London, 1981).

is best in postmodernism in the quest to extend our knowledge of the Soviet past.[2]

Before setting out a research agenda for the next 20 years, it seems appropriate to review developments in the historiography of the Russian Revolution over the past 20 years. Since the 1970s British historians have produced a couple of dozen enlightening, judicious, well-researched and occasionally path-breaking monographs on different aspects of the revolutionary era, along with some excellent articles and a few synthetic studies of high quality. Using the opportunities which emerged for limited work in Soviet archives and libraries, these scholars turned to writing the history of social groups, especially the working class, the history of the revolution in specific localities and the history of political organisations and parties in their social context. Though diverse in subject matter and approach, these works evinced a common desire to explore aspects of the Russian Revolution that had been deemed unworthy of attention by advocates of a totalitarian model and to get away from ideologically driven generalities.

The approach of this generation to the study of the Russian Revolution was profoundly shaped by the political and intellectual conjuncture of 1968. First, they shared a common rejection of Cold War assumptions about the Bolshevik Revolution, a determination to put shrill polemic to one side and a commitment to approaching Soviet society as a 'normal' society. Second, they sought to revitalise Russian history by taking on some of the perspectives and methods of the social sciences – an orientation that characterised the historical profession generally at this time. Third, and most notably, this generation was associated with establishing what might be called a 'social' interpretation of the Russian Revolution – a development that was proceeding apace in North America at the same time. It is this social interpretation – which, incidentally, was waxing just as the social interpretation of the French Revolution was coming under attack – that has drawn the fire of critics, particularly since the fall of communism.

These critics – who generally subscribe to a version of the totalitarian approach to Soviet history – were quick to seize on what they perceived to be the lessons of the fall of communism in order to discredit

2   That most astute critic of postmodernity, David Harvey, summarises the condition as follows: 'The experience of time and space has changed, the confidence in the association between the scientific and moral judgements has collapsed, aesthetics has triumphed over ethics as the prime focus of social and intellectual concern, images dominate narratives, ephemerality and fragmentation take precedence over eternal truths and unified politics, explanations have shifted from the realm of material and political-economic groundings towards a consideration of autonomous cultural and political practices'. D. Harvey, *The Condition of Postmodernity: An Enquiry into the Origins of Cultural Change* (Oxford, Basil Blackwell, 1989), p. 328.

what they called the 'revisionist' approach to the history of the Russian Revolution. The 75th anniversary of the October Revolution passed by largely unnoticed in the Western and Russian media (the general inclination, apparently, being to draw a veil over the awful three-quarters of a century long nightmare). An exception was the *Times Literary Supplement*, which invited half a dozen eminent scholars – all exponents, to a greater or lesser extent, of the totalitarian model – to celebrate the fall of communism.[3] In striking unanimity, they agreed that the latter now proved the October Revolution to have been a 'calamitous accident', a 'model putsch', a 'surgical strike against the vital organs of the state'. A couple reserved their most withering scorn for the 'revisionists', who, they suggested, had been revealed as unwitting dupes of Soviet ideology, and whose advocacy of the 'pretentious disciplines of political and social "science"' had proved jejune.

Such triumphalism seems premature. In the West there is little evidence that the historiographic field is being reconstituted along the lines of warmed-up Cold War dogma. And in the former Soviet Union the totalitarian approach, understandably welcomed in the first flush of *perestroika*, already seems yesterday's news. There are, alas, signs that the tone of historical inquiry is beginning to revert from the dispassionate to the denunciatory – even among scholars associated with 'revisionism'. It is a tendency we should guard against. For if we approach the Russian Revolution with undisguised hostility, it is likely that understanding will be drowned out by our vituperation. Polemic has its place, certainly, and it is cathartic for citizens of the former Soviet Union to engage in it. But in the longer term, a historical practice which abandons its aspiration to explain the past in favour of condemning it will lose any claim to social usefulness.

This is not to demand that we should be 'soft' on the bolsheviks. I would readily admit that there was a political naiveté to some of the work that was done in the first wave of enthusiasm for social history. I think that this was more a fault of those of a social democratic or liberal persuasion than of those who drew inspiration from the New Left, since it was often the mistaken desire to depoliticise the historiography of the Russian Revolution which ended up in apologetics for the Soviet system. Moreover, a failure of moral and political imagination, a myopic social scientism, held sway in some quarters. To this extent, I believe that the critics of 'revisionism' are correct. Indeed, all of us who espoused a 'social' interpretation of the Russian Revolution might concede that we were not always mindful of the ubiquity of power in Russian and Soviet history.

3   *Times Literary Supplement*, 6 November 1992.

But there are other, more serious weaknesses that have characterised Western, particularly British, historiography of the Russian Revolution during the past two decades. If detailed studies of circumscribed topics over relatively short spans of time have yielded dividends in deepening understanding of the social and political dynamics of the revolution, they have also produced a certain blinkeredness, a tendency to shy away from big questions about 'what it all meant'. Consider how few debates and controversies there have been in the field of Russian and Soviet history during the past 20 years: the work of Theodore Shanin was notably fecund, though the debate inspired by it did not last beyond the 1970s;[4] perhaps the debate on peasant living standards during the late-imperial period, though that soon fizzled out also; certainly, the (largely American) debate on the social interpretation of Stalinism. Otherwise there has been remarkably little interest in the kind of big questions that draw students to Russian history. And in so far as these have been discussed, they have been largely the ones first raised by historians two or even three generations ago: reform versus revolution after 1905, and the continuity between Leninism and Stalinism. The terms of these debates, moreover, have remained remarkably unchanged.

Perhaps I can illustrate in more detail what is wrong by looking at the field in which I have worked, that of labour history in the late-imperial and revolutionary periods. Without doubt, this has been the most productive field in which 'revisionists' in Britain, the USA, Canada or Japan have worked. There now exist more than a score of detailed studies of the Russian working class from the late 19th century through to the 1930s, mainly focused on particular cities or regions. Almost all are of a high standard, offering stimulating insights as well as extending our knowledge. Yet hardly any addresses the kinds of questions that bright undergraduates ask in class. Was there something 'special' about the Russian working class? Did it acquire a revolutionary class consciousness in the years after 1905? Or did Russian workers simply have ordinary aspirations that could no longer be accommodated in 1917 without a profound shift in the balance of power? If so, why is it that not all revolutionary situations give rise to revolutionary labour movements (just as often they seem to split them or shift them to the right, as apparently happened in Germany in 1918–19)?

No doubt there are many reasons for the reluctance to face up to big questions. In Britain – perhaps less so in North America – Russian history tended to remain tied to the sub-disciplines of Slavic or Soviet Studies which, while having very different problematics, both fostered a rather narrow set of questions and discouraged wide-ranging and com-

---

4   T. Shanin, *The Awkward Class. Political Sociology of the Peasantry in a Developing Society: Russia, 1910–25* (Oxford, 1972).

parative enquiry. Second, much of the energy of Western scholarship derived from debunking the myths of Soviet historiography. In intellectual terms, this was always a rather low-cost option, but it provided work that was largely empirical in character with a pseudo-conceptual underpinning. A third element in the explanation may relate to the institutional pressures which operate on academic historians – the pressure towards narrow specialisation, the pressure to publish (the tenure hurdle in the USA, the research assessment rankings in Britain), the pressure to net funds from research councils whose priorities are significantly shaped by contemporary exigencies.

More important, in my view, than any of these factors, however, is the general distrust of theory and explicit conceptualisation that is evident among so many historians of Russia. Empiricism still holds sway to an extent that is not true among historians of other countries, notwithstanding the percolation of concepts and approaches from the social sciences from the 1960s onwards. How many of us rose to the challenge to conventional ways of thinking about the Russian Revolution that was posed by the work of Theda Skocpol or Perry Anderson? How many historians in the West engaged with the infrequent but occasionally stimulating debates that took place among our Soviet colleagues (on the nature of the autocratic state, for example)? This evasion of debate about big issues, linked to the reluctance to generalise out of and bring theory into substantive historical research is, in my view, at the root of a malaise that besets our field.

Despite the intrinsic drama of Russian and Soviet history, the writers of its history (and I have Britain mainly in mind) have been depressingly unadventurous. This becomes evident if we compare it with the historiography of other European countries. What parallel is there among historians of Russia to the lively debate on the English Civil War between the exponents of a structural explanation – either couched in terms of constitutional crisis or of class conflict – and the 'revisionists' who emphasise short-term causation and a concatenation of mishaps? What is the parallel to the debate sparked by 'revisionists' of the French Revolution who insist that the political character of the upheavals of 1789–94 cannot be deduced from social phenomena held to be more basic? What is the parallel to the theoretically astute yet empirically dense debates among German historians about the *Sonderweg*, the continuities between the Wilhelmin and the Nazi eras, or about the nature of the Nazi state? Such comparisons are all to our detriment. A cloud of intellectual inertia seems to hang over our field.

Of course, this is a harsh generalisation to make about a field in which the volume of highly professional studies grows exponentially. The work of individuals should certainly be exempt from these strictures, and they do not apply to all areas within the field – women's history, notably, has had a real élan in recent years, due to its intimate relation with feminism as an ongoing political and intellectual movement. But liveliness is not a word that springs readily to mind when one is seeking to characterise the field as a whole.

This judgement is directed mainly, though not exclusively, at British historians. In general, scholarship in the USA has been more lively and innovative during the past 20 years. It is hard to be sure why this is so. In part, it is an effect of the greater number of Russian historians active on the other side of the Atlantic. In part it is a consequence of the excellent system of graduate education which exists in North American universities. It may also reflect the demonstrably superior conditions that academics in the more prestigious institutions enjoy (lighter teaching and administrative loads, better study leave provision, greater access to resources in the form of research assistants, travel money and IREX opportunities). Finally, it may have something to do with the greater status that attaches to higher education in the USA, where an academic career is still seen as something worth striving for.

Setting an Agenda: General Principles

Before specifying areas in which it seems desirable to focus research over the next couple of decades, it is worth making some general comments about what is required if we are intellectually to revitalise our field. A first point to make is that the opening of the archives of the former Soviet Union ushers in unprecedented opportunities for research in new areas. For too long we have laboured at a disadvantage compared with fellow historians of other European countries. It is not just that we have been deprived of access to secret or sensitive information: primary sources of central importance to the study of the Russian Revolution, such as the protocols of the Petrograd Soviet, have been unavailable to us. At the same time, we should not imagine that getting access to new documentation will of itself elevate the quality of historical scholarship. Doubtless, important discoveries will be made (though I am rather sceptical that dramatic revelations await us in the archives): the sticking point will be what we do with them. There is a danger that a fetishisation of the archive will substitute for creative, innovative thinking.

As the implications of the fall of communism work themselves into the collective consciousness, a profound shift in perspective on the Russian Revolution is beginning to take place. Communism in any meaningful sense is a thing of the past – although that is less evident if one is looking west from Tokyo rather than east from London. It is now incumbent on us to use this retrospective distance to set the 70-odd years of Soviet history into sharper focus. This places a premium on intellectual reflexivity. We need to become aware of how our problematics, priorities and categories were shaped at the deepest level by Soviet power. Whether our political leanings were to left or right, a Soviet master-narrative tended subliminally to influence our approach, even as we busily disproved its substantive claims. This does not mean that our problematics were false or that researchers were led up blind alleys, but it does mean that the foreshortened perspective, the taken-for-granted assumptions, the hierarchies of relevance engendered by that master-narrative are only now becoming apparent.

As that master-narrative recedes, we have the possibility to construct radically different ways of thinking about the Russian Revolution. But to do that, we need to start by approaching the Soviet past as something strange and unfamiliar. In our research and writing we should seek to emulate that principle of *ostranenie* which was held in such esteem by the Russian Formalists, since making strange, rather than taking for granted, is a condition of asking interesting questions. One of the besetting sins of Cold War historiography was its implicit presentism: it knew what the Soviet past was about because the odious reality of Soviet power was there for all to see. In a different way, too, for the generation of 1968, the history of the Russian Revolution was always understood through the lens of contemporary political exigencies. Yet within less than ten years the Russian Revolution will have become a fact of the previous rather than the present century. As that happens, the passage of time will of itself make the event seem strange. But we can assist the process of defamiliarisation. This will be in the interests of good scholarship, but will also, I believe, facilitate the renewal of a politics aimed at bettering the world, since political inspiration may be drawn from the Russian Revolution only after its radical alterity is recognised.

In the 1960s the principal intellectual challenge to Russian and Soviet history came from the social sciences, from the need to inject a modicum of economic theory and sociological literacy into historical practice. Since then a fine body of work – particularly on the economic and social history of the Soviet Union in the 1920s and 1930s – testifies to the fact that the challenge was met (in certain quarters, of course, it was never taken up). Today the challenge comes from a different direction, namely, from the geological shift that is taking place in the humanities as a consequence of the 'linguistic turn'. In disciplines as various as philosophy, literary criticism, social anthropology and history the past decade has witnessed a deepening recognition of the ways in which 'reality' is produced through language, a growing concern with the production and communication of meaning in social life. Among historians this is associated with a recognition of the ways in which discourses

– institutionalised modes of speaking and writing, symbolically articulated social practices (the definitions are various) – constitute the economic, social and political spaces in which people in the past acted. In addition, it entails a recognition of the ways in which the historian's own discourse constitutes the objects which he or she purports to describe realistically and analyse objectively. The challenges thrown up by the 'linguistic turn' affect us whether we specialise in Gosplan investment targets, the campaigns on the Eastern Front or the ideology of the Workers' Opposition.

The 'linguistic turn' is but one symptom of the wider cultural transition to postmodernism. Many distinct, contradictory intellectual currents are lumped together under this catch-all term, but whether one is dealing with poststructuralism, deconstruction or certain styles of feminist analysis, these currents all share a tendency to subvert the grounds on which knowledge claims are secured. I do not believe that we can escape this condition of postmodernity, since its roots lie in new forms of capitalist restructuring and political and social readjustment that are making themselves felt at a global level. Indeed, I think that the intellectual challenge to historians of postmodernism is an invigorating one, which we would do well to 'take on' – in the double sense of accepting its force (taking it on board) and of resisting it (squaring up to some of its wilder claims). Over the next 20 years, I believe, much of the most challenging work will come from historians who are trying to face up to the discursivity of history as a discipline, its subordination to the effects of language and writing.[5]

Postmodernity also means facing up to the fact that all knowledge is implicated in the social and political practices of a specific historical and cultural moment. This is already apparent within our discipline in the massive widening of historical subject matter that has occurred during the past 20 years, in the growing interest that historians have shown in what were once considered 'non-topics' – domestic labour, leisure, crime, homosexuality. Such topics have acquired legitimacy as objects of study very much as a consequence of contemporary social and polit-

5   I am steering clear of an extended discussion of history and postmodernism in this article, but it is perhaps worth indicating the general areas in which I have reservations about its claims upon our discipline. There are cogent philosophical grounds – in respect of postmodernism's expunging of agency from the realm of language, in its peremptory rejection of any form of epistemological realism – for defending a distinction between discursive and non-discursive realms. However problematic that distinction may be, its installation seems to me to be the foundational act whereby history consititutes itself as a discipline. And a history that eschewed concepts which rely on that distinction, such as representation, determination or agency – however much those may function largely as rhetorical devices – would be much impoverished.

ical developments. In Russian history the broadening of subject matter has been going on for over a decade. A clutch of recent works treats subjects such as popular entertainment, drink, peasant women and hooliganism. The import of this broadening of historical concern is to undermine taken-for-granted assumptions about what is and is not significant about the Russian Revolution, and to reveal how the apparently marginal, when set in relation to other phenomena, can lay bare the unacknowledged workings of larger systems of power. In other words, an implicit challenge already exists within our field to the hierarchies of relevance that have traditionally structured our intellectual endeavours.

It would be an oversimplification to imply that there was ever a single agreed hierarchy of relevance among historians of the Russian Revolution. The point is that hitherto the issue was not addressed. That is going to change over the next two decades. Indeed it is quite likely that we shall become increasingly uncertain as to what 'a' history of the Russian Revolution should look like. This will force out into the open questions about the organising principles, strategic priorities and forms of writing we adopt. Could one have a synoptic history of 1917 – as opposed to a specialist monograph – that was not axed along the lines of the February Revolution, dual power and the October seizure of power? Could one construct a narrative of that *annus mirabilis* which put the experience of peasants or women at its centre? In my view, the implication of this should not be that 'anything goes'. There may be no possibility of establishing grounds on which a true account can be anchored, or on which incommensurate narratives can be reconciled, yet we shall continue to find some accounts of the Russian Revolution more enlightening than others and to judge their respective merits on technical, substantive, literary or theoretical grounds. The point is that the postmodern condition forces us to be explicit about the strategic decisions we take when constructing our accounts, forces us to recognise that we are not recreating the past, but representing it.

This opens up exciting vistas. Narratives of Soviet history have been organised along axes as different as the abolition of the market and the institution of a planned economy, state-building or the creation of a one-party dictatorship. We are now free to write our histories along radically new lines, to try out startling 'takes' on Soviet reality. To offer an example or two: Mayakovsky compared modernity to a liner daringly splitting the oceans of the future, and the association of bolshevism and modernity is well known. Why not construct the history of the Soviet Union along the organising axis of modernity – commitment to progress, rational control of society and nature, secularisation, the disenchantment of the world? (Incidentally, such a history would need to give equal attention to the counter-modernising thrusts within the bolshevik project – the brake applied to increasing pluralism in society and culture, the resistance to commodification etc.) Or a social historian might wish to write a history of peasants and workers in late-imperial Russian that eschews the organising paradigm of socioeconomic transformation with its supposedly concomitant changes of consciousness, and take as her narrative principle what Francis Fukuyama has called *thymos*, the universal human need for recognition in the eyes of others.[6] This could be a powerful way of analysing the clamorous struggle for dignity and respect which welled up in Russian society after the 1905 Revolution.

We do not all need to adopt radically new paradigms (it was Schönberg who said that there is still plenty of good music to be written in the key of C major!). But if we are to inject vitality into our field, it is incumbent on all of us to engage in more explicit conceptualisation in our work, however delimited its scope or empirical its character, and to seek to relate our findings to wider concerns. In a sense, refusal is not an option, since even the most dyed-in-the-wool empiricist has recourse to abstract terms ('authority', 'state', 'culture'), however much he or she may resist them. But too often among historians of Russia the use of concepts is unreflective or purely rhetorical. In writing about the history of 1917, for example, we need to be far more precise in our use of concepts such as 'state', 'power' or 'democracy'. The generation before us – that of Leonard Schapiro or E. H. Carr – was more attentive to these matters. Similarly, we need to attend to the terms that structure the discourse of the revolution itself – *gosudarstvennost'*, *vlast'*, 'revolutionary democracy'. It is my contention that if we do so, the quality of work and the standard of debate in our field will rise.

The following list of areas for research is deliberately pitched at a high level of generality. There are many substantive topics crying out for research which one could include in such a list – popular religion, food riots, *kustar'* industry, the Black Hundreds, to choose at random. There are also some critically important historical questions to which we do not have satisfactory answers (the elements of conspiracy behind the February Revolution; the extent of profiteering during the war; the significance of the Constituent Assembly). These, too, do not figure on my list, which concentrates instead on selecting ten broad areas which seem to offer potential for advancing knowledge and transforming understanding of the Russian Revolution. In line with my commitment to taking on the challenge of postmodernism, I hope the list is heterogeneous in both subject-matter and approach and that it registers the fact

6 F. Fukuyama, *The End of History and the Last Man* (London, 1992), pp. 162–165.

that pluralism – letting a hundred schools of thought contend – is not only desirable but will be an ineluctable feature of society in the 21st century.

The Agenda

1. We must advance the *social history* of the late-imperial and Soviet periods, first, by continuing to extend its reach. There are topics of central human significance whose history has yet to be written – the history of birth and death, romantic love, childhood, ethics, racial attitudes (to name but a few). Moreover, we should not be afraid to carve out subjects that did not necessarily exist as a unified focus of concern for contemporaries (or, more precisely, which were scattered across different discursive formations). A few stimulating examples of the creation of new historical subjects already exist in the shape of studies of sexuality, utopian visions, iconography and visual representation. Second, we need perhaps to free ourselves from too exclusive a concern with social groups, even though there are important ones, such as the Orthodox clergy, the village intelligentsia, the urban lower middle classes, which await their historians for the revolutionary epoch. One reason is that work focused on groups tends to reinforce a type of social history that rests comfortably on a notion of social/economic determination. By contrast, postmodernism compels us to face the difficulties attendant on reconstructing social groups as historical agents and upon recovering their experience. Third, the next 20 years are going to be critical in tapping the huge potential of oral history for the 1920s and 1930s (for 1917 it is too late). This has already begun in Russia with the activities of groups such as Memorial, but foreign historians need to get in on the act. Historians of the Chinese Revolution have much to teach us in this respect, particularly those hybrid studies which marry social anthropology – for example, extended field work in Chinese villages – to history based on oral and written sources. Let us get talking to the workers, peasants, party bosses and generals before it is too late. And let us also take a leaf out of the recent historiography of Italian fascism, and think ambitiously about the ways in which popular memory itself was formed in Russia.

2. *Class* permeates Russian history in the period from 1905 through to the 1920s. Yet the need for *ostranenie* is nowhere greater than with regard to it. For the enormity of class inequality tends to reinforce a methodology that treats class as a social fact derived from a material base, and class consciousness as something directly induced by the pro-

cesses of industrialisation and urbanisation. Yet these latter processes, which have transformed large parts of the world in the second half of the twentieth century, have not produced the same types of class-based political movements as occurred in tsarist Russia – thereby registering the extent to which class formation is discursively produced. The formation of a working class (or any class) as a historical 'subject' was not just a consequence of social and economic change, but of reconfigurations of discourse in which class became the organising centre for constructing social reality. We need to explore the ways in which class as a particular model of social and political identity was created and communicated.[7] In relation to political history, we should investigate how class came to organise the rhetoric of conservatives and even liberals, and how the discourse of citizenship and rights was marginalised and colonised after 1905 by that of class. In relation to 1917 we can explore the complex interrelations between 'class' and *narod*, in order to pursue the question whether in that year the fundamental rift was one between classes or between popular and ruling forces. Similarly, the fate of the language of class once it became the language of the bolshevik ruling order offers scope for innovative research.

3.   If much work has already been done on class, it has barely begun on the other fundamental lines of social cleavage. *Gender* is a constituent element in all facets of human activity, and Russia in the period from 1914 to the late 1920s provides a remarkable case-study of a profound recasting of gender relations that was both 'objectively' and 'subjectively' determined. War had the paradoxical effect of, on the one hand, intensifying segregation of the sexes (men sent off to the front, women left in the rear) and, on the other, of blurring gender differences (women's entry into public life challenged traditional divisions between home and work, private, and public). This was followed by the bolsheviks' sustained attempt to upgrade the position of women through education, wage-earning, the reform of marriage and divorce laws. Capturing the complex balance between continuity and change, between radicalism and conservatism, is a task that remains to be done, in spite of some fine contributions to women's history that have appeared in recent years. Gender history, however, goes well beyond the history of the social roles and expectations ascribed to women and men. If we construe gender as the social and cultural organisation of sexual difference, then suggestive possibilities for the utilisation of gender as an analytical

7   See, especially, Geoff Eley, 'Is All the World a Text? From Social History to the History of Society Two Decades Later', in Terence MacDonaly (ed), *The Historic Turn in the Social Sciences* (Ann Arbor, MI, 1993).

tool in say, the study of political history are opened up.[8] We can explore how gender was used to legitimise war, how the expending of young men's lives in protection of the state depended critically on notions of manhood, filial duty, (masculine) honour, defence of the (feminine) nation. And we can look at the ways that bolshevik discourse was frequently coded in masculine terms, notwithstanding its commitment to women's emancipation.

4.   The break-up of communism has already forced on to the historical agenda issues of *nationalism and ethnicity*. The Soviet Union never considered itself a new nation-state, but rather a model for a future in which nationalism as a political principle was superseded. This claim was not as ludicrous as it is currently fashionable to suppose. Nevertheless, just as the economic, social, political and cultural developments of the communist era served to foster nationalisms among the non-Russian peoples, so, in one of history's little ironies, it may come to seem that this was also the era which saw the demise of class consciousness among the dominant nationality and the growth of a popular Russian national consciousness.

Both national and ethnic identities must be understood as complex cultural and social creations, as self-conscious projections that entail the selection and appropriation of signs of ethnicity, such as religion, language and history. National identity, like class identity, is discursively constituted rather than a direct product of social and political change. If we follow Benedict Anderson in thinking of nations as imagined communities,[9] as human fictions with real causes and effects rather than as material realities (*pace* Stalin), then we can start to look concretely at the ways in which the ethnic and national groups that comprised the Russian Empire imagined themselves, of how they defined and redefined themselves in response to particular others and of how consciousness of distinctiveness was forged in response to historical events (war and revolution being critical in deepening resentments, firming up loyalties and redefining experience and memory in ethnic terms).

Russian nationalism was intimately linked to an expansive, multinational empire (according to the 1897 census, non-Russians made up 55.7% of the empire's 122.6 million people). Some good work has already been done on the relations between Russians and non-Russian minorities, which shows that these were never ones of straightforward

8   See Joan W. Scott, *Gender and the Politics of History* (New York, 1988).
9   B. Anderson, *Imagined Conummnities: Reflections on the Origins and Spread of Nationalism* (London, 1983).

domination and subordination: they were always criss-crossed by social fissures within the minority groups, by the attractions of assimilation for certain elements etc. We need now to investigate how Russia came to constitute itself in relation to the non-Russian minorities of the empire, to look at how explorers, anthropologists, visual artists and the like constructed these self-constituting others.

It is time, too, to unsettle the unconscious Russocentrism of our accounts of the Revolution and the Civil War by writing its history 'from the margins'. By that I do not mean simply adding to the sum of local studies of the 1917 Revolution (many reliable and some superb studies of most regions and nations of the empire now exist) but using these as a means to deconstruct the assumptions that have been taken as normative for the 'Russian' Revolution as a whole, when this was always a revolution across a multiethnic empire (e.g. the assumption that class was the dominant focus of political identity). Those in the newly enfranchised states, writing as Latvians, Georgians, Uzbeks, or even Siberians, are well placed to do this.

In the case of Russian national identity, it is surprising how sketchy our knowledge is. Because political nationalism was so colonised by the Right in late-imperial Russia, we assume it had little popular resonance (though this is deduced rather than proven). Yet the prevalence of anti-semitism – a key ingredient in one influential rendition of what it meant to be Russian – ought to induce caution. As against that, there are signs that from the 1860s national identity was being redefined in more liberal, less exclusive terms than those of Official Nationality. If we may not speak of popular nationalism, we may nevertheless be seeing a process in which national consciousness was being popularised. Allan Wildman has argued that the mass of peasants drafted into the army during World War I did not share the sense of nationhood to which the Provisional Government appealed, yet we need more research on the meanings that these peasants attached to their native places, the links they made between them and 'Mother Russia', their images of the enemy, their devotion to Orthodoxy.[10]

In 1917 among Russians class consciousness appears to sweep aside national consciousness. But though class loyalty and national loyalty were in tension, they were never as mutually incompatible as either the bolsheviks or their enemies believed. Here is a good instance of how the terms of the Soviet problematic – apparently backed up by 'facts' such as the weakness of socialist defencism, the intense popular hostility to the war, the admirable internationalism of sections of the working class

---

10   Allan K. Wildman, *The End of the Russian Imperial Army: The Old Army and the Soldiers' Revolt, March–April 1917* (Princeton, NJ, 1980).

– have blinded us to the ways in which a deeper attachment to the nation may have underlain the strident expressions of class antagonism. Nor should we forget that the transcendence of nationalism promised by Social Democracy was only ever offered on Russian terms.

5.   The three foregoing topics could all be considered subsets of the larger issue of *social identities*, which was first raised in relation to our field by Leo Haimson.[11] Identity is about who we are. According to anthropological cliche, identity in traditional societies is fixed, solid and stable, whereas in modern societies it becomes mutable, multiple, self-reflexive. It is a complex interaction of identifications based on age, ethnicity, gender, class, religion, whose unstable ordering is managed through language and representation: it involves processes of inclusion and exclusion, of negation and reinforcement. Crucially, it has a temporal dimension: identities are assembled through the meshing together of two types of historical time: the life history and the history of the society. Erik Erikson provides an elaborate documentation of the ways in which 'value in the eyes of others' is at once the general determinant of identity and a determinant which is historically variable.[12] Some groups are more exposed than others to experiences that deny past identities and affirm the possibility of new ones. Politics involves conflict over or acceptance of collective identities as much as it entails conflict over who gets what, when and how. The transformation of social identities by the Russian Revolution offers great scope for research.

6.   Although *power* has figured centrally in narratives of Russian and Soviet history, the critics of the 'revisionists' have, with some justice, accused them of failing to appreciate the extent of coercion entailed in establishing the bolshevik regime, especially in the countryside. The force of this criticism hit me three years ago, when I spent a couple of weeks in the excellent *oblast'* archive in Perm', looking partly at materials relating to so-called 'kulak' resistance in the first half of 1918. Yet I was also struck by the need to extend our concept of power beyond that of simple coercion, and by the ways that historical analysis is handicapped by conceptual dichotomies such as voluntary versus coerced, support versus resistance. It seemed to me that the problem was precisely to understand how the extensive use of brute force meshed with other forms of power, including exhortatory propaganda, bargaining, leverage, opportunism, to establish bolshevik rule in the countryside. We need to enlarge our understanding of power, to understand it as

11   L. H. Haimson, 'The Problem of Social Identities in Early Twentieth-Century Russia', *Slavic Review*, 47, 1, 1988.
12   E. Erikson, *Identity: Youth and Crisis* (New York, 1968).

capacity, as something implicated in all social activity. Only then will we begin to appreciate the complex blend of enthusiasm, hope, fear, violence, neutrality and apathy that was at issue in the consolidation of the bolshevik regime.

The political history of the Russian Revolution, where the existing literature is so rich, would benefit from being rejigged along new axes. A history of the internal passport from the late 19th century, for example, might tell us more about the nature of power in late-imperial and Soviet Russia than another study of the Third Duma or of *raikom* party organisation. (In 1896 in St Peterburg, in a population of 1.2 million inhabitants, there were 23 000 arrests for passport violations, compared to 46 000 for criminal offences.) Or one might take the 'undergovernment' of the countryside as one's theme, looking at the ways in which the coercive and non-coercive organs of state power shaped the lives of peasants before and after 1917. Or more ambitiously, one might try to trace the reproduction of the culture of bureaucracy across the 1917 divide: how corruption, *proizvol*, the lack of a clearly defined system of administrative rules, the near-impossibility of speedy redress of grievances, the overriding of the law by emergency powers, continued to be defining features of the political culture of Russia. By taking new organising themes in this way, we may conclude that the revolution was far less revolutionary than it has appeared if we look at formal institutions.

Since the onset of *perestroika* there has been much interest in the concept of 'civil society', but historical work that looks at its origins is still embryonic. We need to trace the roots of *obshchestvennost'*: not just in relation to demands for representative government, but in relation to the creation of new institutions, discourses and social spaces. Provincial capitals may be a good place to advance this research, for by looking at the role of the press, the rise of a reading public, the improvements in transport, the emergence of new forms of sociability, we may discover that the central bureaucracy was less successful in stifling the sociability and public-mindedness of local elites than we have supposed.

We might also try our hand at using some of the techniques of deconstruction in political history. To deconstruct a discourse is to show how it undermines the philosophy it asserts, the hierarchical oppositions on which it relies, by identifying the rhetorical operations that produce the supposed ground of argument. For example, although Western historians have approached Soviet historiography of the Bolshevik Party with extreme scepticism, emphasising such factors as internal opposition, changes in the party line, the untypicality of Lenin's views, they have tended to assume that it was a single organisation with a continuous history, a reasonably cogent ideology, clear boundaries etc. Perhaps the time has come to look at how the Bolshevik Party's history was constructed in the 1920s, entailing processes of inclusion and exclusion, and how this has fed back into shaping the analytical categories of historians in the West. Following the techniques of deconstruction, historians might find it fruitful to dismantle the Bolshevik Party as a unified subject, and to look instead at the different and competing meanings and strategic usages of designations such as 'bolshevik', 'menshevik', 'SR'; to place 'deviations' at the centre of the party and to push Lenin to the margin (possibly, to position the party's centre of gravity with the 'syndicalists' prior to 1914, or with Kamenev in 1917).

7.   On 19 September 1917 *Russkie Vedomosti* observed: 'on opening the paper every day, the man in the street finds the same torrent of political words and with them forgets about the approaching threat of economic facts'. Following the historians of the French Revolution, it is time that we attended more to the 'torrent of words', the *language*, that gave shape to the Russian Revolution.[13] In revolutionary situations the language of order, like order itself, breaks down. Such situations call forth the 'extraordinary' (the *Ausseralltäglichkeit*, which Max Weber presented as the decisive characteristic of charisma), a discourse capable of giving systematic expression to the gamut of disorienting experiences. And revolutions see the forging of new languages and symbolic practices through which political claims can be made. Close, detailed study of the dominant discourses of politics between 1905 and the 1920s will reap dividends, for discourses situate subjects politically, make sense of their experiences, mobilise support behind particular projects and establish the basis for political, intellectual and moral leadership. Why did socialism become the preferred idiom of politics in 1917? What did different social groups understand by 'democracy'? What conceptions underpinned the democratisation of governmental structures? Why was antipathy to the 'bourgeoisie' so widely dispersed in Russian society?

8.   The collapse of communism has stimulated new interest in the history of the *market* and of entrepreneurship in Russia. We need research on the growth and integration of the national market and its specialised sectors, the monetarisation of the rural economy, 'commodification' of social life. Such research must be attentive to what Karl Polanyi called the 'social embeddedness' of market relations.[14] It must also attend to cultural attitudes towards the market, to the apparently widespread hostility to *kulaki-miroedy, skupshchiki, meshochniki*, nepmen *et al.*

13   See Keith M. Baker, *Inventing the French Revolution* (Cambridge, 1990).
14   Karl Polanyi, *The Great Transformation* (New York, 1944).

The Soviet order firmly subordinated consumption to production, and invested great energy into sustaining the belief that citizens should constitute their collective identity around their experiences at the point of production. In capitalist societies, meanwhile, consumption gradually became the principal site of personal fulfilment, aspiration, alienation. Nevertheless, there is a history of mass consumption to be written for Russia, especially for the late-imperial period, starting with the slow development of a consumer market in textiles, the diffusion of consumer durables, patterns of saving and spending, the rise of the department store, changing popular taste, the market place as a site of cultural affirmation, appropriation etc. What happens to 'consumption' in the Soviet period is unclear: it is largely, but not exclusively, a story of appalling hardship, shortages, shoddy goods. Yet new 'needs' do slowly develop, as a result of urbanisation, education, increase in disposable income, fashion, the emergence of specialised subcultures around youth etc. As Russia becomes a capitalist society, the need for a sociocultural history of consumption that is attentive to gender as well as class, to the mythic as well as material dimensions of commodities will increase.

9.   Is to be hoped that we come increasingly to see *cultural history* not as the icing on the cake but as central to understanding historical change. In a real sense, it logically should not figure as a separate item on this list, since I am concerned to suggest that, whatever our specialist field, we need to put at the centre of our enquiries the processes whereby social life is invested with meaning. However, cultural historians have always been specially concerned with analysing certain types of object, text, artwork (whether of the 'high' or 'popular' variety). And it is to be hoped that the continuance of specialist studies on literature, film, music, sport or whatever, suitably oriented towards understanding how these things were 'read', consumed, used and enjoyed, and also how they were connected with other cultural objects and social practices, will help us better to appreciate the complex processes whereby political power was exercised, whereby social elites were reestablished and whereby social groups were consolidated and identities worked out.

10.   Consciously *comparative study* is a powerful tool in helping us reconsider our assumptions about the uniqueness of Soviet (or possibly communist) experience. Though historians tend to be unexcited by the type of macro-level comparative analysis that is concerned with the structural, the quantitative and with model-building, this by no means exhausts the forms of comparative enquiry available. A more qualita-

tive, middle-range, historically bounded, culturally specific approach to comparison, attentive to questions of agency, meaning and context, would prove invaluable in building new sets of questions into our field of study. Such comparison need not be cross-national, it can be focused on regions, on different social groups, on different moments in time (1905 compared with 1917). The comparative study of communist societies always had an important place within Soviet studies, but tended to focus on institutions and political processes. It also tended to take the Russian experience as the norm. Comparative history should now be used to investigate the uniqueness of the Russian Revolution. Most communist regimes, for instance, were tied to a nationalist or anti-colonial project, which was never true for the Soviet Union. In other words, the 1917 Revolution was quite distinctive. Dual power proved to be the exception, not the rule. Nowhere else did soviets play quite the same role (even in the Bavarian and Hungarian 'soviet' republics), likewise factory committees (cf. Chile or Iran).

Cut loose from the somewhat narrow agenda of sovietology, we need to reintegrate Russian history into European history (and perhaps into Asian history). An older generation of Russian historians, particularly in this country (one thinks of Hugh Seton-Watson or Leonard Schapiro), always thought about Russia in its wider context, and we need to revive that tradition.

Conclusion

It may be appropriate to end by speculating on the relationship over the next two decades between the kind of agenda outlined above and developments in historical writing in the former Soviet Union. I am basically pessimistic about the prospects for Russia over the next 20 years, but since no social transition as complex as the one that is presently underway is an unrelieved tale of woe, there are many positive developments currently taking place. Among them I detect a revival of historical writing. This may seem dubious to those who believe that it will take Russian historians a generation to 'catch up' with their Western counterparts, but I reckon that the dogmatic straitjacket of Soviet historiography has already been sloughed off, at least for the younger generation. Of course, the material conditions of academics, archivists and librarians at present are appalling and this may pose insuperable obstacles to the regeneration of scholarly work. But history still holds a place within the national culture that it has lost in the West (Chekhov wrote in *The Steppe* that 'the Russian loves to remember, but does not like to live'!), and I am hopeful that in spite of all the hardships, honest, critical, questioning work on the history of Russia in this century will develop apace.

If it does, it raises the question of the relationship between Western and Russian historiography. This is where I would make a second point, which somewhat contradicts the first. Although a sharp distinction between 'Soviet" and "Western" ('marxist' or 'bourgeois') historiography has already dissolved, I doubt whether this means that the distinction between Russian and foreign historiography of the Russian Revolution will vanish, at least over the next two decades. Certainly, the distance between the two will be reduced, as intellectual traffic increases, as social contacts expand and as collaboration becomes more common. But historians in Russia and the West will continue to respond to fundamentally different rhythms. I suspect that the agenda that I have set forth will look to my colleagues in the former Soviet Union to be less about history after the fall of communism than about history after the arrival of postmodernity. That cannot be avoided: we in the West write insulated from the exigencies of daily life in post-communist Russia, but under pressures of our own – both institutional and cultural. Until such time as the economic, social and political conditions in which Russian and Western historians work are broadly similar, there is unlikely to be any real convergence in our agendas. Nevertheless, if my optimism about the prospects for historical writing in Russia is not entirely misplaced, then we can expect it to exert increasing influence on our agenda in the West. It is not easy to predict what form that will take – I recognise that I may not like it! – but for the first time Western historians will be forced to respond to a pace set by the research and debates of Russian colleagues in a way that seldom happened in the past.

Glossary

Chekhov, Anton   Preeminent prerevolutionary playwright in Russia.

Erikson, Erik   Psychoanalytic social theorist and author of numerous influential studies in the U.S.

Gosplan   State Planning Committee of the Soviet union.

Gosudarstrennost'   The phenomenon of state authority.

IREX   International Research and Exchanges Board, Supporting research in Russia.

kulaki-miroedy   People who live off others' labor.

Kustar' "Cottage industry," small-Scale artisanship and production.

Mayakovsky, Vladimir Leading poet of the postrevolutionary years in Russia.

Meshochniki "Bagmen" of Russian Civil War who sold and transferred goods in short supply.

Narod Literally, "people" but implying the Russian rural peasantry and non-elites in society.

Nepmen Supporters of Lenin's New Economic Policy of limited capitalism in 1920s.

Oblast' Region or district. Smith is here referring to a provincial archive of manuscripts.

Obshchestvennost' The consciousness and infrastructure of civil society.

Ostranenie Term to describe the phenomenom of estrangement or of "making strange."

Proizrol' Arbitrariness and abuses of power.

Russkie vedomosti Popular Russian newspaper prior to the Bolshevik seizure of power.

Schönberg [Schoenberg], Arnold Major composer of atonal music in the 20th century.

Skupshchiki People who buy goods that are largely unavailable, in order to resell them at a profit.

Sonderweg Concept to describe a "special path" for German national development.

Russian Formalists Avant-garde literary movement of Soviet writers during the 1920s.

Workers' Opposition Group that supported workers' autonomy against Bolshevik centralization policy.

Futher Reading: Historiography

S. Kotkin, "1991 and the Russian Revolution: Sources, Conceptual Categories, Analytical Frameworks," *Journal of Modern History* 70 (June, 1998): 384–425.

R. G. Suny, "Toward a Social History of the October Revolution," *American Historical Review*, 88, 1 (1983): 31–52.

Index